Poetic Will

Poetic Will

Shakespeare and the Play of Language

David Willbern

PENN

University of Pennsylvania Press

Philadelphia

Copyright © 1997 University of Pennsylvania Press
All rights reserved
Printed in the United States of America on acid-free paper

10 9 8 7 6 5 4 3 2 1

Published by
University of Pennsylvania Press
Philadelphia, Pennsylvania 19104-6097

Library of Congress Cataloging-in-Publication Data

Willbern, David.
    Poetic Will : Shakespeare and the play of language / David Willbern.
        p.   cm.
    Includes bibliographical references (p.) and index.
    ISBN 0-8122-3389-1 (alk. paper)
    1. Shakespeare, William, 1564–1616—Style.   2. English language—Early modern,
1500–1700—Semantics.   3. English language—Early modern, 1500–1700—Style.
4. Play on words.   I. Title.
PR2997.P8W55   1997
822.3′3—dc21   96-37484
                                                                                      CIP

Literary creation is that adventure of the body and signs that bears witness to the affect—to sadness as imprint of separation and beginning of the symbol's sway; to joy as imprint of the triumph that settles me in the universe of artifice and symbol, which I try to harmonize in the best possible way with my experience of reality.

—JULIA KRISTEVA

Through artistic expression we can hope to keep in touch with our primitive selves whence the most intense feelings and even fearfully acute sensations derive, and we are poor indeed if we are only sane.

—D. W. WINNICOTT

Contents

Acknowledgments   ix

Prologue: Cordelia's Skirt   xi

Introduction: Hamlet's Inky Cloak   I

1. Limitations of Character, Limits of Language   II

2. Paranoia, Criticism, and Malvolio   26

3. Pushing the Envelope: Supersonic Criticism   39

4. The Famous Analyses of *Henry the Fourth*   55

5. Hyperbolic Desire: Shakespeare's *Lucrece*   76

6. Phantasmagoric *Macbeth*   97

7. Shakespeare's Nothing   125

8. What Is Shakespeare?   143

Epilogue: Yorick's Skull, Miranda's Memory   160

Notes   173

Index   231

Acknowledgments

IN CHRONOLOGICAL ORDER, I THANK the magnificent group of scholars, critics, and teachers at Berkeley, where many years ago I began serious study of Shakespeare: especially Jonas Barish, Stephen Booth, Frederick Crews, Donald Friedman, Stephen Orgel, and Norman Rabkin.

At Buffalo, I thank the following colleagues, some here, some gone, for providing a sustaining environment of learning, wit, and good humor: Charles Bernheimer, Christopher Bollas, Barbara Bono, Kenneth Burke, Amy Doerr, Barbara Freedman, Norman Holland, Claire Kahane, Robert Rogers, Mark Shechner, Marc Shell, Henry Sussman, and Jim Swan.

Among the larger society of psychoanalytic Shakespeareans, I am pleased to express appreciation for the wisdom and example of Janet Adelman, Harry Berger, Lynda Boose, Avi Erlich, Peter Erickson, Coppélia Kahn, William Kerrigan, Peter Rudnytsky, Meredith Skura, Madelon Sprengnether, David Sundelson, Robert Watson, and Richard Wheeler. Regrettably it is too late to share the culmination of this work with two colleagues who supported much of it: the late C.L. Barber and Joel Fineman.

I can only gesture toward an incalculable gratitude to Murray Schwartz, colleague and friend.

Finally, I thank Katherine and Noel, and Joan and David for their patience in the last stages.

Prologue: Cordelia's Skirt

DURING THE LATE 1960S, at the end of the dominance of New Criticism and before the institutionalization of postmodern interpretive styles and challenges to them, I began my apprenticeship as scholar and critic. At Berkeley I read widely in English Renaissance literature, its classical and historical backgrounds (we still used that term in those days), its continental analogues, and its meanings as determined by literary critics. I appropriated the hermeneutic techniques of New Criticism and psychoanalysis in order to develop a "third ear" for language: hearing over and under the manifest words, listening for latent senses, constructing plausible motivations. This psychoanalytic style of reading derives from Freud's fundamental rule for analysts: to maintain a state of "evenly suspended attention" in which normal modes of understanding are relaxed so that unconscious modes of reception can be enhanced.[1] It thereby blends a receptive mode of "free association" with an interpretive mode that mirrors the strategies of Freudian dream-work: what I've referred to elsewhere as interpretation-work.[2]

At Buffalo during the 1970s I became involved in "Delphi Seminars," wherein faculty and graduate students pursued their own personal associations to literary texts, ignoring conventional inner voices (usually parental and professional) that cried, "inappropriate." We read texts not merely as received but as recreated.[3] I can recall the moment, appropriately elucidated by a visiting Frenchman, when I fully understood the elementary distinction between a *book* and a *text*. A book is simply the paper object on a shelf; it exists without being read. A text, another creature altogether, appears when one takes the book from the shelf and begins to read it. That's where literature happens; the rest is interior decoration.[4]

My epiphany about texts was simultaneously enabling and disabling. The full recognition of the power of a reader to energize and interpret language meant that I was now licensed to re-create the words-on-the-page *and* that I was bound to do so in my own individual style, now only too visible to my psychoanalytic eye. Professional criticism, which I had been blithely practicing under the New Critical aegis of the poem-as-

external-object-of-scrutiny, became inextricably wedded to personal response, and the same revelations that powered my private associations in
academic seminars looked embarrassingly confessional as part of the published criticism which as a junior faculty member I was anxious to produce.
I found myself in an uneasy rhythm of primary, free-associative psychoanalytic attention to literature and my responses, which I would record, and
careful secondary revisions of those responses, which involved scholarship,
censorship, and translations into the publicly shareable. This process, I
came to realize, is called *writing criticism*. In my case it was a rhetorical
effort to blend the pleasure of reading with the practice of interpretation.

In the 1970s I began to publish my findings, usually on Shakespearean
topics. My experience has been that Shakespeareans are generally a kindly,
tolerant sort, occupying a large territory with flexible boundaries, whose
tribal disputes rarely flare into long-lasting or irreparable antagonisms
(rather like a very extended and only occasionally dysfunctional family).
Still, I found lines to cross.

One especially memorable trespass occurred when I presented a paper
on "Shakespeare's Wordplay" to a meeting of the Northeast Modern Language Association.[5] In a brief presentation I proposed that underlying
Cordelia's fateful "Nothing" in her answer to Lear's demand in the rhetorical love-test is the same sense the term possesses in Hamlet's bawdy
by-play with Ophelia: *no thing*, or female genitals. From this immodest
observation I proceeded to develop some ideas on the paradoxical interplay of negativity and generativity within the profoundly sexualized imagination that I find in Shakespeare.[6] After my talk, a fellow rose and
sputtered from the audience: "You can't do that! Shakespeare won't let you
do that. What?! Are you proposing that, as she speaks, Cordelia throws up
her skirt?" Startled by such vehemence, I composed myself and responded
on three fronts. First, I allowed that the bit of stage business my critic
proposed was unlikely to work well in performance, and that I had not
thought of it at all. Second, I noted his Foucauldian use of "Shakespeare"
as an author-effect to limit permissible readings. Last, I sketched out an
essential element of my own approach to Shakespeare, namely, that we
might usefully think of two plays occurring simultaneously. One is the play
of action and character: the evident phenomena of *dramatis personae* addressing one another and imitating actions (Aristotelian drama, in short).
In such a scene, Cordelia is not likely to be referring to her genitals, by
either her language or her gestures. The other play is what I call *the play of
language*. The phrase refers not only to localized puns and wordplay but

also to an entire circulation of linguistic meaning, within and without the drama, which subsumes characters or in which characters participate but do not own or control. Outside character and action, there is another site of the play, the play of language. In this larger scene, words refer to—or encourage readers and hearers to respond to—other significances. Today this idea should hardly be startling.[7]

Another way to sketch the question is in terms of character or agency. Does it make sense, for instance, to assert that Cordelia intends any genital significance in her word? As far as I can see, the only way to support such an assertion is to attribute unconscious intention to the character. A great strength and at times a great weakness of psychoanalytic criticism is that it attributes unconscious intentions to literary characters. In this case, I think the weakness is more apparent. I, for one, would not want to have to defend such a contention about Cordelia. But character, as a dramatic construct, has its own great strength and weakness. A weakness is that audiences and critics may come thoroughly to believe that each character owns his or her language and that each dramatic moment provides a limiting context for the language. The illusion of people walking and talking on a stage is powerfully compelling. On the other hand, a criticism that does not privilege character, but instead examines the linguistic matrix within which characters occupy positions from which they speak, such a criticism need not be disabled or inhibited by ideas of intentionality localized in characters (whether conscious or unconscious).

The history of criticism in the twentieth century, and especially of Shakespeare criticism, has variously argued the status of character versus language, play versus poem, *parole* versus *langue*, meaning versus metaphor, symbolic versus semiotic. In the field of traditional Shakespeare studies, A.C. Bradley and G. Wilson Knight may be taken as emblems of apparently oppositional styles of reading. Bradley's devotion to intricacies of character and specific details of dramatic action (such as "Where was Hamlet at the time of his father's death?") contrasts with Knight's celebration of metaphor and image (what he termed "the Shakespeare vision").[8] Contemporary versions of the argument can be found in modern analyses (including psychoanalyses) of characters as autonomous, ambulatory, speaking fictions (*dramatis personae*) versus postmodern studies of such agents as literal figures in a (re)circulating system of supplementary signification.

My intention in this book is twofold: to look again at the issue of character from the perspective of all-inclusive language—treating "char-

acter" as a functional fiction and active figure of speech—and, using various textual examples, to put Shakespeare's language into play in order
to demonstrate how various dramatic characters *in* the plays and critical
readers *of* the plays find themselves (or miss themselves) in relation to
that energy. Finally, this project represents a fuller response to my name-
less NEMLA questioner. After all these years, I still thank him for the
challenge.

My title bears several kinds of sense, which I will sketch here as a quick
preview of the themes of the book. By "poetic" I intend a predramatic
term for imaginative production, whose Greek root pertains to *handicraft,
invention, causation, action*, and *celebration*.[9] The word links intellectual
concept, fabricated text, and rhetorical action. Although the precise term
is not used by Shakespeare, in *As You Like It* the simple Audrey exhibits
her ignorance of aesthetic theory by admitting, "I do not know what
'poetical' is. Is it honest in deed and word? Is it a true thing?" Touchstone,
her dubious suitor, replies that it is not, "for the truest poetry is the most
feigning" (3.3.17–20).[10] The term "poetic" thus joins truth and pretense,
in the necessary guises of representation by figure, trope, metaphor, and
other devices of rhetoric.

As many readers of Shakespeare will know, puns on "will" are frequent in the plays, poems, and criticism. (Sonnet 135 is a notorious and
overworked example of the rudimentary sexual connotations: "*Will* in
overplus.") The term occupies a densely overdetermined semantic nexus
within which notions of erotic *appetite* or *desire*, sexual and procreative
organs, aggression (the will to power), *wish, whim, inclination, volition, conscious intention, purpose*, and *bequest* or *testament* co-exist at varying levels
of potentiality.[11] Paradoxically, in Shakespeare's time the same word meant
"primitive, involuntary desire" and "conscious volition."[12] (Etymologi-
cally, *volition* and *voluptuous* have the same root: in English, *will*.) In
Romeo and Juliet, Friar Lawrence poses a simple opposition in man between "grace and rude will" that relies on conventional theological notions of fallen man saved only by divine power (2.3.28). The subtitle of
Twelfth Night, Or What You Will, indicates both intention and wish. Claudius chastises Hamlet's stubborn persistence in grief as showing "a will
most incorrect to heaven" (1.2.95). Laertes uses the term in two senses in
the same sentence, when he warns Ophelia about Hamlet and possible
stains on "the virtue of his will" (desire), then notes that "his will is not his
own" (choice) because of his royal birth (1.3.14–17) Hamlet's meditation
on that mortal dread that "puzzles the will" conflates anxiety, conscience,

resolution, and thought in the same passage; all motions, affective or intellectual, are paralyzed (3.1.77–87). Iago, sly rhetorician and malevolent psychotherapist, confuses Roderigo and reader alike in his slippery uses of the term. "Virtue?" he exclaims to Roderigo. "A fig!"

'tis in ourselves that we are thus or thus. Our bodies are our gardens, to the which our wills are gardeners, so that if we will plant nettles or sow lettuce, set hyssop and weed up [tine], supply it with one gender of herbs or distract it with many, either to have it sterile with idleness or manur'd with industry—why the power and corrigible authority of this lies in our wills. If the [beam] of our lives had not one scale of reason to poise another of sensuality, the blood and baseness of our natures would conduct us to most prepost'rous conclusions. But we have reason to cool our raging motions, our carnal stings, [our] unbitted lusts, whereof I take this that you call love to be a sect or scion.

When Roderigo objects to this cynical reduction of his love, Iago reiterates the lesson: "It is merely a lust of the blood and a permission of the will. Come, be a man!" (*Othello*, 1.3.319–35). But the clarity of Iago's conventional illustration of psychology and morality—his lesson in ethical husbandry—starts to blur as soon as he begins. His claim that "it is in ourselves that we are thus or thus" apparently counters Roderigo's point that his own frail strength (his "virtue") prevents him from changing: by "in ourselves" Iago evidently means "by our own means." Yet the phrase also means something closer to Roderigo's claim: we are as we are by nature, by what is within. Semantic meaning conflicts with rhetorical meaning.[13]

Iago then develops the traditional trope of balance between reason and sensuality, but it is precisely this psychological "poise" he works to disturb, in Roderigo here and in Othello later. His reference to "the blood and baseness of our natures" alludes to that other register of "will" that counterpoises and conflicts with the "corrigible authority" of the rational will. The subcurrent of carnal will that co-exists with the idealized volition Iago rhetorically proffers hence suggests a turn in the adjectival force of "corrigible authority": not that authority corrects, but that authority itself is subject to correction, reformed or deformed by the pressures of desire.[14] Iago's reiteration that love is merely an offshoot of lust collapses the counterpoised government of rude will and wise volition into a collaboration of "a lust of the blood and a permission of the will." The gardener is no longer neatly planting and sowing according to conscious design; now his hands are dirtied in the baseness of nature.

Subterranean puns even gesture toward the material object that provides evidence for Othello's preposterous conclusions: "nettle" is ety-
mologically equivalent to "needle" (the plant provided both needle and
thread in early sewing) and "sow" echoes the association. Deep in the tex-
ture of Iago's language lie associations to the primitive technology of his
most powerful fabrication: the handkerchief.[15] Iago's phrase, "permission
of the will," also tends to shift from its apparent meaning of volitional lapse
(permission *from* the will, or choice) to a subterranean sense of the release
of desire (licensing *of* the will, or appetite). Ultimately Iago's didactic garden plot produces a perverse shadow moral that avows the virtues of reason
while appealing to the vices of carnality. (His own attitude to the garden
figure may be audible in his initial vulgarization of it: "a fig!") His project
here is to encourage Roderigo to obtain more money ("Put money in thy
purse!") so that he can be separated from it, but the play of the language
prefigures the larger project of ruining Othello by similarly leading him "to
most prepost'rous conclusions."

Iago's slippery use of the term "will" obscurely takes advantage of the
problematic relation the term contains between reason and desire. Another statement of the problem, though couched in conventional rhetoric,
is a summary assertion by the Player King in *Hamlet*: "Our wills and fates
do so contrary run / That our devices still are overthrown, / Our thoughts
are ours, their ends none of our own" (3.2.211–13). The immediate force of
this statement is aimed at the Player Queen and the hypothetical event of
her remarriage after her husband's death (she swears otherwise). The lines
echo through the play, however, and apply to many of the characters. If we
translate the traditional term "fate" into Freudian terms—a translation
this, Freud's favorite play, surely encourages—the other agent that opposes
rational will is the unconscious will, a counterpoised desire that plots the
overthrow of intention so that thoughts and plans eventuate in surprising
ends and effects.[16]

Many of the various meanings of "will" are dramatically demonstrated
in the instrumental and symbolic relation of Mark Antony to Caesar in
Julius Caesar. Antony is most obviously the active instrument of the revelation of Caesar's will in Act Three, Scene Two, when he exhibits that legal
document along with Caesar's bloodied corpse. The actual reading of the
will is subordinate to Antony's brilliant rhetorical transformation of Caesar
as symbolic body and spirit; he performs a critical reading of Caesar and
the conspirators that reverses the previous and presumably stable meaning

installed by Brutus before he unwisely left the podium. Anchored in Caesar's body, his documentary will is actually anticlimactic (he leaves grounds for a public park, along with seventy-five drachmas per capita—a sum later reduced by Antony and Octavius). But the force of Caesar's legacy as transmitted by Antony is formidable. Caesar's will, understood as the extension of his desires after his death, continues to animate the play to the end. Yet Antony is more than the interpretive instrument of Caesar's will and testament. He is also the instrument of will in its other senses, of generative sexuality. His initial entrance into the play is as a naked agent of fertility running the Lupercalian course, who is to touch the barren Calpurnia with his leather thongs, as ordered by the will of Caesar (1.2.1–11). Brutus calls him a "quick spirit" (1.2.28) and "a limb of Caesar" (2.1.165); Antony offers to be "cut off" when he discovers Caesar dead, before he is "prick'd in number of [the conspirators'] friends" (*Julius Caesar*, 3.1.162, 216).

Antony begins as an agent of procreative will; after the assassination he becomes an agent of posthumous will, as the interpreter of Caesar's legacy. This final turn of the term, as in "last will and testament," opens its meanings into the arenas of legacy and bequest while still linked to the procreative sense: "testament" comes from the Latin *testis* or witness, which relates to testes, testicles. The patriarchal law that views virility as sign and surety of legal testimony also understands legacy as an act of posthumous potency, an enforcement of the dead father's will and a governed transmission of patrilineal inheritance.[17] Shakespeare's versions of this last act of patriarchy can be seen in the ritual contest at Belmont in which "the will of a living daughter is curb'd by the will of a dead father" (*Merchant of Venice*, 1.2.24–25) and most significantly in the actual event of Shakespeare's own will, which Richard Willson characterizes as uniquely focused on enforcing primogeniture and patrilineal descent in its bequests, establishing the priority of legal ties as defined by property and described by the testator's desire, over the conventional medieval customs of inheritance through kinship.[18]

Read with the ear as well as the eye, the first two words of the title of this book manage a modest pun on Shakespeare's instrument of writing, using an element of a natural body. The next words, read with the eye, produce a near facsimile of a signature, "Will: Shakespeare." Regrettably, this form is not an extant record of how the man signed his name. Of the very few surviving signatures, only two abbreviate the first name: one has "Will," the other "W^{m}."[19] By "Shakespeare" I mean the person, the author, the literary ideal, the cultural concept, the object of a profession; Chapters Seven and Eight explore these senses. By "language" I aim at personal, historical, and social fields, which I will discuss in Chapter One.

The remaining operative term, "play," is multivalent. As in my extemporaneous response to my NEMLA challenger, I intend a linguistic analogy to the dramatic work: a play of language that parallels and circulates around and through the play on the stage. ("Shakespeare," as authorial agent, is similarly balanced by "language," as inclusive matrix.) The term "play" is both literary and mimetic, both verb and noun, with several senses—*exercise, free movement, amusement, pleasure, recreation, sport, game*, and *trick*. Sometimes "play" is more subtle, as in the flicker of light or the surface of a stream (in Shakespeare's day it also meant "to boil"). Hamlet uses the word when he rebukes Rosencrantz and Guildenstern for trying to play him like an instrument (3.2.350–72). Rosalind uses it in at least two senses (dramatic and extra-dramatic) when she asks the audience "to like as much of this play as please you," and then charges the men "that between you and the women the play may please" (*As You Like It*, Epilogue, 11–17). The term has a lot of play, in the sense of loose, unstable motion within a tolerable range, like the play of an automobile steering wheel, or of a fishing line once the creature is hooked. Playing with lines, of course, is what my style of criticism promotes, and it is just this sort of slippage along associational lines that evokes post-structuralist theories of the "free play" of signifiers in language.[20] But just as a steering wheel that *only* "played" would be useless, indeed dangerous—a disconnected, deranged guidance system—the concept of free play is useful within limits, as Chapter Three explores. A good paradigm is the *playground*, and I ground my understanding of human play in the developmental theories of psychoanalysts, the aesthetic theories of rhetoricians, and the social theories of historians.[21]

Wordplay is the nexus or matrix of interlinked critical theory and practice and, as Viola said to Feste, "they that dally nicely with words may quickly make them wanton" (*Twelfth Night*, 3.1.14–15). I consider the issue of wordplay and puns in Chapter One. The erotic colloquy between Viola and Feste, however, gestures toward a core thesis of this book, or a deep analogy: that between imaginative and physical conception. To sketch with a broad brush ideas I will later detail, *will = unconscious = (female) sexuality*. Ultimately I want to relocate Shakespeare's muse in the re-presented or re-configured body of the mother. Roland Barthes radically and nostalgically claimed that "the writer is someone who plays with the mother's body."[22] As psychoanalytic critics have demonstrated, the maternal body in Shakespeare is a source of generativity and degeneration, pleasure and terror.[23] Analogies between female or maternal sexuality and poetic creativity recur throughout the book, culminating in a playful yet deadly serious juxtaposition of two testimonial containers: Yorick's skull and Miranda's memory.

Introduction:
Hamlet's Inky Cloak

Seems, madam? nay, it is. I know not "seems."
'Tis not alone my inky cloak, good mother,
Nor customary suits of solemn black,
Nor windy suspiration of forc'd breath,
No, nor the fruitful river in the eye,
Nor the dejected havior of the visage,
Together with all forms, moods, shapes of grief,
That can denote me truly. These indeed seem,
For they are actions that a man might play,
But I have that within which passes show,
These but the trappings and the suits of woe.
                        (*Hamlet*, 1.2.76–86)[1]

THIS CELEBRATED PASSAGE, in which Hamlet as character and Shakespeare as dramatist simultaneously demonstrate external style while disparaging it in favor of internal, undemonstrable matter, juxtaposes three large subjects of current criticism: *poetic writing* (character as literary text), *dramatic enactment* (character as performance) and *hidden essence* (character as person). In terms that reduce mourning and melancholy almost to caricature ("the windy suspiration of forc'd breath" gives the appearance of bad acting), Hamlet emphasizes the distance between his acted representations (or his representative actions) and his inner feelings—between "these" (83, 86) and "that" (85), or *ça*, as the French might say.[2] We see (he tells us, he shows us) the *shapes* of grief but not grief's source or senses, its affective or intellectual qualities. The form is visible, but what of the substance? In an earlier, more commonplace statement of the problem, Shakespeare's Richard the Second asserts, "My grief lies all within,"

And these external manners of laments
Are merely shadows to the unseen grief

That swells with silence in the tortur'd soul.
There lies the substance.   (4.1.295–299)

Richard's statement, and the colloquy with Bullingbrook wherein it occurs, employ the tropes of shadow and substance unproblematically. External representation enacts an internal state that can be felt and named, as
grief. Although Richard's "manners of laments" (both mode and decorum) may be inadequate to demonstrate the full pain and pressure of his
inner state, they still represent or shadow it. The link between substance
and shadow remains.

Hamlet suggests a more problematic relation. Forms and actions can
after all be played, or imitated as in a play. (Theater, for instance, consists
largely of "actions that a man might play.") Such external signs are modes
of *denoting*, marking down, and are, Hamlet claims, ultimately inadequate
as true representations of substance. His inner state surpasses show. Taken
literally, what Hamlet's words are here claiming about Hamlet's character
is that the latter cannot be "truly" performed.[3]

What then denotes Hamlet truly? Not the staged play, for all its formal
weight and glory, its centuries-old tradition of brilliant enactments, but
something before and beyond dramatic action, something relating not to
conventional denotations like costume or posture or emotive delivery, but
to the dilating associations of *connotation*: the play of language.[4] Hamlet
is in his language; he is found in it, caught in it, rapt in it, lost in it—as we
are. Dramatic actions are guises, posturings and costumes, trappings and
suits. Words are Hamlet's and Shakespeare's matter, but words freed from
their dramatic denotations and opened into connotations, so that "inky
cloak" points to the character's textual status, and "trappings" and "suits"
become puns that predict his plots (the Mousetrap) and petitions (the
Ghost's to him, his to Ophelia or Gertrude) long before the character can
know or intend these meanings. If Hamlet's enacted character, the role he
plays or that actors play on his behalf, cannot disclose the "that within,"
perhaps Shakespeare's language can. Before Hamlet, *Hamlet*. And before
that play, the play of language. The writing is all. Shakespeare is in the
details.

Hamlet's words are dramatically reflexive; they quote Gertrude back
to herself. He rudely excises one term, "seems," from the discursive flow
and then subjects it to skeptical analysis. By definition, the word he chooses
is easily pressed toward the point of pretense, ambiguous representation,
and secret surplus; it is one core facet of semantic *polysemy*. What Hamlet

specifically knows not, however, is balanced by what he vaguely knows, his "*that* within." Like the "something" that is rotten in the state, it resists naming. This tactic, in which a character treats a word like a symptom and turns it toward an unspecified discontent, looks very like a gesture toward the Freudian unconscious (or the Lacanian *ça*), an internal psychic process that is *inarticulate*: unspoken and not articulated, that is, not organized according to conscious modes of conventional representation or *show*.

In this respect Hamlet is the figural inverse of Iago, who articulates hidden desires by seeming to be what he is not. He takes pride in what Hamlet describes as a limit:

> Were I the Moor, I would not be Iago.
> In following him, I follow but my self;
> Heaven is my judge, not I for love and duty,
> But *seeming* so, for my peculiar end;
> For when my outward action doth demonstrate
> The native act and figure of my heart
> In complement extern, 'tis not long after
> But I will wear my heart upon my sleeve
> For daws to peck at: I am not what I am.
>
> (*Othello*, 1.1.57–65)

Hamlet wants (he tells us) precisely to enact what he is, to suit his outward action to his native figure—as he so instructs the Players (3.2). Of course his current circumstances require that this pursuit be masked, so that he assumes an "antic disposition" that apparently disqualifies his speech, in exact opposition to the "honest" disposition Iago assumes that apparently authenticates his. Iago comfortably impersonates the actions a man might play, easily conflating nature with artifice ("native act and figure"). Both characters boast a hidden self, but discovery of that self means potential ruin for one and potential salvation for the other.

In this book I intend to scrutinize the first of Hamlet's guises—his inky cloak—as delineating a primary arena of linguistic play within which the secondary effects of character emerge. Shakespeare's language, scenes, and characters emerge from his writer's quill, propelled by the genius of his poetic *will*—understood simultaneously as emotional erotic drive and intellectual artistic design (both conscious and unconscious) as well as literary legacy. They are originally products and effects of writing, and the plays, like the poems, are primarily written narratives. Characters like (and unlike) Hamlet occasionally gesture toward their linguistic origins, as when Hamlet the character inscribes the paternal command in the "book and volume of [his] brain," or when *Hamlet* the play opens with a demand to "unfold."[5] When Claudio observes of the pregnant Juliet that "character too gross is writ on [her]" (*Measure for Measure*, 1.2.155), Shakespeare's language equates physical sign (writing) with inferred behavior (interpretation).[6]

Let me be pellucid, even polemical. My goal in this book is to rescue Shakespeare from the lamentable, albeit necessary, limitations and distortions of dramatic performance and to reclaim as fully as possible the rich potential of his poetic language. While it is surely true that stage productions animate the plays and undeniable that the plays were written for the stage, productions are double-edged devices. They deprive a play while they enable it.[7] The deprivations derive not only from actual cuts that reduce the text or emendations that change it, or from directors' and actors' conceptions that provide one consistent character or social and temporal frame at the cost of others, but also from the mere impossibility of staging many of the functional aspects of Shakespeare's language. On the stage, Hamlet's inky cloak is black, the conventional sign of melancholy, the potential guise of impersonation, and it is cloth (textile). On the page, it is *ink* (text). I want to get my hands on Shakespeare's language, to stain my fingers, like the dyer's hand (Sonnet 111).[8]

Consider another instance of textile and text: Desdemona's handkerchief. That particular piece of (stage) property is doubtless real, no mere writing effect, and the material hinge of one of the most classical (Aristotelian) dramas in literature. The first time we see it is when Desdemona drops it; the first time we hear of it is when Othello remarks, "Your napkin is too little" (3.3.287). In the play of language, however, the handkerchief exists long before Desdemona brings it out to bind her husband's symptomatic headache. Prior to the appearance of the material object, Shakespeare's language provides a structure for its significance, a literary preview of a dramatic event. Iago, Othello's ensign, or flag bearer, voices his hypocritical design in terms of his customary duty: "I must show out a flag and sign of love, / Which is indeed but sign" (1.1.156–57). The referential show of the flag constructs a field or frame of reference *before* the crucial referent of that other sign of love, the handkerchief, drops into the drama. In my ink-stained production of this play, Iago's flag *is* Desdemona's handkerchief, whose fabric enmeshes Othello as he follows it to perdition, believing it to be the lost "recognizance and pledge of love" (5.2.214).[9] Such an equation is plausible in the play of language but almost impossible in dramatic production. Even if a director were to bring Iago's flag on stage, it is unlikely he or she would produce a strawberry-spotted one or show it later with a piece cut out.

When the tragedy of *Othello* is complete, its characters gesture from another angle at the textual phenomenon of Hamlet's inky cloak. Upon Othello's surprising yet well-staged suicide, Lodovico and Gratiano exclaim, "O bloody period! All that's spoke is marred" (5.2.356–57). This metadramatic piece of literary criticism judges Othello's action as a final and fatal punctuation to an excellent discourse, a bad end to a good story. By thus marring his own speech, Othello figuratively stains the sheets on which he implored his Venetian auditors to inscribe his sad tale ("Set you down this . . ."). The bloody period, moreover, is not only a metaphor of the written sign. It designates a blood spot, and is hence a mark of female sexuality: of virginity (bridal sheets), murder (deathbed sheets), and menstruation ("napkin" also bears this significance).[10] Linen in Shakespeare's day was used to make paper, so that the maculate handkerchief that emblematizes purity and then defilement becomes the play's reification of Desdemona as "fair paper" stained and begrimed by the name of "whore" (4.2.71–72). The Venetian commentators use a metaphor that has, for them as characters, one specific reference, but which resonates deeply within the inclusive play of language.

Iago too, as an agent in this play of language, has a nondramatic, nonpsychological, merely literary quality. Of course he is a slim shadow of the Christian devil, a re-animation of the medieval Vice, and an envious, devious character. But before he enacts these figures, he represents a linguistic device: the simple principle of negation. His first and last words are negative ("You'll not hear"; "I never shall speak word"), his most famous self-definition is a demonic parody of divine autonomy ("I am not what I am"), and his effect on Othello is to negate the words and image of an idealized Desdemona. In the play of language that is *Othello*, the deepest and most pernicious effects of Iago appear most clearly in Othello's tortured assertion of his wife's fidelity: "I do *not* think *but* Desdemona's honest" (3.3.225). In the play of language, Iago lies in Othello's syntax.[11] (Beyond the negatives over which Othello stumbles toward his unstable assertion of Desdemona's honesty, the sentence veers close to another statement and a deeper truth: something like, "Without my trust in her fidelity, I am incapable of rational thought." As he says later: "Perdition catch my soul / But I do love thee! and when I love thee not, / Chaos is come again" [3.1.90–92].)

The collisions and collusions of linguistic and dramatic play could be demonstrated with many other examples. One classroom incident focuses many of the ideas and tactics of this book. Regularly, while conducting undergraduate courses in "Shakespeare," I have occasion to test students' abilities to identify specific passages from the plays. One common test item is from *Romeo and Juliet*: "No, 'tis not so deep as a well, nor so wide as a church-door, but 'tis enough, 'twill serve." Expert readers will recognize this as Mercutio's last-gasp joking as he lies mortally wounded by Tybalt. A student once responded that the line must be spoken by Romeo to Juliet on their wedding night. Of course this sort of wit is endemic among undergraduates, and I appreciated the Mercutio-like spirit of the response, (that the student was not joking is thinkable, but barely).[12] As soon as I connected his joking with Mercutio's, I realized that this piece of sophomoric cleverness was actually very insightful. The test answer is simply wrong in terms of the play of drama and character but profoundly right in terms of the play of language. For the deep confusion between sexuality and death that permeates *Romeo and Juliet* operates at the level of specific language in ways that precisely correspond to the student's clever response. From the crude phallic joking of the opening scene, the consistent bawdiness of Mercutio and the Nurse, the eroticized construction of Juliet as toddler by the Nurse's dead husband (1.3.39–57), to the stark Freudian symbolism of the graveyard scene and Juliet's final reference to her body as "sheath" (5.3.167–68), the consanguinities of sex and death, womb and tomb, circulate throughout the play.

As this anecdote indicates and the next chapters will demonstrate, I am intrigued by the question of *limits* in criticism. What is "permitted" by a text, or by "Shakespeare," or by an audience? Specifically, what are the interpretive and rhetorical limits of psychoanalytic literary criticism? The various readings that follow—from self-evident to preposterous, commonplace to idiosyncratic—should demonstrate the practical aspects of this question. It can be framed theoretically in terms of two primary structures in psychoanalytic theory. The first involves Freudian models of wish and defense, anxiety, and the ego-ideal or superego. The second is the object-relations model of interactive play.

The Freudian model of limit involves inhibition, repression, and otherwise defensive transformations of thoughts and feelings, along with a mandated repetition of some previous problematic episode, like the Ghost insisting to Hamlet, "Remember me": the *nom du père* that supervises critical representations and rhetoric. The object-relations model describes limits less in terms of restrictive bounds and more as an arena of possibility: a playground of discourse, a holding environment for testing and exploring fantasized relations to others (texts, authors, audiences). The primordial template for this structure is the infant's early relation to the mother.[13]

When I consider the question of the limits of criticism in Freudian terms, my superego anxiety is energized. I worry about censorship, not only about what I'm permitted to say (by whom?), or the degree of outrage I might induce in an audience, but also about how much of my own private and unconscious concerns I exhibit in my writing, especially concerning the densely eroticized language I find in Shakespeare. This is confessional anxiety, or to be melodramatic, the "tragic" form of literary criticism. Conversely, when I consider the question of limits within the object-relations model of imaginative play, then I revel in what I can say, how playfully I can re-create Shakespeare's language and represent my observations. Writing is fun as well as work; this is the "comic" form of criticism. Thus, poised between the tensions and compromises of the interaction of (paternal) inhibition and (maternal) exhibition, I produce psychological and rhetorical compromises, and eventually manage to write.[14]

Writing about Shakespeare is challenging and pleasurable, which is why so many of us do it. The resource is inexhaustible, like language itself. My sense of Shakespeare's language—that is, the words he used within the arenas of Elizabethan vocabulary, syntax, echo, and allusion—is of plenitude and consummation.[15] The texts are full to overflowing. If we mark the Elizabethan moment as the birth of modern English in the sixteenth century, then we can mark its demise in postmodern obituary notices of depletion, exhaustion, and emptiness in the twentieth. Beckett could represent the terminal artist in this grand design (Jan Kott's juxtaposition of *King Lear* and *Endgame* is a crucial moment in twentieth-century criticism), but Joyce is the more appropriate figure. The consummate genius of Shakespeare, tilling the overabundant garden of early modern English—with its vernacular neologisms and classical roots, its humanist storehouse of mythology and theology, its vigorous appropriation of foreign terms, its flexible syntax, its love of analogy and allegory—presides over the (re)naissance of our literature, while the desperate genius of Joyce records the exhaustion of this linguistic potential: he is the mortician of meaning, presiding over radical dislocations in language, celebrating its demise, writ-

ing its wake. Harold Bloom, for whom *Finnegans Wake* is the central ca-
nonical text in what he calls our Chaotic Age, recently asserts that in that
work "Joyce broke with the language of Shakespeare" to produce the
"most successful metamorphosis of Shakespeare in literary history."[16] But,
I would add, Joyce's language wrings such changes on Shakespeare's that
it becomes displaced, fragmented, literally de-composed. (Bloom quotes
Joyce: "a burning would is come to dance inane.")[17]

Evidently Lacan believed that Joyce wrote the *Wake* in an attempt to
rescue himself from the collapse of the symbolic order and a deathly silent
jouissance by creating "a kind of writing that is completely empty of
meaning, noninterpretable." Ellie Ragland-Sullivan continues to summa-
rize Lacan's view of language and Joyce's predicament as follows:

> We all live behind the wall of language, inhabited by a fault or flaw or lack, or in the
> language of the Church, a sin. Every subject is an effect caused by this wall of lan-
> guage (Lacan's structure of alienation) behind which he or she lives more or less
> confidently, not knowing that they [*sic*] retrieve the words by which they live at the
> expense of a lack in being that constitutes them as speaking beings. Lacan gave
> Joyce a new name, "Joyce the symptom"[18]

If this claim is true, as some today believe, then in my view the wall of
language that encloses and "causes" us as modern subjects was built from
the loose stones and pliable mortar of the language Shakespeare had at
hand. The limited mode of word-retrieval to which we are now confined
was once a limitless expanse (at least for Shakespeare) of semantic resources,
an immense field of play not yet enclosed by alienation, lack, or symptom.
What Lacan declaimed as a description of *personal* subjectivity, Shakespeare deployed as an effect of *literary* or *dramatic* subjectivity.[19] He wrote
at a moment of literary genesis, of the opening up of styles of writing and
reading. Joyce and Lacan wrote at closing time. Whereas Shakespeare
comes into language through a doorway he himself constructed (with the
help of his company)—one newly marked "Entrance"—Joyce, Beckett,
and Lacan bump futilely into a wall, where an ancient sign that once read
"Exit" has been prefaced with the nomination, "No." (My idealization of
Shakespeare is elaborated in Chapter Eight.)

Lacan seems to have had a fortress mentality about the effects of living
in language, which Nietzsche once called a prison house. Other constructions are conceivable. The American philosopher Stanley Cavell, for instance, takes a recent occasion of writing about Shakespeare to respond to

this question of the inevitable otherness of language in terms that do not imply alienation, incarceration, or abysmal lack:

Certainly we must not deny it: A word's reach exceeds its speaker's grasp, or what's a language for?

This is to say: words recur, in unforetellable contexts; there would be no words otherwise; and no intentions otherwise, none beyond the, let me say, natural expressions of instinct; nor would there be the expression of desire, or ambition, or the making of a promise, or the acceptance of a prophecy. Unpredictable recurrence is not a sign of language's ambiguity but is a fact of language as such, that there are words.[20]

As I understand this, without the free, unintended, unpredictable circulation of words beyond a speaker's momentary utterance or a writer's inscription, there would be no context to provide linguistic resources for the reception and elaboration of that statement. Where Lacan is immured, Cavell sees doors to relationships: promises, prophecies, plays—kinds of *correspondence*. Where one hears only echoes in a prison house, the other hears the resonance of communal voices.[21]

I prefer Cavell's view. Although there is a deep strain of European theoretical influence in my critical style (primarily Freudian, though I appreciate Lacan, Kristeva, and Bakhtin), there is also an essentially American strain. Alongside the sophistications and sophistries of European theory sit the rough and vulgar contentions of American practice. For decades, critics on this side of the Atlantic have subjected the idealized British Bard to vigorous appropriations, from Twain's mongrel parodies in *Huckleberry Finn* and Melville's virile melodramas in *Moby-Dick*, to Emerson's transcendentalist apotheosis,[22] to the material capitalist confiscations of Horace Howard Furness and Henry Clay Folger, or Phineas T. Barnum's plan to purchase the Stratford birthplace and ship it to New York, to the professional dominance of the Shakespeare Association of America and the pre-eminence of Americans in Shakespeare criticism since mid-century.[23] Recent major "appropriations" include Steven Urkowitz's challenge to the integrity of the existing text, Donald Foster's claim for a new authentic text, and Sam Wanamaker's reconstruction of a New Globe Theater on the banks of the Thames.[24] As Emerson wrote to his brother about his soon-to-be-published grand lectures on "Representative Men," especially Shakespeare: "There is no telling what we rowdy Americans, whose name is Dare, may do!"[25] The British critic Terence Hawkes has even claimed that since the improvisational re-creation of existing structures (like jazz, or literary criticism) is an essentially American style, critics everywhere may be forced "to recognize that criticism makes Americans of us all." [26]

One of the most daring and appreciative readers of Shakespeare's language was the American poet and physician, William Carlos Williams. In *Spring and All*, his improvisational meditation about poetry, the imagination, and Shakespeare, he wrote:

In description words adhere to certain objects, and have the effect on the sense of oysters, or barnacles.

But the imagination is wrongly understood when it is supposed to be a removal from reality in the sense of John of Gaunt's speech in Richard the Second: to imagine possession of that which is lost. It is rightly understood when John of Gaunt's words are related not to their sense as objects adherent to his son's welfare or otherwise but as a dance over the body of his condition accurately accompanying it. By this means of the understanding, the play written to be understood as a play, the author and reader are liberated to pirouette with the words which have sprung from the old facts of history, reunited in present passion.

To understand the words as so liberated is to understand poetry. That they move independently when set free is the mark of their value.

Imagination is not to avoid reality, nor is it description nor an evocation of objects or situations, it is to say that poetry does not tamper with the world but moves it—It affirms reality most powerfully and therefore, since reality needs no personal support but exists free from human action, as proven by science in the indestructibility of matter and of force, it creates a new object, a play, a dance which is not a mirror up to nature but—

As birds' wings beat the solid air without which none could fly so words freed by the imagination affirm reality by their flight.[27]

In the spirit of the two Williams (the American William Carlos Williams and the English William Shakespeare), I intend in this book to free the language of play from its illusory anchors in characters, like prying loose barnacles, so that words can dance and take flight, not in order to abandon reality or referentiality, but by their motion to reaffirm that wider world of reference that is language itself, "as birds' wings beat the solid air."

I

Limitations of Character,
Limits of Language

LET ME ACKNOWLEDGE RIGHT AWAY that it is almost practically impossible to write about Shakespeare's works without employing the notion of character, at least as a rhetorical device. In my own readings I will therefore make free use of character as a functional fiction to discuss the texts: as, in other words, an active *figure of speech*.[1] Before proceeding to such critical practice, it will be useful to review some representative current theories about Shakespeare's language and characters. This chapter is a kind of *bricolage* that aims to assemble and discuss prior scholarly and critical efforts that address these key issues.[2]

An illustrative coincidence saw the publication of two paradigmatic studies of character in the same year, 1974. One was a central scholarly book; the other was a marginal theoretical essay. The first, J. Leeds Barroll's *Artificial Persons*, is an excellent psychological, philosophical, and theological study of the status of "self" and "personality" in relation to dramatic character in Shakespeare's time.[3] Barroll addresses the problem of constructing character from linguistic or dramatic data (words and actions) by examining relations between sixteenth-century and twentieth-century ideas about motive. He argues for a balance between strict historicism and the pertinence of modern psychological views. His book is well anchored in scholarship about early modern ideas: humor psychology, theology, moral types, civil ethics. In an effort to counter A.C. Bradley's "nineteenth-century Anglo-Hegelian" assumptions about individual character, he offers a Renaissance "transcendentalism" whose ideal is the unification of personal identity with supernatural agency. For Barroll, "character" is a consistently conceived agent with an inferable ontology and teleology: a positive goal to be achieved by a person or an author.[4]

In the same year that Barroll's book was published, an essay appeared that undermined many of its assumptions. Written in post-1968 Paris under the banner of feminist responses to Lacanian psychoanalysis, Hélène Cixous's essay on "The Character of 'Character' " was published in English in 1974.[5] Cixous posits "character" as the social placing of a subject, "I," that is fluid, evasive, "always on the run"; it is "the product of a repression of subjectivity . . . under the aegis of masterdom of the conscious." For her, the effect of "character" produces a limited reading-construct of literary communication: it "organizes 'recognition' " and "patronizes meaning." Characters are "to be *figured out*, understood, read" as vehicles for conventional identifications. "As soon as we say 'character,' or *personnage*," she writes, "we are in the theater, but a theater that offers no exit, that takes in everything, that substitutes itself for a nonrepresentational reality." The counter to such restrictive, patronizing meaning is the aesthetic elaboration of the subject: " 'I' must become a 'fabulous opera' and not the arena of the known." Reading Cixous's manifesto is like reading fiction in which a character named "character" suffers the limitations of mere consciousness and meaning while another figure named "the subject" is liberated into a protean, unconscious aria of possibility.[6]

As such radical challenges to conventional critical ideas and practices began to appear in Shakespeare criticism, traditional critics responded. A powerful example is A.D. Nuttall's *A New Mimesis*, a philosophical and aesthetic extension of W.H. Auden's working thesis that Shakespeare's characters are deeply analogous to persons.[7] As a corrective to what he judges the "naive relativism" of much Shakespeare criticism, Nuttall posits pellucid representation of objective reality. His stated goal is to rehabilitate older critical postures: "The eighteenth-century critics were right." His book is an update of Maurice Morgann on Falstaff, as he is well aware. After rebuking L.C. Knights and E.E. Stoll for relativist notions, he writes: "Falstaff is quite clearly presented, through fiction, as a human being. To strive to dislodge such fundamental and evident truths as this is a kind of critical idiocy."[8] Nuttall's polemic has the virtue of clearly stating some fundamental assumptions about Shakespeare's characters on which many readers have relied over the centuries. When a critic imitates Dr. Johnson and begins knocking on skulls (Falstaff's or L.C. Knights's) to prove the reality of characters, one may infer that a previously self-evident epistemological position is under attack.

The postmodern assault continued, as represented by Catherine Belsey's *The Subject of Tragedy*, which shifts critical attention from the dramatic figure of "character" to the psychological figure of the "subject."[9] Her book is premised on the assumption that speaking subjects, historical or fictional, are previously determined by existing cultural discourses, of which language must be presumed a primary one. Belsey sees the early modern precursor of the modern "subject" as an effect of Renaissance humanism and its patriarchal bias. She uses examples from drama, specifically Hamlet and the Duchess of Malfi, as efforts to map out an interior space of inviolable identity, or at least delineate such a space for later, more durable inhabitants, such as Descartes's *cogito*. But, she continues, "the humanist subject is always other than itself, can never be what it speaks."[10]

Differences between conventional and postmodern conceptions of character are well drawn and discussed by Robert Knapp, in *Shakespeare—The Theater and the Book*.[11] Knapp offers an "account of the reasons both for Shakespeare's peculiar indeterminacy of meaning, and for the way he taunts us with the disappearing prospect of modernity."[12] Noting a tendency toward distortion and caricature in much current critical debate that pits "pure formalists" against "new historicists," he argues that the peculiar tension we find in Shakespeare does *not* emerge from differences between early modern and postmodern styles of representation, production, or reception. Those tensions and ambiguities in Shakespeare's meaning are instead effects of the "tension inherent in language" between two poles, variously named metonymic/metaphoric, or symbolic/semiotic. Collapsing centuries in a move that A.D. Nuttall would approve (though he would likely disagree with the conclusion), Knapp asserts that the primary issue at Shakespeare's historical moment was "the question of whether an individual actor is a nonunitary sign in some larger writing, or himself . . . a writer of signs."[13]

Three recent books sustain a certain resistance to postmodern perspectives, each taking a different approach. In *Reading Shakespeare's Characters*, Christy Desmet blends Aristotelian concepts of character with Burkean notions of agency-through-action to counter the idea of character as "an effect of language, a textual character." Bert States, in *Hamlet and the Concept of Character*, insists on the theatrical necessity of creating psychological consistency in order to act out a character and extends this necessary premise to the reading experience. The opening chapter of William Kerrigan's *Hamlet's Perfection* offers a subjective overview of the debate, then comes down on one side (the working necessity of character) while still acknowledging that "an awareness of literary devices, and behind them the raw energy of language itself, combining and splitting, is not inconsistent with the apprehension of character."[14]

The fact (or the experience) is that Shakespeare's characters evidently answer very well to either humanist or postmodern critical assumptions. Unlike other early modern authors, Shakespeare offers a spectrum of character that extends from medieval *psychomachia* to conventional *dramatis persona* to identifiable person to protean postmodern subject. Especially his most loquacious characters, such as Falstaff and Hamlet, can be located at various positions along this spectrum. Chapters Four and Five examine the decomposition or disintegration of character in *Henry IV Part One* and *The Rape of Lucrece*. As a current brief example, Hamlet may suffice. This character, in whose image Freud first designed the Oedipus complex and in whose speaking figure Harold Bloom designates the origin of modern self-reflection, has its narrative origin in northern European legend and a dramatic model in enacted allegory or *psychomachia*.[15] For the character of Hamlet can be decomposed into corollary figures that act out potential behaviors of which "Hamlet" principally only speaks: the Ghost enacts his fears and suspicions, Ophelia his madness and suicide, "Hecuba" his unendurable grief, Laertes his fierce revenge, Horatio his words, words, words, Fortinbras his strong succession. Hamlet is thus a character that simultaneously condenses a bright focus of spoken self-consciousness *and* is split or decomposed into several other figures that surround him. He is besieged by instructive examples of his own possibilities as he protects an apparent inner "self."

Such a character can be profitably viewed from either medieval, early modern, modern, or postmodern aesthetic and critical perspectives. Hamlet is hence an emblem of Shakespeare's position at the juncture or threshold of modernity, or of represented self-consciousness. Schematically put, the question whether "character" is located externally (e.g., as social or theological inscription) or internally (e.g., as individual expression) was precisely the question Shakespeare investigated in a play like *Hamlet*—in a dramatic prefiguration, not only of Descartes and Locke (born in 1596 and 1632 respectively) but of Freud (see Chapter Six). Like Hamlet, Shakespeare looks both before and after, and his gaze extends to each horizon.

Along with Falstaff, Hamlet remains the character most adduced in critical arguments about character. He represents early modern conventions about body, mind, and soul, and he augurs postmodern metapsychologies of the subject. For instance, in *The "Inward" Language*, Anne Ferry notes that Shakespeare gives Hamlet the illusion of "a continuous inward existence [even though] there was no theoretical formulation" of the concept available in 1600. Not until Locke's *Essay Concerning Humane*

Understanding (1689), she argues, do we find a philosophy of "modern consciousness."[16] Ferry believes that Shakespeare explored "a new conception of inward experience" in the Sonnets and in *Hamlet*: Hamlet is "a new kind of figure in English literature," yet produced with premodern "verbal resources."[17] She argues that in the Elizabethan vocabulary the term "self" typically meant "the same," or was used as a synonym for "soul" or "body-and-soul." But even if early modern terms like "inner," "inward," and "secret" typically referred to such components as heart, soul, or other subdivisions of sixteenth-century physio-psychology, Hamlet's key reference is to "*that* within": an unspecified substance or agency. His language is not tied to particular referentiality; it points, but to what?[18]

In an intriguing, sometimes obscure meditation on the status of incipient modern selfhood as outlined in the character of Hamlet, Francis Barker distinguishes the "penumbra of solitude" that surrounds and highlights the solitary Hamlet from a modern psychological interiority.[19] Although Hamlet's "Seems, madam," speech asserts "an essential interiority," the effect is merely gestural, according to Barker. The prince's serial enactments of apparent subjectivity in *Hamlet* are rather desperate and clever evasions of roles others provide for him. Hamlet's asserted interior subjectivity is an anachronism, a projection of a psychic posture as yet unavailable psychologically or socially. Post-Shakespearean criticism has then replaced the unstable outline of Hamlet's proto-subjectivity with its own bourgeois presumptions, filling a void and answering questions that Shakespeare's *Hamlet*, truly read, actually destabilizes.

Although working from radically different critical assumptions, both Ferry and Barker agree that a dramatic representation of authentic, subjective interiority was historically unavailable to early modern writers, even Shakespeare. Recently, Katherine Eisaman Maus has reconsidered the question, both historically and theoretically.[20] She explores the differences "between an unexpressed interior and a theatricalized exterior" in Renaissance England and challenges the claims of Barker and Belsey that ideas of subjective inwardness did not exist in 1600, arguing on the contrary that gestures like Hamlet's toward an interior secret were "almost [truisms] . . . and a very familiar rhetorical tactic." The issue was a serious one in the emerging philosophy of skepticism and "the problem of other minds," as well as in general theological questions of faith in the unseen, or in the doctrine of equivocation. Maus speculates about the working assumptions of new historicist or cultural materialist critics and their need to devalue "bourgeois subjectivity," and she points out that demonstrating prevailing conditions of social production does not logically require the "vaporizing" of an inward self.[21]

Precocious as usual, Joel Fineman a decade ago provided a way to think through the problem of dramatic and literary mimesis that Shakespeare presents to critics.[22] In *Shakespeare's Perjured Eye* he argued that Shakespeare invented "a new first-person poetic posture" now considered conventional. Fineman's book describes a paradoxical progress by which a posture of rhetorical subjectivity is achieved through a self-conscious and refined deployment of literary effects that call into question, even as they brilliantly exploit, the duplicitous nature of language itself.[23] As the speaker of the Sonnets re-presents himself, he opens up an interior space so that his experience of himself is precisely "his distance from himself. His identity is an identity of ruptured identification"—the perjured eye/I. This moment of Shakespearean poetics Fineman cites as the origin of the "modernist literary self, . . . the poetic psychology of the subject of representation."[24] Such an exclusively *literary* definition of "the subject" is especially helpful in thinking about dramatic characters without succumbing to the Scylla of mimetic human representation or the Charybdis of sheer textual effect. As Fineman puts it, Shakespeare's persuasive psychology succeeds "not because [his characters] are the imitation of a real human nature, but because they enact the *only* logic through which subjectivity can be thought or represented in our literary tradition."[25] In other words, Shakespeare's linguistic and dramatic reformulations of character forged the template by which are measured subsequent Western representations, both in terms of literary creation and critical response. This is a large claim, but the ground of *Hamlet* is large enough to accommodate it.

Similarly, Robert Weimann, noting a "crisis in the continuity of the liberal tradition in both criticism and the theater," suggests that *Hamlet* is both before and beyond contemporary terms of mimesis or representation.[26] For him, Shakespearean mimesis is in a special category that subverts or transcends our theoretical categorizing; it is not "representation" or "non-representation," "classical" or "literary" or "carnivalesque." *Hamlet*, Weimann implies, is the central radical interrogation of representation in Western culture. It creates, then explores, the disruption between exhibition and meaning that has become the frame and focus of its criticism.[27]

"I have that within which passes show," Hamlet declares. "All right, then," we might ask, "what is it?" "Who's there?" "Unfold yourself." But

to reiterate the play's inaugural demand for explication (*explicatio*, unfolding) is already to shape and limit responses: the interrogative "who" pre-
sumes agency. Perhaps, as Barker and Belsey assert, no one is there: "At the
centre of Hamlet, in the interior of his mystery, there is, in short, nothing."[28] Other critics have filled the vacancy by characterizing it as *loss*—
more specifically, mourning.[29] Turning the inaugural question of *Hamlet*
against the key postmodern question of Foucault, "What matter who's
speaking?"—itself a version of Lacan's "*Qui parle?*"—Annabel Patterson
argues that the key issues of voice and agency were critical for Shakespeare
and fin-de-siècle Elizabethan culture, and that Hamlet finally provides an
answer of sorts when he responds to Laertes that it was not Hamlet who
wronged him but "Hamlet's madness."[30] Whether mourning or madness,
the implicit psychological trajectory of Hamlet's gestures is toward another
place or agent of being or action, something inarticulate, unavailable to
conventional demonstration or "show."

Of Hamlet, Fineman remarks that the character demonstrates an
"eroticization and suspicion of the rhetorical that begins to manifest itself
toward the turn of the century."[31] Because I believe that just this attitude
toward language maps the ground of Shakespeare's literary play, not just in
Hamlet, I want to turn now to a brief survey of the concept of "language"
in Shakespeare, and specifically the theory and practice of wordplay.

Studies of Shakespeare's English are a large subcategory of studies of
English itself; it would be a project beyond an author's energy or a reader's
patience to review them all.[32] Aside from the regular adduction of Shakespearean instances in philological and linguistic studies, sustained and systematic attention to the particulars of Shakespeare's language did not
really appear until Caroline Spurgeon's 1935 study, *Shakespeare's Imagery
and What It Tells Us*.[33] Spurgeon's book is an important original work on
the "stuff" (her word) of Shakespeare's images, that is, their substantial,
manifest content. She charts the types and frequency of evident images in
order to sketch a stylistic profile of Shakespeare the writer.[34] A related
study published a decade later, Edward Armstrong's *Shakespeare's Imagination*, is an effort to get behind Spurgeon's image categories to discover
"image clusters," primarily from nature, that offer insight into Shakespeare's creative process.[35] Armstrong's psychology is adamantly not psychoanalytic; he relies on commonsensical notions of subliminal effect and
hierarchical layers of meaning. Although he is sensitive to the "streamy
associations" of Shakespeare's poetic style, his ideas about the interrelation
of text and reader are sublimely vaporous.[36]

Following Spurgeon, Clemen, Armstrong, and G. Wilson Knight, later critics of Shakespeare's language focused on the function of image and metaphor in individual plays. For example, Madeleine Doran examines the speeches of individual characters, such as Richard the Third or Richard the Second, and networks of image patterns, for instance in *Romeo and Juliet* or *A Midsummer Night's Dream*.[37] Although Doran offers sensitive readings of several plays, especially the tragedies, she confesses that her ultimate question about the specific distinctiveness of Shakespeare's language from play to play is unanswerable.[38] In *The Shakespearean Metaphor*, Ralph Berry isolates the "controlling metaphor" of individual plays, such as the sonnet and formalized eroticism in *Romeo and Juliet* or devouring time in *Troilus and Cressida*.[39] Although these are fine rhetorical distillations of controlling critical insights, they still restrict many surplus meanings even as they highlight a particularly salient one, just as an actor animates one convincing dramatic possibility while subduing others. (Berry knows this, of course, and chooses rightly to exhibit the powerful, visible insight.) In a sophistication of Spurgeon's cataloguing of images, Berry distinguishes between active metaphor and passive symbol, thus complicating any elementary assumption of a simple, transparent, interpretable relation between literal and figurative language.

Robert Weimann provides a thorough survey of main trends in twentieth-century Shakespeare criticism as they relate to studies of imagery.[40] Noting that interest in Shakespeare's imagery is "of curiously recent origin," Weimann suggests that previous styles of criticism—Romantic and Neoclassical—held different assumptions about language and drama, largely derived from Aristotle. Beginning in the 1930s, with the work of Clemen and Spurgeon, image studies were folded into the techniques of New Criticism and the practices of mid-twentieth-century poetry (such as "Imagism"), and prior foci on plot or character were replaced by discoveries of underlying structures or patterns ("the figure in the carpet"). A new "spatial aesthetic" flattened the plays into a two-dimensionality that could then be (atemporally, symbolically, subjectively) mapped.[41] Writing in the mid-1970s, Weimann sees a transition period in Shakespeare criticism: dissatisfied with readings of texts as ahistorical, autonomous artifacts, critics are not yet possessed of new methods that could create the synthesis between past and present, text and play, literature and society, that Weimann ideally seeks. "How to link the theory of metaphor and the mode of historical criticism?" he asks.[42] His essay is a prolegomenon to an answer.

From the premise that society and history are neither background nor frame to artistic works but "in" the works as a "dimension," he focuses on the *link between* metaphoric tenor and vehicle. Following Rosemond Tuve, he argues that modernist assumptions about the relation of tenor to vehicle are opposite from those of poets in Shakespeare's time; whereas the tenor, or primary basis of the image, was once emphasized, modern critics emphasize the vehicle, or secondary analogy.[43] For instance, modern critics typically follow associative links *from* the vehicle, whereas the Renaissance focus was on the relation of the two components in the original metaphor. Modern criticism thus produces a "second world" of primarily pictorial referents, a proliferation of blossoms from the initial metaphoric plant.

After many pages of close historical and theoretical argument, Weimann examines a few bare examples, such as the metaphor of "sea-walled garden" in the famous garden scene in *Richard II* (3.4). "What is the 'content' or . . . 'subject-matter'?" he asks. Is it garden or nation, or a synthesis of both? Considering the historical dimension, Weimann asserts that a medieval understanding of "sea-walled"—as in *Beowulf*—would have been "opposite" to an early modern comprehension. A medieval view would see the wall as "denoting the coast, which, as it were, surrounds the sea, not the land." An Elizabethan view would see the protective, unifying quality of the wall—thus reflecting a different social and political world. Although I am not clear just how Weimann constructs this reading or this opposition (his interpolated "as it were" suggests some uncertainty even on his part), I am willing to believe that medieval and early modern understandings of the social or political nature of walls could differ to *some* degree. To construe the poetic argument about metaphor as only about the particular nature of the link between "garden" and "state," however, is to exclude a rich field of reference—discoverable in biblical, classical, medieval, Renaissance, and Shakespearean literature, including especially *Richard II* (Gaunt's speech in 2.1)—rooted in another core metaphor (garden as body or womb). His reading privileges *production* (garden as political ground to be managed) over *origin* (garden as ground or source). The encyclopedic mind of Robert Weimann of course knows this other area of metaphor, but it is not in the trajectory of his project here to notice it. Neglecting it, however, is to ignore a key realm of Shakespeare's imagery, thereby inhibiting and in my view eventually disabling a full reading of the play-texts. The metaphor opens multidirectionally, toward society, poetry, theology, and psychology. Readers need to follow it everywhere they can.

If there is a presiding genius (besides Shakespeare) behind my own assumptions about language, it is Theodore Thass-Thienemann, whose *Interpretation of Language* is a psychoanalytic study of the "unconscious" of language, or "the forgotten language of unconscious fantasies."[44] Inverting Lacan's claim that the unconscious is structured like a language, Thass-Thienemann investigates how language is structured like the unconscious. His erudite and unruly volumes construct a linguistic archaeology or paleontology by which he examines verbal symbolism and the fields of semantic (free) association rooted in etymology. His style is a blend of psychoanalytic theory and practice, philosophy, phenomenology, and linguistics: an expansive philology that combines multilingual erudition with a willingness to explore all plausible (and less plausible) etymological branchings of words. Essentially the work is a study of the cultural and linguistic bases of the verbal and symbolic resources Freud employed in *The Interpretation of Dreams*. For Thass-Thienemann, "etymology is . . . not a historical discipline, but the study of motivation. It is the key to the understanding of unconscious fantasies which have been accepted by the language community. They underlie all speech activity."[45] His examples come from various languages, including Greek, Latin, and Hebrew, and Romance and Germanic languages, but his primary focus is English. He cites many examples from the early modern period, including Spenser, Donne, Milton, and especially Shakespeare.

The quintessential emblem of Shakespearean linguistic play is the pun, which condenses the "eroticization and suspicion" of language that Fineman noted in Hamlet, that character whose opening words are a pun. As M.M. Mahood writes in her classic study, "most of the witty wordplay in Shakespeare is either wanton or aggressive."[46] In Shakespeare, she continues, "words heat and burn with a connotative energy"; his poetic practice indicates a growing awareness of the power of "the conceptual world of words built by poetry [which] has its own validity and worth."[47] Mahood is an extraordinarily sensitive reader of multiple senses in Shakespeare's language, although she mostly limits herself to the manifest lexical meanings of words and resists temptations to larger analyses. While she provides excellent elucidations of puns and metaphoric associations in the text, she is concerned about the dangers of being "over-subtle": "It is fatally easy," she writes, "to fall into the 'personal heresy' of substituting an amateur psycho-analysis of the writer for a critical analysis of the work."[48] My own assumptions about the relation of writer and reader to the literary work, and the interrelations of psychoanalysis and criticism, make such caution a style of resistance that I tend to resist.[49] Further, my project is not to psychoanalyze Shakespeare, but to explore how Shakespearean and Freudian assumptions about language and psychic structure correlate.

The Shakespearean pun is a potent device, expansive and explosive—like Hamlet's "less than kin and more than kind" (1.2.65).[50] It is partly, as Sigurd Burckhardt observes, "an act of verbal violence, designed to tear the close bond between a word and its meaning. . . . It denies the meaningfulness of words and so calls into question the genuineness of the linguistic currency on which the social order depends."[51] But puns and wordplay are not merely a threat to meaning or a release of repressed energies. They are also creative linguistic acts that call for active response, or interpretation. Weimann makes a distinction between metaphor, where a relation between two levels of meaning is apparent (a type of mimesis) and wordplay, where the link between expression and association is not apparent (a type of confusion, or riddle). Like the riddle, wordplay exerts on its auditors a demand for interpretation.[52]

A key question in Shakespeare studies, then, is just how particular instances of wordplay are to be interpreted. This question opens out into the arenas of both language and character, where I will pursue it by examining the interpretive practices of critics whose work pertains to the issue of latent senses in language, and the question of agency or intention in character. For instance, in her excellent book on Shakespeare's language, Hilda Hulme shows a willingness to relax some formal semantic codes and entertain additional meanings to words and phrases, in a cautious and scholarly dilation of lexical meanings within the particular dramatic context.[53] As an example, she considers the unusual verb in Macbeth's wish to "trammel up the consequence" of regicide (1.7.3) and suggests that in addition to the common gloss of "to catch in a fishing or hunting net," we consider an ancillary meaning of "to bind a corpse in a shroud." Her defense of this reading offers a succinct statement of my own working assumptions about the play of language in Shakespeare:

Whether or not it is accepted that Shakespeare intends the trammel image to show something of the less conscious mind of his created "character," I hope it may be agreed that the text itself gives evidence that such a meaning of "trammel" as I have suggested was known to the dramatist and to some of his audience. . . . What [Shakespeare] writes can serve as sufficient evidence for what he knew. But it should be noted also that I cannot *prove* either Shakespeare's knowledge or his purpose; I can only show that the external dictionary evidence ties in neatly enough with the internal contextual evidence.

Later she admits that her "method is extravagant; one cannot know in advance which intuitions are most worth following; one can only hold firm to the postulate that every 'full' word in the Shakespeare text has its quota of meaning." There is a special plenitude in Shakespeare's language: "no word in his text is meaningless or muted."[54] Stopping to ponder and associate to other meanings is necessary to comprehend the full sense of a line or passage. (By "association" I intend both the lexical researches of Hulme and the free responses of Freud.)

E.A.M. Colman begins his book on *The Dramatic Use of Bawdy in Shakespeare* by noting the timidity of previous critics in acknowledging the scurrilous features of Shakespeare's language, which he attributes to "the middle-class upbringing of many a sensitive critic."[55] But he himself draws lines of propriety, for example rejecting any double entendres in the opening lines of Sonnet 129 ("Th' expense of spirit in a waste of shame / Is lust in action . . . ")—for instance, "(*spirit* = spermal [sic] fluid, *waste* = waist, *hell* = vagina)"—as "super-ingenious" adolescent trifling.[56] At precisely the same time, in the early 1970s, on the other side of the Atlantic (indeed on the Pacific coast), Stephen Booth was preparing his magnificent edition of *The Sonnets*, wherein he devotes almost three single-spaced pages to an exhaustive analysis of all the puns and senses, salacious and scientific, that resound in this extraordinarily rich opening phrase of Sonnet 129.[57] Both Colman and Booth notice the same senses (though Booth's readings are much more extensive). The American, however, is more willing to trust his ingenuity, following his eyes and ears into the dense network of semantic association that the Shakespearean and Elizabethan vocabulary provides, until the "latent" bodily meanings rise to the surface and become at least equally "manifest" with those simple moralistic pronouncements about spiritual economy that Sonnet 129 also affords. The British reader, on the other hand, will acknowledge sexual senses only by repudiating them as "super-ingenious" and judging them unworthy of mature contemplation.[58]

Colman's caution is driven in part by an assumption of the necessary intentionality and communicability of "indecent" meanings, from character or author to audience or reader (as his utilitarian title implies). Such an assumption can be hazardous, as Harry Berger demonstrates in a trivial yet useful illustration from *Henry IV, Part Two*. Quoting the famous line, "Uneasy lies the head that wears a crown" (3.1.31), Berger notes a pun in "lies," then asks if Henry is aware of it. Such a question goes straight to the concept of Henry's character and may also play a part in any actor's decision of how to say or "deliver" the line. Berger observes that positing a pun in "lies" is "strictly a semiotic decision" that precedes later issues like character or acting. "Meanings or messages may be excavated from the language," he continues, "before the excavator decides whether they are meant or unmeant, heard or unheard, by speakers and auditors and before he decides what kind of psychological framework he will use to condition the development and dramatic articulation of the meanings."

For if the language exists "before" and "outside of" any character or consciousness we construct on the basis of the evidence we find in it, then, during interpretation, the language comes to "speak" the character and to speak *about* him. In no way is it an immediate expression of his "interiority." Rather, it offers suggestions and directions for a portrait or a set of portraits that readers, actors, and directors proceed to draw. From this standpoint speech is not the property of the speaker; the speaker is the property of the language. The language may be "psychoanalyzed" apart from the speaker, and readers may agree in their analysis—may agree, for example, on the presence of a specific set of effects, motives, or "moves" in a stretch of language—but still disagree when it comes to deciding what that analysis tells them about the speaker.[59]

While the critical assumptions and practices of Booth and Berger are quite congenial to a psychoanalytic style of reading Shakespeare, another typical objection is that this style does injustice to the historical conditions in which Shakespeare wrote. When we reify and re-animate a Shakespearean text as a literary document, and "psychoanalyze" its language, not only may we be in danger of ignoring the dramatic function of the language but we also may be making a weak assumption about Shakespeare's audience. Some scholars have claimed that Elizabethan society was "*virtually* non-literate."[60] Terence Hawkes argues that an equation of literature with writing is historically hazardous and misleading, a modern presumption itself created by a modern, highly literate, culture or subculture that privileges the printed book and the phenomenon of reading as a private experience, thereby producing a sense of a self separate from society—an assumption alien to an "oral" culture like Elizabethan England.[61] Even if Shakespeare's plays were more frequently seen and heard than read (as they are today), we might keep in mind that early modern styles of attention to spoken language likely exceeded our own, enervated as it is by our hyper-visual culture. When "Shakespeare" is more and more frequently becoming a visual art (for example, in film) or a commodified icon (as in advertising), perhaps the only way to recuperate or preserve the full intellectual and emotional properties of his work is by reading it. In a crucial way, the project of the insistently textual critic is a conservative one, devoted to the production and preservation of the fullest senses of Shakespeare's language. If an audience member, Elizabethan or contemporary, literate or illiterate, does not hear Shakespeare's language all the way through, any limitation here likely resides in the audience member, not in the author. If the full meanings of Shakespeare could be presented and received on the stage, then why do we have courses in "Shakespeare?"[62]

Reading, after all, is the practice Shakespeare's original editors so eloquently proposed for us. In their prefatory address "To the Great Variety of Readers" in the *First Folio* (1623), John Heminge and Henry Condell wrote: "For his wit can no more lie hid, than it could be lost. Read him therefore; and again, and again: and if then you do not like him, surely you are in some manifest danger, not to understand him." To be sure, Heminge and Condell were likely motivated less by a critic's desire to recuperate and imaginatively animate the texts than by a seller's desire to market the product. But their words are wise across the centuries. Milton heard them, when he wrote that "the readers of Shakespeare took over from the fickle players the trust and inheritance of his fame." Nietzsche opined that Shakespeare's intellectual richness, his philosophical "reflection," was "too remote and refined for the eyes of the theatrical public." Charles Lamb went so far as to claim that Shakespeare's plays are better suited to reading than seeing.[63]

But this is to incite a dispute I want to subdue. Better to avoid insisting on one definition of the plays as either texts or dramas, or on one style of response, either reading or watching. As Hawkes usefully puts it, Shakespeare's works are *play-texts*. They can be treated like novels or plays or poems, precisely because they are "the site of a competition between different ways of reading": "They stand outside—and thus call into question—the only categories we have available to describe them."[64] In this way the works are like the characters. They can be formulated according to categories from various historical periods and aesthetic or critical genres, and once they are so categorized they begin immediately to push against the limits of their definition.

Often surplus meanings in Shakespeare's language are available to attentive eyes and ears from their first appearance (unlike, say, Cordelia's "Nothing"). One well-known moment occurs in Macbeth's first line, "So foul and fair a day I have not seen" (1.3.38), spoken immediately before he and Banquo encounter the witches, who moments before were chanting "Fair is foul, and foul is fair." Only the most obtuse of critics could resist the uncanny inference that Macbeth as a character is already subsumed within a language that pre-exists and literally prefigures him. But his open-ing line more than echoes the witches. The last phrase, "I have not seen," also prefigures those future uncanny phenomena that Macbeth sees and does not see: the dagger, Banquo's ghost. The line places the character within a demonic pre-script and indicates the paradoxical epistemology that will victimize him. In this case, the play of language is presumably undeniable, since the dynamic is thematized in the play and comprehen-sible, for instance, as a displaced expression of unconscious motivation (see Chapter Six).

Another notable instance of a character using language beyond pre-sumable conscious intention is the Moorish general's grand farewell la-ment: "Othello's occupation's gone" (3.3.357). Hilda Hulme was one of the first critics to hear the full sense of the term "occupation." She noted that whereas Othello intends to refer to his military career, "as Iago and the rest of us understand it" the word must also refer to Desdemona. She then notes that the "indecent" meaning of "occupy" as "to cohabit with" would have been known to Shakespeare's audience (she cites 2 *Henry IV*, 2.4.159), so that the meaning of the word "which Othello himself ignores would be the more vividly present" to them. Hulme considers this "a tiny point." [65] Twenty years later, at the 1981 World Shakespeare Congress in Stratford-upon-Avon, the British critic Andrew Gurr read a paper on "The Many-Headed Audience" in Shakespeare's playhouse, during which he worried the term "occupation" for many minutes as he entertained the possibility of its sexual meaning. I cannot recall his conclusion, though I believe he was ambivalent. What I do recall was my own (American) amazement that the meaning should even be in question. [66]

My occupation is here. These various arguments, responses, and ex-amples should provide a sketch of the terrain and techniques by which I intend to map out some possibilities of the play of language in Shakespeare. The project is full of hazards and benefits. One way to begin is by study-ing the talents, techniques, and trials of that clever and cantankerous hermeneut, Malvolio.

2

Paranoia, Criticism, and Malvolio

AN AMERICAN FILM OF THE 1970S, *The Seven Per-Cent Solution*, portrays Sherlock Holmes and Sigmund Freud as fellow detectives, tenaciously worrying stubborn details until they yield their uncanny clues.[1] The consanguinity of these two investigators is apt. They are the modern sires of a hermeneutic brotherhood whose members include many literary critics. As the Wizard of Baker Street once remarked to Dr. Watson: "the more *outré* and grotesque an incident is the more carefully it deserves to be examined, and the very point which appears to complicate a case is, when duly and scientifically handled, the one which is most likely to elucidate it."[2] Like Holmes, Freud too was a systematic and intuitive detector of telltale clues in strange events, constructing a psychoanalysis of parapraxes (errors, omissions, slips of the tongue), from which he derived—or in which he discovered—complex yet repudiated intentions. For both Holmes and Freud, every human action has a meaning, a motivation, an explanation. Final discovery becomes revelation; the problem is solved, everyone is enlightened, and the culprit is caught (he slips up).[3]

Yet the conclusive discovery of secret meaning and hidden motivation can be perceived differently. Another film of the same period, *They Might Be Giants*, stars George C. Scott as a respectable judge gone mad, believing himself to be Sherlock Holmes. Roaming New York City in deerstalker cap and greatcoat, accompanied by his faithful psychiatrist, one Dr. Watson (played by Joanne Woodward), he pursues the trail of the villainous Moriarty. Clues are literally everywhere, in almost any chance event. When a bag of groceries splits and spills on the sidewalk before him, the would-be Holmes quickly retrieves a can of vegetables and finds a secret message in its label. Other leads are cleverly hidden in the telephone directory. He is relentless in pursuit, a genius at discovering clues, and he is also hopelessly paranoid. Indeed, to be paranoid means to see intention everywhere and

to fit events into the scheme of meaning required by the system of suspicion. This paranoid Holmes melodramatically illustrates an intriguing aspect of psychoanalytic theory and practice: its paranoid potential. Freud at
least once acknowledged the hazard. Speaking in 1915 about the sorts of
evidence psychoanalysts discover and use to support their claim that all
behavior, conscious or unconscious, is intentional, he warned:

> And one other point. To work from slight indications, as we constantly do in this
> field, is not without its dangers. There is a mental disorder called *combinatory para-
> noia* in which the practice of utilizing such small indications is carried beyond all
> limits, and I naturally do not contend that the conclusions which are built up on
> such a basis are throughout correct. Only by the breadth of our observations, by
> the accumulation of similar impressions from the most varied forms of mental life,
> can we guard against this danger.[4]

Not only is this assumption—that all behavior is motivated, that all acts
have meaning, that everything provides a clue for detection—a potentially paranoid presumption, but guarding against the potential danger
requires intensifying its strategies. In Freud's terms, *combinatory* paranoia
is avoided through the *accumulation* of more details. Paradoxically, we
must be on guard to avoid being overly suspicious.

Psychoanalysis, of course, has been characterized as a school of suspicion.[5] And nowhere is Freud's epistemology of suspicion more acutely displayed than in his essay on paranoia, the "Psycho-Analytic Notes upon an
Autobiographical Account of a Case of Paranoia (*Dementia Paranoides*)
(1911)," or the "Schreber case."[6] In fact, Freud's essay is not an actual case
history but an interpretation of the history Schreber himself wrote (his
Memoirs of a Neurotic, published in 1903). Freud never met Schreber and,
with the sole exception of the date of his birth, all of the material Freud
had to work with came from the *Memoirs*. In effect, Freud's analysis and
diagnosis derive from his meticulous reading of a book. The essay on
Schreber is thus particularly analogous to an act of literary criticism.

More specifically, Freud's central theory of paranoia as a defense
against homosexual wishes is presented as a set of linguistic transformations of a single sentence—or as Freud put it, "contradictions of the single
proposition: 'I (a man) love him (a man).' " He offers four possible contradictions, all described in terms of the grammar of the basic sentence, "I
love him." Contradiction of the subject leads to jealousy ("she loves him");
contradiction of the verb leads to delusions of persecution ("I hate him.
Why? Because he hates me"); contradiction of the object leads to eroto-

mania ("I love her. Because she loves me"); contradiction of the whole sentence leads to megalomania ("I don't love anyone. I love only myself").

Without arguing the validity or value of these assertions, I want merely to point out the linguistic and literal form in which Freud puts his theory. He is not only "reading" Schreber through his literal reading of a book. Freud is also formulating a general psychological theory in terms of the various ways a sentence may be written and read.

There are other analogies in the Schreber essay to Freud as a literary critic. When, for instance, he begins to suspect a transference neurosis in Schreber's reported behavior toward a physician, he hunts through the *Memoirs* for some reference to Schreber's father or brother. "After a prolonged search," Freud writes, "I was delighted when I came at last on a passage . . . "—a passage that supports his suspicion. Literary critics, I imagine, do this sort of thing frequently. We begin with an expectation, or suspicion, or structure, or interpretive bias, and then we search and re-search for passages that support us. Imagine our delight when, so very frequently, we come upon exactly what we need, not always on first perusal, and sometimes we must polish our discovery a bit so that others might see it shine, but we find it.

This activity, I submit, is a type of nonpathological paranoia. I believe that Freud was aware of the similarity. Add to his remark about the dangers of "combinatory paranoia" the remarkable concluding paragraphs of the essay on Schreber. Here Freud explicitly notes salient similarities between Schreber's elaborate delusional system and Freud's own suspicious interpretive strategies that explain the meaning of Schreber's paranoia. At this point, Freud writes:

> I can nevertheless call a friend and fellow specialist to witness that I had developed my theory of paranoia before I became acquainted with the contents of Schreber's book. It remains for the future to decide whether there is more delusion in my theory than I should like to admit, or whether there is more truth in Schreber's delusion than other people are as yet prepared to believe.[7]

After pages of scrupulous suspicion, ingenuousness here is almost touching. To reach to a friend and fellow specialist as witness to the priority of Freud's theory could be evidence *for* a charge of paranoia. Theory first, evidence later is after all the structure of paranoid interpretation—even if those "other people" remain skeptical.[8]

Paranoia is basically an ingenious, albeit delusional, *system of coherence*.

Such a system discovers and interprets causes, motives, intentions, and meanings in events perceived to relate directly to the subject. (Persecution is one such construction.) The paranoid person, writes the analyst David Shapiro, "regards a communication or a situation not to apprehend what it is, but to understand what it signifies." He continues:

A subjective world comes into being that is a peculiar blend of the autistic and the factual. The paranoid person's picture of the world is interpretively autistic, but it is usually accurate in its factual details. He imposes a biased and autistic interpretive scheme on the factual world. His interest is not in the apparent world, but in the world behind the apparent world to which the apparent world only gives clues. Thus, the subject matter of his interest has to do with hidden motives, underlying purposes, special meanings, and the like. He does not necessarily disagree with the normal person about the existence of any given fact; he only disagrees about its significance.

Acute, narrow attention that is rigidly directed toward certain evidence can extract it and can impose its own conclusions virtually anywhere. Thus, the suspicious person can be at the same time absolutely right in his perception and absolutely wrong in his judgment.[9]

The assumption of hidden significance and its resulting discovery can thus be aspects of pathological strategies of perception and thought. I am suggesting, following Freud's hint, a corollary paranoid assumption in psychoanalysis, and further, an analogy to literary criticism. For instance, there is an implicit process in therapeutic interactions that might be termed the primary paranoid assumption of psychotherapy. It functions according to a simple logic:

A.   If I, as a therapist, listen or otherwise relate to a patient, and
B.   I respond with, say, a feeling (not necessarily verbalized, but felt), then
C_1. My feeling is *caused* by the patient, or,
C_2. The patient is *doing something to me with the intention* of arousing this feeling in me.

(Therapists often talk about being "manipulated" by their patients, or about their efforts to avoid being manipulated.) This dynamic has even been aphorized: "In the result lies the intention."

I find an analogy to the way in which some literary critics apparently perceive their relationship to a text. The logic is identical:

A. If I read a text, and
B. I respond (whether or not, indeed before I articulate my response), then
C_1. My response is caused by the text (or in some models by the author), or,
C_2. The text's (author's) intention/message/meaning/significance is to cause that response in me.

Together with its corollary assumption—that there *is* a message in the text, and I, properly trained in sophisticated methods of detection, can discover its traces and decipher it—this assumption of intention underlies much literary criticism, past and present, conservative and avant garde. I am suggesting the proximity of these assumptions to paranoid processes. Here are the steps of this potential process:

1. "There is a message here." (The Assumption of Intention)
2. "There is a message here, for me to discover." (The Critic as Detective)
3. "There is a message here, for *me*." (The Critic as Paranoid)

Let me hasten to add that I am not arguing that psychoanalysts and literary critics are paranoid, but that a potentially paranoid assumption underlies some of their basic interactions with people and texts. As Shapiro admits, paranoia is pathological at its extremes, but its fundamental perceptual and cognitive strategies are necessary components of normal functioning. Wariness is after all a useful attribute in life.

Moreover, this logic of therapeutic assumptions is admittedly simple. While many therapeutic interactions may be based on such assumptions, many are not. Those therapists who conceive a more complex relationship with their patients are more likely to achieve the therapeutic results they both desire. A more complex process of perception would relate the patient's actions to the therapist's feelings, not in a simple cause-and-effect mode but because there is a (to-be-determined) correspondence between the therapist's perception of the patient's actions and the therapist's perception of his own feelings, understood through his own self-knowledge. It is such self-knowledge that may enable a relationship to emerge and develop (in a manageable "transference" and "countertransference"), and that may eventuate in a new self-knowledge for the patient, and even the therapist. A similar complexity modifies my analogy to literary criticism.

The central defense mechanism of paranoia is *projection*: the attribution to others of feelings, thoughts, wishes, and fears within oneself but repudiated. As Shapiro puts it:

The projective process is completed and a projection may be said to exist when the paranoid person, in a certain state of tension and biased expectancy vis-a-vis the external world, turns his attention toward an object and seizes on a clue the significance of which convinces him of some motive, intention, or the like, and thereby crystallizes his biased expectancy in some concrete shape.[10]

I should stress that this projection is unconscious; the repudiation and externalization are unknown, unacknowledged. This is important because one difference between paranoid people and us sane, sensible critics is that our projections can be acknowledged. We can accept our own share in constructing meanings from texts and recognize that when we read, *we* read. We literally inspire a poem by giving it our breath and voice as we read aloud. We discover and understand its significance in our own terms, in terms of ourselves and the contexts of our relationships (which may include literary history, biography, psychoanalysis, and so on). We "make sense" out of what we read by making sensible links between the terms of the text and our style of understanding them. It's not that we "make up" or create the text; that's a psychotic position. It's that we use the text to create our response to it, and the only way we can articulate our critical relation to the text is through that response. Otherwise we could just read the text aloud and say, "It speaks for itself." Conversely, we could criticize the text without reading it at all, thereby speaking for ourselves. Literary criticism exists between the poles of a reified, animistic text and an empty, ignored one.

The strongest form of this argument in critical theory can be instanced by Edward Wasiolek, who argues that "texts are made and not given": metaphorically they are empty structures waiting to be in-formed by the expectations a reader brings to them.[11] Geoffrey Hartman has called interpretation the act of "finding" texts.[12] A text is an occasion for discovery. Or it is a corpse (*corpus*) waiting to be newly inspired and re-energized by a reader. Hence Cary Nelson's definition of criticism as "a special way of projecting individual experience through the medium of pre-existent texts."[13] To make such acknowledgments is to avoid many of the hazards of paranoid or unconscious projection (although some aspects of any reading will remain unconscious). Paranoid projection provokes the idea of an autonomous, animistic text: the words-on-the-page that are objectively out *there*, signifying or containing meaning. *Res ipsa loquitur*: not I, but the text that talks to me ("the words say"). A more sophisticated version of this unconscious assumption imagines an omni-operative text that controls the reader, meticulously manipulating him or her into paradox or revelation.[14] Now the text talks not to me but through me; the reader becomes a ventriloquist's dummy.

I believe it is possible for us as critics to modify if not avoid such potentially paranoid object-ifications of the text by remaining consciously aware of our own individual styles of making sense out of what we read. (After all, the individuality of our styles has much to do with why we read one another.) By recognizing and acknowledging our projections, our own personal investment in the meanings we construe, we can open fields of interpretation without losing touch with the texts we interpret. Literary critics speak of being anchored in or to the text; psychotherapists speak of being anchored in or to their own feelings. My ideal reader has both anchors out and floats naturally in between—immersed but not drowned in his or her medium.

Some readers, however, may be engulfed by their unacknowledged, paranoid projections. The plight of Shakespeare's Malvolio in *Twelfth Night* offers a dramatic paradigm of the risks of unconscious projection as a style of reading. As a character, the puritanical steward is humorless, affected, austere: "sick of self-love," as Olivia says of him (1.5.90). Indeed, many of his characteristics seem like textbook paranoia: rigidity, secrecy, suspiciousness, lack of spontaneity, humorlessness, arrogance, narcissism, hypersensitivity, intolerance of others and their play.[15] In the famous forged letter scene, when Malvolio happens across the note conveniently planted by Maria and Sir Toby, his paranoid characterization ultimately subjects him to the very ridicule the defense initially protected him from. Imagine, if you will, Malvolio as a literary critic confronted with a text, and take note of his interpretive style.

Certainly he has the affectations of a scholar ("I will read politic authors"), a critical eye (witness his harsh evaluation of Feste as a professional Fool), and a good ear for the jargon. Disturbed by the nocturnal noises of Sir Toby and the merrymakers, he demands, "Is there no respect of place, persons, nor time in you?" (2.3.97–98). In other words, he asks, "Can't you observe the traditional three Unities in your play?"[16] With his consistent concern for formality, order, and decorum, Malvolio becomes an Aristotelian dramatic critic of the play he inhabits. His scene with the forged letter—which Maria calls "some obscure epistle" (2.3.155)—gives him an opportunity to display his skills at textual exegesis as well. They are remarkable.

After studying the handwriting of the letter, and confidently identifying it as Olivia's, Malvolio proceeds to his reading.

> By my life, this is my lady's hand: these be her very C's, her U's, and her T's; and thus she makes her great P's. It is in contempt of question her hand. (*Reads.*) "To the unknown beloved, this, and my good wishes." Her very phrases! By your leave, wax. Soft! and the impressure her Lucrece, with which she uses to seal: 'tis my lady! To whom should this be?

Soon after asking this question, he wishes an answer: "If this should be thee, Malvolio?" Then he reads further.

> "I may command where I adore;
>   But silence, like a Lucrece knife,
> With bloodless stroke my heart doth gore.
>   M. O. A. I. doth sway my life."
> "M. O. A. I. doth sway my life."—Nay, but first let me see, let me
>   see, let me see.

(At this point, of course, Malvolio closes his eyes.)

> "I may command where I adore." Why, she may command me; I serve her, she is my lady. Why, this is evident to any formal capacity. There is no obstruction in this. And the end: what should that alphabetical position portend? If I could make that resemble something in me! Softly! "M. O. A. I."—
> "M"—Malvolio. "M."—Why, that begins my name! But then there is no consonancy in the sequel; that suffers under probation. "A" should follow, but "O" does. And then "I" comes behind.
> "M. O. A. I." This simulation is not as the former: and yet, to crush this a little, it would bow to me, for every one of these letters are in my name. Soft! Here follows prose. (*Reads.*)   (2.5.86–143)

Now he reads and accepts the written instructions to dress in yellow stockings, to be cross-gartered, and to smile incessantly upon his lady. His reading fools him; it makes him a fool.

"M. O. A. I. . . . If I could make that resemble something in me." The strategy of projection is clear enough here (it is the major defense mechanism of this play of *Twelfth Night, or What You Will*).[17] What is fascinating is that the strategy is so catching. Malvolio is not alone in puzzling over the "fustian riddle" of alphabetical positions. More than a few Shakespearean editors, scholars, and critics have succumbed to this "graphomania" and caught the urge of infectious exegesis.[18]

Of course Malvolio's projections are not unsupported by textual reality, just as the various scholarly solutions rest on variably secure linguistic foundations. The letters are in his name; Maria is an excellent forger; there is evidence to detect. Such evidence, combined with the detective's own aspirations for advancement, make it easy, even reasonable, for Malvolio to arrive at his happy conclusion. It is "evident to any formal capacity."[19] (We may even have noted the alphabetical links before Malvolio, and marvel at his stupidity.) Yet it is also projection—and worse, projection denied.

> I do not now fool myself, to let imagination jade me; for every
> reason excites to this, that my lady loves me.   (2.5.164–66)

From the inverted perspective in which reason excites rather than informs, Malvolio finds the way to shape the letter(s) in terms of himself, and then to reform himself in terms of the letter. It requires only a little "crush" to make the fit, yet Malvolio will soon find himself uncomfortably constricted by his cross-garters and painfully confined as a madman in a cell—a paranoid schizophrenic, surely. As Elizabeth Freund puts it, in what is "a warning to all interpreters," "Malvolio digs his own hermeneutic grave"; he is "a casualty of the carnival of letters."[20]

Malvolio's fate is a consequence of his own desires, projected outward and then returned against him in humiliation and punishment (mortification). Those desires are both social and sexual: "to be Count Malvolio" and to possess Olivia. His apparently random manipulation of alphabetical positions spells out one of the bawdiest moments in Shakespeare, echoed in his next phrase, "in *cont*empt of question."[21] Further, his breaking of the letter's seal (a wax impression of Lucrece, the classic personification of both Chastity and Rape) is a symbolic transgression: a rending of the virginal seal to know its contents, and when the contents prove intractable, a further forcing of Olivia's letter to his own will. As he says when he breaks the seal, "By your leave, wax. . . . 'Tis my lady." What is hereby dramatized could be termed The Tale of the Violated Letter, where the violated letter

represents the alphabet, Maria's forgery of Olivia's writing, Malvolio's reconstructions, and ultimately our own readings of the scene and its cryp-
tograms.[22] In order to render meaning, the text is rent. Perhaps Malvolio
and we fellow critics are, like Feste, not so much fools as "corrupters of
words" (3.1.40).

I'll join the crowd, though not around "M. O. A. I." Instead, I want
to follow Malvolio's projective interpretation of his "found" text with my
own verbal corruption of *Twelfth Night*'s opening speech, whose themes
relate to Malvolio's plight. My reading will also be projective, as I believe
all readings are. Whether it will be paranoid as well remains to be seen.

> If music be the food of love, play on,
> Give me excess of it, that, surfeiting,
> The appetite may sicken, and so die.
> That strain again, it had a dying fall;
> O, it came o'er my ear like the sweet sound
> That breathes upon a bank of violets,
> Stealing and giving odor. Enough, no more,
> 'Tis not so sweet now as it was before.

Orsino, carried on stage (I imagine) lounging on a couch, begins in a state
of absolute dependence yet absolute control: "Give me" ("feed me").
Kenneth Burke, in a wonderfully whimsical and insightful "translation" of
this opening speech, terms Orsino's initial state "larval receptivity": he lies
passively ingesting his harmonious environment—yet also, I would add,
commanding it.[23] The announcement of appetite, however, and the response of satiation lead to surfeit: "Enough, no more." Note how the
rhythm of the lines shifts from languid flow to abrupt completion. The
primal rhythm of hunger and satiety is here expressed in languid lyrics of
music and flowers. Yet, in that odorous "sound that breathes," my carnal
ear hears a belch, the sign of surfeited appetite, soon to be personified by
Sir Toby Belch.[24]

This dynamic structure of desire, excessive fulfillment, and a resulting
sickness or "dying" has other analogies beyond the oral and aural (food
and music). As Orsino admits, he wants the symbolic food of *love*, and his
own poetic images of "a bank of violets" (auguring Viola, and perhaps
violation) and "a dying fall" have conventional roots in Elizabethan erotic
poetry, where their references are more clearly sexual. As the Arden editors
note, "surely Orsino, like other lovers, may wish also to have the pangs of

love itself allayed."[25] Orsino's next lines develop these potential meanings and allude metaphorically to the sexual allaying of the pangs of love.

> O spirit of love, how quick and fresh art thou,
> That notwithstanding thy capacity
> Receiveth as the sea, nought enters there,
> Of what validity and pitch soe'er,
> But falls into abatement and low price,
> Even in a minute.

These lines are typically read as more of Orsino's sublime romantic ruminations. I want to undermine their sublimations, to note the carnal appetite under the romantic yearnings, to find the food beneath the music. Accordingly, I want to point out the potentially venereal vocabulary of the lines—to subject them to verbal corruption and translate their sexual senses, freeing them into the larger play of language.

The word "spirit" can have sexual connotations (as in Sonnet 129), and in at least two places Shakespeare uses "spirit of love" as a genital euphemism.[26] Terms such as "quick" and "fresh" also have sexual meanings: recall Mistress Quickly, or Cressida as "a woman of quick sense"; Shakespeare uses "fresh" to refer both to whores and virgins.[27] (I am not denying the simultaneous innocence of these terms, just adding another potential context.) The entrance into a capacious receptacle by an object of "pitch" (height) that soon "falls into abatement" is sexually analogous to intercourse followed by detumescence. In other words (or in other contexts of the same words), my reading of Orsino's speech symbolically enacts the emergence and satiation of appetite at various levels: oral, aural, genital, romantic. The "spirit of love" is simultaneously a sublime romantic image of Eros *and* the carnal embodiment of Venus. At one very basic level, Orsino's capacious "sea" is also Malvolio's cryptic "C."[28]

After his lyrical and symbolic satisfaction, Orsino moves out of the posture of passive dependence and begins to make puns about hunting. Desire now shifts from one kind of appetite to another—from the desire to rest and be fed ("Give me excess of it") to the desire to go out and find food, an aggressive, predatory desire that has an absent object. In this play, when such desires are revealed or released, they typically turn back upon their source. Orsino—"little bear" in Italian—is the creature of boundless appetite who is also the object of the hunt, as his pun on "the hart" further indicates. A metaphoric version of what happens to Malvolio is emblematized in Orsino's allusion to Actaeon, the hunter devoured by his own hounds as a consequence of a forbidden carnal vision (the naked Diana). Like Malvolio, he is victimized by his own projected desires.

> O, when mine eyes did see Olivia first,
> Methought she purg'd the air of pestilence!
> That instant was I turn'd into a hart,
> And my desires, like fell and cruel hounds,
> E'er since pursue me. (1.1.17–22)

Carnal appetites and their symbolic metamorphoses are the implicit subjects of *Twelfth Night*, just as they are the subjects of the Feast of Twelfth Night, or the Epiphany. Such transformations are, if you will, the meat of the play. The dynamic of the return of the repressed—distorted desires projected outward only to return to victimize their source—is a primary structure throughout Shakespeare's works.[29] *Twelfth Night* is a play about the comic and potentially tragic results of such desire and projection.

Yet there are less catastrophic versions of projection, which may benefit rather than victimize and which also relate to literary criticism. All criticism, as I experience it, originates in projection, an *outering* into a text that generates a critical utterance.[30] When this outering is denied, the inviolable objectivity of the text may be decreed and a pattern of potentially paranoid processes can develop. When the outering is acknowledged and accepted, an interrelationship of reader and text, self and other, can be opened up rather than closed off. If I start to interrogate a text with a question, like "What does this *mean*?"—even with the psychoanalytic third-ear third degree—I am really asking myself a question: "How am I relating to this text?" And since in this instance I began with a question, my relationship is interrogatory and can soon involve potentially paranoid assumptions about significance and intent: where there is a question there should be an answer. Such a critical posture constructs one relationship but closes others. *Hamlet*, chronologically and psychologically *Twelfth Night*'s tragic twin, opens with a charge to its critical interrogators. It begins with a primal question, then repudiates it and offers an alternative.

> Who's there?
> Nay, answer me. Stand and unfold yourself.

As the history of *Hamlet* criticism amply demonstrates, critics have done just this for centuries, folding and unfolding themselves with varying degrees of awareness and revelation, without wearing out, or even putting any creases in the text. Ultimately, if I ask a book, "What's here?," it answers, "You are."[31] Explication is reflexive.

The model of Malvolio and the letter, or the text as pretext for projection, is one we can all recognize. Those of us who do so, admitting both the risks and benefits of our obsessive critical scrutiny of words, may be less in danger of succumbing to Malvolio's fate. Malvolio suffers finally because his narcissism rejects community: "You are idle shallow things," he snarls. "I am not of your element" (3.4.123–24). Analogously, he misreads because he can *only* read in terms of himself; he cannot consider his text in relation to anything except his own selfish wishes.[32] For readers who can acknowledge private wishes *and* imagine public community (the community of other readers, for example), projection can be a way into a text without getting lost in narcissism and paranoia. Authors, literary and critical, test reality through their audiences. Malvolio's audience is literally unseen and unknown (the hidden tricksters), and the audience before whom he chooses to exhibit himself (Olivia) is mistakenly perceived. He can never move beyond his habit of "practicing behavior to his own shadow" (2.5.17), literally a narcissistic projection. The ground on which he projects his image reflects and imitates him perfectly, but it does not communicate to him. He only talks to himself. Writing criticism is a bit like talking to oneself, too, but teaching and publishing are communicative gestures toward real audiences. If we as critics must sometimes seem to be Malvolios obsessed with letters, at least we can try to be Malvolios who know we're on stage.

3

Pushing the Envelope:
Supersonic Criticism

A GENERATION AGO, IN 1963, ALFRED HARBAGE remarked that "in general, Shakespeare's puns shade into his serious word-play by such imperceptible degrees that we cannot pinpoint the place where joking ends and poetry begins."[1] This view of a rhetorical continuum from low to high, base to sublime, has value, yet its assumption of *classes* of language and intent undermines its perception. A better idea may be to consider Shakespeare's language not as a hierarchy or spectrum—however shady the threshold between levity and gravity, crude joke and serious poetry—but as an arena of linguistic play in which pun and profundity coexist: a field of deep wit, wherein the nature of particular rhetorical events is as much a function of our attitude toward them as of their intrinsic semantic qualities, or Shakespeare's inferable intent. This chapter aims to test some boundaries in our rhetorical attitudes, to draw provisional lines around licit and illicit uses of Shakespeare's language and to propose some models of close reading. One might call them pilot projects.

Nowhere have the hazards of close reading been more effectively and hilariously dramatized than in *Twelfth Night*, in the scene of Malvolio and the forged letter, where, as a result of his ambitious efforts at literary criticism in the service of personal advancement and sexual adventure, the humorless steward transforms himself into a cross-gartered fool, to be treated as a lunatic. The moment offers itself as an emblem. It is both joke and enigma, a moment of deep wit staged clownishly, obscenely. It may even be that the crudity of the joke disguises the depth of the wit.

Before embarking on a few exercises in practical criticism (pushing the envelope), I want to examine another crucial and pivotal moment in Shakespeare. It occurs in *Troilus and Cressida*, when Ulysses is trying to persuade the sulking Achilles to join the Greek forces against Troy. Ulysses, pretending to be reading philosophy, conventionally notes that virtue must demonstrate itself in order to be valued, and Achilles agrees:

> *Achilles.*   What are you reading?
> *Ulysses.*   A strange fellow here
> Writes me that man, how dearly ever parted,
> How much in having, or without or in,
> Cannot make boast to have that which he hath,
> Nor feels not what he owes, but by reflection;
> As when his virtues, aiming upon others,
> Heat them, and they retort that heat again
> To the first giver.
> *Achilles.*   This is not strange, Ulysses.
> The beauty that is borne here in the face
> The bearer knows not, but commends itself
> To others' eyes; nor doth the eye itself,
> That most pure spirit of sense, behold itself,
> Not going from itself; but eye to eye opposed,
> Salutes each other with each other's form;
> For speculation turns not to itself,
> Till it hath travell'd and is mirror'd there
> Where it may see itself. This is not strange at all.
> *Ulysses.*   I do not strain at the position—
> It is familiar—but at the author's drift,
> Who in his circumstance expressly proves
> That no man is the lord of any thing,
> Though in and of him there be much consisting,
> Till he communicate his parts to others;
> Nor doth he of himself know them for aught,
> Till he behold them formed in th' applause
> Where th' are extended; who like an arch reverb'rate
> The voice again, or like a gate of steel,
> Fronting the sun, receives and renders back
> His figure and his heat. I was much rapt in this . . . .   (3.3.95–123)

Underlying Ulysses's speech is an analogy central to Shakespeare's art: that of theatricality, or acting on a stage. The phrase, "communicate his parts to others," opens a comparison made manifest in the terms "applause" and "arch" (of the sky or heavens, like the arch under which

"Achilles" and "Ulysses" stand as actors before an audience at the Globe). Underlying the theatrical analogy is another simile, the *mirror*:

> . . . or like a gate of steel,
> Fronting the sun, receives and renders back
> His figure and his heat.

Vividly sensual, the simile presents a brilliant sign of the reflected image ("figure") and power ("heat") of the eye of heaven as it gazes into the metal surface. It is a design perfectly suited to both Ulysses and Achilles, for it simultaneously models antagonism and mutuality (two styles of reciprocity). In Ulysses's production of the image—call it his reading—the primary meaning is a mirror, a shiny metal surface reflecting the shape and energy of the sun. But it is also a gate, alluding to the Gates of Troy which the Greeks seek to demolish, or perhaps even the Scaean Gates, before which Achilles will eventually meet his own fate. This simultaneous figure of *gate* and *mirror* offers a way to construct apparently opposed positions of literary response.[2] That is, does the reader enter into the text and engage it on its own terms (text as gate), or does the reader find reflected in the text those familiar features he or she brings to it (text as mirror)? Having thus naively put the question, I propose that it, like the image, is only apparently oppositional. Shakespeare's figure is *both* gate and mirror, and so is my ideal reading. The choice between "the words on the page" and readerly interpolation ("reading into") is a false dilemma, since in practice the only way we *can* read is to engage the words from within various frames of reference that can never wholly exclude the "personal." That is, when we read, we make sense of what we read, and making sense is partly a constructive activity.[3] Imagine looking through a window at an external scene. Not only is your perspective framed by the architecture of the window (like a gate), limited by the angle of your view, and subject to your own qualities of apperception, but the scene may also be infiltrated through a reflection of your own image as you look out (a mirror). This is a sketch of the psychological and epistemological idea of a *frame of reference*.[4]

If the text is thus partially a personal reconstruction, then how do we know if or when we are bending it to our own wills, distorting its sense beyond recognition? Are there no limits to readerly re-creation? Rather than belabor such familiar questions, let me turn to some specific examples of Shakespeare in an effort to test the bounds of plausible interpretation—pushing the envelope, in test-pilot idiom.

After Bassanio has accosted Shylock with his need for money, Antonio enters. The Jew thus greets the merchant: "Rest you fair good signior," he says. "Your worship was the last man in our mouths" (1.3.60). Now a necessary way to read this line is to translate it into its conventional equivalent (the necessary evil of paraphrase): "We were just speaking of you." Of course this is what the phrase does mean, and is the tenor of the typical editor's note. Yet to translate into common idiom is to veer from the immediate and pervasive meaning of the words. How are we to respond? Can Shylock be voicing a wish to put Antonio into his mouth—that is, to eat him? Before any production of the pound-of-flesh contract, before Shylock begins to whet his knife and grind his teeth in vengeful anticipation of Antonio's sacrifice, can he be thinking of eating the Christian? Or should we consider the phrase an unconscious admission, wherein Shylock speaks no manifest intention to devour Antonio, but betrays a latent cannibalistic desire? Or should we finesse the issue of Shylock as a character with an analyzable psychology and suggest that the phrase is part of the overall *play of language*, an early sounding of a theme and image that will echo throughout *The Merchant of Venice* and that may arouse primitive fears of being attacked and devoured by a monstrous creature (similar to medieval Christian constructions of murderous Jews)?[5]

If we accept that the greeting ("Your worship was the last man in our mouths") is a key moment in the play of language, further questions arise. I could argue, with substantial evidence, that a fantasy of Shylock carving and eating Antonio is "in" the play. But what if we were to press the image? For example, what if (given plausible homosexual readings of the play, and many modern performances), our associations led us into fantasies of oral sexuality? To many readers such a proposal would be unpalatable. Or, given the obvious theological registers of the play, what if a reader were to connect the term "worship" with that peculiar ritual of divine cannibalism known as the Eucharist (in which Christians symbolically eat a Jew), and find in Shylock's greeting a keenly ironic allusion to that holiest of religious rituals that provides the reciprocal carnal analogy to the raw fantasy of the Jew eating the Christian? Or what if this emerging complex of carnality, sexuality, and theology were connected to the famous question of the pound of flesh, "to be taken in what part of [Antonio's] body pleaseth [Shylock]," and the standard psychoanalytic reading of castration were recalibrated as a central issue of cultural difference marked on the body—namely, circumcision?[6] I could argue that the cutting of flesh as a mark of difference is a crucial theme "in" the play, and that within the play of language, Shylock is honing his knife in order to turn Antonio into a Jew. (The Christian, of course, turns the tables by inflicting Christian charity on Shylock, demanding that he convert.) Shylock's language when he discovers his stolen treasure suggests that he feels the deprivation as much more than a material loss:

> My daughter! O my ducats! O my daughter!
> Fled with a Christian! O my Christian ducats!
> . . . .
> A sealed bag, two sealed bags of ducats,
> . . . .
> And jewels, two stones, two rich and precious stones . . .   (2.8.15–20)

(Shylock's own banker is named "Tubal.") Given this barely latent context of castration and circumcision, I might introduce the late medieval "cult of the holy foreskin" (Christ's prepuce) and such mystical visions as that of Catherine of Siena, who imagined marrying Christ with a ring of his holy foreskin, or the fourteenth-century Viennese nun who had a vision of receiving the sacred prepuce in her mouth and who reported that it tasted like honey.[7] To me these are pertinent associations to the full play of language in the play; to others they may be impertinent, illegitimate readings—perverse distortions of Shakespeare's sense.[8]

As another kind of example, consider the famous question of the origins of Leontes's jealousy at the beginning of *The Winter's Tale*. Critics have proffered various explanations for the sudden onset of the jealousy, from the dramaturgical observation that the tragicomic events of the play must depend on the character's actions, and that a character can arrive on stage without benefit of psychological coherence in the modern sense, to psychoanalytic diagnoses of Leontes's displaced homosexual affection for Polixenes, the suspected rival in the love triangle.[9] I suggest that another source for the character's reaction may be found in the play of language, apparently outside any character's putative agency. Listen to Polixenes's opening lines:

> Nine changes of the wat'ry star hath been
> The shepherd's note since we have left our throne
> Without a burthen. Time as long again
> Would be fill'd up, my brother, with our thanks,
> And yet we should, for perpetuity,

> Go hence in debt. And therefore, like a cipher
> (Yet standing in rich place), I multiply
> With one "We thank you" many thousands moe
> That go before it.   (1.2.1–9)

As several critics have noticed, the references to nine months, to the moon as "watery star," the images of "burthen," "filled up," "standing in rich place," and "multiply" evoke highly suggestive associations to procreation and pregnancy.[10] Without pressing the point further into the scene, where similarly suggestive language continues, I suggest that the origins of the *character's* jealousy lie in the *reader's or audience's* associative responses to the language. Of course a reader devoted to analysis of character might argue that Polixenes's language indicates a wish to reveal his guilt to Leontes (a guilt he expressly does reveal in Act Five, in terms of deep fraternal sympathy: 5.3.53–56), but surely that would be a strange speculation in a scene where the whole dramatic point is that Leontes is sadly, horribly, wrong.

In the next instance, Isabella has come to Angelo to plead for her brother, who is condemned to die for the crime of fornication (*Measure for Measure*, 2.2). Her first words are not about Claudio but about her own views of sexuality and justice:

> There is a vice that most I do abhor,
> And most desire should meet the blow of justice;
> For which I would not plead, but that I must;
> For which I must not plead, but that I am
> At war 'twixt will and will not.   (2.2.29–33)

Since Isabella's first words in the play concern the limits to her liberty when she joins the convent (she wants in fact more restraint than the already strict rules require), one reading of her initial words to Angelo reinforces a psychological view of the character as one who wishes to repress sexual energies. Her image of "the blow of justice" could be connected to her later notorious statement to Antonio that, rather than submit her body to shameful lust, "th' impression of keen whips [she'd] wear as rubies, / And strip [her]self to death as to a bed / That longing have been sick for" (2.4.101–3). Such a psychological reading could speculate about sado-masochistic ambivalences in Isabella, and call into question the posture of severe purity she maintains.[11] A more intimate audition of her opening line

("There is a vice that most I do abhor") could hear the genital meaning of "vice" (used more directly in her charge to Claudio, "Wilt thou be made a man out of my vice? / Is it not a kind of incest, to take life / From thine own sister's shame?" [3.1.138]),[12] and an aural echo of the term she cannot say but that characterizes the flip side of the nunnery she intends to join (the play even has a character named "Abhorson"). But to really push the envelope, let me re-form the lines in a way that their sequence provisionally permits but that many readers may judge out of bounds: "There is a vice that most I do abhor, and most desire." (Period.) Now, can I do that? Will Shakespeare let me? The syntactic moment evanesces, resolved into the succeeding clause. But for an instant the line captures the precise paradox of desire that energizes *Measure for Measure* and most of its characters, "at war 'twixt will and will not" (notice as well how the word "will" oscillates between its senses of desire and volition). But can she mean to have said this? Or is it unconscious? Is it an aspect of the play of language? Or is it merely beyond the pale of permissible readings?[13]

Now for the acid test. As the first interview is about to conclude, Isabella suddenly offers to bribe Angelo. "How?" he returns. "Bribe me?" "Ay," she says,

> with such gifts that heaven shall share with you.
> Not with fond sicles of the tested gold,
> Or stones, whose rate are either rich or poor
> As fancy values them: but with true prayers . . .   (2.2.146–52)

Editors tell us that "sicles" derives from the Hebrew "shekel," that "tested gold" is gold proved true on a touchstone, and that "stones" are precious jewels. Fine. And my psychoanalytic third ear, by this time acutely attuned to the extraordinarily suggestive language of the entire scene and further sharpened by Angelo's own quick response to Isabella's offer (in terms of his character's psychology, her answer may respond to his wish that she bribe him with sexual favors)—my third ear, now listening in supersonic registers, breaking sound and syntax barriers—hears Isabella referring to something that she cannot plausibly be referring to: these contiguous syllables, only slightly re-arranged, evoke the term "testicles," immediately glossed by the common synonym of "stones."

Now what am I to do with this response? It's on the edge, marginal even for me. Does it make sense to construct an unconscious intention in the character, whereby she produces a brilliant Freudian moment that discloses her own desires, while appealing to Angelo's, in a kind of unconscious conversation such as real people may have but rarely become aware of outside an analyst's consulting room? (Earlier she exclaims to Angelo, "I would to heaven I had your potency" [2.2.68].) I could argue that the moment catches a radical ambivalence in Isabella, placed on the threshold between one state (the silence and repression of the nunnery) and another (sudden entry into the slippery sexual economy of Venice).[14] Or I could argue that the moment demonstrates how the sexually charged language of that erotic economy invades Isabella's speech even as she tries to deny it, as if it were unavoidable, a natural contamination by carnality (this is a condition common to characters in *Measure for Measure*: see for instance the Duke at 1.3.1–6). Or I might contend that Isabella's language, like the character herself, is a masculine invention, constructed with the purpose precisely of invading the privacy of her "true prayers" by a denied and displaced profanity.[15] The textual moment replicates in miniature the large-scale project of the play, which is to move Isabella out of the nunnery and into the Duke's bed. The moment may be a prime instance of the play of language, beyond character, outside local intentionality. Or is it rather a prime instance of a reading distorted by what Timon of Athens, referring to another character's bawdy comments about procreation, calls "lascivious apprehension" (1.1.207)?[16]

The two interview scenes between Angelo and Isabella are dramatized instances of the problem of *reading*. Both Angelo and Isabella are trying to read the other's character, to detect through language and gesture the other's intention, to discover underlying meaning. When senses and intentions that neither suspects gradually emerge, as when Angelo finds himself aroused by Isabella, who is the agent of this newly constructed meaning?

> What's this? what's this? Is this her fault, or mine?
> The tempter, or the tempted, who sins most, ha?
> Not she; nor doth she tempt; but it is I . . .   (2.2.162–64)

From the perspective of character, Angelo's location of meaning-construction is apt and plausible. He is guilty of "reading into" Isabella's speech and gesture, of imposing his own wished-for sense on the text that she presents to him (like Malvolio and the forged letter).[17] During the second interview, the readings of the situation by Angelo and Isabella become more obviously a struggle between competing meanings, as Angelo approaches the raw proposition of his scheme and Isabella seemingly is unable to comprehend. "Nay, but hear me," he says to her: "Your sense pursues not mine: either you are ignorant, / Or seem so, crafty; and that's not good" (2.4.73).[18] At this point both characters may be negotiating "lascivious apprehensions": Angelo is trying to bring them to the surface, while Isabella tries to keep them suppressed. What I suggest is that both characters are subsumed within a play of language wherein such meanings are already in play. Perhaps the characters arrive belatedly at understandings an attentive audience already entertains.[19]

By no accident are my examples predominantly sexual. An aspect of my reading style is that my third ear is especially attuned to sexual meanings. It is also my theoretical conviction that the deep metaphoric core of language is carnal.[20] At root, many terms relate to the body and to physical action, like Angelo's word, "conception"; "genius" and "genital" have the same root. The phrase "lascivious apprehension" literally means to grasp or lay hold of wanton pleasures. Indeed, tracking the etymology of "lascivious" through Latin *lascivia* and Anglo-Saxon *lust*—both terms cognate with *ludere* (to play, to sport)—I realize that my personal and professional reading project is to conjoin the ludic and the lascivious. My own interpretive style involves a working compromise between literary learning and unconscious response, or (as a colleague has put it) a rhetorical co-production of my intellect and my primary process.

Yet I would argue that connections between language and sexuality in Shakespeare's texts are not only reflections of my interpretive style or aspects of the carnal core of language. Recent feminist and psychoanalytic studies of Shakespeare suggest that masculine efforts to manage meaning and to control female sexuality (for instance, *Measure for Measure*) are powered by an anxiety about threats to the boundaries of conventional significance represented by the exorbitant surplus of "femininity." In an essay on *Hamlet* and *Measure for Measure*, Jacqueline Rose remarks that "slippage of meaning and sexuality as excess seem . . . to be the subtext of the critical focus on Isabella and Gertrude."[21] The figure of woman presents a destabilizing effect within the conventional system of representation known as masculine hegemony or patriarchy. Femininity or female sexuality, as the site of excess, the ludic and lascivious realm of the infinitely marginal, may embody a powerful background against which traditional (masculine) critical projects enact their exegetical searches for stable meaning. Commenting on T.S. Eliot's famous remark that *Hamlet* is "the Mona Lisa of literature," Rose extrapolates her study of the place of sexuality in the plays into an hypothesis about the hermeneutic need for articulatable meaning and recognizable aesthetic form as a defense against anxiety about destabilized, excessive feminine significance. This is a large and provocative claim, one that likely intimates Rose's personal notions of the power and place of her own interpretations. Even traditional criticism of Shakespeare, however, as the poet of "mixed metaphor" and the all-too-willing victim of puns, suggests a similar point. For example, consider Samuel Johnson's famous criticism of Shakespeare's wordplay:

A quibble is to Shakespeare what luminous vapours are to the traveller; he follows it at all adventures; it is sure to lead him out of his way, and sure to engulf him in the mire. It has some malignant power over his mind, and its fascinations are irresistible. . . . A quibble is the golden apple for which he will always turn aside from his career, or stoop from his elevation. A quibble, poor and barren as it is, gave him such delight, that he was content to purchase it by the sacrifice of reason, propriety, and truth. A quibble was to him the fatal Cleopatra for which he lost the world, and was content to lose it.

Johnson's mini-allegories of linear progression and erroneous detour, of engulfment, malignancy, and fascination, his allusion to a goddess's temptation, his assumption of the debilitating power of pleasure over reason, produce a Shakespeare literally bewitched by puns.[22]

Cleopatra—that occult agent of femininity who stretches the boundaries of passion and discourse, who figures infinite variety, who teases Antony and us with her "immortal longings," who makes men hungry even as they are satiated—the figure makes a powerful emblem of Shakespeare's language. And could there be (dare we hear it?) a pun in Dr. Johnson's own decorous objection to the "low" art of punning ("and was *content* to lose it")? Does the ghost of the sixteenth-century puritan, Malvolio, haunt the eighteenth-century guardian of reputable language? We are back at Malvolio's bawdy spelling lesson, or Hamlet's notorious byplay with Ophelia, his "country matters." If the pun is there, did Johnson intend it? Or is it an irruption of the good Doctor's unconscious associations? As editor of Shakespeare, Johnson glossed the notorious lines in *Hamlet*, proposing to amend the phrase to "country *manners*," as follows: "Do you imagine that I meant to sit in your lap, with such rough gallantry as clowns use to their lasses?" (Presumably by "rough gallantry" Johnson intended a sublime euphemism.) A later eighteenth-century editor rejected Johnson's emendation, attributing it to "casual inadvertence," and went on to state that "what Shakespeare meant to allude to, must be too obvious to every reader, to require explanation." Hilda Hulme, in whose study of Shakespeare's language I found these editorial opinions, remarks:

In this particular instance the post-Victorian student who notes the country pun will escape the charge of reading into Shakespeare's text some new obscenity, self-invented. . . . It is likely also that the eighteenth-century editors were aware of some implications in the Shakespearean text which, because of the narrower code of verbal decency imposed in Victorian times, no longer have a place in the ordinary language of protected academic life.[23]

Professor Hulme wrote this in 1962. Today, not only post-Victorian but also self-consciously post-Freudian, it is practically inevitable to acquaint the ordinary language of current unprotected academic life with those textual implications not traditionally noted in public.[24]

Let us return, therefore, to that gate of steel and reflect more on it. A deeper psychoanalytic reading of the passage notes Ulysses's appeals to Achilles's virility and exhibitionism, to his "parts" and their extension before an audience.[25] As a corollary to the latent phallic play of the language, the arch or gate that receives and reciprocates masculine energies may plausibly be imagined as a body (vaginal) image. Underlying this traditional Freudian reading would be the traditional Shakespearean reading of besieged cities as feminine enclosures threatened by masculine force: the (sexual) rape of Helen, for instance, that spurs the (martial) rape of Troy, to which action Ulysses is slyly urging Achilles. Such an interpretation replicates a style of Freudian readings that have by now found a relatively acceptable place in Shakespeare criticism. I think the gesture can be extended.

Achilles's recital of conventional optics and the confrontation of forms relies on a naive assumption of accurate specular reflection in which the reciprocal circuit of mutual speculation leads to a clear picture. Ultimately the eye does "see itself" through the recognition of others. Achilles's beauty and prowess are evident, even self-evident, since they are always and obviously remarked by his admirers. Achilles's mirror is a narcissistic one.[26]

Ulysses shifts the traditional position toward a skeptical challenge. It is no longer a mutual salutation of self-evident forms, but an interactive process of re-cognition in which the nature of a self is actually formed and echoed by the social matrix wherein that self communicates, extends, or performs itself. Pushed only slightly, these lines can be read as a poetic evocation of a primary site and scene of identity formation: those repeated moments in infancy when a baby extends itself toward its mother and is met with echoing approbation. (A brief fantasy: The little Achilles reaches out to Thetis and grasps her finger. "Oh, how strong you are," she exclaims. "How beautiful! You're my hero." The infant's gesture, the mother's response, constituting his identity.)[27] Ulysses reconfigures Achilles's narcissistic surface into a relational dynamic.[28]

From various psychoanalytic perspectives, then, the scene can be read in terms of exhibitionism, narcissism, and object relations. In my view, none of these perspectives is fully explicative, nor does one contradict another. (I will further develop the senses of this passage in Chapter Eight.) The model of reading Shakespeare that I am here testing, based on various responses to the "gate/mirror/body" image in *Troilus and Cressida*, is one that invites entry into a world of apparently autonomous characters (the Greek camp, the Viennese court) while offering frequent chances for self-reflection (I can see myself in Ulysses and Achilles, Isabella and Angelo, and, yes, Malvolio) and while arousing and shaping sexual energies. In short, reading Shakespeare is for me the nearest thing to the process of erotic identification that literature provides. Testing the limits—playing in the margins of Shakespeare's text—is a means of simultaneously questioning and validating the boundaries of language *and* of sexuality.[29] At origin (if I may imagine origin), such an erotics of reading Shakespeare rests on a fantasized apprehension of the maternal body: Cleopatra's infinite variety, or Cressida's embodied discourse ("There's language in her eye, her cheek, her lip" [4.5.55]). "By my life," Malvolio says, "this is my lady's hand."

But Malvolio, of course, is mistaken—another critic taken in by a facsimile of re-presentation. The steward pushes the envelope until it tears. His reading, which discloses his own private desires as he attends obsessively to the letter of the text, exhibits a posture of autoerotic fantasy that is also metaphorically a rape. If Feste is the clownish yet ultimately benign corrupter of words, Malvolio is the foolish and finally malevolent debaucher.

In the spirit of benign corruption then, I propose three models of critical reading based on these three emblems. One: the figure of Malvolio and the letter, which demonstrates the pleasures and perils of solitary monologic reading. Two: the figure of Isabella and Angelo, which offers a dramatic dialogic episode in which meaning is negotiated, or solicited within a contest of opposed forces. Three: the figure of Ulysses and Achilles, not quite a dialogue but rather pedagogic, as one reader subtly instructs another in a hidden agenda. (Ulysses sets out to seduce Achilles, whereas Angelo is apparently unaware of his initial motives.) Each of these interpretive moments blends understanding and obtuseness, arousal and inhibition, wish-fulfillment and defensiveness, within a play of language whose deepest strata are carnal, and whose layers of overdetermined meaning reach to the margins, and beyond.

Coda: Close Reading Redux

The 1989 meeting of the Shakespeare Association of America, in Austin, Texas, highlighted a plenary session on "Close Reading." One of the profession's finest practitioners of that art, Stephen Booth, provided a dazzling demonstration of its possibilities while asserting a refutation of any theoretical grounding for the practice.[30] His initial example was the opening line of Edmund's soliloquy in *King Lear*, Act One, Scene Two: "Thou, Nature, art my goddess. . . ." Booth pointed to the abrupt coupling in this line of two quintessential terms in *Lear* and in the largest philosophical quarrels of the Renaissance: "nature" and "art." Of course, in this instance "art" serves grammatically as verb, not noun, but once the acoustic-visual event is noted, such linguistic conventions may seem, to some very close readers, subordinate. The juxtaposition of the two words is an observable textual event. It may be an illegitimate, even "bastard" reading, but it is nonetheless an event. (To use Edmund's own argument, are ear and eye to be shackled by "the plague of custom" [1.2.3]?) What are we to do, Booth asks, with this event? Is it an accident of language? Did Edmund intend it? Did Shakespeare? Does it carry meaning? Booth went on to argue that it cannot be ignored (just try to forget it now) and that it need not carry a character's or author's intention, or thematic meaning. It is simply there: a momentary phenomenon that we observe or bypass in our readerly traversal of the line. He continued to state that his style of close reading is thus "merely academic," not tied to theoretical schools or hermeneutic assumptions.

At the conclusion of this session, someone in the audience asked Booth about the place of unconscious receptivity in his notions of literary response—and by implication in his argument for a merely academic literary criticism. Booth's response was to rise from the panelists' table, walk to the podium, look at the questioner, and enact a lengthy moment of silence. He then joked, in his marvelously deadpan manner, about not having had time to explain the workings of the unconscious. Then he extended his arm to his side, turned his hand palm up, and stared at it—like

Hamlet gazing at Yorick's skull, or like Macbeth interrogating his own vision. Finally he spoke. "I don't know," he said. "I don't know [about the
unconscious] any more than I know how I can do this." And here he closed
his fingers in a grasping motion, a visceral apprehension that mimicked his
acknowledged ignorance of the unconscious—literally, the un-known.

Of course the gesture deflected the question. Both Booth and his
questioner must have known it was unsatisfactory. Yet I thought it was a
good move. It simultaneously disclosed Booth's inability to speak about
"the unconscious" and the power of the unconscious to speak. For the
gesture of sustained silence followed by recourse to pure physicality
does display the unconscious. It is something apparently strange ("I don't
know") yet fundamentally part of one's nature (like an extended append-
age). It is a primary means by which we handle experience without thinking about it.

I liked the moment, yet I think its message, however interpretable,
omitted a core issue. Booth's gesture evidently proclaimed that the workings of the unconscious are like the workings of the nervous system, or
the ineluctable connections of synapse and muscle that enact articulations
of the will upon the body. What the gesture omitted, and what Booth was
unable to talk about, was the issue of *motivation* that underlies and in psychoanalytic theory defines "the unconscious." In Freud's original formulations, the "System Ucs." was the result of the dynamic repression of
wishes: it was an arena of desire whose energies had gone underground but
that continued to shape the acts and language of conscious life. The unconscious, in short, situates our most basic and personal wishes and fears,
motives and anxieties. It grounds *why* we speak; it harbors images of *to
whom* we speak; it adumbrates earlier moments and situations *when* we
spoke. The proper place of the unconscious in psychoanalytic criticism is
as the locus of primary, unacknowledged desire. So described, the concept
of the unconscious has no place in the critical theory of Stephen Booth as
he asserts it. A poetry and criticism of pure structure, of interacting patterns of potential coherence and subliminal significance, needs no concept
of dynamically repressed unconscious motives. Booth's is a motiveless
criticism—or so he insists.

Another prominent expert in Shakespearean close reading provides
another kind of example: Harry Berger. Both Berger and Booth describe
the moment-by-moment enactment of a text—in a dramatic production,
or reading, or interpretation—as reifying latent possibilities within the
text, possibilities that are simultaneously expressed and disguised. For

Berger, Booth, and myself, a particular production or reading necessarily limits textual potential even as it enables some privileged significances to emerge. Berger refers to this process as "a defensive transformation of latencies in the text." Both Booth (implicitly) and Berger (explicitly) recognize the convention of dramatic character to be a linguistic and dramatic device, subsumed by and smaller than the larger play of language within which characters seem to live. Audiences reify and imagine as persons those characters they see on stage, or read on a page, but a prior and primary agency of audience evocation is not character, but language, which refers beyond any single character's momentary articulation of it.

Berger, for instance, brilliantly evokes ("excavates" is his favored term) the displaced oedipal agon of the Bullingbrook-Gaunt relation in the opening scenes of *Richard II*. He demonstrates through meticulous attention to words and images how the unconscious contest between one father and son enacts itself in a scene of political rivalry. Using as well his earlier work on *King Lear*, he shows how intrafamilial contests get displaced onto contiguous nonfamily relationships. Berger speaks the sense of a scene that the scene itself can only hint at. For example, he says of the opening scene of *Richard II*: "Mowbray serves as the medium in which are condensed Bolingbroke's darker purpose, to accuse the king, and his darkest purpose, to rebuke his father." [31]

It seems to me that Berger has a working theory of the unconscious that Booth lacks—or displaces to deferred, absent explanation. Berger feels himself speaking for other characters in the play; he is "charmed" or "tempted" into an interpretive ventriloquism through which unheard meanings are articulated. Booth gestures toward the "undelivered meaning," he notes the unheard echo in a line, but then he insists on deferring interpretation, since to fall into interpretation is to give up the momentary juggling of multiple meanings. Booth evokes possibilities but resists meaning. Structure, not content, is all.

For Berger, as I read him, Shakespeare's text is a dark and mysterious place, in which meanings need to be excavated, disinterred; silent characters need to be given speech; repressions and displacements need to be undone. Light can be brought to the dark moments, but an attentive archaeologist of buried meanings can find as well motivations. This is a psychoanalytic style—a Freudian style—of listening to language as a symbolic expression of complex human relationships.

For Booth, as I read him, Shakespeare's text is both a beautiful puzzle of wondrously intricate patterns, and a hazardous place. In his SAA talk he described it as a "mine field," where meanings relevant or irrelevant, sensical or nonsensical, are likely to go off. Our best job, then, is to try to keep our wits about us amid the mêlée of possible meanings, to traverse the territory (the mind-field mine field) without succumbing to the pitfalls of conclusion. (The Bible warns, "He who digs a pit will fall into it, and a serpent will bite him who breaks through a wall" [*Ecclesiastes*, 10.8].) [32]

Booth, I surmise, has no use for a theory of the unconscious. His practice assumes varying thresholds of subliminal apperception, building up accretions of sound and sense (he likes the musical analogy). The process is purportedly neutral: without active desire, without intention, without preferred result. A merely academic, motiveless criticism is like free association without tears. To repeat: the psychoanalytic idea of the unconscious is precisely that which partly motivates an action, a word, a reading, *and* that which responds to or enables interpretation, eventually achieving that privileged yet provisional moment called "meaning."

Another question arises: that of psychoanalytic criticism releasing or taming subversive energies of a text or play, by paradoxically making "the unconscious" available to knowing. Insofar as any conclusive criticism, by structuring such energies, thereby stabilizes and defensively transforms latent meanings into reified significances (such as "Freudian symbols"), psychoanalysis can be charged with complicity in such defensive management of the anxieties and emotions it interprets. One might also claim this as a general function of literary criticism.

Meanings, like Robert Frost's slippery definition of a poem riding on its own melting, can be momentary stays against confusion. This is a point on which Booth and Berger and I agree (at least I think so). Yet insistently avoiding meaning can be as risky and dubious as too quickly falling into it. Stephen Booth steps warily through his mind field, pointing out potentially explosive moments, while Harry Berger happily and helplessly slides into any and all possible excavations. Perhaps one sees Ulysses's gate of steel as a mirror, reflecting intricate and fair designs at a distance, disclosing a quick glimpse of a figure, while the other sees the gate as an invitation to enter, in an ardent search for hidden energies. Together, both interpretive styles generate light and heat.

4

The Famous Analyses of
Henry the Fourth

ONE OF THE EARLIEST CRITICISMS of Shakespearean character is Maurice Morgann's well-known but rarely read "Essay on the Dramatic Character of Sir John Falstaff," published in London in 1777 as a bold defense of the corpulent and witty knight against the charge of cowardice.[1] Morgann assumed that Shakespeare's characters were like people and that Falstaff was like an historical person, with a history and an inner life that corresponded to common human nature, which he termed "certain first principles of character," and who therefore could be understood and judged through the critic's emotional responses to that nature, which he called "mental Impressions" as opposed to rational "Understanding." Since then both Falstaff and his fellow sportsman, Prince Hal, have attracted scrutiny from traditional character critics like A.C. Bradley, L.L. Schucking, and J.I.M. Stewart, and psychoanalytic critics like Ernst Kris.[2] My plan in this chapter is less to review various analyses of characters in *Henry IV, Part One* than to sketch categories of psychoanalytic interpretive strategies that have been deployed in the effort, and then to consider the large issue of psychological versus (new) historical or cultural approaches.[3] I find four major categories of psychoanalytic explication: (1) *structural*, (2) *oedipal*, (3) *pre-oedipal or object-relational*, and (4) *linguistic or semiotic*.

The first, or structural view, is an early approach that considers the play as a kind of intrapsychic allegory, analogous to medieval *psychomachia*. The Freudian model of id/ego/superego can be mapped onto characters in the play, roughly as follows: The id is represented (or symbolized, in this terminology) by Falstaff and Hotspur, figures of unrestrained appetite and uninhibited reaction. The superego is symbolized by King Henry as a judgmental, restrictive father, the basis for an internal imago or ego-ideal based on an introjected paternal image. The King's rebukes sound early in the play and are echoed in Prince Hal's famous soliloquy, "I know you all . . . ," in Act One (1.2.195–217), a rationalizing monologue that presents self-rebuke as self-justification, promising future reformation and reconciliation with the father. The ego is embodied by Prince Hal, the gradually heroic son who learns to mediate among the demands of impulse, restraint, and his various social worlds (tavern, court, battlefield).

Within this structural design, the psychological progress of the play can be seen to enact a gradual working-through and accommodation of id and superego to the framework of the ego; it is, by this design, a process of maturation. This progress occurs over the course of the play, but the interplay of the three elements or agencies can be seen in the initial tavern scene (1.2), where Hal plays at being Falstaff, then announces in soliloquy that he knows better and rebukes the "unyok'd humor" of his friends.[4]

Such a psychoanalytic reconfiguration may seem old-fashioned and allegorical, relying on Latinate Freudian terms that, after these many years, creak when flexed, and unexamined assumptions about symbolism and dramatic representation. Still, a benefit of this style of reading is that it is *pre-characterological*, that is, it does not get caught up in personality-analyses of those reified linguistic complexes conventionally identified as "characters." In some ways this primitive mode of psychoanalytic reading is close to more recent methods that will be addressed later.

The second, or oedipal view focuses on the various father-son conflicts in the play, primarily re-enacted in terms of King Henry's initial wish to replace Hal with Hotspur (1.1.85–89) and Hal's rejection of his filial role and his symbolic replacement of King Henry with Falstaff. The primal scene of these reversals is the role-playing in the tavern (2.4), where Hal dethrones the King and repudiates Falstaff. These oedipal displacements turn the father into a comic scapegoat figure who is eventually sacrificed (Falstaff), while the figure of the rebellious son is displaced onto a character (Hotspur) who is sacrificed for the sake of resolution of conflict and the reunion of father and son, dramatized at the end of *1 Henry IV* by Prince Hal fighting with and for the King, and at the end of *2 Henry IV* by Prince Hal becoming King and banishing Falstaff.[5]

The oedipal reading is dramatically privileged by the play, and made manifest at least in terms of contests between fathers and sons. Through a series of rivalries, alliances, and victories, a proper new balance or filiation is achieved, so that Hal can attain the position of prince as support for his father before he eventually succeeds him. The success of the oedipal project, in short, culminates in a relatively untroubled succession. However, just as the structural reading reasonably assumes the virtue of psychic coherence and mature development, I suggest that most conventional readings of Hal's glorious progress toward heroic monarchy in *Henry V* are fueled by an unexamined complicity in the oedipal project that the plays dramatize. We can largely thank feminist readers, as well as psychoanalytic critics—such as C.L. Barber, Coppélia Kahn, Richard Wheeler, and Peter Erickson—for helping to de-idealize this unacknowledged masculine identification.

The third, pre-oedipal or object-relational interpretive strategy considers the play's primary dyad of Hal-Falstaff as reconfiguring a more intimate familial bond than father-son, that is, the mother-child relation. As many critics have noted, *1 Henry IV* is notably without effective female presences. There are no manifest mothers, and wives are either mute (Mortimer and his Welsh wife share no language)[6] or muted (see Hotspur's playful yet cruel neglect of Kate). Mistress Quickly is subordinate to Falstaff, who plays both host and guest. It is Falstaff, virtually, who assumes the maternal role, becoming an all-providing source of food, fun, discourse, and self-reflection. He is an androgynous, magical figure, a hall of mirrors for Hal to play in. Falstaff's relation to his world is basically childish; he seeks instant gratification for primitive impulses like eating, drinking, and sleeping. One way to imagine the character is as a big infant (although wondrously precocious in speech) who focuses solely on the sources of his own pleasure (primarily oral—his next cup of sack) or on opportunities to display his magnificent narcissism.[7]

Hal's fondness for the world of Falstaff and the tavern hence represents a wish to reconstitute a simpler, basic bond of mother and child, wherein each mirrors the other. Falstaff is a buffer between Hal and the world, a wall of flesh that encloses him from the demands of harsh reality. W.H. Auden describes Falstaff as a pre-social being, whose rotundity brings together mother and child and is therefore fantastically self-sufficient.[8] Hal's rejection of Falstaff thus becomes a rejection of the seductions of childishness, the irresponsibilities of narcissism and instant gratification. Hal grows up by growing beyond the child within himself. The repudiation, however, is only superficial. Hal incorporates his relation to Falstaff, so that, as Wheeler puts it, "Falstaff sustains Hal at a deep level comparable to the power of dreaming to keep intact the essential knowledge of the infantile past."[9]

In an important new analysis of the figure of Falstaff, Valerie Traub

deepens and extends previous psychoanalytic criticism of the Hal-Falstaff
dyad to include "a projected fantasy of the pre-oedipal *maternal* whose
rejection is the basis upon which patriarchal subjectivity is predicated."
Using Bakhtin's idea of the grotesque, carnivalesque body, and precise textual details, she refashions "Falstaff" in terms of the female reproductive
body and suggests similarities between his magical language and Kristeva's
"semiotic." Traub's analysis also extends the social realm of the play—its
symbolic politics—beyond evident issues of adult masculine rivalry and
succession and into questions of the repression of infantile connections to
maternal dependence.[10]

Combining the oedipal and object-relational approaches produces a
view of the character of Falstaff as a fantastic, substitute, familial environment: brother, father, child, and mother. The tavern then becomes a *playground* of wishes (and fears) within which Hal can enact various fantasies
(of stealing, killing, lying) and styles of being (controlling, submitting,
pretending). It is an arena of innocent acts, a safehouse, or *playhouse*, that
offers refuge from the dangerous and bloody world of civil war that surrounds it. The opening lines of the play characterize this world:

> No more the thirsty entrance of this soil
> Shall daub her lips with her own children's blood.
> No more shall trenching war channel her fields,
> Nor bruise her flow'rets with the armed hoofs
> Of hostile paces.   (1.1.5–9)

The image of a devouring and abused maternal figure is thus evoked
at the start of the play, but only through denial: "No more. . . ." The
insistent absence of manifest female power in *1 Henry IV* and throughout
the second tetralogy is telling. These opening lines hark back to sanctioned
images of a maternal England from *Richard II* (for instance, Gaunt's nostalgic evocation of "this blessed plot, . . . this teeming womb of royal
kings / Fear'd by their breed and famous by their birth" [2.1.40 ff]). The
appropriation of a benign, creative version of this ground by Falstaff permits Hal a magical playspace within which he can marginally encounter but
largely bypass the world of women, as Kahn has noted.[11] In *1 Henry IV* this
world is either repressed or fantastically transformed; but what is repressed
will return. *Hamlet* is the most significant site of this return of repressed
femininity, yet it is suggested at the end of this play, as I will show.

The fourth, linguistic or semiotic approach focuses on the question of *identification* as a mode of human development. Psychologically and socially, the ways we represent ourselves publicly are learned in the context of primary childhood identifications within our families. As small but telling examples, consider personal vocal intonation, or handwriting. Our voices mimic those we hear; our handwriting is unique yet derivative, based on imitating parents, teachers, and other ego ideals. In handwriting each of us can see the singular sign of our individuality—it legally identifies us—that also carries indelible traces of its sources.[12] The linguistic approach thus resituates the structural, since Hal's project is to move among various identifications—with Falstaff, Hotspur, and Henry—and to select aspects of each that he can amalgamate in order eventually to define himself as "the true prince." It also resituates the oedipal, since identification has ambivalent motives: (1) becoming like (liking), and (2) taking over (incorporating, replacing).[13]

These examples of voice and handwriting are overdetermined, for Shakespeare portrays the process of identification in *1 Henry IV* literally in linguistic terms, that is, in terms of the rhetorical styles of his central characters. Prince Hal is expert at imitating the terms and tropes of Falstaff and Hotspur, and later the King. When he arrives in the play, he speaks the language of Falstaff as well as that character himself. Rhetorically, the first "Falstaff" in the play is performed by the Prince.

> *Falstaff.*   Now, Hal, what time of day is it, lad?
> *Prince.*   Thou art so fat-witted with drinking of old sack, and unbuttoning thee after supper, and sleeping upon benches after noon, that thou hast forgotten to demand that truly thou wouldest truly know. What a devil hast thou to do with the time of the day? unless hours were cups of sack, and minutes capons, and clocks the tongues of bawds, and dials the signs of leaping-houses, and the blessed sun himself a fair hot wench in flame-color'd taffata; I see no reason why thou shouldst be so superfluous as to demand the time of the day.   (1.2.1–12)

This linguistic mimesis is exact in terms of comparisons and metaphors, but it is identification with a difference. Hal's insistence on the passage of time, his criticism of Falstaff's habits (he simultaneously expands and deflates the character as delimited by the pleasure principle), and the pun in "blessed sun" all point to his later repudiation of both style and character.

Hal similarly mimics and places Hotspur in his brief foray into an imitation of that character:

> I am not yet of Percy's mind, the Hotspur of the north, he that kills me some six or seven dozen of Scots at a breakfast, washes his hands, and says to his wife, "Fie upon this quiet life! I want work." "O my sweet Harry," says she, "how many hast thou kill'd today?" "Give my roan horse a drench," says he, and answers, "Some fourteen," an hour after, "a trifle, a trifle."   (2.4.101–8)

This parody is in prose, perhaps because Hal's own verse will need the tropes of ambition and bravery when he achieves the princely goal. But Hal catches Hotspur's unrealistic fantasies of simplistic aggression, his need (like Falstaff) for an appreciative audience, and his tendency to think about his horse when responding to his wife (see 2.3.89–102).

Falstaff and Hotspur are exemplary stylists of one figure of speech, hyperbole. Hotspur is an hyperbolist of linear ambition, an overreacher; Falstaff is an hyperbolist of all-inclusive rotundity and comparison. Hotspur drives aggressively at his topic with figures; Falstaff surrounds it with similes. Hotspur seems to be pursuing some grandiose heroic identity; Falstaff is instantly ready to re-compose his descriptions of himself in terms of some other person, thing, or possibility. To use a mythological parallel, Hotspur has Mercury's speed, Falstaff his mutability.[14]

The most poignant instance of Hal's mimetic appropriation of his rival's language is at the moment of Hotspur's death, when Hal literally completes his last line: "No, Percy," Hotspur says to himself, "thou are dust, / And food for—/ For worms, brave Percy," Hal continues. "Fare thee well, great heart" (4.4.85–87). The moment merges two styles of identification: affection and aggression, sharing and taking. Hal takes Hotspur's last breath and substitutes his own in order to speak Hotspur's last word, an honorable theft that authentically replaces what was taken ("worms" is surely the word Hotspur would have said; the trajectory of thought and language requires it).

In a word, Hal's project in the play is to find, take, or make his own language—or more precisely that language with which he can identify in such a way as to become "the true prince." The most dramatic moment of this discovery or production is the scene of Hal's magnanimous and mature speeches over the fallen bodies of Hotspur and Falstaff on the battlefield. Here is the inception of his own "authentic" discourse, his "winning of his own" (the final line of the play) in language.[15] Before this dramatic moment, however, Hal enters another register of language at the beginning of Act Five, when King and Prince cooperate to produce a verse description of the new day:

> *King.*   How bloodily the sun begins to peer
> Above yon bulky hill! the day looks pale
> At his distemp'rature.
> *Prince.*   The southren wind
> Doth play the trumpet to his purposes,
> And by his hollow whistling in the leaves
> Foretells a tempest and a blust'ring day.
> *King.*   Then with the losers let it sympathize,
> For nothing can seem foul to those that win.
>
> (5.1.1–8)

This shared poetic construct (the two voices co-produce line three) is a linguistic emblem of what Kahn calls the "reciprocal validation of each other as father and son, king and prince."[16] The validation is tempered, however, by Erickson's inference that "neither father nor son can securely know exactly who the other is because of his theatrical sense of himself."[17] This little poem-within-the-play thus serves well as an indicator of characters (both Henry's and Hal's) and climactic evidence of Hal's achievement of the language of a prince, properly subservient to his father. The lines echo beyond character, however, and beyond the dramatic moment into the domain of the play of language. Psychoanalytic attention should disclose these echoes. The rhetorical set-piece description of the dawning of day on the battlefield coalesces at least two central themes: the manifest theme of oedipal resolution and emerging harmony between father and son, and the latent theme of repressed relations with a maternal image.

King Henry opens the set-piece with a regal observation: "How bloodily the sun begins to peer / Above yon bulky hill! The day looks pale / At his distemp'rature." The King's conventional identification with the sun, the royal eye of day, extends to his projection of his own anger into the hot blood of the dawn's distemperature. Prince Hal joins in, literally in mid-line, to accompany the paternal observation. His forecast deflates the royal appearance of the sun by shifting the trumpet of regal annunciation to "hollow whistling," and his imagery also suggests the question of his own heroic actions to come. Will he "play the trumpet" to his father's purposes, or whistle in the leaves (perhaps with Falstaff)? King Henry ignores any subtleties in Hal's comment, however, and closes the speech with a conventional battlefield homily about the blessings of victors.

This moment of masculine martial harmony occurs on the site of another scene, the literal ground of authority on which the staging of masculine conflicts and resolutions will occur. Typically, a Shakespearean pun discloses this scene. The appearance of the bloody "sun/son" above the "bulky hill" echoes Hal's previous description of himself (to Henry) "wearing a garment all of blood":

> I will redeem all this on Percy's head.
> And in the closing of some glorious day
> Be bold to tell you that I am your son.
> When I will wear a garment all of blood,
> And stain my favors in a bloody mask,
> Which wash'd away shall scour my shame with it.
> And that shall be the day, when e'er it lights,
> That this same child of honor and renown,
> This gallant Hotspur . . .   (3.2.132–40)

As Watson and Traub have noted, this imagery promises a magical regeneration of the Prince through a fantasy of birth. Watson situates the moment in a series of autochthonous Caesarean births of the hero, including Glendower, Richard III, Macbeth, and Coriolanus. Traub notes that the fantasy provides the newborn son with a bloody baptism that washes away any maternal connection, so that Hal becomes "his father's son and his nation's hero."[18] One motivation for this fantasy of masculine birth and its implicit rejection of maternity lies in previous metaphoric evocations of violent mother-child interactions (as Watson notes): "No more the thirsty entrance of this soil / Shall daub her lips with her own children's blood. . . ." Yet the new day that Hal prophesies (the dawn of the bloody sun) rises over this same ground of maternal presence and power. The very ground of masculine authority, then, the "bulky hill" whose soil will once again "daub her lips with her own children's blood" in the ensuing battle, adumbrates the ubiquitous yet invisible primordial female presence in the play, a type of *mons martialis* (whose dangerous confusion of sexes may reciprocate Falstaff's comic version of androgyny). Against the notice of evident feminine/maternal absence in *1 Henry IV*, then, can be placed the deeper observation that the maternal ground is both nowhere and everywhere.[19] As Janet Adelman puts it, in a distillation of her theory of Shakespearean tragic ambivalence:

> The problematic maternal body can never quite be occluded or transformed: made into a monster or a saint, killed off or banished from the stage, it remains at the center of masculine subjectivity, marking its unstable origin. For the contaminated flesh of the maternal body is also home: the home Shakespeare's protagonists long to return to, the home they can never quite escape.[20]

Shakespeare's dramatization in *Henry IV, Part One* of the linguistic production of masculine styles of speech and action provokes useful questions in terms of contemporary theories of the historical origins and psychological structure of identity. Masculine identity as displayed in this play enacts itself generally through contest and cooperation among men, and particularly through careful linguistic identifications. Hal finds and situates himself through sequential identifications with Falstaff, Hotspur, and King Henry; he knows them all. Yet the climactic identification with the father that apparently culminates and completes heroic masculine identity occurs on the site of a repression—the buried relation to the mother, the bulky hill that supports the sport of heroes.

Theoretical Interlude

This dramatic moment in *1 Henry IV* impinges on a central question in current psychoanalytic theory. Does primary identity emerge from a series of linguistic identifications whose continual repetition it requires in order to maintain or re-create itself? Or does identity rest on the solid, repressed ground of a preverbal relation? Is identity primarily theatrical, whereby we each play the trumpet to an other's purpose, or is it genuine, the expression of a self from which we truly proceed? Is the self a series of defensive poses, temporary enactments within particular social contexts, a *dramatis persona* we maintain from one discontinuous moment to another? Or is there a core "true self" from which we speak, write, act, and otherwise present ourselves? Such a self recuperates a primitive connection to a matrix of identity—the mother-infant relation as felt and learned in early childhood. We are approaching, from other angles, the primary question of Hamlet's "*that* within," in terms of psychoanalytic theories of the origins of ego, self, subject, or (for lack of a better term) character.

At this point I will embark on a brief theoretical interlude, to define terms and to fashion the argument. This interlude is relevant to Shakespeare's plays only if one supposes that mimesis, identification, and representation—in terms of language and performed behavior—are relevant to the plays, or if one considers that the question of Hamlet's "that within" might be clarified by psychological concepts.

Very briefly, let me rehearse some general psychoanalytic ideas about human development. Over time, and uniquely for the human animal this is a very extended time, the interaction of innate psychobiological processes (similar to the species but unique to the individual)—call it *nature*—and social modes of caretaking (similar to the culture but unique to the individual caretaker)—call it *nurture*—produces patterns of behavior that form the characteristic blueprint of the person, her or his "character." These characteristic patterns inform psychic and emotional structure, unconsciously. As we grow, experience, and learn, we retain images, memories, and styles—not simply out of who we are "inside" or from whom we encounter "outside"—but from the interactions of inside and outside. These internalized representations of relationships form a template that informs how we feel, think, speak, and act. The primary dispute in current post-Freudian theory is between those who think that this internal template of unconscious identifications is grounded in a core emotional relation (the infant-mother dyad of object-relations) and those who think that the template is a distorting mirror of imaginary identifications (Lacanian psychoanalysis).

A brief sketch of key terms will be useful here: the Freudian *ego*, the object-relational *self*, and the Lacanian *subject*. As Freud described it in *The Ego and the Id* (1923), the ego is a boundary concept, a "frontier creature," analogous to the skin.[21] As such it is a managing agent or interface between internal energies (somatic events, affects) and external reality. In its defensive modes it may seek withdrawal or magical modification of stimuli, but its goal is the integration of outside and inside in a manageable synthesis. In the gradual development of such boundary maintenance, a perceptible and negotiable difference between inside and outside, "me" and "not-me," self and object world, is produced. The ego is the agent or process of this negotiation. Object-relations theory extends this basic Freudian idea of boundaries into a notion of the relational *self* as a style of managing needs, demands, and wishes in the context of an other person (mother) or environment (family, society). Over the course of time, a history of internal relations is experienced, practiced, and established, which produces an idiomatic, individual epistemology, in terms of the environment the person comes to expect. As Christopher Bollas puts it: "The concept of self should refer to the positions or points of view from which and through which we sense, feel, observe and reflect on distinct and separate experiences in our being. One crucial point-of-view comes from the other who experiences us."[22] For Lacan, as I understand him, the impingement of the other's perspective is structurally less benign. (Of course there is plenty of room in the object-relations model for malign impingement and a distorted self, but this would be categorized as pathology.) The Lacanian *subject* is already a pun: both active, thinking agent (though this may be an illusion) and passive victim of domination. Rather than relating across a negotiated distance or absence, the Lacanian subject is faced with a primordial lack, gap, or division from an aboriginal unity ("the imaginary"). The basic organization of the subject is in terms of alienation.[23]

These various concepts, interrelated as they seem, are significantly different. For an object-relations theorist like D.W. Winnicott, an identity of temporary, serial identifications is a skeptical self, a compliant and canny structure of defenses—what he calls a "false self system." It is very like the Lacanian subject, generated by slippery language, constructing an illusory context of relations against a shifting background of irrecoverable loss. As for the ego, that for Lacan is "the sum of the identifications of the subject . . . like the superimposition of various coats borrowed from . . . the bric-a-brac of its props department."[24] The identity that connects to an inner core self, unconscious, expressing a consistent and coherent idiom of being, presents another kind of subject, constructed by object-relations theorists like Winnicott. Lacanians view this self as a nostalgic fiction, a wish and a defense. Winnicottians see it as a ground of being.

The psychological argument, I believe, may be haunted by theology. For the idea of a "true self" is like an article of faith—a residue of the Christian theology of *presence*, a type of psychic Holy Spirit within that relates to a Madonna-like internalized object.[25] Stripped of its adjectival ethic of "true" and "false," Winnicott's ideas of the production of self through a history of repeated transactions with the world (initially the maternal matrix) could be refashioned in other terms, such as "active" or "passive," "aggressive" or "submissive," "managing" or "accommodating." Such modifiers indicate a style of relationship, not a quality of self. By contrast, if the Winnicottian true self is a residue of Christian fictions—an angel in the psyche—then the Lacanian subject is a piece of the devil's work, made of lies and illusions, forever alienated, fragmented, faced with phantoms and lack. Where Winnicott inscribes a Madonna at the source, Lacan reiterates the expulsion from the garden, under the *nom du père*. Between these rival caricatures of theories about the origins of identity, choice is problematic. Shall we be naive or cynical, embraced or estranged, saved or damned? Is there no middle ground?

I think there is. The philosopher and psychoanalyst Heinz Lichtenstein has developed a theory of identity that provides crucial intermediate concepts. Briefly, Lichtenstein theorizes an *instrumental primary identity*, generated through iterative behaviors and emotions, that connects an individual to his or her (maternal) environment in functional terms.[26] We learn how to be *for* an other; we identify with the (unconscious) desires *of* the other *for* us. This primary identification is mimetic in the Winnicottian sense (the recursive mirroring of the mother), and it is derivative in the Lacanian sense (the Desire of the Other). Lichtenstein writes about "the mirroring quality of the infant's sensory responsiveness to the mother's libidinal attachment":

This mirroring cannot, of course, be understood in terms of any visual perception, but a reflection through touch, smell, and other primitive sensations. What is dimly emerging in this mirror is, at least in the beginning, not a primary love object, but the outlines of the child's own image as reflected by the mother's unconscious needs with regard to the child. In this first, archaic mirroring experience of the child a primary identity emerges which may be called narcissistic. It is not as yet a sense of identity, for that presupposes consciousness. I see in it rather a primary organizational principle without which the process of developmental differentiation could not begin.

The mother, in contrast to the nonhuman environment, reflects back to the child a configuration of its own presence. I have suggested . . . that this primary identity has the form of an identity theme, i.e., the specific reflection received from the mother conveys to the child a primary identity defined as instrumentality in relation to the mother.[27]

The idea of identity as a belated reflection of an original source achieves splendid evocation in Wallace Stevens's poem, "Description Without Place," which is in my view a precocious postmodern gloss on Hamlet's remarks about seeming and being as well as a poetic illustration of psychoanalytic theories of identity and language.[28] The poem is difficult, and relies on contemporary science (solar position and energy) and philosophy (being and consciousness). It begins by side-stepping Hamlet's paralyzing quandary about the unbridgeable difference between seeming and being.

It is possible that to seem—it is to be,
As the sun is something seeming and it is.
The sun is an example. What it seems
It is and in such seeming all things are.   (1–4)

After thus setting a stellar scene of projected and reflected reality, Stevens
personifies the agent of reflective energy as "a queen that made it seem /
By the illustrious nothing of her name."

Her green mind made the world around her green.
The queen is an example . . . This green queen
In the seeming of the summer of her sun
By her own seeming made the summer change.
In the golden vacancy she came, and comes,
And seems to be on the saying of her name.   (7–14)

Later in the poem influential *noms du père*—like Nietzsche and Lenin—
figure prominently. Initially, however, the source of being and seeming (or
their coincidence) is this archaic (m)other who comes on call, literally corresponding to the speaking agent who calls. In the full ambiguity of the
term, she *appears*. "Such seemings are the actual ones," the poem continues (17). Even "if seeming is description without place," "it is a sense / To
which we refer experience, a knowledge / Incognito"; "it is an expectation, a desire" (99–107). We construct and experience the reality of our
lives in terms of this earliest reflection, which is not precisely ourselves nor
an illusory replica.

Description is revelation. It is not
The thing described, nor false facsimile.
It is an artificial thing that exists
In its own seeming, plainly visible,
Yet not too closely the double of our lives,
Intenser than any actual life could be,
A text we should be born that we might read,
More explicit than the experience of sun
And moon, the book of reconciliation,
Book of a concept only possible
In description, canon central in itself,
The thesis of the plentifullest John.   (121–32)

   As this penultimate section makes clear, Stevens is writing about the human experience of living a life mediated through language, a language that exists before us and that we learn as new ("a text we should be born that we might read"). Language enables description, a conscious awareness and articulation that intensifies the natural, sensory phenomena of "actual life." The poem ends with a section that praises the particular nature of language ("men make themselves their speech" [139]) while it simultaneously returns human invention to its natural origin: language or description must "be alive with its own seemings, seeming to be / Like rubies reddened by rubies reddening" (151–52). If *being* is natural existence ("actual life"), then *seeming* is consciousness of that existence. Paradoxically, until we seem we cannot fully realize being. Seeming is self-reflection, a secondary enlightenment that mirrors the archaic dawn of existence, in which we are held, warmed, and *shown* "in the golden vacancy" of an archaic maternal matrix. In the final lines of Stevens's poem, the quintessential human verb (*to be*) is reabsorbed into the lustrous reflections of visual similitude and acoustic rhyme (ru*bies*). Are rubies red, or do they only seem to be so within the spectrum of visible light that human eyes require? Absent such light their redness vanishes, but so too does our sight. The redness of rubies is hence a blend of seeming and being, "as the sun is something seeming and it is." Without the primal *lux* that shows us the world, we cannot see it. Without the archaic (m)other that originally describes our place in the world, we cannot experience it as a coherent self.

   Hamlet dramatizes the problems of being and seeming from at least two perspectives. From one view the hero is apparently paralyzed by his perception of an unbridgeable gulf between inner self and external representation, and from another he leaps that gulf by casting thought away, trusting in spontaneous reaction. In his book about Hamlet and *Hamlet*, the psychoanalyst André Green observes:

Dans le deuil qui l'affecte Hamlet oppose les actions qu'on homme peut jouer, c'est-à-dire feindre sans doute, mais surtout représenter au théâtre et ce qu'il a en lui qui dépasse tout ce qui peut se représenter. "Play" et "show": la metaphore du théâtre est en sous-texte.

   Voilà donc le paradoxe rencontré par Shakespeare. Donner à jouer, à représenter ce qui dépasse les possibilités de la représentation: la douleur psychique. Toute la pièce va devoir soutenir ce défi. Le langage poétique va servir de médiateur entre le monde intérieur indicible et son extériorisation sur la scène.[29]

Within the grief that affects Hamlet are opposed the actions that a man could play, that is, feign, undoubtedly, but above all represent in the theater, and what he has within, which goes beyond anything he can represent. "Play" and "show": the metaphor of the theater is in the subtext.

There is the paradox Shakespeare encounters: to put into play, to represent, that which surpasses the possibilities of representation—psychical pain. The entire play must sustain this challenge. Poetic language will serve as mediator between the inexpressible interior world and its exteriorization on the stage. (my translation)

Caught in the paradox of representing that essential "Hamlet" who cannot be truly enacted, language mediates between intrinsic inarticulation and extrinsic behavior. How does one show what cannot be shown? And if shown, how will it be perceived?

> *Oph.*   Will 'a tell us what this show meant?
> *Ham.*   Ay, or any show that you will show him. Be not you asham'd
>   to show, he'll not shame to tell you what it means. (3.2.143–46)

Display first, criticism after. Both modes of exhibition involve shame. The witty moment gestures toward the problem of interpretation (and its confident inevitability) as well as toward the potentially shameful bodily bases that may underlie both textual and critical display. Yet what Hamlet cannot show through deliberate speech or demeanor he is ultimately able to show through sudden action.

>   Rashly—
> And prais'd be rashness for it—let us know
> Our indiscretion sometime serves us well
> When our deep plots do pall, and that should learn us
> There's a divinity that shapes our ends,
> Rough-hew them how we will—   (5.2.6–11)

What Hamlet terms "rashness," then "indiscretion," and then "divinity" is a spontaneous expression of an inner state without conscious articulation: unmediated, thoughtless action, show *sans* tell. Considered psychologically, the Hamlet who reacts to Laertes's histrionic display of grief, his astounding "phrase of sorrow," by leaping into Ophelia's grave and claiming, "This is I, / Hamlet the Dane" (5.1.254–58), has moved from an initial assertion of inward authenticity that cannot be shown to a sheer declaration and exhibition of self in action: "*that* within" becomes "*this* is *I*." [30] This is the moment, tragically short-lived, of Hamlet's assumption of an identity of his own, not one located elsewhere ("I'll call *thee* Hamlet," he said to the Ghost).

"The spontaneous gesture," wrote D.W. Winnicott, "is the True Self in action."[31] For Winnicott, the core self is paradoxically the point of deepest connection and isolation: it is a secret, sacred essence to be expressed through genuine, spontaneous gesture and to be preserved and protected from manipulations and violations from without.[32] For Lacan, on the other hand, the "that within" is a *lack*, a mark of the mourned object that constitutes an always alienated subject. For Winnicott it is a pristine *presence*. As Adam Phillips understands Winnicott (and he does), "the self is by definition elusive, the player of hide and seek."[33] "Hide fox, and all after!" (*Hamlet*, 4.2.30). Hence Hamlet's bold assumption of identity at graveside is also a broad histrionic exhibition; his "show" is both theatrical and authentic. His seeming now fully displays his being. This *complication* (folding together) becomes both the question and the answer for Hamlet's problem of (re)presentation.[34]

"Rough-hew them how we *will*." Hamlet's remarks in praise of rashness modulate among several registers of unconscious, conscious, and supraconscious. The volitional project of plots is bracketed by the sudden gesture of indiscretion and the final design of divinity. A full appreciation of the term "will" includes this range of motivation and agency. Conscious intention occupies a shifting mid-range along a spectrum that spans unconscious spontaneity (a glimpse of unknown genuineness) and suprapersonal structure, whether understood in vague theological terms, as here, or in psychological and social terms, as in contemporary psychoanalysis.

I insert this theoretical interlude in order to provide current psychoanalytic ideas about identity and its origins as background to corollary arguments in current criticism, not merely about *Henry IV Part One* but about Shakespeare and the Renaissance, and in larger debates about the relation of the personal to the social, or of psychology to history. For instance, Stephen Greenblatt discusses the Henriad in terms similar to a linguistic approach, but draws different inferences.[35] He sees one mode of the plays, especially the two parts of *Henry IV*, as a " 'recording' of alien voices," those disempowered or illiterate characters who compose the lower elements of society. Hal studies the language of these others from a position of mastery and contempt. As his brother says in *Henry IV Part Two*: "The Prince but studies his companions / like a strange tongue . . ." (4.4.68–9). Rather than noting a style of identification, however, Greenblatt stresses the construction of difference and cites contemporary sixteenth-century compilations of glossaries of marginal vocabularies, like "cant language."

Following his argument of self-fashioning, he then remarks about Hal and the notion of *self*: "Hal's characteristic activity is playing, or, more precisely, theatrical improvisation . . . , and he fully understands his own behaviour through most of the play as a role that he is performing." Greenblatt hence wonders if "such a thing as a natural disposition exists in the play as anything more than a theatrical fiction." For instance, in Falstaff's case even an appeal to "instinct" becomes a histrionic artifice, a rhetorical device.[36]

In its largest form, the argument about natural disposition and socially constructed artifice is an argument about the developmental priority of psychology or history. Greenblatt presents one test case in his essay on "Psychoanalysis and Renaissance Culture."[37] His fundamental argument is that psychoanalytic interpretations of the Renaissance must be "marginal and belated" because psychoanalysis itself, and the concept of self from which it proceeds, are historical developments whose sources can be located in the Renaissance. Psychoanalysis is hence a "product" of the Renaissance and not privileged as an interpreter. One of Freud's primary assumptions—a coherent, continuous and authentic "self"—did not exist or was not assumed in Shakespeare's time. In the sixteenth century, Greenblatt asserts, such an idea of an irreducible physical and psychological self was "irrelevant to the point of being unthinkable."[38] By contrast, he argues, Freudian psychoanalysis credits a "dream of authentic possession," "a primal, creatural individuation" anchored in the personal body, "the fixity, the certainty, of our own body."[39]

As historical evidence, he presents the story of Martin Guerre, the sixteenth-century Frenchman whose identity was claimed by another. The dispute was resolved in a public trial, through communal judgment and legal authorization. The impostor was eventually executed because he laid claim to Martin Guerre's social place. The man's "subjectivity does not any the less exist," Greenblatt acknowledges, "but it seems peripheral, or rather, it seems to be the *product* of the relations, material objects, and judgments exposed in the case rather than the *producer* of the relations, objects, and judgments." Guerre's identity was an effect of external social framing and not of an adduced interior subjectivity; identity was a "placeholder in a complex system of possessions, kinship bonds, contractual relationships." Toward the end of his essay Greenblatt notes a shift in the "body-property-name" relation: "this slow, momentous transformation of the middle term from 'property' to 'psyche.'" In a note he adds that this transformation "is at once a revolution and a continuation: 'psyche' is neither a mere mystification for 'property' nor a radical alternative to it."[40]

The essay is provocative and problematic. Before addressing specific problems, let me suggest that even if the main argument were true, the interpretive pertinence of psychoanalysis to Renaissance culture and texts is not thereby disabled. In the discussion of *Macbeth* (Chapter Six) I posit an *isomorphic* relation between Freud and Shakespeare that uses similarities in their models of psychic structure to elucidate meanings in both. But I do not believe that Greenblatt's argument holds up, for several reasons. First, his reductive restatements of the Freudian ego and his brief oedipal reading of Guerre's case indicate a limited familiarity with psychoanalytic theory. He sketches an analysis of Guerre's anxious sexuality and uncertain masculine identity that precipitated an oedipal rebellion against his father, the failure of which caused him to flee—"classic materials of Freudian speculation," as Greenblatt sees them. His inference that Guerre's flight "abandoned" a social identity while retaining a personal one is not, however, the paradox or problem Greenblatt represents it to be. His argument stresses the biophysiological components of Freudian theory (real aspects, to be sure) and ignores the social, interrelational aspects of identity-formation through identification. The Freudian ego develops simultaneously "from the inside," through its mediation of instinctual derivatives and the pleasure principle, and "from the outside," through its identifications with others and its management of external exigencies (the reality principle).[41] Greenblatt constructs an antagonism between personal body and social place, where Freud theorized a cooperation—troublesome though it was.

Second, in historical terms, why is one sequential arrangement of "body-property-name" so privileged? Why is "property" or "psyche" a middle term? One might rearrange the terms to demonstrate alternative ways of thinking about the interrelations of each, thereby questioning an assumption of priority. Socially, name customarily precedes body, and name is a function of property. Humans are never entirely outside culture, nor did Freud think they were. When the real Guerre's identity was established in a sixteenth-century court, is this an instance of historical difference? Even today identity is established in similar ways. Finally, who could think that individual subjectivity would be the *producer* of social relations and material objects? A solipsist, perhaps, but not a Freudian. In brief, what Greenblatt's version of psychoanalysis lacks is a sophisticated idea of *identification* whereby individual identity is produced through the interrelations of self and others, understood in familial, linguistic, and social contexts.

Yet although Greenblatt's version of psychoanalysis in this essay is reductive, his conclusion recuperates much of its validity and value:

> But if we reject both the totalizing of a universal mythology [of psychoanalysis] and the radical particularizing of relativism, what are we left with? We are left with a network of lived and narrated stories, practices, strategies, representations, fantasies, negotiations, and exchanges that. along with the surviving aural, tactile, and visual traces, fashion our experience of the past, of others, and of ourselves.[42]

This is not a bad definition of psychoanalysis, both in terms of its theory of self and the analytic process. Rather than providing historical precedent to devalue psychoanalysis, I think Greenblatt's essay offers substantial evidence to enrich the theory: indeed, as he asks, to "historicize" it, to amplify its relevance beyond the reductive modes in which it is sometimes employed and adjudged.

The issue of history (or sociology) versus psychology can be further examined by citing another contemporary, nonpsychoanalytic critic, Terry Eagleton, who states, citing Hamlet:

> The self lives an irresolvable division between its desire, which conducts it along an endless chain of inflated signifiers, and its effort at "imaginary" unity with the fixed signified of its social position. As far as Hamlet is concerned, such efforts are hardly worth the trouble.[43]

Compare this statement with Greenblatt's famous Epilogue to *Renaissance Self-Fashioning*:

> But as my worked progressed, I perceived that fashioning oneself and being fashioned by cultural institutions . . . were inseparably intertwined. In all my texts and documents, there were, so far as I could tell, no moments of pure, unfettered subjectivity: indeed, the human subject itself began to seem remarkably unfree, the ideological product of the relations of power in a particular society.[44]

These statements rest on differing yet connected assumptions about the relations of "self" and "society." Eagleton's assumptions lead him to describe a self torn between endless desire and stable unity, where both desire and unity are illusory. The former is an endless series of steps along an ultimately tautological linguistic system, and the latter is a projected integrity of fixed social identity. In the Lacanian terms the passage deploys, the self circulates within the symbolic order while wishing to restore itself to the imaginary. It is a *subjected self*, conducted by desire and not actively desiring—although it may delusively credit the fiction of such an independent agency. The effort is troublesome and possibly futile, a lost cause, a burnt-out case. This self can find no satisfaction, because it is looking in a narcissistic mirror for a relationship with a genuine other.

Greenblatt's assumptions permit him to describe a less constrained, more complex subject, based on the interrelationship of self and others. He rejects, albeit to some degree regretfully, the fiction of self-creativity or of the individual, subjective production of language or literature. The work of art is a co-production of individual consciousness and the shared social customs and internalized relationships within which individuals develop. For Greenblatt these relationships are the residue of ideology, a product of systems of power. His rhetoric presses toward tragic limitation, whereby pure unfettered subjectivity is shackled by deterministic social forces.

The implicitly Marxist bias of this language can be refashioned, however, to allow the trajectory of the concept to incline another way. For there is a more positive theoretical statement of the interdependence of self and society, or subject and other. That is the domain of object-relations psychoanalysis, where subject and other are originally (re)presented by infant and mother, in a prolonged and productive construction—not of binary oppositions like "self" and "society," or "desire" and "unity," but of a style of relationship that underlies and informs all emotions and actions of the individual as he or she grows out of the maternal and familial arena and enters the wider social world. Persons are thus truly "products of relations," but not necessarily as slaves stamped by ideology or subjects chained to paranoid projections of illusory unity. Object-relations are co-productions, primary attachments to and losses of objects (persons and internal representations of persons) that produce the experiential reality of self, object, and the relationships that link them.[45] Although psychoanalysis posits a basic and prior human, interpersonal relation, it does not thereby reject the formative functions of what Lichtenstein calls "the nonhuman environment." The special value of the mutually reflective relation is that it offers the child an initial "configuration of its own presence" that gradually enables it to interact with the larger social world.[46]

Large designs of the "history versus psychology" debate can thus be found in contemporary criticism of Shakespeare's plays *and* in those plays. Of course, our tendency to discover such issues in Shakespeare is itself a reflection of our current modes of framing critical questions.[47] Perhaps the relation of "Shakespeare" and "Shakespeare criticism" is analogous to the interrelation of subject and society. That is, does criticism derive from a clear reading of Shakespeare, so that it reproduces the truth of the texts, or does criticism produce a "Shakespeare" answering to its own current needs? Is criticism a window onto the Bard or a mirror wherein we practice behavior to our own shadows? From my perspective, it's both.

Hyperbolic Desire:
Shakespeare's *Lucrece*

> Her maid is gone, and she prepares to write,
> First hovering o'er the paper with her quill;
> Conceit and grief an eager combat fight,
> What wit sets down is blotted straight with will:
> This is too curious-good, this blunt and ill.
> Much like a press of people at a door,
> Throng her inventions, which shall go before.
>   (1296–1302)[1]

THIS MOMENT OF ANXIOUS COMPOSITION belongs to Lucrece, as she considers how to inform her husband Collatine of her rape by Tarquin. The Narrator shares the moment as well, sympathizing not only with the victim's plight but also with the poet's occupation, addressing questions of style that face any writer. Implicit in this stanza is an aesthetic of narrative invention that controls the reading of *Lucrece* I will present in this chapter.

From the conventional allegorical combat between "conceit and grief" (or, loosely, invention and passion) and the standard opposition between "wit" and "will," Shakespeare's description of writing moves to questions of style ("curious-good" versus "blunt") and then to a personification of composition itself. The writer's stylistic struggle illustrates an intrapsychic tension within the character: Lucrece's dilemma of self-presentation is translated into issues of linguistic representation. The craft of "wit" is sabotaged by the "blot" of "will," a subversive agent of emotional revision that undoes intellectual design. The final simile, of poetic inventions as people, indicates how I will read the poem. I intend to treat the personae of Shakespeare's *Lucrece* not as characters ("people at a door") but as rhetorical and psychological constructs ("inventions"), thereby describing circulations of desire through the poem as independent of and prior to those nominal agents that conventionally articulate them.[2] In effect I will conflate "Tarquin," "Lucrece," and "Collatine" into one superagent whose actions and reactions trace the psychology of desire itself. The text thus becomes a metaphoric demonstration of the play of language.

As a dramatic poem, *Lucrece* enacts an elementary psychology: the sudden emergence of obsessive desire, its progression into action, and the physical and emotional consequences. While relating a classic story of violation and revenge, the poem simultaneously explores primary issues of imaginative conception and linguistic creation. Poetic convention, such as the narrative "complaint" and the humanist tradition of rhetorical "copiousness," allowed Shakespeare free license for hyperbole, for extended investigations of linguistic possibility unsuitable in dramatic monologue or dialogue. Paradoxically, being limited to the printed page provided Shakespeare an authorized occasion for elaborate and intensive poetic excess, a limitless field for the play of language. Constructed thus midway between poem and drama, *Lucrece*'s collocation within both genres makes it easier to erase the superficial convention of *dramatis personae* and to treat literary characters who enact paradramatic scenes as linguistic representations of intellectual and emotional states. The poem thus becomes a dramatic narrative of self-division, or fragmented self-representation. Such an interpretive perspective derives of course from much earlier conventions, such as medieval allegory and psychomachia, and contemporary Renaissance practice of extended allegory.[3]

Collapsing the poem's fictional agents into a circulating flux of desire displaces critical emphasis from character to event, where the event becomes not a narrative of rape but a fantasy of violation: of ideals imagined and debased, wounds inflicted and suffered, taboos broken, thresholds crossed. Such a style of interpretation considers the poem as an intrapsychic debate, or a before-and-after design of a powerful desire followed from impulse to drive to fulfillment to reaction. "Tarquin" and "Lucrece" thus become reciprocal and inseparable aspects of the same trajectory of lust and guilt; they trace a hyperbolic curve, a rise and fall, of desire itself. (Although in the interest of readability I shall maintain the convention of referring to "Tarquin" and "Lucrece" as dramatic characters, the names always carry invisible quotation marks.)

The figure of hyperbolic desire can be illustrated by the geometric design of the hyperbola. The ascending curve is occupied by "Tarquin," while "Lucrece" occupies the descending curve: the mirrored rise and fall of desire.

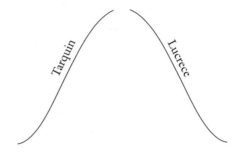

That the action of *Lucrece* occurs simultaneously on external and internal planes is clear from the beginning, when Collatine's urge to idealize spurs Tarquin's lust to debase. This structure is reinforced by the language of the poem, as when Lucrece's house retires, "every one to rest themselves . . . , / Save thieves and cares and troubled minds that wake" (125–26). External agents (thieves) parallel internal events (cares and troubled minds)—"As one of which doth Tarquin lie revolving" (127). Tarquin here exists coequally as both (outer) agent and (inner) impulse. A similar moment extends into allegory, when "pure thoughts are dead and still, / While lust and murder wakes to stain and kill" (163–67). The description reciprocally portrays both Lucrece and Tarquin, partially allegorized into sleeping Purity and wakeful Lust, while it reflects the psychology of dreaming and the release of repressed impulses.[4]

A durable tradition of medieval psychomachia underlies Shakespeare's quasi-allegorical dynamic of passion, as when Tarquin is "madly toss'd between desire and dread" and leaps vigorously from his bed to strike his phallic "falchion" on a stone flint to ignite the torch that lights his way to Lucrece's chamber (169–82), or when he is momentarily disabled by "disputation / 'Tween frozen conscience and hot burning will" (246–47). Here the tradition of psychomachia blends with conventional Petrarchan conceits, vividly hyperbolized. Yet Shakespeare always does more than merely employ conventions; he explores and ultimately exhausts them.

> Within his thought her heavenly image sits,
> And in the self-same seat sits Collatine.
> That eye which looks on her confounds his wits;
> That eye which him beholds, as more divine,
> Unto a view so false will not incline,
> But with a pure appeal seeks to the heart,
> Which once corrupted takes the worser part:

And therein heartens up his servile powers,
Who flatter'd by their leader's jocund show,
Stuff up his lust, as minutes fill up hours;
And as their captain, so their pride doth grow,
Paying more slavish tribute than they owe.
    By reprobate desire thus madly led,
      The Roman lord marcheth to Lucrece' bed.   (288–301)

These stanzas describe a passage from idealization to violation that is abrupt and linear, emerging from a con-fusion of self and other, Lucrece and Collatine, thought and object. Preceding his outward action, Tarquin looks within, where he discovers a version of Collatine's "sky of delight" (12)—the idealized Lucrece. She is already occupied, however, by Collatine. This highly sublimated primal scene seeks denial in "a pure appeal," but base eroticism is already released and quickly transforms mental images into physical arousal, as Tarquin's lust is "stuffed up" with blood in growing "pride."[5] Quick shifts from imagination to arousal to motion sketch the genesis of a basic drive that propels Tarquin along his linear course: "The locks between her chamber and his will, / Each one by him enforc'd" (302–3). Here is the rape played out in symbols both Shakespearean and Freudian; the imagery continues with the conventional sexual tropes of glove and needle (316–22).[6]

A keen delineation of desire's hyperbola is in two stanzas of the poem that prefigure similar erotic trajectories elsewhere in Shakespeare:

O deeper sin than bottomless conceit
Can comprehend in still imagination!
Drunken desire must vomit his receipt,
Ere he can see his own abomination.
While lust is in his pride no exclamation
    Can curb his heat or rein his rash desire,
      Till, like a jade, self-will himself doth tire.

And then with lank and lean discolour'd cheek,
With heavy eye, knit brow, and strengthless pace,
Feeble desire, all recreant, poor and meek,
Like to a bankrout beggar wails his case.
The flesh being proud, desire doth fight with grace;
    For there it revels, and when that decays,
      The guilty rebel for remission prays.   (701–14)

The model of oral appetite, prominent throughout *Lucrece*, vividly evokes the brute pleasures of sheer gratification, contrasted with the "abominable" perceptions of post-satisfaction guilt. The two stanzas present a metamorphosis of similes; the conventional equine image of unrestrained lust modulates via attributes shared by man and beast (cheek, eye, brow, pace) into the human image of the beggar, his spirit spent. Desire's hyperbola is quickly sketched by pride (rise) and decay (fall). Another stark "before-and-after" contrast recurs in *The Merchant of Venice*, yet with a major difference. The uncurbed "jade" of the above stanzas exhausts himself through his own efforts, while the prodigal ship (by convention feminine) in the passage below is enfeebled by the harsh elements of "the strumpet wind":

> All things that are,
> Are with more spirit chased than enjoy'd.
> How like a younger or a prodigal
> The scarfed bark puts from her native bay—
> Hugg'd and embraced by the strumpet wind!
> How like the prodigal doth she return
> With over-weather'd ribs and ragged sails—
> Lean, rent, and beggar'd by the strumpet wind!
> (*The Merchant of Venice*, 2.6.12–18)

Here the hyperbola is only suggested, traced from initial spirited prodigality, through embrace, to lean beggardom. Shakespeare's most famous and most complex elaboration of desire's hyperbola is in Sonnet 129 (though the geometric figure is faint):

> Th' expense of spirit in a waste of shame
> Is lust in action; and till action, lust
> Is perjur'd, murderous, bloody, full of blame,
> Savage, extreme, rude, cruel, not to trust;
> Enjoy'd no sooner but despised straight;
> Past reason hunted, and no sooner had,
> Past reason hated, as a swallow'd bait
> On purpose laid to make the taker mad,—
> Mad in pursuit, and in possession so;
> Had, having, and in quest to have, extreme;
> A bliss in proof, and prov'd, a very woe;

Before, a joy propos'd; behind, a dream.
All this the world well knows, yet none knows well
To shun the heaven that leads men to this hell.

The sonnet well describes the lust-maddened Tarquin, "fancy's slave" (200), who damns himself through his blind drive toward the hellish heaven of Lucrece. For Tarquin enlists in the army of passions: "Affection is my captain, and he leadeth" (271). His march to Lucrece's chamber begins with the illusion of orderly direction, but soon the metaphor of martial leadership collapses into the bestial rush of compulsion: "But nothing can affection's course control, / Or stop the headlong fury of his speed" (500–501). No longer following an impulse, Tarquin is now impelled. Like Macbeth, he is carried by his own intent (*Macbeth*, 1.7.26); like Othello, he is swept up in the compulsive current of his rash desire (*Othello*, 3.3.460–67). The model of Affection shifts from allegorical persona to psychological drive. Shakespeare later echoes this sense of "affection" in Leontes's violent and obscure ravings in *The Winter's Tale*:

Affection! thy intention stabs the center:
Thou dost make possible things not so held,
Communicat'st with dreams;—how can this be? . . . (1.2.138ff)

Considered within the context of *Lucrece*, these lines suggest the consanguinity of lust and fantasy, desire and dream, while they also evoke intersecting images of rape and suicide ("stabs the center") or of an outer-directed passion that reflexively returns to injure its source.

At the source of Tarquin's affection, or the erotic compulsion culminating in the rape of Lucrece (the object of his affection), lies the idealization of her boastful husband, Collatine. Sublimely constellating Lucrece in the "sky of his delight," he "unlock'd the treasure of his happy state" in Tarquin's tent (12–15). As the Narrator questions, "Why is Collatine the publisher / Of that rich jewel he should keep unknown / From thievish ears, because it is his own?" (33–36). An answer to this question is that the impulse to idealistic display derives precisely from the pleasure of possession: as the proud owner of such a gem, Collatine cannot hide its virtue under a bushel. Shining in his private constellation, her "pure aspects did him peculiar duties" (14).[7]

Such contamination of virtue by possession is hence the first "rape of Lucrece," as she is seized (*rapire*, to seize) by Collatine's imagination and displayed for the admiration of others. His fantasy of ownership leads to the verbal exhibition that fires Tarquin's lust; the initial violation is linguistic. Recent feminist readers have focused on this point. Catherine Stimpson terms Collatine's boasting "an act of excess that is a rhetorical analogue to Tarquin's sexual will." "Rape," concludes Nancy Vickers, "is the price Lucrece pays for having been described."[8] Collatine's boasting amid his comrades is an imaginative sharing of his wealth while arousing jealousy and envy. In effect, he offers his ideal possession to the potentially lewd admiration of his companions. The offshoot of such admiration is embodied in the lascivious Tarquin, who enacts the implicit climax of Collatine's discourse. Tarquin carries the shadowy subtext of a message sent post-haste from Collatine: "From besieged Ardea all in post / Borne by the trustless wings of false desire" (1–2). Although deep and invisible here at the beginning, the pun on "post" gradually surfaces as the poem develops its parallels with imagination and writing, and becomes manifest in the echoes of Lucrece's message on the outside of her letter to Collatine after the rape: "Her letter now is seal'd, and on it writ / 'At Ardea to my lord with more than haste.' / The post attends" (1330–32).[9]

The observation that Tarquin consummates Collatine's discourse restates as a structural principle the Narrator's opinion that Tarquin acts, literally, at Collatine's *suggestion*: "Perchance his boast of Lucrece's sovereignty / Suggested this proud issue of a king" (36–37). In Elizabethan vocabulary the transitive verb "suggest" carried a stronger sense than it has today; it meant "urge," "prompt," "motivate," often to questionable acts (see Sonnet 144). From this perspective, the poem has a structure similar to *Measure for Measure*, where a presumably virtuous agent (the Duke) employs a lustful substitute (Angelo) as a tool to debase an idealized woman (Isabella). Tarquin represents the displaced enactment of an unconscious wish, or "suggestion," proceeding from Collatine. The poem gestures toward this signification when Tarquin worries, "If Collatine dream of my intent" (218–20). The rape enacts the trauma of debasement that shadows the dream of idealization. "Thoughts are but dreams till their effects be tried" (353).

It is an axiom of psychoanalysis that idealization requires denial or repression and that what is repressed will return, usually in another form. As the Narrator of *Lucrece* asserts: "No perfection is so absolute / That some impurity does not pollute" (853–54). The maxim carries both internal and external senses. It states that impurity endangers perfection from without, as the Narrator continues to warn ("What virtue breeds, iniquity devours" [872]), and it implies that impurity already resides within perfection; no ideal is unalloyed. Here is the ambivalent psychology of idealization. It is just such a thought—that some impurity pollutes his divine Desdemona—that maddens Othello and drives him to a murder that is also a symbolic rape. In a world of imperfect relationships, any idealization of an other requires denial of conflicting characteristics, thus intensifying a potentially unstable ambivalence. If the ideal cracks, repressed energies erupt through the flaw. When Cordelia is not Lear's perfect child and nurturer she becomes a monster of ingratitude. When Desdemona is not Othello's faithful angel she becomes a lying whore. When Imogen is not Posthumous's innocent Diana she becomes a vicious devil. Idealization demands denial, yet what is denied inevitably reasserts itself as the dark ghost of the paragon, the satyr to Hyperion (to use Hamlet's terms).[10]

Within the intrapsychic circulations of unconscious desire configured by the nominal agents of *Lucrece*, every external misdeed is an internal trespass and every violation is a self-violation. As soon as he "yields to [Collatine's] suggestion," Tarquin finds his "single state of man" divided, so that "himself himself he must forsake" (*Macbeth*, 1.3.134–42; *Lucrece*, 156–60). He "pawn[s] his honour to obtain his lust," and at the moment he commits the rape, "his soul's fair temple is defaced," becoming a "spotted princess" (719–23). These terms precisely prefigure Lucrece's response to her rape, where "her sacred temple [is] spotted, spoil'd, corrupted" (1172). As Tarquin rapes Lucrece, he also violates himself.[11] Beyond her standard typology of wifely virtue, "Lucrece" represents an *internal* figure, an icon of classical purity and integrity as well as a female imago of the Christian soul. Psychoanalytically, she represents an internalized image of maternal perfection, whose vehement consecration to virtue is motivated by the pressures of oedipal desire. What *Lucrece* demonstrates is the frailty and failure of the repression of such desires.

Tarquin's rape of Lucrece represents self-violation on several levels. It is a crime against his own integrity and valor, against the Roman state ("Rome herself . . . doth stand disgrac'd" [1833]), against his sworn friendship with Collatine, and against Collatine's honor as embodied by Lucrece; her chastity was her husband's possession, therefore its theft and enjoyment is an assault on him (834–40). Under the strict fictions of patriarchy, rape is a type of theft, an act of envious rivalry between men.[12] This patriarchal economy persists to the end. On the site of Lucrece's death, Collatine and

Lucretius (her father) dispute the primary right of grief: "'Woe, woe,' quoth Collatine, 'she was my wife; / I ow'd her, and 'tis mine that she hath kill'd'" (1802–3).

The theme of self-division pervades the figures of both Tarquin and Lucrece. From the beginning the duplicity of Tarquin as friend and betrayer, visitor and violator, augurs a psychological doubleness: "Tarquin comes to Lucrece as two persons."[13] Reciprocally, Lucrece's responses to the rape demonstrate analogous self-divisions, as she debates suicide ("with herself is she in mutiny" [1153]; see also 1196) and implicitly imagines the act as self-rape: "To kill myself . . . alack what were it, / But with my body my poor soul's pollution?" (1156–57). When she finally does kill herself, her act formally re-enacts the rape (and not merely through the sexual symbolism of the dagger).[14] As she stabs herself, Lucrece exclaims of Tarquin, "He, he, fair lords, 'tis he / That guides this hand to give this wound to me" (1721–22). Lucrece's climactic posture culminates in an exact identification with her rapist, in a poetic implication of the binary consanguinity of victim and aggressor. The implicit co-action denotes a symbolic coitus that leads to an actual and figurative commingling of bloods, as Lucrece's blood, "bubbling from her breast," divides into two streams and encircles her body like an island (1737–43).[15] Some is red (Lucrece's pure blood) and some is black (defiled by Tarquin), but the two, red and black, are not in separate streams (as some critics mistakenly read). The emblem is not simply of division but also of confluence, not simply opposition but also identity—a literal consanguinity. Lucrece, in the last half of the poem, includes and encloses Tarquin, who has vanished from the narrative as manifest agent. In terms of our geometric mnemonic of the hyperbola, "Lucrece" takes over where "Tarquin" leaves off; her agency subsumes her shame and his guilt.

"Tarquin" and "Lucrece" thus figure a binary unit, a balanced pair of apparent opposites that mirrors an identity. Such structural symmetry informs the elaborate rhetorical balancing of those stanzas immediately following the (absent) scene of the rape (736–49). After Tarquin leaves Lucrece's bed, he "bear[s] away the wound that nothing healeth" (731). *She* has been wounded (externally), and *he* bears the wound (internally). "She bears the load of lust he left behind, / And he the burden of a guilty mind" (734–35). Although Tarquin now disappears from the poem, his "guilty mind" is not in fact borne away; it remains behind, now reposited in Lucrece, who immediately bewails her "offence," "disgrace," "sin," "guilt," and "shame," and who launches into her hyperbolic tirades against Night, Opportunity, and Time. Referring to "the iterative transfer-ral of these topics from Tarquin to Lucrece," A. Robin Bowers remarks that "the traditional *de casibus* theme has become internalized . . . to include the notion of *de casibus mentium*."[16]

The inclusion of "Tarquin" by "Lucrece" changes the language and style of the poem. Simply, the rape effects a violent epiphany. The poem initially presents an idealized, virtually virginal Lucrece,[17] who can neither discern nor imagine any duplicity in her sudden guest. She is an innocent reader, unable to gloss the "subtle shining secrecies" of Tarquin's false book (99–105). After the rape, a new, darkly erotic language reveals carnal contamination, as when she imagines Night as a demonic ravisher who smothers the sun in poisonous mists "ere he arrive his noontide prick" (764–84), yet wishes that night would never end, in an ironic performance of the traditional lover's wish (*"Lente, lente, currite noctis equi"*).[18] After the rape, her eyes are opened to the ways of the world; she can now read signs of deceit in the Troy-painting whose visages she scans—especially Sinon, the traitor who convinced the Trojans to admit the wooden horse. Her new knowledge positions her in an unfamiliar post-sexual context. Suffused by a complex of arousal and guilt, she becomes momentarily caught in a thick interchange of looks, thoughts, and blushes in her en-counter with the "sour-fac'd groom" who provides direct contact with her husband, the first agent to whom she entrusts her "confession." During their brief encounter she imagines that he perceives her guilt, and he, though ignorant of her stain, responds to her embarrassment with a blush, which she augments by reciprocation:

> His kindled duty kindled her mistrust,
> That two red fires in both their faces blazed;
> She thought he blush'd, as knowing Tarquin's lust,
> And blushing with him, wistly on him gazed.
> Her earnest eye did make him more amazed;
> The more she saw the blood his cheeks replenish,
> The more she thought he spied in her some blemish. (1352–58)

Contrasted with her prior innocent inability to read Tarquin's libidinous look, this post-sexual gaze combines guilt, self-suspicion, and projection. Violently, she has been transported into a new register of erotic imagina-tion; she is now possessed by knowledge, where before she was "unknown" (34). This brutal fracture of her conventionally virtuous relationship to

Collatine creates a sudden and poignant estrangement when they meet, at
Lucrece's mysterious summons:

> He hath no power to ask her how she fares;
>   Both stood like old acquaintances in a trance,
>   Met far from home, wond'ring each other's chance.   (1594–96)

The power of this alienation derives unconsciously from the sudden awareness of the other's sexual knowledge, the wish/fear that she knows and is
known, the ambivalent recognition of oedipal history.

> Being so caught up,
> So mastered by the brute blood of the air,
> Did she put on his knowledge with his power
> Before the indifferent beak could let her drop? [19]

The example of Yeats's modern revision of another classic rape resituates the event in terms of a Freudian epistemological trauma. For one way
to describe the Oedipus complex is to say that "knowing" the mother
sexually means to know that she has a sexual history, to recognize her as
erotically experienced and available—to others and therefore potentially
to oneself. Such a discovery or admission carries the awareness of rivalry
(the knowledge of prior possession). When this recognition is coupled
with fantasies of the primal scene, the sudden awareness of maternal sexuality becomes a kind of erotic epistemological assault, like a rape. One
could also theorize that shifting the image of the mother from a position
of idealized and solitary possession to a position of debased and shared
rivalry (with the father, with other men) can be felt as a violent disruption.
Violently participating in this transition from what Lacan called the Imaginary Register to what he called the Symbolic, the child in fantasy can simultaneously act out and enjoy sexual participation, while punishing this
newly conceived image of the mother through assault and death—consequences that can then also be avenged by rebelling against and casting out
the father.

The dynamic of this post-sexual knowledge is vividly portrayed in Lucrece's studied reading of the Troy-painting. [20] The rhetorical energies of
this set-piece simultaneously dilate outward from the formal debates of
Tarquin and Lucrece into the large-scale scene of the Rape of Helen and
the Sack of Troy, while they contract and distance the trauma of Lucrece

into the static realm of (apparent) pictorial representation.[21] Whereas before Lucrece could read nothing beyond the bland civilities of Tarquin, now she perceives affect and motive in the pictured faces of the Greeks and Trojans: Ajax's "blunt rage and rigour," the "deep regard and smiling government" in the look of "sly Ulysses" (1394–1400), and especially "despairing Hecuba" who becomes a mirroring figure:

> In her the painter had anatomiz'd
> Time's ruin, beauty's wrack, and grim care's reign;
> Her cheeks with chops and wrinkles were disguis'd:
> Of what she was no semblance did remain.
> Her blue blood chang'd to black in every vein,
>   Wanting the spring that those shrunk pipes had fed,
>   Show'd life imprison'd in a body dead.   (1450–56)

Here the post-sexual image of Lucrece is reflected in the ruined maternal figure of Hecuba (herself a morbid reflection of the mirrored face the poet imagines in the initial sequence of the Sonnets). Lucrece identifies with Hecuba and speaks for her: "'Poor instrument,' quoth she, 'without a sound, / I'll tune thy woes with my lamenting tongue'" (1464–65). This identification serves dual functions: it provides Lucrece with a character she can imitate, and it offers her an option beyond lamentation—revenge. Her typology shifts from patient Penelope, through victimized Persephone, to vindictive Philomela.[22] Immediately after her identification with victim and avenger, she turns her imagination to Helen:

> Show me the strumpet that began this stir,
> That with my nails her beauty I may tear!
> Thy heat of lust, fond Paris, did incur
> This load of wrath that burning Troy doth bear.   (1471–74)

A metaphor of pregnancy expresses the genesis of Lucrece's own wrath from the "load of lust" that Tarquin left her (734). Yet insofar as the woman receives the initial blame, an implicit identity of Lucrece, Helen, and Troy emerges. Helen becomes a debased image of Lucrece, a woman upon whose questionable virtue empires turn. When Lucrece transfers her "load of lust" to Troy's "load of wrath," she identifies with Troy, a city invaded and violated by male deceit. Next she identifies with Priam, as the master of Troy (1546–47). Lucrece's stream of confluent identifications

(Hecuba, Helen, Troy, Priam) follows her previous relation to Night, whom she first blames but soon conjures and identifies with, as "the silver-shining Queen" who would also be raped by Tarquin, himself "night's child," thereby becoming Lucrece's "co-partner" in victimage (785–89). The complexity of this particular con-fusion—Tarquin would rape his own mother (Night), if he were her (Night)—produces one of the most intense cross-identifications within the flux of shifting representations in this poem.

The momentary consanguinity of Lucrece and Helen, "the strumpet that began this stir," developed in later decades into a subterranean, liber-tine counter-image of Lucrece as sexually experienced, bawdy, even whor-ish. Tracing the evolution of this counter-image in Aretino, Carew (his notorious pornographic poem, "A Rapture"), and anonymous authors, Saad El-Gabalawy notes the vigorous translation of this emblem of virtue into a defense of lust. Through its desublimation of erotic (romantic) con-vention, this strain of seventeenth-century libertinism effected "a kind of metamorphosis in the figure of Lucrece, transforming the virtuous matron into a coquette." [23]

Further shifting cross-identifications within the poem parallel the fig-ures of Sinon and Priam as iterative representations of Tarquin and Colla-tine; Sinon/Tarquin is the deceitful traitor and Priam/Collatine is the master of the "sweet city" that is Troy/Lucrece. Just as Collatine's story inflames Tarquin to ruin Lucrece, so Sinon's narrative burns Troy:

> The well-skill'd workman this mild image drew
> For perjur'd Sinon, whose enchanting story
> The credulous old Priam after slew;
> Whose words like wildfire burnt the shining glory
> Of rich-built Ilion, that the skies were sorry,
> And little stars shot from their fixed places,
> When their glass fell, wherein they view'd their faces.   (1520–26)

The language echoes the initial rhetorical contest wherein Collatine's praise of Lucrece inflamed Tarquin (his agent) to "bear the lightless fire" that would pluck chaste Lucrece from the "sky of his delight" (4–12). Since the inflammatory narrative belongs to Sinon and to Collatine, our reading of the Troy-piece becomes knotted. Sinon clearly represents Tar-quin, but he also represents Collatine. Whereas Sinon talks the giant Greek horse within the walls of Troy, Collatine talks Tarquin into Lucrece. In both cases, a deceitful male rhetorician introduces an engine of ruin into a presumably well-fortified (feminine) city. The result is a violent debasement, the collapse of a pure constellation and the fracture of the mirror of idealization.[24]

Even before her confrontation with the Troy-piece, Lucrece's latent connection to its history is marked by her typology as Penelope, the spinner-weaver who waits with virtuous patience for her husband's return from war, though she is besieged by suitors. This story also carries a climactic chapter whereby the husband tests his wife by visiting her as a disguised substitute. The Troy-piece can thus be seen as Lucrece's production, or a projection of the poem's fantasies about marriage, war, fidelity, trust, disguise, and language onto a mute screen that mirrors unspoken motives of the poem itself. When Lucrece addresses the painting, she gives it voice, in a stark schematic of the basic aesthetic division between poem and drama that Shakespeare explores and entertains in *Lucrece*. Whereas the poem has no visual enactment (Shakespeare has only page, not stage), the painting has neither voice nor text.

The emblem of mute display that rouses others to voice and action finds its ultimate locus in Lucrece's body. After Collatine, Lucretius (her father), and Brutus have sworn on the bloody knife pulled from Lucrece's body to avenge her shame and purge Rome of Tarquin kings, they propose to carry the corpse into the streets, "To show her bleeding body thorough Rome, / And so to publish Tarquin's foul offence" (1851–52). On the statement of this intention, the poem abruptly ends. The ritual vindictive gesture rests on a crude signification whereby *res ipsa*, the body, represents the crime done to it. Lucrece's corpse is simultaneously an icon of violation and of purity. Her wound symbolizes both her suicide and Tarquin's offense: the Rape of Lucrece objectified, both as suffered and as inflicted. This public display of her wound is an ultimate seizure and display of her body within a masculine system of signification; it is the final rape. It is also the culminating publication of Collatine's "rich jewel he should keep unknown" (34), now known to all Rome. Ovid's phrase (which Shakespeare read) suggests a deeper, carnal meaning: "*vulnus inane patet*" (Ovid, *Fasti*).[25] Literally, "the gaping wound lies open, is exposed." Thus reduced to passive display of her wound—her void or vacancy—Lucrece becomes a vaginal signifier, an empty "inanity" made sensible by the vigorous admirations, lewd or legitimate, of men who possess her.

The crude carnal significance of this display of violated virtue returns the poem to the paradox of praise. For chastity praised is immediately chastity defiled. Just as the essence of true virginity is that the virgin is wholly unknown (e.g., veiled), the deep nature of chastity is that it is never announced. Praising chastity already enters the virtue in the lists of its opposition; it calls it into question, admits alternatives, and thereby (to use the language of Sonnet 116) admits impediments. Praising chastity is implicitly equivalent to testing it. *Lucrece* plays out this dynamic of tribute and trial through the cooperative agencies of Collatine and Tarquin.

One of the best examples of hyperbole in *Lucrece* is a stanza devoted to Lucrece asleep on her pillow:

> Her lily hand her rosy cheek lies under,
> Coz'ning the pillow of a lawful kiss;
> Who therefore angry, seems to part in sunder,
> Swelling on either side to want his bliss:
> Between whose hills her head entombed is,
>   Where like a virtuous monument she lies,
>   To be admir'd of lewd unhallowed eyes. (386–92)

Among conventional critical evaluations of this sort of poetic excess, Douglas Bush's objection is typical. "Such a conceit as this," he writes, "is in Marlowe's worst vein. . . . As often in the early plays, the author has quite forgotten the situation; he is holding the subject at arm's length, turning it round, saying as much as he can about every side of it. Almost every line gives evidence of a self-conscious pride in rhetorical skill."[26] It is of course just such pride in rhetorical skill that is the central subject of *Lucrece*, in matter and in form, beginning with Collatine's proud praise.[27] The vigorous manipulation of the subject that Bush describes is hardly a forgetting of the situation; it *is* the situation. Moreover, the elaborate hyperbole of the pillow inscribes in miniature the complex motivations that prefigure the rape itself. The sleeping Lucrece, in all innocence, prevents her pillow from its "lawful kiss." Such deprivation results in anger, division, and swelling, as a response to the "want" (lack) of "bliss." Thus surrounded by an emblem of angry arousal, both erotic and violent, Lucrece is rhetorically murdered, transformed into a tomb, "a virtuous monument." She is then subjected to the lewd admiration, not only of Tarquin (who is gazing on her at this moment), but also of the reader, before whose eyes Shakespeare's highly eroticized rhetoric will exhibit all of Lucrece's charms: her hair, her breasts, "her azure veins, her alabaster skin, / Her coral lips, her snow-white dimpled chin" (400–20). This elaborate inventory of Lucrece's various beauties idealizes and simultaneously dehumanizes her; it is another rhetorical appropriation or "rape," analogous to Collatine's public exhibition of his pure jewel. As the pillow's swelling mimics Tarquin's arousal, it becomes a displaced expression of his "will," a symbol of his erotic gaze: "But Will is deaf . . . ; / Only he hath an eye to gaze on beauty" (495–96). Here is lewd admiration reduced to its anatomical organ, the ruthless gaze of the monocular phallus.[28]

The stanza enacts a model of the poem itself. It condenses a pattern of denial and frustration that Joel Fineman discovers throughout the narrative, a "logic of 'let' that links Lucrece to Tarquin and that makes Lucrece responsible for her rape by virtue of the energetic and energizing resistance that she offers to it."[29] The dynamic of deprivation and arousal that Fineman describes accords with the trajectory of hyperbolic desire, which collates "Lucrece," "Tarquin," and "Collatine" as co-producers of the complete event. When Collatine arrives home, summoned by Lucrece's letter, her first words allude to her own culpability: "'Few words,' quoth she, 'shall fit the trespass best, / Where no excuse can give the fault amending'" (1613–14). She then proceeds to confess that "in the interest of thy bed / A stranger came" (1619–20). These at best ambiguous phrases twist the nature of her victimage so that the crime is not initially rape but infidelity.[30]

In her lament to Night, Lucrece earlier described her position as both agent and victim:

> "Make me not object to the tell-tale day:
> The light will show character'd in my brow
> The story of sweet chastity's decay,
> The impious breach of holy wedlock vow;
> Yea, the illiterate that know not how
>   To cipher what is writ in learned books,
>   Will quote my loathsome trespass in my looks."   (806–12)

The ambiguous diction, through which such terms as "decay," "breach," and "trespass" are both objective and subjective, active and passive, constructs a Lucrece whose rape is literally her "fault": it is a flaw, written in her face and on her body. "Poor women's faces," the Narrator opines, "are their own faults' books" (1253). Lucrece's face is from the beginning an ambivalent ground of shame and arousal, demarcated by that blatantly ambivalent physical sign, the blush.

> When virtue bragg'd, beauty would blush for shame;
>   When beauty boasted blushes, in despite
>   Virtue would stain that o'er with silver white.   (54–56)

This conventional contest between heraldic signs of purity and beauty, that "silent war of lilies and of roses" (71), now transmutes into a darker image of the *stain* on a white surface, an implicit sign of *writing*.

> Her maid is gone, and she prepares to write,
> First hovering o'er the paper with her quill;
> Conceit and grief an eager combat fight,
> What wit sets down is blotted straight with will:
> This is too curious-good, this blunt and ill.
>   Much like a press of people at a door,
>   Throng her inventions, which shall go before.   (1296–1302)

Lucrece's writing posture emulates her rape. This stanza precisely delineates the process of the rape, both as endured event and as composed narrative. The image of Lucrece "hovering o'er the paper with her quill" exactly mirrors Tarquin "shak[ing] aloft his Roman blade . . . like a falcon tow'ring in the skies" above the subject whose purity he means to stain, to "blot" with his "will." The pressure of invention at Lucrece's door reflects Tarquin's insistent drive to cross her threshold. These postures of rapist and victim replicate an original moment, I conjecture: the posture of Shakespeare at the instant of composition. Though deeply buried, linguistic associations further connect the rape with the process of writing. For instance, to silence her outcries, Tarquin wraps Lucrece's face in her bedlinen: "For with the nightly *linen* that she wears / He *pens* her piteous clamours in her head" (680–81). (Paper in Shakespeare's time was made primarily from linen: see *Othello*.) The effort of her tears to cleanse the stain of Tarquin's lust then becomes a wish to erase her shame from the historical record.

Precisely this intersection of rape and writing may return us to the figure of the hyperbola, and to the missing moment at the climax or apex. For the poem traditionally known as *The Rape of Lucrece* does not in fact

describe that event.[31] The actual rape, insofar as it may be surmised or projected, occurs literally between stanzas, in lines 683–84.[32] Our geometric
figure draws a blank at this moment. Of course issues of propriety and
decorum pertain here, but these are not exhaustive explanations. *The Rape
of Lucrece* is not about rape but about the motivations and feelings that
precede and succeed the event. It is a "before-and-after" design, pivoting
on a central act that is not described (in this design it resembles *Macbeth*).
The pivotal moment divides "before" from "after." It marks a gap or fault,
intersection or union, violation or disjuncture; it highlights a moment of
fusion that also forces separation, the illusory division between inside and
outside, idealized and debased, sacred and taboo. It is like a membrane
that joins primary oppositions, that marks—like the use of walls, doors,
and gloves in Shakespeare's poem—the fecund interval, the threshold of
oedipal sexuality.

My metaphor becomes transparent; it is the *hymen*, especially as elaborated by Derrida in his philosophical reverie out of Plato by Mallarmé, in
which he analogizes crossing the threshold of the hymen to blotting the
virginal blank page with writing. Mallarmé provides the fertile text:

La scène n'illustre que l'idée, pas une action effective, dans un hymen (d'òu procéde
le Rêve), vicieux mais sacré, entre le désir et l'accomplissement, la perpétration et
son souvenir: içi devançant, la remémorant, au futur, au passé, *sous une apparence
fausse de présent.* Tel opère le Mime, dont le jeu se borne à une allusion perpétuelle
sans briser la glace: il installe, ainsi, un milieu, pur, de fiction.[33]

The scene illustrates but the idea, not any actual action, in a hymen (out of which
flows Dream), tainted with vice yet sacred, between desire and fulfillment, perpetra-
tion and remembrance: here anticipating, there recalling, in the future, in the past,
under the false appearance of a present. This is how the Mime operates, whose act is
confined to a perpetual allusion without breaking the ice or the mirror: he thus sets
up a medium, a pure medium, of fiction.

While the precise relevance of these Symbolist meditations to Shakespeare's
poem may be obscure, Mallarmé's rich confusions (idea and action, sacred
and vicious) and his potent evocation of a medium, or space between, that
separates yet connects desire and gratification, past and future, through an
illusory present, apply to those images of motivation and of writing that
Shakespeare explores in *Lucrece* and elsewhere, in terms of rape. From the
grimly absurd scene in *Titus Andronicus* of the mutilated Lavinia writing
"stuprum" ("rape") in the sand with her stumps, through the tragic melodrama of Othello's efforts to keep Desdemona's "most goodly book" free

of the grimy term "whore," to the parody of rape and debased reputation by a "Iachimo-in-the-box" in *Cymbeline*, Shakespeare correlated the
themes of despoiled innocence and inscription. *Lucrece* may be his most
extended investigation of the hinge of this correlation: an elaborate study
of the mediating moment between innocence and knowledge, purity and
corruption, unity and disintegration. *Lucrece* is constructed on the principle of the climactic hinge, the sharp shift in direction from desire ("Tarquin") to response ("Lucrece"). Its pivotal point is literally absent (in
terms of literary representation), yet crucially present as a structural principle. It is a moment of traumatic deprivation—for both Lucrece and
Tarquin—and simultaneously a moment of sudden plenitude. Desire is
satisfied, delay terminated, the hyperbolic trajectory given final shape.
"Hymen" symbolizes both membrane and marriage. Derrida's ornate, hyperbolic rhetoric suggests the power of this conceit: "The hymen," he
writes, "the consummation of differends, the continuity and confusion of
the coitus, merges with what it seems to be derived from":

> the hymen as protective screen, the jewel box of virginity, the vaginal partition, the
> fine, invisible veil which, in front of the hystera, stands *between* the inside and the
> outside of a woman, and consequently between desire and fulfillment. It is neither
> desire nor pleasure but in between the two. Neither future nor present, but be-
> tween the two. It is the hymen that desire dreams of piercing, of bursting, in an
> act of violence that is (at the same time or somewhere between) love and mur-
> der. (212–13)

Derrida's aggressive eroticization of Mallarmé translates the hymeneal
conceit into those two arenas that Shakespeare hyperbolizes in *Lucrece*: the
mirroring hyperbolas of desire traced by (1) the fantasy of rape and (2) the
act of writing. It is as though when writing what we now call *The Rape of
Lucrece* Shakespeare married the hyperbolic description of rape (the body's
praise and violation) with hyperbole itself, or with the act of inscription.
The image of Lucrece at her writing desk, hovering over her paper while
inventions press" her, not only imitates the scene of rape; it also replicates
a primal scene of Shakespearean composition.

   The violent intersection of "Tarquin" and "Lucrece," as a primal scene
of composition, enacts an energetic collision between two aspects of the
Shakespearean imagination that can provisionally be distinguished by gender: the "dramatic" (male) and the "poetic" (female). The two agents of
Lucrece personify traditional divisions: male/female, active/passive, sadis-

tic/masochistic, doing/being. Linear action (Tarquin's line) is masculine, while convoluted verbal display (Lucrece's lines) is feminine.[34] Whereas Tarquin demonstrates his identity through action, Lucrece discovers her identity through reflection (e.g., the Troy-piece). Tarquin acts, while Lucrece reacts. Such conventional gender division is in fact a manifest subject of *Lucrece*. It is evident in the characters, in the narrated action, in the figure of desire's hyperbola, and expressly examined in a stanza in the middle of the poem:

> For men have marble, women waxen, minds,
> And therefore are they form'd as marble will;
> The weak oppress'd, th' impression of strange kinds
> Is form'd in them by force, by fraud, or skill.
> Then call them not the authors of their ill,
>   No more than wax shall be accounted evil,
>   Wherein is stamp'd the semblance of a devil.   (1240–46)

Through such Neoplatonic psychology the Narrator imposes his own logic and morality on the poem. The thoughts echo Spenser's Garden of Adonis, and are echoed in *A Midsummer Night's Dream* when Theseus warns Hermia that her subjection to her father is "but as a form in wax / By him imprinted" (1.1.49–50). As Katharine Maus notes, the metaphor, by insisting on absolute female passivity, effectively removes all agency from Lucrece. If she has no will of her own, Maus asks, "then what can Tarquin have violated?" The rape of passive women by active men then becomes "in the nature of things," and Tarquin's assault is "excusable." [35] The passage implicitly suggests rape, but explicitly it describes inscription, not marring but marking. Beyond the Narrator's conventional complacency about gender relations lies a powerful metaphor of compliance, the equation of writing and rape.[36]

Shakespeare's *Lucrece*, then, is not merely about a classic rape, or about the hymeneal intervals between wish, deed, and response, but also about the process of writing—or of imaginatively conceiving a traumatic act and inscribing that conception on the page. Inscription leaves a permanent mark or stain—unlike the vital yet ephemeral voices and gestures of a staged play. It is essentially emblematic that Shakespeare's two intended poetic publications conclude with images of stains and indelible memory—the blood-stained purple anemone in *Venus and Adonis* and the bloody corpse of

Lucrece. Both are emblems of innocence re-marked by lust; both enter cultural mythology as images of victimized virtue, polluted yet consecrated, violently memorialized as monuments to chastity defiled.

If Shakespeare imagined publication as leaving a permanent mark, and if his imagination of that mark was characterized by a sadomasochistic confusion of figure and disfigurement, love and violence—that is, by a fantasy of rape—then his conspicuous indifference to or ambivalence about publication acquires new significance. It may be that writing for Shakespeare, when fixed in published form, did not represent a purely positive emblem of textual procreativity that would "bear his memory" through time (Sonnet 1). Shakespeare's is no mere erotics of poetry. His potent coupling of rape and remembrance suggests publication as a kind of violation—an arrest of the imagination, an insult to time, a blot on the stream of (dramatic) creativity. Such speculation is a grand, indeed hyperbolic conjecture. That reading Shakespeare should tease us into such thoughts is a major motive for our continued study of him.

6

Phantasmagoric *Macbeth*

IMAGINING MACBETH IS A BLOODY LABOR. With its oneiric style, gory passages, and sinister issues, the play taxes imaginative conceptions and critical perceptions. An answering criticism may require, as G. Wilson Knight insisted, "a new logic," a perspective beyond rational orders of causality, sequence, or choice. In place of a conventional analysis that traversed the two-dimensional plot of the play, Knight called for a three-dimensional mapping of its irrational dreamscape.[1] In this chapter I will sketch such a map, through a style of imagining *Macbeth* that is vivid and visceral, psychoanalytic and phantasmagoric.

I begin with the still point and turning point of the play: the murder of King Duncan. Although the event offers powerful dramatic possibilities, Shakespeare does not stage it. Among the effects of omitting this potent scene is to displace it into fantasy—to make an audience imagine it—and thus to expand the range of responses. What we fantasize can be more vivid and affecting than what might be staged. To recast Macbeth as aesthetician: "[Re]present[ed] fears are less than horrible imaginings" (1.3.137–38).[2] As D.J. Palmer notes of the offstage regicide, "instead of distancing the deed from us, . . . the effect is to intensify its sacrilegious horror."[3] Unstaged and unseen, yet horribly imaginable, the central regicide may affect an audience at deep psychological and emotional levels.

Psychoanalytic interpretations offer various intrafamilial reconstructions of the crime. Imagining Duncan's murder as symbolic patricide is commonplace in psychological (as well as religious and political) readings. In this case the patriarch heads a violent masculine hierarchy that excludes women: there is no Queen of Scotland. Macbeth poses initially as a dutiful son who advances by the death of his own father (Sinel: see 1.3.71, 1.4.25). Lady Macbeth makes the patricidal analogue explicit by calling attention to the king's resemblance to her father (2.2.12–13). Duncan's actual sons flee after the murder and are blamed for the crime. Such a standard psychoanalytic reading is based on Freud's oedipal triangle, including his brief remarks about *Macbeth*.[4] In this geometry of unconscious desire, Macbeth represents the rebellious oedipal son, Duncan the father, and the maternal angle prefigures Lady Macbeth, or (via conventional symbolic characterization of a country as feminine, maternal) Scotland herself.[5] Actual geometric figures may make these symbolic intrafamilial relations easier to imagine:

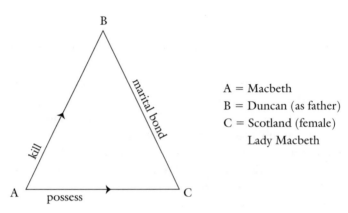

A = Macbeth
B = Duncan (as father)
C = Scotland (female)
    Lady Macbeth

In this, the classic oedipal triangle, side AB indicates the patricidal wish, side AC the incestuous wish, and side BC the marital bond of husband-wife (father-mother, King-Scotland). The lines of force are unidirectional, driving the son along his one-way career.

By shifting perspective and reconfiguring the oedipal triangle, we can imagine the intrafamilial drama in another way—as symbolic matricide. Such a view focuses on Duncan's loving and generous nature and envisions his murder as an assault against maternal providence. Macbeth murders Sleep in its innocence, the agent that "knits up the ravell'd sleave of care," a bath, a balm, "great Nature's second course, / Chief nourisher in life's feast" (2.2.34–39). Duncan himself is "the spring, the head, the fountain" of his country's and his countrymen's blood. As Macbeth remarks of the king's death, "The wine of life is drawn" (2.3.95). The phrase evokes a fantastic union of murder (spilled blood) and feast (filled cup). In this reconstruction of king as mother, Duncan becomes identified with Scotland: "it weeps, it bleeds; and each new day a gash / Is added to her wounds" (4.3.41). Duncan's own "gash'd stabs look'd like a breach in nature / For ruin's wasteful entrance," and the actual instruments of entrance are "daggers / Unmannerly breech'd with gore" (2.3.113–16). Linguistic associations here suggest regicide as rape, making Macbeth's grim reference to "Tarquin's ravishing strides" suggestively apt (2.1.55). The imagistic combination of parricide and sexual assault indicates the incestuous component of matricidal fantasies.[6]

This imagined re-vision of regicide as matricide generates a more complex dynamic to which I will return. For the moment, note that the interpretation posits maternal authority as the source and target of the play's violence. While there is no queen, there are demonic emblems of female power in the witches and Lady Macbeth. Assaults on Duncan and on Lady Macduff (the only actual mother in the play) then become displaced attacks on more dangerous and less accessible maternal evils. This dynamic suggests in psychoanalytic terms a failed splitting. The division between benevolent maternal support (Duncan) and malevolent manipulation (the witches, Lady Macbeth) breaks down, so that Macbeth kills what is fair and trusts what is foul.

Geometrically this design presents mirroring images, or the reflection of a subliminal, shadowy figure. In the diagram, side AB indicates the ma-

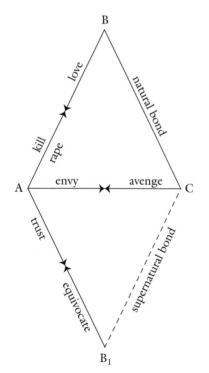

A = Macbeth
B = Duncan (mother)
B_1 = Witches/Lady Macbeth
C = Malcolm/Macduff/Banquo/Fleance

tricidal impulse of erotic assault. Its diabolic mirror, side AB_1, suggests the bond of fatal trust. Side BC represents the natural familial bond of mother and sons (analogous to the sacral bond of king and subject), while side B_1C evokes the supernatural connection of witches and avenging children. Side AC marks a mutual contest (fraternal rivalry); as AC it indicates Macbeth's envy of his rivals and his violence toward them, while as CA it indicates their reciprocal vengeance against him.

Combining these patricidal and matricidal readings suggests King Duncan as a magical composite parent, both father and mother; his murder then becomes a complete parricide. Such a revision is appropriate to the style of splittings and recombinations inherent in the play, which can also reconstitute Macbeth and his wife as a unit (this is Freud's reading). This interpretation would stress the ambivalent androgyny of the bearded weird sisters, or Lady Macbeth's vigorous gender-straddling. Duncan's effort to idealize masculine authority and power is an attempt to subsume or repress chthonic feminine energies, which yet return in force.[7]

The most intriguing psychoanalytic reconstruction, and the most complex, is of the regicide as symbolic infanticide. In this interpretation, the King becomes a satiated then victimized infant. For instance, as Duncan prepares to visit Inverness, he savors his "plenteous joys, / Wanton in fulness," and announces that Macbeth is "full so valiant, . . . I am fed; / It is a banquet to me" (1.4.33–34; 54–56). Together Duncan and Banquo describe the Macbeths' home: "This castle hath a pleasant seat; the air / Nimbly and sweetly recommends itself / Unto my gentle senses. . . . Heaven's breath / Smells wooingly here" (1.6.1–10). Their references to beds and procreant cradles and breeding impinge immediately on the entrance of Lady Macbeth, who has just warned that "the raven himself is hoarse, / That croaks the fatal entrance of Duncan / Under my battlements" (1.5.38–40). The imagery evokes a typically Shakespearean fusion of architecture and anatomy, a fusion furthered by Duncan's conversation with Banquo. Inverness is the scene of hospitality and hell, and the castle becomes (fantastically) Lady Macbeth's body, the battlements her transfigured woman's breasts.[8] The locus of gratified desire and gratuitous death is the same—a pattern repeated in Duncan's bed (the place of healing rest and fatal assault) and in the witches' cauldron (where ministry and murther coalesce).

When Banquo retires, he remarks that "the King . . . hath been in unusual pleasure . . . and shut up / In measureless content" (2.1.12–17). We can imagine the sequence: Duncan is drawn seductively into the attractive, nurturing locus of the fragrant castle, fed full to satiety, and (smiling in his sleep) brutally murdered. This event is exactly analogous to Lady Macbeth's fantasized murder of the infant at her breast, another crucial moment of gratification and violence that we do not actually see but that may arouse our imaginations to horror and disgust.

These last two reconstructions of regicide—as matricide and as infanticide—offer reciprocal perspectives on the central event of the play. We can see the core assault from both sides of the mother-infant bond: that is, the mother is murderous and the infant is victimized, *and* the mother is potentially murderous but the infant is the avenger who retaliates by killing her (or others who represent her, since Lady Macbeth dies offstage, apparently by her own hand, and the witches are beyond assault). Reciprocity turns easily into retaliation. The geometry of this design is complex, as the triangle of manifest relations is circumscribed by the arcs of supernatural bonds.

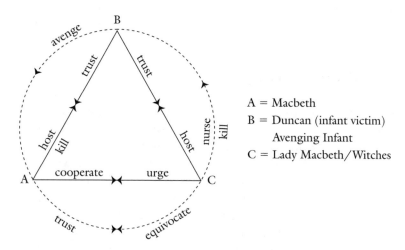

A = Macbeth
B = Duncan (infant victim)
    Avenging Infant
C = Lady Macbeth/Witches

The triangle indicates manifest motives, while the circle suggests their shadows. For example, side AC indicates the relations of Macbeth and his wife, while its shadow (arc AC) marks the pattern of his trust and the witches' "paltering." The diabolic consanguinity of Lady Macbeth and the witches is suggested by the lines of force diverging from point C. Side AB represents the relation of murderous Macbeth and victimized Duncan (imagined as infant), while arc BA traces the trajectory of revenge.

In brief, the sleeping king and the nursing infant are analogous and reciprocal. The avenging infant takes revenge for both figures. As the nursing babe is ripped untimely from his mother's breast, so the avenging son is ripped untimely from his mother's womb. Macduff's birth repeats yet survives the fatal bond of nurturance and negation that Lady Macbeth's fantasized infanticide forges. Unlike her child, who suffers traumatic disintegration, Macduff is the "child of integrity"—so-called by Malcolm, another son who is proudly "unknown to woman."[9] As Cleanth Brooks notes, before appearing ultimately as Macduff the avenging infant manifests itself most dramatically in the apparitions of the bloody child and the child with tree in hand, as well as the unending line of Banquo's progeny.[10] The apparitions are ironic verification of Macbeth's fear that "Pity, like a naked, new-born babe" will disclose the crime and take up Duncan's cause.

These various associations of nursing, murder, and revenge in primitive, infantile terms may explain the curious criminal strategy of deflecting the blame for Duncan's murder by gilding the faces of the grooms with the king's blood. Juxtaposing such lines as "The wine of life is drawn" with the nightmarish query, "Who would have thought the old man to have so much blood in him?" suggests a phantasmagoric confluence of liquids: wine, blood, milk, gall. Fantastically, it is as though Duncan's blood is sacrificially drunk from his wound, in a ritual union of murder and feast. Hearing sacramental tones in Macbeth's speech before the murder of Duncan, Richard Ide suggests that the phrase, "The bell invites me," echoes the ritual Invitation to Holy Communion, leading to "Macbeth's crude sacrilege, the perversion of the Lord's Supper."[11] David Barron writes that "the drink to which his wife summons him is the blood of Duncan."[12] Banquo's murderer also has blood on his face, and when Macbeth stares at his friend's apparition, its head and face gashed all over, "the blood-bolter'd Banquo *smiles* upon him" (4.1.123). This smile reflects the helpless, victimized infant ("smiling in my face"), but now no longer helpless. Its potency lies in the regal lineage over which it proudly presides. It is a smile of vengeance and vindication, a smile to reciprocate and retaliate the communal but ambiguous smile of friends ("There's daggers in men's smiles") or mothers or infants. Then there is Lady Macbeth's infamous contention:

> I have given suck,
> And know how tender 'tis to love the babe that milks me:
> I would, while it was smiling in my face,
> Have pluck'd my nipple from his boneless gums,

And dash'd the brains out, had I so sworn
As you have done to this.   (1.7.54–59)

This catastrophic moment of violent disruption and death is also one of loving union and nurturance. It presents the icon of Charity shattered by maternal malevolence.[13] The phrase, "while *it* was smiling in *my* face," linguistically replicates the perfect mirroring of mother and infant that founds familial harmony; it locates the infant's smile "in" the mother's face. Lady Macbeth's brutally broken nursing scene is a feast disrupted by a murder, the most vivid (or morbid) representation of a central and recurrent event in the play.[14] This catastrophic weaning conflates in a single moment a disturbance that Shakespeare earlier separated. Juliet's Nurse recalls that her charge's weaning occurred on the very day of a memorable earthquake (*Romeo and Juliet*, 1.3.20ff). Moreover, the Nurse's practice of putting wormwood on her nipple places poison at the source of maternal nourishment, in an analogy to Lady Macbeth's murthering ministry, or to the Captain's remark that "from the spring whence comfort seem'd to come / Discomfort swells" (*Macbeth*, 1.2.26–27). Such weaning practices were customary in Shakespeare's time, and much folklore attached to them. Robert Burton lists "Bad Nurses" as the first accidental cause of melancholy, followed by "Education," then "Terrors and Affrights."[15] Beyond Renaissance beliefs in actual "engrafting" and "imprinting" (Burton's terms) of characteristics through the nurse's milk lie some home truths. Current developmental theory could well agree with Burton that "the strange imagination of a woman works effectually upon her infant." It may not be precisely that "minds are altered by milk," but they are by mothers, in the nursing relation. The chemistry is wrong but the psychology is right.[16]

In psychoanalytic terms, this primal relation is a "dual unity" wherein mother and infant are bound "symbiotically" in nurturance and trust (the ideal paradigm).[17] Perversions of the dual unity afflict *Macbeth* throughout, as community degenerates into hostility: for instance, the "two spent swimmers who do cling together / And choke their art," or Duncan's horses that turn on one another as predator and prey. Critical commentary echoes psychoanalytic terms. Stephen Booth notes that the two swimmers, "thus intertwined, become an entity in which the two independent beings are indistinguishable." Harry Berger stresses the "symbiotic" and "destructive" bond of the swimmers and the equation of comrade with enemy.

Moreover, his close-focus reading of Rosse's description of "Bellona's bridegroom, lapp'd in proof" offers an image of striking perception and relevance. The phrase "Bellona's bridegroom" is paradoxical, he writes, "because the archaic goddess of war was a fierce unyielding virgin the opposite of Mars's Venus; 'lapp'd' means wrapped, swathed (like a baby?), clothed, as in a soft blanket or robe, or as in waves, but the proof is gore. The image is not only gigantic, but also erotic and infantile." [18] This intimacy of care and gore recurs in the Captain's report of Macbeth's heroism. His actions demonstrate the instant transmutation of courtesy into carnage. Macbeth, "like Valour's minion,"

> carv'd out his passage,
> Till he fac'd the slave [(Macdonwald)];
> Which ne'er shook hands, nor bade farewell to him,
> Till he unseam'd him from the nave to the chops,
> And fix'd his head upon our battlements.   (1.2.19–23)

Duncan responds to this gory tale by praising Macbeth as a "worthy gentleman," yet the Captain's allusion to true gentlemanliness (shaking hands) in the midst of war reciprocates Lady Macbeth's moment of carnage in the midst of womanly nursing. Both images present a dyad of violent community and the bloody disruption of natural order by monstrous inhumanity.

Macbeth carving out his passage is a most suggestive image. Not merely does he hack his way through rebel soldiers to confront and unseam the merciless Macdonwald, but more generally he knifes his way to the throne and beyond. Moreover, the phrase "carv'd out his passage" evokes the mystery of Caesarean section that resonates throughout the play. Macbeth opens up Macdonwald in a grotesque parody of this procedure, as well as other surgical practices of "bleeding." He becomes both butcher and surgeon (the London Company of Barber-Surgeons had organized in the sixteenth century, under the sign of blood). What emerges from the act of unseaming Macdonwald is both Macbeth's glory and his treachery. Fantastically, one can imagine the issue of Macdonwald's Caesarean section as the avenging infant "not of woman born" that returns to kill Macbeth. That is, Macbeth "unmans" Macdonwald by subjecting him to battlefield gynecological surgery, thus making him the fantastic origin of the agent of revenge.

Shakespeare's imagery evokes still more bizarre imaginings, of Macbeth like an infant *in utero* forging his way into the world through the containing body of his source. His carved passage effects a Caesarean section from within, incising his world from navel to neck in a simultaneous assault on and escape from the maternal matrix that holds (embraces and limits) him. This is a carnal metonymy of the whole tragedy. Macbeth carves his career in an element that ambiguously supports and surrounds him, that offers him advancement while confining him to decreasing circles of motion (like a bear at the stake). Although his emphasis differs, Barron's metaphors effectively enwomb Macbeth: "Macbeth determines to break out of his strangling situation through violence . . . and thus cut his way out of the female environment which chokes and smothers him." "He is already caught up in the witches' world. He is *cabin'd*, *cribb'd*, *confined* in the entrails of devouring woman, and must therefore cut his way out with the sword."[19]

The claustrophobia of cabin, crib, and confine in *Macbeth* may even allude to specific beliefs in Jacobean obstetrics, which held that a male fetus "was faster tied and bound [within the womb] then the female, because the ligaments which hold and fasten him are stronger and dryer then they that bind and support a wench."[20] Fox notes that the "birth-strangl'd babe" whose finger the witches add to the bubbling cauldron was not an unusual phenomenon in Jacobean obstetrics; in breech births the mother's pubic bone could constrict the infant's breathing passage.[21] Furthermore, Caesarean section in early seventeenth-century England was literally a matricidal procedure, performed only on mothers already dead or certain to die,[22] so that the gruesome battlefield surgery transforms the enemy other into a woman while it murders him/her.

This paradox of advancement and restriction informs Macbeth's style of acting out his martial identity through violent aggression against others who reflect his own violence: Macdonwald, Cawdor, Banquo, Macduff. Macbeth literally and figuratively *mirrors* his antagonists by his posture of facing and imitating them, making the violent dyad an embrace of doubles. He confronts the traitor Cawdor "with self-comparisons, / Point against point, rebellious arm 'gainst arm," and he faces Macdonwald in a similar posture in which antagonists are imagistically and grammatically confused. (Shakespeare's lines do not distinguish whose point and whose arm; the pronoun in the line, "Which ne'er shook hands . . . ," is Janus-faced.) Antagonists become mirror images or doubles, enemy twins who yoke themselves in a bond both aggressive and erotic. (Coriolanus and Aufidius are the clearest instance of the tenacity and tension of this bond.)[23]

From a psychoanalytic perspective the image of rival twins represents a later manifestation of wishes and fears evoked in the early mirroring of (male) infant and (female) mother. Later re-enactment in valiant violence is a paradoxical attempt at release, an aggressive "heroic" struggle against an enemy who represents an original, inexorable matrix. In Freudian terms, oedipal revenge is a repetition of oral desires and dreads. In Shakespearean terms, Coriolanus's heroic autonomy and hysterical virility are efforts to escape or transcend maternal dependence, yet at the same time they are instruments of Volumnia's wishes. The more he tries to author himself, the more he is his mother's son. No exit, only repetition. Macbeth is caught in a similar bind; as he carves his independent passage he simultaneously sinks into the controlling maternal matrix that, like the witches, both nurses and curses him. In psychoanalytic terms, violent aggression and the maintenance of difference through repeated enactments of violated union may be a defense against a basic fear of undifferentiation or the state of no-difference, for example, between rival twins, or infant and mother. This defense is doomed to endless repetition in identities that paradoxically act out autonomously yet follow an embryonic script, like the tragic careers of Coriolanus or Macbeth.

This paradoxical pathology suggests a potential hazard of the necessary reciprocity between mother and infant in human development. Identity is based on identification, but it must emerge from mimesis if genuine separateness is to develop. "The precursor of the mirror," writes D.W. Winnicott, "is the mother's face."[24] At first this mirroring reflects no difference for the infant between self and other (or mouth and breast). Perfect reciprocity institutes no difference. Individuation is therefore a process of breaking out of this exact mirroring without breaking the mirror (the reflecting relationship). Winnicott terms it a gradual process of "disillusionment." Establishing externality or otherness requires separation, which may present itself or be perceived as deprivation or aggression. A distance must be forged, then bridged, or the infant may not establish boundaries of its own self as distinguishable from the nurturing matrix. In the Ovidian myth, Narcissus died, deprived by his own apparent abundance: "*inopem me copia fecit.*" A persistent "no difference" psychically murders a child. The mother who mirrors her child exactly, who gratifies instantly and perfectly her infant's every need, becomes a magical provider whose effect is ironically damaging: "she is dangerous, a witch."[25]

As Winnicott describes it, the necessary distance can normally be forged by the infant's "attack" on the object (breast or mother)—an attack that represents in fantasy its destruction.[26] When the object survives, proving that it is not vulnerable to the infant's fantasies of omnipotence, its externality becomes apparent, thereby creating a space for interrelationship between ego and object, self and other. A process of self-other differentiation can thus emerge from a moment of violence (though not necessarily anger) and can result in the beneficial "use" of the object as a distinguishable other. An example is the infant who attacks the breast, through hungry sucking or perhaps even biting, but does not injure the mother, because the infant is weak and toothless. When the mother neither retaliates nor withdraws, the breast survives the infant's "destruction" and begins to become marked off from the subject's field of self.

Lady Macbeth's imagined infant has "boneless gums," yet she reacts to its nursing with gratuitous violence in apparent retaliation. Or, from another view, she rejects its developing identity by using it to demonstrate her own ruthlessness. Here the space of difference is neither initiated by the infant nor mutually sustained by the mother but suddenly and catastrophically created by her—from mother's breast untimely ripped. As Adelman puts it, "Lady Macbeth and the witches fuse at this moment, and they fuse through the image of perverse nursery." [27] This fantasy of a bloody break at the origin of relationship provides a scheme for the style of masculine identity in *Macbeth* that seeks confirmation in violence. ("What bloody man is that?") To be a man, in this tragedy's central terms, means to be bloody or bloodied. Wounds are the mark of manliness; fighting establishes virility in the face of and at the expense of a mirroring rival. At play's end, with butcher and fiend safely dispatched, this fatal ideology of masculinity persists, as Old Siward, pleased that his dead son "had his hurts before," exclaims, "Had I as many sons as I have hairs, / I would not wish them to a fairer death" (4.9.14–15). Fair is still foul, and the ironic pun ("hairs"/"heirs") emphasizes the confusions of self and other, issue and excrement (to use Shakespeare's vocabulary).

In her extended commentary on this crucial scene of malignant nursing and challenges to virility, Adelman concludes that "the play's central fantasy of escape from woman . . . unfold[s] from this moment: for if Macbeth's bloodthirsty masculinity is partly a response to Lady Macbeth's desire, in effect an extension of her will, it simultaneously comes to represent the way to escape her power." [28] It may *represent* such a way, but the trajectory is soon cut off. Any mode of escape that Macbeth seeks or finds is always enclosed by the space he is caught within; the way out is ultimately another way in.

When Lady Macbeth, like Old Siward, wishes her son to death by throwing the fantasized infant to the ground, she cancels and tears to pieces that greatest bond of all (3.2.49). Her imagined gesture annihilates the fluid field within which human relationships emerge and develop. Her sudden rupture of that "potential space" closes the intermediate area between perfect mirroring (the magical unity of no difference) and the establishment of self-other boundaries and the lessons of difference.[29] In Winnicott's terms, the resulting absence of a dependable "holding environment" disables normal symbolic representation or leads to an invasion of projected "persecutory material." With the ruin of this playspace and the loss of an intermediate provisional arena where things *may be* (for example, both real *and* imagined), the capacity for normal relationship suffers pathological distortion.[30]

For Macbeth this space is horribly distorted. He finds no mediating ground where things *may be*; instead, things *are* and *are not* in maddening equivocation. There is no place for fantasy, no interim for the provisional play of wish and deed. As Shakespeare's Brutus puts it,

> Between the acting of a dreadful thing
> And the first motion, all the *Interim* is
> Like a phantasm, or a hideous dream.
> (*Julius Caesar*, 2.1.60–62)

The word "*Interim*" is capitalized and italicized in the Folio texts of this passage and *Macbeth* 1.3.154–56 (below), and nowhere else in Shakespeare:

> Think upon what has chanc'd; and at more time
> The *Interim* having weigh'd it, let us speak
> Our free hearts each to other.

Macbeth never keeps this promise to Banquo—unless murder speaks his heart.

Like Macbeth, Brutus (who cannot sleep and who speaks these lines immediately after a knocking at the gate) endures the anxieties of the interim between the initial proposal ("motion") of a deed and its eventual enactment, during which interval he suffers a psychic insurrection that shakes his single state of man. But even as Macbeth suffers doubts, he moves inexorably toward Duncan's bedchamber, drawn by a fantastic replica of his own dagger. For him the phantasmagoric interim displaces reality; dreams replace deliberations, and the distinction between wish and deed is blurred, then erased. The normal process of desire → interim → act (or inhibition) is distorted. Other characters in *Macbeth* endure their interims more normally. Banquo puts his uncanny experience in its proper place when he dreams of the three weird sisters (2.1.90) and asks the "merciful powers" to "restrain . . . the cursed thoughts that nature / Gives way to in repose" (2.1.5–7).[31] Once he begins to ponder his profit in the witches' predictions, he stops himself and says, "But hush, no more" (3.1.10). Banquo can recognize his desires yet inhibit his deeds, as can Lady Macbeth. They provide places in dream or fantasy for their dangerous wishes (such as Lady Macbeth's infanticide, or her somnambulism). But Macbeth, having murdered sleep, cannot dream. Instead he acts out his dreams in his nightmarish waking life. As a character, "Macbeth is helpless as a man in a nightmare," as Knight put it.[32] As a play, *Macbeth* is like a psyche turned inside out, its fantasies actualized as external events, agents, and obsessive repetitions.[33]

The normal psychological process of admitted and inhibited fantasy is crudely yet effectively illustrated in Malcolm's long speech to Macduff, where he purportedly tests Macduff's loyalty by pretending to be more villainous than Macbeth, finally disclaiming the heinous character he constructs (4.3). Malcolm can pretend. He can out-Herod Herod and then relegate the fantasy to its proper, repudiated place. He can imaginatively inhabit the phantasmagoric interim and then inhibit its dreadful action. Anyone can do this. It is within our imaginative range to express the most vile character and most wicked act, in thoughts or words. Malcolm's speech demonstrates onstage the validity of Auden's claim that "watching *Macbeth*, every member of the audience knows that the possibility of becoming a Macbeth exists in his own nature."[34]

Macbeth, however, is not free to imagine or play himself. Compelled to enact his fantasies, he must be and do. "Strange things I have in head, that will to hand, / Which must be acted, ere they may be scann'd" (3.4.137–38). Like a hurried player he must act out his role before the script is clear to him.[35] He becomes an unread but ready actor in a phantasmagoric tragedy of blood—a Jacobean adumbration of the modern theater of cruelty—wherein his actions are determined before he can reflect upon or choose them. "The theater of cruelty," writes Derrida, "is indeed a theater of dreams, but of *cruel* dreams, that is to say, absolutely necessary and determined dreams, dreams calculated and given direction."[36] Once embarked on his compulsive career, Macbeth becomes even more determined (as both agent and victim) after he sees the apparitions. "From this moment," he swears,

> The very firstlings of my heart shall be
> The firstlings of my hand. And even now,
> To crown my thoughts with acts, be it thought and done.
>   (4.1.146–49)

This is simple pathology, a compulsion. It signifies the closure of the interim, or of normal imaginative playspace, and its restriction to instantaneous acting-out. Francis Fergusson puts it one way when he isolates the concept, "to outrun the pauser, reason," as the action or motive of the play. Norman Rabkin puts it another way when he describes Macbeth in "purposeless subjection to drives he does not understand and goals he does not want." Jerald Ramsey characterizes this design of compulsive (re)activity as Macbeth's "doom of reflex and repetition." Harold Bloom terms it "the Macbeth complex" and connects it to the Freudian death-drive.[37]

Where there is no viable potential space, then in Winnicott's terms the psychological efficacy of "transitional objects" is limited. (A transitional object is an emblem of exchange in the playspace between infant and mother, such as a blanket or doll. It represents an essential con-fusion of wish and gift. The child does not ask, "Is this me or other?" or, "Did I make [wish, hallucinate] this or was it given to me?" A transitional object is both inner creation and outer presentation, with no attendant anxiety about its ontological status.) In these terms, the world of *Macbeth* becomes a field of transitional phenomena in which the hero asks the impossible question: "Is this real or am I hallucinating it?" He interrogates his own vision: "Is this a dagger which I see before me, / The handle toward my hand?" That dagger is the perfect transitional object, both there and not there, real and not real, provided and imagined, his and not his. It appears in authentic answer to his own intent, mirrors his own instrument, and then, as he watches, transforms itself from present replica to future image; it drips blood. As he shifts from subject ("I see") to object ("before me"), his description echoes this fantastic reciprocity: "the *hand*le toward my *hand*." What is without is also within, what is not also is, in an unsettling ontological equivocation. The phenomenon will not abide his question, because (like Birnham Wood and the man not of woman born) it is beyond any terms he can imagine.

Macbeth seeks futilely to establish boundaries in a world where things won't stay put—like Banquo's bloody ghost that rises to unseat the king. But whereas Macbeth moves through a world and a play in which he can only *do* and not play "as if," we as audience can entertain the paradoxical nature of Macbeth's world, imagining witches, daggers, babes, and ghosts as both there and not there. They are images spawned from Macbeth's desires and dreads, *and also* from the supernatural agency of the weird sisters. For us these phenomena can be transitional, while for Macbeth they are obsessive, haunting visions. In the play of *Macbeth* Shakespeare provides his audience with a framed potential space wherein he presents a character, Macbeth, for whom such space is closed off. This suggests one feature of tragedy as a psychological genre; it can demonstrate the failure of psychic strategies (or defenses) while strengthening its audience's abilities to manage those strategies. The play of *Macbeth* occupies our own potential space (thereby filling it) with manifestations of its own violation, closure, or emptiness: it signifies nothing.

Of course I am projecting an audience from my own conceptions. Not all audiences are so play-full as mine nor may they tolerate ambiguity and equivocation so eagerly. Some may wish to establish boundaries and provide answers to questions that the play leaves invitingly open. They want either to grasp Macbeth's dagger or blink it away.[38] Similarly, they want either to certify or reject the existence of Lady Macbeth's mysterious child. One veteran of hundreds of productions of the play has no doubts on the issue. Of course Lady Macbeth has a child, he asserts, because she says so, and it's by Macbeth and not any former husband. Marvin Rosenberg continues to stage the scene in his conception, setting an actual infant on the boards, in a crib, whose timely cries and gurgles contribute momentous sound effects during Lady Macbeth's speech.[39] Fox imagines a pregnant Lady Macbeth, whose condition gradually shows by play's end.[40]

Rosenberg's reaching for an actual infant to match the one Lady Macbeth conjures up imitates Macbeth's reaching for his actual dagger to match the one he sees before him. Just as Macbeth's action imitates the vision (Is the dagger leading him or is he projecting it in his way?), so an audience's imaginative response may realize (make real) the fantasy held out by the scene. "The bloody business informs thus" to our minds' eyes. Although I consider Rosenberg's staging unwise, his reification of a phantasm is certainly within the range of audience response to (and directors' conceptions of) the scene, as the history of ongoing debates about this and similar problems in *Macbeth* amply demonstrates. "An essential feature of transitional phenomena is a quality in our attitude when we observe them."[41] Some audiences cannot tolerate dramatized paradoxes of transitional phenomena. As a result, their attitudes toward radically questionable plays like *Macbeth* or *Hamlet* or *Othello* may be to seek after certainties, in an apt imitation of the tragic characters' own doomed quests. Other audiences, such as the one I am projecting, are more comfortable with unanswerable questions, or recognize that wonder and worry over such questions can be part of an effective response to the play—not problems to be solved but responses to be experienced and examined.[42]

Consider the famous riddle of Lady Macbeth's child. Does she have one or not? I offer a reply if not a solution. First, the dramatic world of *Macbeth* is phantasmagorical, inhabited by witches, phantom daggers, ghosts, apparitions (of children), bloodstains real and imagined. It evokes an environment where our most basic differentiations and boundaries are jeopardized by the mutual coexistence of and antagonism between such primary distinctions as "real/imagined," "inside/outside," "alive/dead," "animate/inanimate," "male/female," "fair/foul," even "day/night" ("What is the night?" asks Macbeth; his wife replies, "Almost at odds with morning, which is which" [3.4.125–26]). In brief, "nothing is but what is not"; existence is a function of impossible opposition.

In such a world of apparitions and violated boundaries, Lady Macbeth's infant may be an *extradramatic* apparition, a transitional phenomenon proffered to us, the audience, as our own quandary, just as Macbeth's dagger is held out to him. Do we accept it as real or do we reject it? Do we search for historical clues (say, in Holinshed) or do we acquiesce in the fantastic moment? Critical assessments of the actuality of the babe are well known. For my audience, the resulting dilemma of "Is it or is it not?" iterates the central question of and for this play. The question has two appropriate answers, each at odds with each. What is a reasonable response to such dramatic equivocation?[43] Rather than argue about the historical or dramatic authenticity of Lady Macbeth's child, we might take another view. "It is impenetrably ambiguous whether she means it," writes Nicholas Brooke, "let alone whether it is true or not. But as an imaginative fact that babe is certainly very vivid to us in ways that are no part of Lady Macbeth's consciousness: it takes its place, with Macbeth's naked new-born babe, and all the other babes of the play that Cleanth Brooks enumerated, in a dimension well beyond the reach of the characters."[44]

This dimension, outside consciousness and beyond its reach, might well be termed the play's "unconscious." More precisely, it is a dimension where logical questions have no force, where *is* and *is not* coexist. In Freudian terms, it is a domain of primary process representation: a field of fluid, shifting representations, where every similarity tends toward identity. Boundaries are indeterminate and unstable; images appear, disappear, and reappear; wishes and fears materialize out of thin air. Time defies temporal rules; past, present, and future cohere in an instant, or the moment of the deed subsumes all time before and after. Contradiction is merely a style of unification; denial or negation does not exist.

Various psychoanalytic terms and concepts describe such a domain, including "the unconscious," "primary process," "potential space," and "transitional phenomena." Keats's idea of "Negative Capability," whereby Shakespeare sustained his creative tension of imaginative contradiction, is applicable here, as is Stephen Booth's elaboration of that idea to include the mind of the audience, momentarily enduring perplexing experiences within the comfort of tragic form.[45] As a key to Shakespeare's "dialectical dramaturgy," Norman Rabkin borrowed the concept of "complementarity" from twentieth-century physics (light, for example, must sometimes be treated as a wave, sometimes as a particle; each perspective contradicts the other).[46] Although Rabkin usually applies the term to competing values and value-perceptions, the concept characterizes the epistemological style of *Macbeth*; the reified hallucination of the dagger exemplifies complementarity, as the *object* complements the *fantasy*. Both perspectives are valid, yet each logically invalidates the other. Or consider the directorial issue of showing or not showing a levitating dagger or a bloodied Banquo. Either choice determines an idea of the play incompatible with the other.[47]

Lady Macbeth's apparent infant can be seen from a similar perspective. Through the device of the phantom child, Shakespeare places his audience at the psychological center of *Macbeth*'s dreamscape. Lady Macbeth's infanticide generates a fantastic apparition *for the imaginations of the audience*. By so radically playing "is / is not" Shakespeare provisionally dislocates those conventional theatrical gratifications we as audience might expect. He has made the play itself equivocate, resulting potentially in a radical questioning of the status of our own response.[48]

Shakespeare's tragedies typically encourage epistemological skepticism in his audience. The plays raise questions in order not to answer them, or to provide contradictory answers. (Is the specter of Hamlet the King a genuine ghost or the devil? Did Gertrude know of the murder? Is Prince Hamlet mad? How old is he?) *Not knowing* may then become the response-state of an audience, and dealing with the experience of not knowing and being unable to find stable answers further complicates that response. As Stanley Cavell has argued about a famous question in *Othello*, what is important is not whether the Moor's marriage to Desdemona has been consummated, but that we may doubt it, whatever the evidence.[49] (This is an audience's version of Othello's quandary of doubt and evidence.) Similarly, the question is not whether Lady Macbeth has a child; it is that she says she does and we may doubt it. "Doubtful it stood" (1.2.7) is a comment on more than specific questions in the play; it is a description of my projected audience's general response posture. We stand, secure, in doubt, unsure. Lady Macbeth's infant both is and is not, in a pregnant paradigm of the whole *Macbeth* experience. She is mother in surmise and in skepticism. A.C. Bradley's authoritative ruling on the question seems to me, then, exactly wrong: "Lady Macbeth's child," he asserted, "may be alive or may be dead. It may even be, or have been, her child by a former husband. . . . It may be that Macbeth had many children or that he had none. We cannot say, and it does not concern the play."[50] Exactly the contrary. It may be all of these possibilities, or none, or some. Our inability to say—our dubious stance—is a central concern of the play because it compels us to share Macbeth's epistemological and psychological disorientations.

In this sense we can simultaneously "be" and "not be" Macbeth, sharing his vision while seeing more clearly. By such devices Shakespeare has made *Macbeth* his most boldly psychological play—even more than *A Midsummer Night's Dream* or *Hamlet* or *The Tempest*. *Macbeth* is Shakespeare's dramatic version of the dynamic relation of unconscious process to ordinary thought. In an historical period when fictions of supernatural agency (such as Fate or witches) were beginning to be challenged by emerging notions of individual pathology (consider the unstable evolution of the theology of "possession" into the psychology of "hysteria"), Shakespeare re-imagined and dramatized the ambiguous interaction of fate and desire. In *Macbeth*, he merged externality and internality, not only in the paradoxes of the hero's vision (the dagger) but also in the relation of "witches" as supernatural agency and "wishes" as personal (unconscious) desire. Both represent the unknowable mystery of motivation; both situate the arena of compulsive action. *Macbeth* collocates these arenas, so that the unconscious becomes a source of (feminine) equivocation, or undifferentiation, or most properly "de-differentiation." [51]

The idea of a "feminine" or undifferentiated unconscious is implicit in Lady Macbeth's urgent solicitation of her husband's desire. She enters the play speaking her husband's words (reading his letter); she announces what is unspoken. Hers is the voice of wishing: "Art thou afraid / To be the same in thine own act and valour / As thou art in desire?" (1.7.39–41). At one point, in an uncanny augury of de Beauvoir and Lacan, Shakespeare puts her precisely in the position of the "Other." After imagining the whirlwind vision of naked Pity, Macbeth complains:

> I have no spur
> To prick the sides of my intent, but only
> Vaulting ambition, which o'erleaps itself
> And falls on th' other—
>   *Enter Lady Macbeth*   (1.7.25–28 S.D.) [52]

Linda Bamber argues that, unlike the other tragedies, *Macbeth* and *Coriolanus* present no genuine Other for the masculine Self. Instead, the feminine Other actually corresponds to the hero's pathological projections of her. In the absence of a real self-other dialectic, Macbeth cannot engage with a real outside world; instead he is "entirely taken up by internal dialogue." [53] I suggest a related idea: *Macbeth* manifests a fatal con-fusion between "feminine" otherness and "masculine" ambition. One controls and expresses the other, but which is which? Like the embrace of two spent swimmers, the intimate bond of (female) other and (male) desire becomes one of unstable support and struggle. It threatens to degenerate into a process of de-differentiation. Like the witches, unsexed Lady Macbeth, or unmanly Macbeth, both agencies (other and desire) are of neither gender, or of both. Complementarity here threatens to collapse into critical mass.

Lady Macbeth's consanguinity with the unconscious is of course most evident through the witches, who are the supernatural reflection and dilation of her persona. Macbeth's language actually identifies the witches with unconscious process, in imagery that characterizes as well his relation to both agencies:

> Now o'er the one half-world
> Nature seems dead, and wicked dreams abuse
> The curtain'd sleep: Witchcraft celebrates
> Pale Hecate's off'rings; and wither'd Murther,
> With Tarquin's ravishing strides, towards his design
> Moves like a ghost.   (2.1.49–56)

Macbeth's bisection of the world inscribes a geography of reciprocal hemispheres: natural and unnatural, day and night, life and death, waking and sleeping. Such a geography holds throughout the play, literally in terms of landscape (battlefield, castle, cave) and metaphorically in terms of surface deceit (hospitality) and subterranean desire (hostility). It takes its theological form in the re-vision of Inverness as Hell (2.3) and transforms suggestively in Donalbain's remark that "fate [is] hid in an auger-hole" (2.3.123–24). The proximity of hidden depths and prophecy ("auger" echoes "augur") becomes most evident in Shakespeare's description of the three weird sisters, their cave, and their cauldron.[54]

What Macbeth sees in the witches' cave (4.1)—one form of the "deed without a name"—is in effect the mystery of generation, "the seeds of time" ripening into the future. He envisions the germination of others, while he himself is cut off from it. His own "doing" is an impotent de-generation that imagines the tumbling of Nature's germens; his "first-lings" will be bloody deaths. The bubbling cauldron most vividly and viscerally signifies the mixture of generativity and destruction. It is a source of energy and insight, poisonous motivation and prophetic vision; a "hell-broth" of unconscious desire; a distilled, degenerative, demonic womb. Its ingredients give a taste of its symbolic value; composed of fragments of dismembered bodies (particularly appendages), it represents a fatal mater-nal enclosure, or a nursery brew with an insatiable appetite:

> Witches' mummy; maw and gulf,
> Of the ravin'd salt-sea shark.
> Add thereto a tiger's chaudron,
> For th' ingredience of our cauldron.   (4.1.22–34)

Shakespeare's rhyme echoes an unconscious identity of inorganic and or-ganic vessels, or of cauldron and womb.[55]

Beyond their location (cave) and equipment (cauldron), the witches' rhetorical and dramatic style suggests their emblematics of the unconscious. These "imperfect speakers" talk in rhyme, rhythmic repetition, alliteration; their speech is fragmented, allusive, incantatory, ritualistic; they present themselves in an eerie song and dance.[56] The language and action of the three sisters can be imagined as an intrapsychic triadic confabulation, a primary-process conversation of separate yet unified parts (similar to Freud's model of the unconscious). Unlike their uncanny roundabout, the rest of the play is narrative and sequential—like the history play it also is. The contrast in styles is like the difference between unconscious and conscious representation, or between dreaming and waking, or primary and secondary process.[57]

The complementary figure to this "feminine" unconscious is the "masculine" desire it seems to urge and oversee. In Macbeth's tale of Witchcraft and Murther, Witchcraft presides over Murther's design. The manifest content of "wicked dreams" involves female invocation and celebration, followed by male motion and doing (imaged as Tarquin's rape). Macbeth's role in this allegory is as "wither'd Murther": *wither'd* suggests Murther's timeless age, echoes the witches ("so wither'd and so wild" [1.3.40]), and prefigures Macbeth's decline into "the sere, the yellow leaf." It also suggests his implicit impotence as a tool of supernatural agency; he thinks he is vital ("striding") but actually he is wasted ("like a ghost").[58]

The theme of impotence, implicit in the issue of Macbeth's childlessness, becomes most evident in the dagger scene. A Freudian interpretation of the dagger as symbolic phallus is valid, though it needs elaboration.[59] Macbeth, who wants to "make love" to murder (3.1.123), complains that he has "no spur / To prick the sides of [his] intent." Charged by his sexually transfigured wife with being too womanly for his manly task, he confronts in the dagger an image that is simultaneously the sign of castration and the means to restore potency. To regain his masculinity, Macbeth must match the fantastic, separated dagger with his own instrument, and kill Duncan. The symbolic identification of dagger with phallus further explains why the regicide is also rape, as it restores Macbeth's aggressive masculinity.

Moreover, as an emblem of Macbeth's "external" motivation the dagger represents a split in his consciousness, a projection of his wishes and fears. Beyond symbolizing castration or displaced potency, and equating sexuality with murder, it displays a style of representation that animates the whole play.[60] For instance, Macbeth and his Lady are (as Freud saw) splits of a single entity, as are Lady Macbeth and the witches, or the various victimized and avenging children. The primary split between conscious and unconscious reflects that other primary (and in this play ambiguous) split—between male and female, or even between sexed and unsexed. Shakespeare has combined these divisions to suggest the interrelation of each, in an almost Freudian way.[61] That is, *Macbeth* dramatizes simultaneously a dynamic of conscious and unconscious desire and a dynamic of sexual difference. From the beginning of the play, unconscious forces bubble up into consciousness, blurring boundaries and distorting reality. As well, the concept of sexual division becomes obscure and mutable. The witches especially blur boundaries even as they draw them; a blend of female and male, their basic style is equivocation. From the start their language makes distinctions that do not hold: "When shall we three meet again, / In thunder, lightning, or in rain?" The nature of storms makes such a choice impossible. A diabolic Trinity, the witches represent unity and splitting simultaneously.

Splitting is perhaps Shakespeare's preeminent strategy of representation, or his favored mode of defense. It animates an early play, *The Comedy of Errors*, where it develops potentially psychotic divisions before the conventional re-pairs of comic form.[62] It designs the tragedy of King Lear, who fractures his kingdom, his family, and his psyche in one catastrophic gesture. It inaugurates a late play by the similar disaster of stormy separation: "We split, we split!" (*The Tempest*, 1.1.60). *Twelfth Night*, almost contemporary with the obsessively divisive *Hamlet*, presents a brief comic vision of *Macbeth*'s nightmare in its "natural perspective, that *is and is not*" (5.1.217). In this case comedy provides rational answers to the quandary, in the image of an illusory optical device or the ultimate solution of twinning. Equivocation becomes duplicity and finally actual duplication. But in the tragedy of *Macbeth*, splittings are not rationally resolved, and the potentially psychotic realm of undifferentiated objects becomes real. Shakespeare dramatizes what psychoanalysis theorizes.

Although Shakespeare was not a Jacobean psychoanalyst, his modes of representing human behavior reflect and elaborate concepts of contemporary analytic theory. Shakespeare's attention to human behavior, language, thought, feeling, and fantasy was as intense and insightful as Freud's, though in a different style of representation. One way to think of the relation between Shakespearean and Freudian representations of psychic, familial, and social structures is through the idea of isomorphism. When two apparently different complex structures can be mapped onto each other with close similarities in nature and function between corresponding parts, mathematicians and logicians term the structures isomorphic.[63] It is at least metaphorically plausible to see Shakespearean drama and psychoanalytic theory as isomorphic. They are two variant representations of human behavior, uncannily similar when examined in relation to each other.[64] The durable example of *Hamlet* is the most prominent demonstration of this isomorphism; I suggest *Macbeth* as another compelling instance. These plays are manifestly about psychic structure and symbolic representation; their imaginative domain is also that of psychoanalysis.

Michel Foucault, in the first volume of his *History of Sexuality*, offers a wider social analogy. He suggests that during the eighteenth and nineteenth centuries European society moved from "a *symbolics of blood* to an *analytics of sexuality*."[65] That is, cultural "regimes of power" shifted from the evidence of sanguinity (blood-relations, inheritance, the ritual symbolism of physical violence) to the control of sexuality (procreativity, concern for human life, definitions of sexual difference). What *Macbeth* suggests is that for Shakespeare this shift was already imaginable in the early seventeenth century.[66] He had at hand a "symbolics of blood"—his play is awash in it—but what he must invent is an "analytics of sexuality." He knew (I imagine) that the problematic issue of sexual difference underlay his play—in terms of procreativity, sterility, masculinity and femininity—and he enacted an "analysis" of its problems through imaginative drama. As Freud often averred, analysis was available to poetry before theory found its language. In this sense, Shakespeare prefigures Freud. Drama enacts what theory affirms, in an isomorphic relation.

A case in point is the doctor who observes Lady Macbeth's "slumbery agitation" in Act Five. He is looking at a dramatic enactment of "the unconscious," though he cannot quite see it. Her sleepwalking scene begins with the blood-spot and its psychological persistence ("Yet here's a spot"), translating reality (the stain) into its mnemonic sign. She enacts a mode of re-presentation whereby traces of past events return, unbidden and ineradicable. But they return not merely in memory; the recurrence of the past effects a fantastic alteration in her perception of reality. Macbeth sees the dagger (and follows it); Lady Macbeth sees and smells the blood-spot (and tries to remove it). Outside its normal psychic confines, memory manifests itself in her senses and on her flesh. The sign of the memory trace is the hallucinated mark of blood. Here is another emblem of the psyche turned inside out that is *Macbeth*. Lady Macbeth's compulsion recalls Macbeth's, except that she sleepwalks and curses a blood-spot while he wades in blood. He is active, she is passive. He acts out the unconscious; the unconscious acts out on her. Now split off from the demonic matrix of the witches, Lady Macbeth no longer actively manifests the unconscious, but is passively subjected to it. The doctor, like a good professional, takes notes on her associations to blood, time, doing, Duncan, the Thane of Fife. But he can offer no help. He lacks a theory of hysteria, a sexualized view of the female that could address her pathology, read the language of the stain (her "thick-coming fancies"), and analyze her bloody mindedness.[67] "This disease is beyond my practice," he concludes.

> More needs she the divine than the physician.
> My mind she has mated, and amaz'd my sight.
> I think, but dare not speak.   (5.1.71–76)

The doctor's words recall Macbeth's circumstances, to the point of amazed sight (the witches, the dagger, Banquo's ghost, the serial apparitions) and the division between hidden thought and the audacity of expression. The doctor is also like Banquo standing before the witches, fascinated yet forbidden to interpret their mystery (1.3.46). His reference to his "mated" mind may allude to the *pia mater* (the membrane enveloping the brain), implying the subduing of the medical mind by the maternal element and a suggestive identity between brain and womb. (In *Love's Labour's Lost*, Holofernes describes his poetic "gift" as "begot in the ventricle of memory, nourish'd in the womb of pia mater, and delivered upon the mellowing of occasion" [4.2.65–60]).[68] Just this identity lies behind the mythology of hysteria—a displacement upward from abdomen to head that pathologizes conventional analogies between womb and psyche or between uterine and lunatic conception. *Hysterica passio*, most dramatically embodied in the rising of Lear's "mother" (2.4.56–7), represents the metaphoric relocation of unconscious psychic disorder at its imagined maternal origin.[69] In Shakespeare similar metaphors are commonplace: from the "unborn sorrow, ripe in fortune's womb" that Richard the Second's Queen foresees (2.2.10), to Falstaff's multitongued "womb" that speaks his name (2 *Henry IV*, 4.3.22), to "the foul womb of night" that the Chorus in *Henry V* envisions (Act 4), to Cleopatra's image of "the memory of my womb" (3.13.363), to Iago's conception of "events in the womb of time" and the "monstrous birth" he "engenders" in Othello's unconscious (1.3.370, 403). A moment in *Antony and Cleopatra* neatly suggests the connection between projection and procreation. The Soothsayer is entertaining Cleopatra's attendants, and Charmian asks him to predict the number of her future children.

Sooth.   If every of your wishes had a womb,
         And fertile every wish, a million.
Char.   Out, fool, I forgive thee for a witch!   (1.2.37–40)

In *Macbeth*, the witch of wishing is both fertile and sterile.[70]

Shakespeare's dramatic enactments of wishing—or of the struggle between fact and desire—call into question the status of imagination and of imaginative revisions of the self. The place of fantasy in Shakespeare's historical world—in theater, politics, religion, alchemy, geography—involves questions that an inquisitive drama like Shakespeare's could powerfully raise and explore. In its challenge to imagine a world of simultaneous being and nonbeing, reality and fantasy, creativity and destruction, *Macbeth* offers its audience opportunities for momentary psychic disorientation. The play confronts our imaginations with a risky yet rewarding interrogation of the very assumptions of our worlds of experience and play. Lady Macbeth may scoff at "the eye of childhood / That fears a painted devil" (2.2.54–55), but even if adult vision may learn such a distinction, the existence of devils and witches was a real issue for Shakespeare's audience. (Seventeenth-century western Europe was zealously finding, trying, and killing witches.)[71] Moreover, what if a devil, painted or pure, were both there and not there—or both within, in psychological space, and without, in theatrical or theological space? Potentially more frightening than the existence of devils is the radical discontinuity of existence itself. In a recent essay on *Macbeth*—a piece of his continuing study of skepticism and the limits of the human—Cavell reads the play (and its criticism) as a "contest over interpretations, hence over whether an understanding is—or can be—intellectually adequate to its question, neither denying what is there, nor affirming what is there (a deed, a dagger). As if what is at stake is the intelligibility of the human to itself."[72] Or as Marjorie Garber puts it, "*Macbeth* presents us with what is in effect a test case of the limits of representation."[73]

At an historical moment when theatricality was inextricably blended with representations of the self and the world ("All the world's a stage," says the poor player, strutting and fretting), the issue of imagination was seminal. For Shakespeare himself it may have been personally acute. As a poet whose imaginings were given local habitation, nomination, and enactment by players, he may have felt sharply the questions of private fantasy and public display. Commenting that Macbeth "cannot maintain the distinction between fantasy and action," so that "what he can imagine he must perform," Murray Schwartz speculates that "such a character expresses a central problem for a playwright, for any playwright must be concerned with the dynamic relationship between what can be imagined and what can be performed in word or deed."[74] *Macbeth* dramatizes the pathology of this dynamic relationship when it is short-circuited, when it lacks the buffer of a proper interim. (By contrast, *Hamlet* dramatizes the pathology of "all interim.")[75]

In every play, especially in the later tragedies and romances, Shakespeare plays with questions of fantasy and representability. *Macbeth* enacts extreme possibilities. *The Tempest* is Shakespeare's ultimate portrayal of the play-maker who has at his service "spirits, which by mine art / I have from their confines call'd to enact / My present fancies" (4.1.120–22). Prospero's fantasies are sometimes kindly (the Masque of Goddesses) but often cruel (the concluding antimasque of attacking dogs). Vengeance underlies the tempestuous anger that inaugurates and animates the play.[76] These fantasies of entertaining and punishing, involving spirits that enact present fantasies with no mediation (Prospero writes no script) represent an immediate translation of wish and fear into action. Such instant transmission of desire into deed is analogous to Macbeth's compulsive creativity ("Strange things I have in head, that will to hand, / Which must be acted, ere they may be scann'd"). A difference is that Prospero's fantasies have "confines" (he still threatens Ariel and Caliban with confinement). For Prospero, the demon of unconscious compulsion (the witch of wishing) is under guard, whereas for Macbeth she and her representatives are free, within and without. Prospero and Macbeth are reciprocal figures of the fantast. One is an image of the artist controlling his shaping fancy (though sometimes only barely), whereas the other is an image of the artist out of conscious control, compelled and ultimately victimized by his own unconscious projections.

Two centuries ago, Maurice Morgann noted the potential hazards of such a connection between dramaturgy and thaumaturgy in Shakespeare's art. Commenting on Prospero's abrupt dismissal of the masque and rejection of his magic, he wrote: "We are to remember that this Play was performed in the Reign of James I[st], when it behoved Shakespeare to look about, lest He, Himself, sho[d] be taken up for a Magician, and it was therefore necessary to unveil the Dangers of this unholy Art."[77] In an elegant essay on the interrelations of early modern witchcraft beliefs and the social and psychological emergence of "the zone of the imaginary," Stephen Greenblatt refines Morgann's observation:

Witches, then—imagined as real or imagined as imaginary—are a recurrent, even obsessive feature in Shakespeare's cultural universe. It seems that he could not get them out of his mind or rather out of his art, as if he identified the power of theater itself with the ontological liminality of witchcraft and with his own status as someone who conjured spirits, created storms, and wielded the power of life and death.[78]

Greenblatt continues to assert that "*Macbeth* manifests a deep, intuitive recognition that the theater and witchcraft are both constructed on the boundary between fantasy and reality" (123).[79] Cavell envisions the boundary as a surface or screen, suggesting that "the witches' cauldron . . . appears as the origin of theater, as the scene of apparition or appearances" (2.5).[80] (I will consider the imaginative relation between theater and conjuration in Chapter Seven.)

At issue are the limits of imagining—a process dramatized in the words and acts of Shakespeare's characters but potentially most fully developed in the thoughts and feelings of his audience. By arousing basic doubts about the psychological boundaries of theatrical playspace, a play like *Macbeth* may evoke responses beyond the conventional Aristotelian pity and terror. Even Francis Fergusson, in demonstrating that "Aristotle was right" by showing the unity of action in *Macbeth*, admits that the play "shows modes of the spirit's life undreamed of by Aristotle himself."[81] To test the limits of our own potential spaces is a process not fully characterized by a term like *catharsis*.[82] Macbeth himself has passed beyond conventional responses. "The time has been," he muses,

> my senses would have cooled
> To hear a night-shriek, and my fell of hair
> Would at a dismal treatise rouse and stir
> As life were in't.   (5.5.10–13)

He has moved from a conventional perspective in Act One, when he confronted the alarming apparitions of the witches, to a radically new vision in which nothing finally can surprise him. His expectations, like Birnham Wood, have been uprooted. Trapped in a nightmare of compulsively enacted fantasies whose origins elude him, he succumbs. We, however, as privileged spectators to his plight, may be able to use Shakespeare's dislocations of theatrical experience to acknowledge and exercise our own capacities for fantasy, positive or negative.[83] Nietzsche, in his critique of Aristotelian tragic theory, speculated fervently about such a possibility: "Not in order to escape from terror and pity, not to purify oneself of a dangerous passion by discharging it with vehemence—this is how Aristotle understood it—but to be far beyond terror and pity and to be the eternal lust of Becoming itself—that lust which also involves the lust of destruction."[84] Not simply to release emotion, but to enter a realm of desire in which "becoming" and "destruction," generativity and degeneration, *is* and *is not*, forge their disturbing coexistence: such is the potential experience of *Macbeth*.

7

Shakespeare's Nothing

Hamlet.	Do you see nothing there?
Gertrude.	Nothing at all; yet all that is I see.
Hamlet.	Nor did you nothing hear?
Gertrude.	No, nothing but ourselves.

(3.4.131–33)

"THE QUALITY OF NOTHING," ACCORDING TO GLOUCESTER, "hath not such need to hide itself. Let's see," he commands Edmund, who is displaying his forged letter by obviously concealing it. "Come, if it be nothing, I shall not need spectacles" (*King Lear*, 1.2.32–35). Gloucester looks at the letter, but does not see that it is nothing (a hoax); only when he is blind, cruelly enlightened, does he finally see nothing. Paradoxically, for us to see Shakespeare's Nothing we do need spectacles, or rather a spectacle: the play of nothing in Shakespeare's theater. His tragedies enact scenes in such a spectacle; they are Renaissance No-drama.

To see Shakespeare's Nothing we must open our eyes. A familiar geometrical figure offers an opening glimpse of its form. We can start with the circle: sign of nothing and all, cosmos and zero. Then we can divide it into two equal parts (zero divided is still zero), marking the division not with a line but with a curve (*curve* derives from *circle*): not ◐ but ☯—to suggest mutuality and not bifurcation of the halves. "Two distincts, division none." We can even give each "half-zero" a mathematical sign: positive and negative, or negative and positive; they are reciprocal yet equal.

This fanciful mathematics and geometry inscribe a structure for this chapter—a circle that is also a point of departure. Since usual order puts absence before presence, zero before one, I begin with the negative sign of nothing: the notion of absence, negation, denial, or lack. The most dramatic appearance of this sign in Shakespeare occurs in Cordelia's fateful silence and voiced "Nothing": her refusal to give Lear what he asks for, to pretend, as her father and sisters do, that words are like things, given and received, a reified rhetoric that wins property. Cordelia's answer doesn't add up; it is not proportional to the third part of the kingdom Lear has reserved to reward the part she was to play. It does not fit the ratio of his irrationality.

Yet Cordelia's answer signifies more than these arithmetical or geometrical metaphors can directly suggest. Shakespeare's overdetermined language typically includes bawdy meanings, and there is a specific, though latent, bodily sense of Cordelia's "Nothing"—as *no thing*—the sense Hamlet intends in his notorious joking with Ophelia just before the play-within-the-play (his by-play is verbal fore-play).

> Lady, shall I lie in your lap?
> No, my lord.
> I mean, my head upon your lap?
> Ay, my lord,
> Do you think I meant country matters?
> I think nothing, my lord.
> That's a fair thought to lie between maids' legs.
> What is, my lord?
> Nothing.   (3.2.112–21)[1]

This genital sense of "thing" functions in *King Lear* most evidently in the Fool's traditional phallic jokes ("She that's a maid now, and laughs at my departure, / Shall not be a maid long, unless things be cut shorter" (1.5.51–52).[2] It relates to ubiquitous anxieties in the play concerning bodily injury or loss, such as Gloucester's eyes, Lear's "cut off" train of soldiers, naked unaccommodated man as a "poor, bare, fork'd animal"—"the thing itself"—Lear himself as nothing, "an O without a figure" (3.4.106–08; 1.4.192–93). Moreover, Cordelia's defense of her spoken "Nothing" alludes to the latent notion of no thing as some thing missing. "I yet beseech your Majesty," she says to the father who has just banished her,

> If for I want that glib and oily art
> To speak and purpose not, since what I well intend,
> I'll do't before I speak—that you make known
> It is no vicious blot, murther, or foulness,
> No unchaste action, or dishonored step,
> That hath depriv'd me of your grace and favor,
> But even for want of that for which I am richer—

A still-soliciting eye, and such a tongue
That I am glad I have not, though not to have it
Hath lost me in your liking.

(1.1.223-33)

One deprivation (her banishment) follows others (her "Nothing," her lack of eye and tongue). Shakespeare's imagery is significantly organic and sexually suggestive. Not having, or having nothing, is Cordelia's loss, and ultimately Lear's. Through its imagery of licentiousness denied and organs deprived, the language of Cordelia's defense glances at the hidden genital significance of her "Nothing." Against this bodily background, France's previous words to Lear also disclose hidden senses. "This is most strange," he notes, that Cordelia

should in this trice of time
Commit a thing so monstrous, to dismantle
So many folds of favor. Sure her offense
Must be of such unnatural degree
That monsters it . . .

(1.1.213-20)

Shakespeare's imagery evokes a vision of Cordelia stripped ("dismantled") of her father's love ("folds of favor")[3] and a hint of some secret sin ("a thing so monstrous . . . , of such unnatural degree"), which Cordelia then denies ("it is no vicious blot . . . "). Hidden in the folds of Shakespeare's imagery is a vision of a woman disrobed and the sight of something monstrous and unnatural—an early glimpse, through metaphor, of that later image of woman and female genitals that incites Lear's rage and terror in ensuing acts. "Thorough tatter'd clothes small [great][4] vices do appear; / Robes and furr'd gowns hide all," he exclaims in Act Four (4.6.164-65), but nothing is hidden to his maddened sight, which uncovers no thing.

Down from the waist they are Centaurs,
Though women all above;
But to the girdle do the gods inherit,
Beneath is all the fiends': there's hell, there's darkness,
There is the sulphurous pit, burning, scalding,
Stench, consumption. Fie, fie, fie! pah, pah!

(4.6.124-29)

Lear's response to this malignant and demonic image of no-thingness is first rage, then insanity, and then a kind of infancy (*infans*, speechless). Confronted with his own grotesque fantasies of destructive female "organs of increase," facing the face he cannot banish from his unsweetened imagination ("whose face between her forks presages snow"—presages "no" [4.6.119]), he lapses into inarticulation, trying, as I hear him, literally to spit out what disgusts him: "*Fie, fie, fie! pah, pah!*" Another moment of nonverbal infancy occurs in the next scene (4.7), when Lear, clothed and carried by others, is brought silent to his reunion with Cordelia. A similar event is enacted at their final meeting, in Lear's last vision of Cordelia's face and lips, which leads him back—a regression—into fantasy and final delusion: seeing what is not there, as he exclaims, "Look on her! Look her lips, / Look there, look there!", and hearing what is not there, as he reaches through the ultimate silence for her voice, "ever soft, / Gentle, and low, an excellent thing in woman" (5.3.273–74).

From her voiced "Nothing" to her mute voice as "an excellent thing," Cordelia's discourse traces a circle of absent presence. She is the queen of silence, reciprocating Lear's tragic stature as the king—"every inch"— of nothing (Hamlet: "The King is a thing . . . of nothing" [4.2.28–30]). *Rex* becomes *res* becomes *rien*. Or in the uncanny wisdom of Lear's Fool, "uncle" is "nuncle" (*none*-cle): "Can you make no use of nothing, nuncle?" (1.4.130).[5] Cordelia's nothing, at beginning and end, circumscribes or pinpoints the elemental absence at the center of Lear's world. She is, to use Kent's phrase, "the true blank of [his] eye" (1.1.159). Her silence and absence describe the center of the target of his sight; and the "blank" (target center) is blank (empty, nothing). Lear's banishment of Cordelia shuts out a symbolic vision he cannot bear to see. "We / Have no such daughter," he says to France, "nor shall ever see / That face of hers again" (1.1.262–64). Its features remind him of nothing (the "face between her forks"). Eventually he will meet its most traumatic mask, represented by Gloucester's bloody eyeless face, into whose vacancy he stares as he delivers his "down from the waist" diatribe.

Yet this design of denial and negation traces only half of my original circle. Its reciprocal, the positive half, represents fullness rather than emptiness, presence rather than absence, whole rather than hole. It rests on or borders its negative twin in a relationship of primary creativity. Nothing, in other words, is the very ground of being, just as silence is the ground of speech. Speech happens in silence, silence happens in speech (without intervals of silence, speech is gibberish). Silence, too, can speak; it is, as we say, pregnant. And when silences are broken, they are also filled. They are spaces or times for talk, occasions for creation.[6]

I want now to consider the potential positive generativity of Shakespeare's Nothing—although what is generated is not always benign. For instance, in *Romeo and Juliet*, after that fairy fantasy turned nightmare of the "Queen Mab" speech, Romeo interrupts Mercutio's barely controlled words by insisting, "Peace, peace, Mercutio, peace! / Thou talk'st of nothing." Mercutio replies,

> True, I talk of dreams,
> Which are the children of an idle brain,
> Begot of nothing but vain fantasy . . . .
> (1.4.96–98)

Nothing, begot of itself. As Lear warns Cordelia, "Nothing will come of nothing." Yet even Lear's words imply a generativity of nothing; his verb is future imperative. This ability of nothing to generate other versions of itself attains its most potent moment in *The Winter's Tale*, as the product of Leontes's barely coherent jealous obsessions.

> Affection! thy intention stabs the centre.
> Thou dost make possible things not so held,
> Communicat'st with dreams (how can this be?),
> With what's unreal thou co-active art,
> And fellow'st nothing. Then 'tis very credent
> Thou mayst co-join with something, and thou dost
> (And that beyond commission), and I find it
> (And that to the infection of my brains
> And hard'ning of my brows).   (1.2.138–46)

Moments later, after watching Hermione and Polixenes converse, he demands of Camillo, "Is whispering nothing? / Is leaning cheek to cheek? is meeting noses?"

> Is this nothing?
> Why then all the world and all that's in't is nothing,
> The covering sky is nothing, Bohemia nothing,
> My wife is nothing, nor nothing have these nothings,
> If this be nothing.   (1.2.284–96)

"Nothing" gets obsessively repeated into thing-ness, an abstraction made concrete that subsumes everything else. It becomes a self-reflexive, self-generating agent of its own creation, produced out of the mysterious, violent, sexual "co-action," or coitus, of "dreams," "unreal[ity]," "something," and "nothing."[7] Like Othello's "cause," which grounds itself on a nonreferential pronoun, "it," Leontes's obsessions and fantasies have a literal and reified "nothing" at their origin.[8] Still, this nothing accompanies something, or hints of "possible things." These hints reside in latent connotations of the "innocent" language of the play, just as Leontes perceives other meanings in the "innocent" behavior of his wife and friend. For instance, when Polixenes enters the world of *The Winter's Tale*, he immediately emphasizes "Nine changes of the wat'ry star" (the human gestation period), refers to "burthens" and to being "fill'd up," and concludes:

> And therefore, like a cipher
> (Yet standing in rich place), I multiply
> With one "We thank you" many thousands moe
> That go before it.   (1.2.1–9)

Shakespeare's language is literally pregnant with connotation.[9] The verb "multiply" carries sexual as well as arithmetical sense, and the simile of "standing in rich place" symbolically imitates Leontes's own carnal fantasies of Polixenes's secret relationship with Hermione. In a real sense, the origins of Leontes's jealousy lie in the vocabulary of the scene. Leontes's "nothings" complement the potent nothing of Polixene's "cipher"; they both multiply meanings.

Leontes has created something out of nothing, or he has deciphered a hidden meaning in Polixenes's simile of the cipher.[10] His creation, like Othello's green-eyed monster, is a destructive progeny; yet the fact of its existence represents a version, however malignant, of the generativity that linguistic or dramatic production ex nihilo involves.[11] "Nothing" signifies the opportunity, indeed the imperative, to create "something"—some meaning or sense: a name for absence. This play of occasion and necessity characterizes various aspects of Shakespeare's plays. While Leontes's creation is dangerous and potentially tragic, others seem initially heroic, like Coriolanus's self-nomination: "He was a kind of nothing," says Cominius: "titleless, / Till he had forg'd himself a name" (5.1.13–14). (Of course, Coriolanus's "forg'd" name is also a forgery, since it denies his family origin.) This naming of nothing manifests itself in happier terms in the assertions of Duke Theseus, whose characterizations (but not use) of imagination and poetic creativity make him a benevolent version of Leontes:

> And as imagination bodies forth
> The form of things unknown, the poet's pen
> Turns them to shapes, and gives to aery nothing
> A local habitation and a name.
> (*A Midsummer Night's Dream*, 5.1.14–17)

(Again, metaphors of physical procreation: birth and baptism.)

The idea of naming nothing is coincidentally built into the very word through its probable pronunciation in Shakespeare's time. That is, "nothing" would have sounded like "noting" (hard "t"). So that *noting* (knowing, naming, or designating) coexists with and represents the awareness of *nothing*.[12] Moreover, the sound of "noting" includes the aural aspect of the shape of nothing. That is, Shakespeare's Nothing looks like "o" (zero) and sounds like "O" (oh), the basic ejaculation that pre-dicts speech, the infant's Word. Its functions range from trivial to extreme, from the common, "Oh, I see," to Albany's "O, see, see!" or to Lear's final howling "O" (*King Lear*, 5.3.258, 305). It is an almost infinitely meaningful phoneme, in which are rooted our most basic words about speech. The Latin *os* (mouth) and *orare* (to speak) are sources for many of our words about speech and the mouth ("orator," "orality"). "Orifice" means literally to make a mouth. To say "O" we make the shape with our own mouths. "O," the sign and sound of nothing, underlies speech itself. Its design underlies writing as well. The circle is found at the origin of almost all alphabets or ideograms.[13] *Ab ovo*, zero.

Psychoanalytic theories of the origins and acquisition of language, of perception, of reality testing, of the capacity to symbolize or to interact creatively with an environment, all start from the primary fact of absence, separation, loss. The loss of an immediate, felt relationship to an object or person stimulates a need to restore the relationship, to bring things symbolically to mind when they are not really present or to make them present through some communicative act (like a cry). Awareness of absence thus results in imagined or re-enacted presence, a re-collection or re-membering of what was lost.[14] Contemporary French psychoanalysis emphasizes this primary myth of loss in specifically linguistic terms. Describing Lacan's "diacritical theory of meaning," whereby words rest finally not on any-thing real (that is, not on any thing) but only on the circularity of mutual inter-definition, Anthony Wilden explains that "it is this implied circularity and autonomy of language that leads Lacan into postulating a sort of fault in the system, a hole, a fundamental lack into which, one might say, mean-ing is *poured*." This is Lacan's "primordial *manque*." It corresponds to Derrida's idea that "the signature is a *wound*—and there is none other at the origin of the work of art." These metaphors of an original lack, hole, defect, or wound signify that anatomical manifestation of presence and ab-sence that demonstrates the fact of genital difference (*la différence* in the Derridean "*différance*"). The sexual, bodily senses of Shakespeare's Noth-ing and O thus connect to various myths of symbolic origins.[15]

Psychoanalytic theorists frequently refer, in their discussions of the development of symbolic representation, to what has become a Freudian exemplum: the little game of discarding and then retrieving a wooden reel (with string attached) which Freud's grandson invented at the age of one-and-a-half (the so-called "*Fort! Da!*" game).[16] Freud interpreted the child's activity as a re-presentation of his mother's disappearance and reappear-ance, events originally only suffered but now under the child's symbolic control. When he threw the reel away, or dropped it beneath his crib, it was *fort* (gone); when he pulled it back to his hands, it was *da* (there). Actually, the little boy seems not to have uttered these words. Instead, he made the sounds "o" and "ah," which Freud and the child's mother heard as childish efforts at the adult terms "*fort*" and "*da*." This is a good, reasonable interpretation by two good analysts, yet it distances us from the verbal (or preverbal) reality of the event. What the child actually did, according to Freud, was to "give vent to a loud, long-drawn-out 'o-o-o-o.'" Our first language, as Lear reminds us, is a cry: "We came cry-ing hither . . ." (4.6.178–80).

This primal dialectic between absence and presence, loss and recrea-tion, sounds its opening note in a pun I hear (thanks to Peter Brook's film) at the very beginning of *King Lear*. Brook's Bergman-like, black-and-white, Scandinavian production opens in absolute, wintry silence, as the camera slowly pans past Lear's waiting subjects and moves into the throne room. It gradually focuses on a slowly-closing door at one end of the room. When the door swings shut, the heavy repercussion of its closing is the initial sound in the film. Paul Scofield, as Lear, then speaks a single word: "Know." He waits several seconds before continuing the line: " . . . that we have divided in three," etc. (1.1.37). The cinematic sequence sounds like this: *slam*/"Know"/silence. For an instant, Lear's word "Know" is separate from the rest of his sentence, so that what we hear first, before the ensuing words resolve the ambiguity, is the single word, "No," accentuated by a closing door. In that brief moment, "No" and "Know" coalesce in the same audible syllable, harmonizing the dialectical theme of knowledge and negation that *King Lear* proceeds tragically to play out and that Shakespeare's Nothing subsumes as part of its whole.

Of course, most productions of *King Lear* will disable the salient significance of this "Know"/"No" pun. Yet that brief auditory event can be considered paradigmatic of an audience's response, moment by moment, to a play. That is, knowing or noting fills up the space of nothing in at least three ways: through the genius of the poet (Theseus's argument), through the events of the production and the theatrical locus within which it happens, and ultimately through the imaginations of the audience who see and hear (and read) the play. A better model of such an audience, filling silence and nothing with meanings (notings), is available in a Gentleman's report of Ophelia's mad discourse. "Her speech," he says, "is nothing,"

> Yet the unshaped use of it doth move
> The hearers to collection; they yawn [aim] [17] at it,
> And botch the words up fit to their own thoughts,
> Which as her winks and nods and gestures yield them,
> Indeed would make one think there might be thought,
> Though nothing sure, yet much unhappily.
>
> (*Hamlet*, 4.5.7–13)

The ways in which we give meaning to nothing, botching up words to fit our own thoughts, are essential processes of seeing, hearing, or reading plays. We also give airy nothing a habitation and name; we also make "nothing sure" by interpreting it, just as Freud interpreted the sounds and senses of his grandson's game. The passage from *Hamlet* provides its own demonstration of its point. For instance, does "which," or "them," in line eleven ("Which as her winks and nods and gestures yield them") refer to *her* words or *their* (the hearers') thoughts? Syntax and sense are obscure here. The best and fullest reading, I would claim, rejects exclusivity and accepts all the possible senses (there are at least four permutations) in an effort to appreciate how speaker and hearer get con-fused in the act of communicating and interpreting symbolic discourse.

To interpret Shakespeare's Nothing is a much larger task. One way to begin is to collect several senses of "O" as sign and sound and symbol—various significations that circumscribe and circulate through Shakespeare's Nothing, especially in *King Lear*. These various meanings coexist and interpenetrate throughout Shakespeare's text; their con-fusions are elaborate. In an effort to sustain the complexity while undoing the confusion, I have isolated separate sets of meanings and briefly characterized them. The ensuing fragmentation in my own text is a result of the necessarily artificial disintegration of Shakespeare's inimitable linguistic integrity.

NOTHING/ZERO/CIPHER

These mathematical terms include various synonyms of "nothing," like "nil," "null," "none," "naught" ("nought"), "aught" ("ought"). "Zero" and "cipher" share the same Arabic root: *sifr*, meaning "empty." The two meanings of "cipher" convey the primary dialectic of presence and absence. As synonym for zero it means "empty," "nothing"; it also means "secret letter" or "code" (it signifies the absence of a specific and salient presence). Nothing by itself, in context its meanings are multiple, like Polixenes's "cipher . . . standing in rich place."

VOID/VACANCY/ABSENCE/LACK

These terms occupy the primary ground of nothing, which can be perceived as a threat ("negative nothing") or as a potential for recreation ("positive nothing")—from Lear to Lacan. In psychoanalytic terms, they represent an occasion for castration anxiety or primitive fears of dissolution, and/or the potential reconnections of symbolic relationships.

HOLE/WHOLE

A primary pun, catching in a single sound the dialectic of nothing and all. Shakespeare's play of language is insistently homophonic.

CIRCLE/CYCLE/ORB/RING/WHEEL

These words describe both objects and motions. Circles and circlings are crucial throughout *King Lear*, especially. For instance, "the orbs / From whom we do exist and cease to be" (1.1.111–12) symbolize a whole matrix of elements, such as stars, planets, orbits, celestial (Ptolemaic) spheres—as well as womb, testicles, semen, eggs, or eyes. Other circles include Lear's crown, the sun ("nothing like the sun" [Sonnet 130]), and the Wheel of Fortune which becomes the wheel of fire (4.7.46) as it and the play come full circle.

WOMB/GENITALS/MOUTH/EYES/EGG

These are the organic embodiments of the dialectic. In *King Lear*, they underlie Cordelia's spoken "Nothing" and her final silence ("Look there! . . . her lips") and Gloucester's "bleeding rings, / Their precious stones new lost" (5.3.190–91)—an image that re-emphasizes the symbolic connection between eyes and genitals. A reciprocal image—the symbolic castrating threat—underlies Edgar's words to Edmund about their father: "The dark and vicious place where thee he got / Cost him his eyes" (5.3.173–74). Less darkly, the womb is traditionally the circle incarnate: see religious representations of the Virgin's womb, or the medieval *topos* of the enclosed circular garden.[18] Our word "egg" is *ovum* in Latin, *oion* in Greek. Zeros are commonly known as "goose eggs," suggesting their imagined procreative powers.

TOMB/PIT/HELL

The tomb is the womb's reciprocal, as *Romeo and Juliet* and hundreds of medieval and Renaissance poems proclaim. Shakespeare often connects the theological hell with the genital one, as places where men are consumed by fire (venereal burning): see Sonnet 144. In *Titus Andronicus* the symbolic identity of the "detested, dark, blood-drinking pit" (2.3.224), destructive female genitals, and the devouring maternal mouth (Tamora) is explicit.[19] Lear's tirade against women repeats these connections. Recall that Shakespeare's stage had a trap-door hell-mouth at its center. (Dante's Inferno is built of descending concentric circles, an abyss that leads to Satan's mouth.)

God/Heavenly Spheres

As the church fathers held, God is a circle (or a sphere) whose center is everywhere and whose circumference is nowhere. An inversion of the geometry of Hell, Dante's Mount Purgatory consists of ascending concentric circles, leading to Beatrice's smile and the gates of Paradise. Paradise itself is a perfect Ptolemaic cosmos of concentric spheres.

Necromantic Circle

This is the magic circle that summons up spirits and protects the summoner from them. It represents a parody, or blasphemy, of God's creative powers and is one of the basic geometric and symbolic figures that structures the theatrical stage itself. Speech (dialogue) gives life to (inspires) spirits (actors). Prospero is magician, stage director, and actor.[20]

Speech/Glottis/Globe/Theater

The sound of "O" and its shape coalesce in these two primary potencies, of the spoken word and dramatic representation on a stage: Shakespeare's *wooden O*, his global theater.

Here is much ado about nothing. Indeed, almost too much. As Laertes remarks of his sister's mad, bawdy songs, "This nothing's more than matter" (4.5.174). Like the widening circles that emanate from a single disturbance in the surface of a pond, or like some protean Joycean process of "the abnihilisation of the etym," my divisions of O multiply into an almost "infinite deal of nothing."[21] I researched "O," and discovered that research itself is circular. Knowledge is not linear but curved.[22] It all becomes an unending *histoire d'O*, of which I can trace only a part. Where I have carefully to sort out various meanings of "Nothing" and "O," Shakespeare's incredibly inclusive language reintegrates this variety into a unified word or metaphor. For instance, as Romeo lies prostrate in Friar Laurence's cell, the Nurse urges him to "stand up, stand up, stand, and you be a man. / For Juliet's sake, for her sake, rise and stand; / Why should you fall into so deep an O?" (3.3.88–90). Shakespeare plays here with several senses of O as sound and shape and symbol—the naughty meanings.[23] Romeo's "O" is his hyperbolic moaning and groaning; the Nurse's meanings include that female (genital) "O" for which rising and falling defines virility and that grave "O" into which Romeo ultimately will fall (Act Five is a set of variations on the theme of womb and tomb). Mercutio earlier teases Romeo in similar bawdy terms. "This cannot anger him," he says:

> 'twould anger him
> To raise a spirit in his mistress' circle,
> Of some strange nature, letting it there stand
> Till she had laid it and conjur'd it down.
> (2.1.23–26)

Mercutio's bawdiness, like the Nurse's, plays with sexual senses of "stand" and further imagines copulation as conjuration. Exactly this latter image, of conjuring up and raising spirits within a female circle, is elaborated in Burgundy's remarks to King Henry in *Henry V*. When the King laments that he "cannot so conjure up the spirit of love" in Katherine, so "that he will appear in his true likeness," Burgundy replies:

> If you would conjure in her, you must make a circle; if conjure up Love in her in his true likeness, he must appear naked and blind. Can you blame her then, being a maid yet ros'd over with the virgin crimson of modesty, if she deny the appearance of a naked blind boy in her naked seeing self? It were, my lord, a hard condition for a maid to consign to. (5.2.288–99)

The genital meanings are straightforward; "naked seeing self" combines eye and vagina, through their physical similarities.[24]

With this naughtiness in mind, and an ear to further bawdy punning, we can now attend to Shakespeare's famous Prologue to *Henry V*, often considered his most glorious evocation of the magical relationship between actor, stage, and audience. It begins with an "O":

> O for a muse of fire, that would ascend
> The brightest heaven of invention!

A kingdom for a stage, princes to act,
And monarchs to behold the swelling scene!
But pardon, gentles all,
The flat unraised spirits that hath dar'd
On this unworthy scaffold to bring forth
So great an object. Can this cockpit hold
The vasty fields of France? Or may we cram
Within this wooden O the very casques
That did affright the air at Agincourt?
O, pardon! since a crooked figure may
Attest in little place a million,
And let us, ciphers to this great accompt,
On your imaginary forces work.
Suppose within the girdle of these walls
Are now confin'd two mighty monarchies,
Whose high, upreared, and abutting fronts
The perilous narrow ocean parts asunder.
Piece out our imperfections with your thoughts;
Into a thousand parts divide one man,
And make imaginary puissance;
Think, when we talk of horses, that you see them
Printing their proud hoofs i' th' receiving earth. . . .
                                        (Prologue, 1–27)

The speech begins with a dramatic wish for fiery ascent and a "swelling scene"—a wish that is initially frustrated by the fact of "flat, unraised spirits" who lack the (phallic) potency to "bring forth" their object. The actual "cockpit" (a genital juncture in pun) is too small: the "wooden O" of the Globe Theater cannot physically contain the objects it wishes to represent. Yet through a metaphoric shift from geometry (the architectural "O") to mathematics ("O" as number, zero)—bridged by the shared image of shape ("a crooked figure")—Shakespeare transmutes impotence into omnipotence. The actors who are nothing in themselves become representative "ciphers to this great accompt," and now they count for something. They symbolically multiply, through the reciprocal paradox of being divided; one man becomes a thousand. That multiplication involves sexual as well as mathematical senses (like Polixenes's cipher). The wooden O then re-presents itself as "the girdle of these walls," which now confine high, upreared, mighty monarchies—an image of potency (male within female) that mirrors and is made possible by the "imaginary puissance" of the audience. That imaginative potency is very fertile, as Shakespeare's image suggests. We translate a mere word, "horses," into a symbolic vision of fecundation that condenses the procreative relationship between word, drama, actor, and audience into a poetic image—one that also alludes to the written text: ". . . *printing* their proud hoofs i' th' receiving earth."[25]

Just as "O" as exclamation represents a primitive word at the threshold of speech, and "O" as mark designates the origins of writing, so the various symbolisms of "O" as creative no-thing, or circle, mouth, or womb, underlie primitive conceptions of the theatrical stage itself, thus connecting human procreation and reproduction with stage production. "O" is the germinal image of Shakespeare's stage (hence the other meaning of my title: "Shakespeare is Nothing"): "this wooden O," the oral stage, and the womb from which that primary relationship develops. Shakespeare's O, his Nothing, thus becomes a dialectic, circumscribing the fruitful interplay between the theatrical mode (what is actually onstage) and the imaginative mode (what is represented to and in the minds of an audience). His O describes a relationship, whose original models are infantile and maternal, involving the "primal cavities" of womb and mouth.[26] The image of the stage as pregnant enclosure (*"cette enceinte de bois,"* in J.P. Petit's felicitous phrase[27]) lies at the basis of Shakespeare's conception of theatrical space as generative—and destructive—female interiority. For him, the metaphor of dramatic and poetic creation as procreation was more than merely metaphor: it was the ground, the primary embodiment, of his art.[28]

Images of feminine enclosures appear throughout Shakespeare's works, sometimes in extreme manifestations. At the negative extreme are such catastrophic enactments as the witches' cauldron in *Macbeth*, or the devouring and dismembering pit in *Titus Andronicus*—an image that returns to its bodily locus in Lear's maddened vision of female genitals, just as Gloucester's ravaged and bleeding face mirrors Lavinia's—or the remembered hazards of the foul witch Sycorax, "grown into a hoop" (*The Tempest*, 1.2.258–59). This terrible image of "negative nothing" never vanishes from Shakespeare's dramatic vision. The tragedies of course shape themselves in terms of the negative or destructive conception of nothing. *Hamlet, Macbeth*, and *King Lear* occupy a stage that seems to offer only danger, confinement, and ultimate death. Yet even the tragedies do not wholly surrender to nihilism. The sheer fact of their existence, as dramatic works that re-present nihilism, is an assertion of some potency (compare

Shakespeare's boasts of poetic immortality in the Sonnets). The creative power of poetry and drama provides a positive balance to the images of negation the tragedies construct.[29] Even that most desperate and apparently nihilistic statement of the nothingness of theatrical significance, which Macbeth utters at the end of his play, sounds some positive notes of affirmation; that is, it is the player, the stage, and the tale that *signify*, award significance to, exist within and create images for, nothing. ("For poetry," Yeats reminds us, "makes nothing happen.") Macbeth's famous moment of despair is the reciprocal negative version of Theseus's more positive characterization of drama as that which gives airy nothing a habitation and name.

> Out, out, brief candle!
> Life's but a walking shadow, a poor player,
> That struts and frets his hour upon the stage,
> And then is heard no more. It is a tale
> Told by an idiot, full of sound and fury,
> Signifying nothing.   (5.5.23–28)

All comes to nothing, as nothing comes to all. Yet this is not solely the darker or tragic vision. The implicit sense of creative power in the images of nothing that tragedies like *Macbeth* or *King Lear* ambiguously suggest becomes explicit in a play like *The Tempest*, where "the great globe itself" contains and becomes a world, an every-thing, while in itself it is a no-thing, airy nothing, "melted into air, into thin air": an all-inclusive sphere whose fragility encloses emptiness, like the emblematic bubbles and dew-drops of Metaphysical and Baroque poetry.[30] Dissolved, insubstantial, the stuff of dreams, both the stage and our lives are finally "rounded"—like a circle or a cipher—"with a sleep" (*The Tempest*, 4.1.148–58). Joyce's pun is perfect: "Shapesphere" (*Finnegans Wake*, 295.4).

The spherical world of Shakespeare ultimately re-integrates all the circles and semicircles of my fragmented vision. Finally I must abandon the fanciful mathematics of plus and minus zero, since what Shakespeare actually attempts is to incorporate the malignant images of "negative nothing" into the "positive nothing" of the global theater he creates. He erects a sphere (thus being symbolically both father and mother) that contains and momentarily controls those catastrophic fantasies of death and dismemberment that underlie his tragedies, and other plays as well. Nothing, ultimately, is what the plays are *about*, in a spatial as well as thematic sense.

Yet Shakespeare's theatrical playspace, with all its positive procreativity, is also simultaneously the most encompassing representation of that "unmanly," "female" Nothing that arouses tragic anxiety. In other words, Shakespeare cannot escape the primary ambivalence of his global image. All he can do—and he can do almost all—is to work within the voluminous confines of that figure's largest spaces (the theater, the world), constructing in imagination and dramaturgy smaller versions of its powers and paradoxes. Shakespeare's imaginatively vast theatrical space simultaneously symbolizes a female interior heroically occupied by male "spirits" (actors, phalli), a maternal womb inhabited by playful children (such as the Forest of Arden), a malignant mouth consuming its victims, or the interior of a confined male psyche—as in *Hamlet*, where the actual Globe Theatre becomes a mirror of the hero's mind, and vice-versa: "Remember thee! / Ay, thou poor ghost, whiles memory holds a seat / In this distracted globe" (1.5.95–97). It also, and most importantly, complements the "mind's eye" of the audience, enclosed within the theater and imaginatively re-creating the play. The particular predominance from play to play of any one symbolic significance does not dissipate the resonant energies of others. All these symbols of Shakespeare's Nothing coexist in each specific dramatization of his idea of the theater. His movement from tragedy to romance demonstrates a shift from a dark, malevolent perspective on this idea to a brighter, more benign one—or from tragic denial to philosophical acceptance of the inexorability of being "rounded with a sleep," surrounded and finished by the inevitable nothing of death. Yet the primary ambivalence never disappears.

Prospero's final dissolution of his own theatrical magic, though hardly an unambiguous evocation of the positive values of dramatic generativity, does offer an alternative, reciprocal view to the darkly tragic perspective of *King Lear*. Both Lear and Prospero, as old men approaching death (and with daughters to give away, reluctantly), confront the fact of inevitable nothing, but in different ways. Lear tries heroically to stand up to the threat, to assert his power in the face of its decline, to say "I" in the midst of nothing ("They told me I was everything"), to be the integer "one" alongside the zero. Yet he becomes, in the Fool's words, "an O without a figure; . . . nothing." ("Power," notes Sigurd Burckhardt, "was the integer before the zero.")[31] "I" (the first person pronoun) equals "one" (both subject and number), equals "1" (the cardinal number). Hamlet epigrammatizes the tragedy of heroic assertion in the midst of nothing when he claims that "a man's life's no more than to say 'one'" (5.2.74).[32] The fearful

idea of being *no one* (none, noun)[33] motivates tragedies of identity like
Hamlet and *King Lear* and the rest of Shakespeare's tragedies. *Coriolanus*
is the extreme example of the denial of circularity (family relationship,
origins) in favor of hyperbolically heroic "one-ness." Heroic assertion in
such a world culminates in tragedy; it adds up finally to nothing. In the
shorthand of psychoanalytic terminology, oral disintegration encompasses
phallic affirmation. Shakespeare's romances entertain another alternative.
Prospero's willing surrender of his "most potent art," his admission of loss
and awareness of ultimate nothingness ("Every third thought shall be my
grave"[5.1.312]), represent a will, not to power, but to surrender power: to
give up, to lose, to be lost. Prospero gives up his daughter, while Lear holds
on to his to the end, and beyond. Lear refuses to surrender, to mourn, to
learn to die. Prospero's exit, and his return as Epilogue, enact the enduring
value of philosophical acceptance instead of heroic denial in the face of
inevitable nothing.[34]

How can I sum up? An infinity of nothings is nothing, and infinity.
The totality of Shakespeare's Nothing cannot be circumscribed by any figure of speech or design, unless it is his own wooden O. Shakespeare's
Nothing is a paradox, a living world that willingly announces itself as a
mere bubble, words that disappear into a void. Shakespeare's theater is finally only a momentary enactment of sight and sound and symbol, surrounded by silence and a bare stage, at the last returning to where it began,
in emptiness and absence. Yet while it is there, in the playspace of creative
nothingness, it is wondrous: beautiful or dreadful, ruinous or renascent,
and uniquely worth noting.

8

What Is Shakespeare?

DURING THE SPRING OF 1819 a young American writer visited Shakespeare's birthplace in Stratford-upon-Avon. While in what he termed the "squalid chambers" of the actual birth-room, Washington Irving noted "a striking instance of the spontaneous and universal homage of mankind to the great poet of nature." Such veneration displayed itself on the walls of the chamber, which were covered with the handwritten names of previous visitors. A garrulous old woman showed Irving through the house, displaying various authentic relics (Shakespeare's tobacco box, his sword, his very chair), while her visitor listened with that "resolute good-humoured credulity" that befits a tourist. As was the custom, he sat in Shakespeare's chair. Afterwards he wandered the Stratford countryside, where he felt the spirit of the Bard pervade the spirit of the place, suffusing the landscape like a Romantic muse, illuminating forests, hills, and houses in "the prism of poetry." [1]

A few decades later another American author made the requisite literary pilgrimage. In the summer of 1855, having been appointed by President Franklin Pierce as the American Consul at Liverpool, fifty-year-old Nathaniel Hawthorne visited Stratford. He was surprised by the small size of Shakespeare's birth-room, and like Irving noted that the ceiling, walls, and even windowpanes of that famous chamber were "entirely written over with names in pencil, by persons . . . of all varieties of stature." Unlike Irving, Hawthorne maintained a skeptic's stance. He refused to add *his* name to the scribblings of the multitude, and had "Shakespeare's chair" still occupied the scene he would have been unlikely to occupy it. While in the house, he "felt no emotion whatever—not the slightest—nor any quickening of the imagination." Though he could now envisage a more solid idea of the man, he was "not quite sure that this [was] altogether desirable." [2]

Fifty years later, at the turn of the century, two more American writers followed the footsteps of their predecessors. They were more skeptical yet. Samuel Clemens and Henry James were both anti-Stratfordians. Clemens's contribution to the question was a volume entitled *Is Shakespeare Dead?*, wherein he advanced the cause of the Baconians. Though James preferred no particular rival candidate, he spoke of "the lout from Stratford" and wrote that "the divine William is [a] fraud." Still he suffered torment at the unguessed riddle of Shakespeare's genius.[3] So fascinated was James by this mystery that he wrote a story about it. "The Birthplace" (1903) represents his challenge to Bardolatry and his idea of transcendent authorship.[4]

The story concerns an English couple hired to look after the birthplace of "the supreme poet, the Mecca of the English-speaking race." The poet is never named. The caretaker, Morris Gedge, is charged with presenting "the Facts," established over centuries. Of greatest interest to Gedge and tourists alike is "the low, the sublime Chamber of Birth": "It was empty as a shell of which the kernel has withered, and contained neither busts nor prints nor early copies; it contained only the Fact—*the* Fact itself."[5] Morris Gedge takes to sitting in the birth-room alone, in the dark, and gradually begins to lose faith in the room, in the Birthplace, in the birth—in short, in the Facts. His lapse of both "piety and patriotism" is encouraged by the arrival of a young American couple from New York. When the husband asserts that "'The play's the thing.' Let the author alone," Gedge fervently agrees and adds:

"It's all I want—to let the author alone. Practically . . . there *is* no author; that is for us to deal with. There are all the immortal people—*in* the work; but there's nobody else."

"Yes," said the young man—"that's what it comes to. There should really, to clear the matter up, be no such Person."

"As you say," Gedge returned, "it's what it comes to. There *is* no such Person."

The evening air listened, in the warm, thick midland stillness, while the wife's little cry rang out. "But *wasn't* there—?"

"There was somebody," said Gedge, against the doorpost. "But They've killed Him. And, dead as He is, They keep it up. They do it over again, They kill Him every day."[6]

James's story is about God, paternity, authorship, and the mystery of sexuality. It is also about Shakespeare and the developing Shakespeare mythology of the late nineteenth century. James's mysterious idea of Shakespeare so fascinated him that he re-animated it in an Introduction to *The Tempest* composed for Sir Sidney Lee a few years later.[7] Here James writes that "the man himself, in the Plays, we directly touch, to my consciousness,

positively nowhere: we are dealing too perpetually with the artist, the monster and magician of a thousand masks." Instead of a withered kernel in an
empty shell, we find the author "at the centre of the storm":

There in fact, though there only, we find that serenity; find the subject itself intact
and unconscious, seated as unwinking and inscrutable as a divinity in a temple, save
for that vague flicker of derision, the only response to our interpretive heat, which
adds the last beauty to its face.[8]

What is Shakespeare? Where do we find that subject and make it visible? How do we distinguish the proper name from the authorial name,
Shakespeare from "Shakespeare?" How can we make the inscrutable subject itself respond more respectfully to our interpretive heat? Irving and
Hawthorne observed with admiration or dismay the autographs written
over every surface in Shakespeare's birth-room, as though a sacred space had
been honored or violated. In "The Birthplace" James overwrote Shakespeare by erasing him from the story and then re-creating "Him" in the
author's own transcendent image of idealized Author. Is Shakespeare then
an inscrutable divinity, a being before whom, as Yeats claimed, "the world
was almost as empty . . . as it must be in the eyes of God?" Is he "a ghost,
a shadow now," as Joyce's Stephen Dedalus would have it, "a voice heard
only in the heart of him who is the substance of his shadow, the son con-
substantial with the father?" Perhaps he was "just like any other man," as
Hazlitt wrote, "but that he was like all other men. . . . He was nothing in
himself; but he was all that others were, or that they could become. . . .
He was like the genius of humanity." This idealization is epitomized in
Borges's parable: "There was no one in him; . . . there was only a bit of
coldness, a dream dreamt by no one. . . . No one has ever been so many
men as this man, who like the Egyptian Proteus could exhaust all the guises
of reality." In this parable Shakespeare becomes finally a secondary deity, a
demiurge who dreams his world as he himself is dreamed by God.[9]

Erased, written over, mythologized, and apotheosized, Shakespeare
has become the critical *occasion for idealization*. His is the exemplary authorial space we whitewash over and where we inscribe our names.[10] A generation ago Alfred Harbage described Shakespearean idolatry as a wish for
a secular theology in an age buffetted by the loss of faith. Lately, in the
tradition of Nietzsche, Barthes, and Foucault, "Shakespeare" has begun to
signify the ultimate instance of the author as dead father—a corpus that
speaks from an absence, the author who arrives, if at all, D.O.A. (though
perhaps reports are exaggerated). As the primal patriarchal agent of au-

thorship he becomes a transcendental anonymity.[11] Or he represents the seminal spirit of modern literature, a source without origin or rival, a Shakespère of the Western world.[12]

These contemporary models of transcendent patriarchal authorship are powerfully adumbrated by Shakespeare. Enter, stage left, the Ghost of King Hamlet. This spectral narrator unfolds a tale that his listener inscribes in the "book and volume" of his brain, incorporating this story as his own, making it the motive and the cue for his passion and (re)action. The Ghost is first a "questionable shape," but Hamlet identifies it in his own terms: "I'll call thee Hamlet" (1.4.43–44). A similar moment opens the play: the question "Who's there?" is met with the charge, "Nay, answer me. Stand and unfold yourself." Reflective self-identification is legitimate, yet it is also faulty, an identity mistook, an act of *méconnaissance*. Stage tradition holds that Shakespeare himself played the role of King Hamlet's Ghost. If so, then the principle of authorship thus displayed posits a ghostly and questionable narrator who is backed by a substantial and identifiable actor who authors his own player's speech. Shakespeare enacts an answer to the question of authorship even as he dramatizes its dilemmas. The figure of the actor, Shakespeare, reciting the lines of the author, "Shakespeare," from within a royal suit of armor that holds both absence and presence embodies a simultaneous invention of modern and postmodern ideas of authorship. His figure in not in the carpet, but behind the visor, or the arras.

Shakespeare wrote during a period when modern ideas of the author were being invented, or historically re-designed. As Renaissance printers invented the book, Renaissance poetics invented the author. Between the conventional anonymity of Spenser's *Calendar* (1579) and the personal exhibitionism of Jonson's *Works* (1616), Shakespeare explored (behind the scenes) the aesthetic space between the "speaking fiction" (character) and the "real writer" (person)—to use Foucault's terms. During this time the cultural significance of what Foucault called "the author function" was changing.[13] Literary texts were becoming identified by author, owned by producer or authorizing agent; anonymity was becoming intolerable. The grounds of literary creation were being enclosed, like sixteenth-century English pasture land. Unlike his contemporaries Marlowe or Jonson or Chapman, Shakespeare did not attempt to aggrandize himself or to construct an idealized image of himself as author. He preferred to work *within* the dramatic arena rather than boast of his mastery *of* it.

For Shakespeare, "actor" and "author" were literally synonymous: in the variable spelling of his day, "auctor." He was simultaneously player and poet, not merely in his profession but in his concept of his art. Whereas today Shakespeare's text is the *writing*, and dramatic productions are the *reading*, in 1600 writing and reading, or inscription and representation, were unified in dramatic production at the Globe. Shakespeare's plays had an immediate, here-and-now origin and enactment in which he participated. As poet, his plays were not separate from him, since he was also their reader, actor, producer, director. As a player, his scripts were not strange to him, since he wrote and revised them as he and his company performed. He embodied the perfect merger of "author's pen" and "actor's voice" (*Troilus and Cressida*, Prologue 24). He could physically animate his own text, or he could retire from it, in a gesture of absence, while maintaining an active presence in it. His is the new and privileged position of the modern "playwright" (the term did not exist before Shakespeare). In order to conceptualize the genius of Shakespearean authorship in its historical moment, we need a theory of "auctorship."

The historical invention of the modern author as secular authority for the production of individualized texts correlates with developing Renaissance concepts of personhood, or what Barthes called "the prestige of the individual."[14] Shakespeare occupies an original position in such concepts. Whereas Marlowe invented the dramatic egotist, Shakespeare invented the dramatic ego. *Hamlet* is of course the central enactment. A more limited example comes from the penultimate scene of *Richard II*. Confined to his cell, Richard prefigures the Cartesian ego attempting to imagine its existence, and implicitly its death. Richard searches for himself in analogy (comparing the prison to the world, or his time to a clock) and in drama (he plays in one person many people). Identity for Richard is theater, role-playing; he plays himself and thereby (re)creates himself. Mere language is insufficient in the world, however, and he, as Hamlet, fails. Philosophy surrenders to action; bare thought cannot confer being. Shakespeare would have restated the Cartesian axiom: "I *act*, therefore I am." The claim carries its own irony, since acting is simultaneously genuine and pretense.

Of course Shakespeare did not invent the concept of the theatricality of everyday life. It was a cultural phenomenon that invoked a medieval *theatrum mundi*. Yet Shakespeare knew, better than anyone else, how deeply rooted was theatricality in the development of human behavior and relationships, not merely as stages on or through which we strut and fret to enact numerable "ages of man" but as a central construct in forming our selves.

Is the self then only a series of masks and poses? Is there no person behind the persona? The question dilates into psychology and philoso-phy.[15] At a lower stage the history of Shakespeare productions offers a theatrical emblem of the problem. When a critic leaves a contemporary production of *Twelfth Night*, performed in a futuristic subway system to punk rock and strobe lights, muttering something to the effect that "It was interesting, but it wasn't Shakespeare," what does he mean? Can he be measuring the production against an original standard which he or Shakespeare criticism considers authentic? Surely not, since no reader of Shakespeare criticism could hope to find such a standard. The history of Shakespeare productions, like the history of Shakespeare criticism, traces a trajectory of cultural values; particular stagings mirror their historical cir-cumstances. Yet however unique or bizarre a particular production may be, most directors and actors proceed from some idea of an authentic, original Shakespeare. Who is he? What is that?

In his discussion of Derrida's theory of representation, Edward Said recounts a travesty of *Hamlet* described in *Great Expectations*.[16] The per-formance is quintessentially Dickensian. Characters are woefully miscast and comically attired; actors forget their lines or butcher them; audience members heckle uproariously (poor Mr. Wopsle plays the Prince). There are in fact several other, extraneous plays vying with *Hamlet* for attention and applause. Yet even as it is being mangled, violated, travestied, Shake-speare's play not only survives but controls its distortions. It sounds through the *mêlée*; the text asserts itself through its misquotings. Like the Ghost beneath the stage, an idea of original authority underlies all its variant rep-resentations. That idea persists in memory. In Dickens's narrated travesty "the royal phantom also carried a ghostly manuscript, to which it had the appearance of occasionally referring." We measure textual or dramatic dis-tortions against an ideal that we cannot wholly recover. As Terence Hawkes suggests, the idea of an authoritative body of Shakespeare's authentic works is the "Holy Grail" of scholarship; all versions of Shakespeare's texts are mediated in some way.[17]

Idealization is the cardinal temptation for anyone conceptualizing Shakespeare. Efforts to surpass predecessors in quotable praise are note-worthy and notorious in the critical tradition from Jonson's day to our own: "To draw *no envy* (Shakespeare) on thy name, . . . I *confess* thy writings to be such, / As neither Man, nor Muse, can praise too much."[18] Like Jonson's primary tribute, most idealizations contain a germ or viru-lent agent of ambivalence. Idealization requires denial, which then resur-faces, like the return of the repressed. (Such a scheme, by the way, helps in understanding the interplay of Bardolatry and anti-Stratfordianism in nineteenth- and twentieth-century Shakespeare criticism.) Shakespeare is *the* occasion for idealization in English literature. Given conventional evaluative hierarchies, with their need for a pantheon, some author must represent the head. That Shakespeare is unarguably the appropriate figurehead attests both to his genius and to our need to mythologize authors as cultural heroes. The only times in which Shakespeare's genius went without saying were those periods when he was undervalued as an author. Today, when his genius is assured, it goes with saying repeatedly.[19]

Anti-Stratfordians persist, of course, long after Delia Bacon's demise. New books regularly champion the usual claimants. Like "the Facts" of Shakespeare, the evidence of these debunkers is of minimal interest. What is of interest is the sheer persistence of the myth of debunking. That challenges to Shakespeare's identity should persist so tenaciously in the face of lucid evidence to their contraries indicates a significant critical and historical phenomenon. Manic skepticism about Shakespeare as genuine author represents the lunatic fringe of a real issue in Shakespeare scholarship, the issue of conjecture or speculation. The identity question is the wildest instance; a milder one is the birthdate. We all know that Shakespeare was born on April 23, 1564, and that he probably was not. The birthdate has an aesthetic, not an historical veracity. April 23 is Saint George's Day; it is the day on which Shakespeare died in 1616, rounding his little life with an artistically pleasing sleep. It is thus the best conjectural date. Shakespeare's historical life *begins* with conjecture. That conjecture matches the known facts is precisely what is so fascinating about the case. Shakespeare, like Hamlet's Ghost—a character the author is conjectured to have played— originates in a questionable shape that answers to our identifications.

Another set of emblems is the various portraits. All of them—the Chandos, Droeshout, Jannsen, Flower, Felton—are attempts to paint a *like*ness. They are still-life versions of performances of Shakespeare's plays; they re-present an original in acts of variant authenticity, where neither original nor authority remains. (My favorite is the Chandos. I admire the healthy complexion, the neatly-trimmed beard, the penetrating yet playful eyes, the simple yet elegant clothes, and that burnished gold hoop in the left ear. The face is almost a perfect oval, like an egg or a zero. The power and serenity of the gaze enchant me.) The several portraits possess varying legitimacies according to experts. Like the birthdate, they emblematize the place of conjecture in Shakespeare studies. They offer a sign of Shakespeare and are therefore more than mere portraits. They are also mirrors. Samuel

Schoenbaum relates that "Desmond McCarthy has said somewhere that trying to work out Shakespeare's personality was like looking at a very dark glazed portrait in the National Portrait Gallery: at first you see nothing, then you begin to recognize features, and then you realize that they are your own."[20]

Signs can be deceptive; they often carry more weight than what they signify, yet they are often all we have. Eighteenth-century reports indicate that the wooden signboard of the Globe Playhouse was a painting of Hercules with the world on his shoulders. This sign signifies more than global theater, or the equation of stage with world. It is the sign of deception, of momentary usurpation, of displacement (Hercules first tricked Atlas into gathering the Golden Apples of the Hesperides, then tricked him again into resuming his fated burden). It signifies an essential aspect of the idea of Shakespeare: the author as usurper.

Shakespeare's first public notice describes him as a thief. He is the upstart crow beautified with others' feathers, a player with a tiger's heart.[21] Another contemporary writes: "Shakespeare, that nimble Mercury thy brain, / Lulls many hundred Argus-eyes asleep."[22] (Mercury put Argus to sleep by telling him the tale of Pan and Syrinx as he played on a pipe; he then decapitated him in order to steal Io, the white cow loved by Zeus.) Dryden called Shakespeare "the very Janus of poets; he wears almost everywhere two faces."[23] Nietzsche remarked that "dramatists are in general rather wicked men" and that Shakespeare in particular had "close relationship with the passions."[24] Yeats, in his famous thesis about "some one myth" for every man, wrote that "Shakespeare's myth, it may be, describes a wise man who was blind from very wisdom, and an empty man who thrust him from his place, and saw all that could be seen for very emptiness."[25] (Hamlet and Fortinbras, or Richard and Bullingbrook, exemplify the pattern.)

Nineteenth-century phrenologists, following Renaissance science, believed that the organ of robbery and the organ for dramaturgy were the same.[26] Shakespeare's career offers evidence for the correlation; almost all of his plots are taken from elsewhere, and much of his language consists of magically transmuted passages from Holinshed or North into perfect iambic pentameter. Trained from boyhood in classical modes of *imitatio*, as a playwright he turned others' workmanlike prose into his own flawless poetry. His goal was not traditional translation, but transformation (from history or romance to drama). Shakespeare adapted many but was influenced by few. Instead of simply imitating previous styles, he used them.

Whereas Jonson imitated classical dramatic forms and Spenser imitated medieval allegory, Shakespeare explored, examined, and finally exhausted previous genres. He not only used them, he used them up. His approach to tradition was aggressive and exhaustive: he explored, found the limits, and then exploded conventional categories of dramatic and poetic expression.[27] This pattern of development persists from *Titus Andronicus* and *The Comedy of Errors* through *King Lear* and *The Tempest*. Shakespeare vigorously manipulated dramatic categories, styles, and devices until they wore out under his handling. He played with the history of literary genres; he was *homo ludens* incarnate. He did not boast of novelty, as Marlowe did, nor did he expect veneration, as Jonson did. Whereas Marlowe translated Ovid with the goal of releasing subversive erotic energies, and Jonson translated with the goal of sustaining Latinate fidelity and grace, Shakespeare used translations to create his own narrative in an individually metamorphosed language. Rather than make translations, he made them over. In this sense he was the truest translator of Ovid because he metamorphosed *Metamorphoses* into drama.

Shakespeare's earliest appreciator, Francis Meres, went so far as to claim reincarnation. "The sweet witty soul of Ovid," wrote Meres in 1598, "lives in mellifluous and honey-tongued Shakespeare."[28] Meres's praise was echoed in ensuing years, as Shakespeare was regularly described as honey-tongued, or mellifluous, or flowing sweetly and freely. The upstart crow became the sweet swan of Avon. In Ovid's *Metamorphoses*, the tales of Cygnus, changed to a swan, and of Corone, changed to a crow, are successive stories (Book II). Various myths suit the metamorphic, polytropic Shakespeare: Hercules, Mercury, Proteus. One that fits best, however, is suggested in Coleridge's famous characterization of Richard II: "he scatters himself into a multitude of images."[29] Though Coleridge does not make it explicit, the image or event that enacts this idea is Richard's breaking of the mirror. He scatters his own image into fragments; he shatters his narcissism in a psychic disintegration that he tries futilely to repair in prison.

The myth of Narcissus lies at the heart of Shakespeare's dramatic art, as it lies at the heart of much current psychoanalytic theory. Shakespeare is not Narcissus, but he *is* the reflecting pool, the surface for projection. By looking at Shakespeare's enactments, we can see ourselves. "Who is it that can tell me who I am?" asks Lear. "Lear's shadow," replies the Fool (1.4.230–31). Actors reflect our identities, as shadows projected on the ground; they give us back images of our selves. We in turn attribute to Shakespeare all that we are. "They told me I was everything" (*Lear*, 4.6.104–05) could well be Shakespeare's comment to his readers. To characterize Shakespeare's identity, read his critics. One of them goes so far as to state that "Shakespeare has no existence apart from the various forms constructed by our critical practice."[30]

Shakespeare is a ground for narcissistic projection and our echoing song; he is the mirror in which we see our idealized selves. For literary critics, idealization cooperates with identification. By re-creating Shakespeare in our own images, critic by critic and age by age, we reconstitute an icon of linguistic perfection, thereby re-animating an aesthetic ideal while participating in its production. Proclamations of Shakespeare's linguistic omnipotence abound; Hazlitt, for instance, wrote that Shakespeare "has a magic power over words: they come winged at his bidding. . . . His language is hieroglyphical. It translates thoughts into visible images."[31]

My own style of idealization follows Hazlitt's, though it falls short of attributing magical animism. For me, Shakespeare simply personifies the English language. His genius represents English at its most flexible and creative. That Shakespeare was born in a period and culture that enabled and encouraged such linguistic creativity is an accident of history wonderful to contemplate. Elizabethan English was a polyglot, protean tongue, developing during a period that experimented simultaneously with vernacular novelties and classical neologisms. It consisted of ageless proverbs and contemporary inventions; its idioms came from humanist scholars and local shopkeepers. Its literary styles, rooted in medieval allegory, blossomed into profusions of analogy before being pruned by eighteenth-century rules of decorum and poetic diction. Syntax, punctuation, spelling—the smaller codes of discourse—were amorphous boundaries to be established or trespassed according to creative will or whim. Vocabulary was a flux of significance; words were almost too full of meaning. Not until the eighteenth century would they be codified within the systematic confines of dictionaries, sentenced to terminal de/finition, buried in a linguistic graveyard where proper usage was carved in the tombstones of convention and precedent.

Elizabethan English was a language of imperial acquisition. Foreign terms that strayed too close were quickly appropriated. The contrast with Renaissance Latin, in which salutary toil Shakespeare early labored, was sharp. As William Kerrigan puts it: "Humanist Latin boasted a barren immutability—all but completed, intolerant of novelty—while English was forever coming into being."[32] This historical moment precedes seventeenth- and eighteenth-century applications of the "author function" as a principle of limitation to restrict "dangerous proliferations of meaning."[33] At the core of Shakespeare's linguistic genius lies polysemous proliferation. Henry James, although he doubted the poet's identity, most admired Shakespeare's medium of "Expression": he had access to a storehouse of language that burst "out of all doors and windows"; his use of it was "something that was to make of our poor world a great flat table for receiving the glitter and clink of outpoured treasure."[34] James's metaphor conveys the tangible weight of Shakespeare's style, its connection to a fundamental economy of Midas-like transmutation, and the rich scope of piratical plunder Shakespeare's expansive expression achieved.

What best symbolizes Shakespeare's English—the language of his time and his uses of it—is its analogical base: its love of metaphor. Shakespeare *thought* in metaphor, analogy, terms of likeness; he re/presented, re/sembled one thing by another.[35] Like Homer's Odysseus he was polytropic, a man of many ways whose language had many turns. He is *l'homme aux modes*, the Proteus of poetry. Analogy is the broad quality of this style, as the pun is its smaller emblem. The pun is a sign in miniature of Shakespeare's uses of and attitude toward language; it is equivocal and multivocal, it dilates significance rather than restricts it. Compared to a plain style of straightforward, controlled discourse, puns represent misdirection and liberation. They create layers of polysemous significance. Shakespeare's puns remind us that his language is never superficial. To the extent that the pun symbolizes Shakespeare's seminal, serpentine linguistic medium—the creative matrix of his thought—then Samuel Johnson was uncannily perceptive when he complained: "A quibble was to him the fatal Cleopatra for which he lost the world, and was content to lose it."

Johnson's objection reveals the aridity of his own eighteenth-century idea of language while suggesting the fecundity of Shakespeare's. An erotics of Shakespearean writing marries a masculine ideal of verbal virility to a seductive style of feminine polysemy. Of course Shakespeare criticism, primarily a male tradition, has erected forms of veneration that imitate masculine ideals. My own idealizations participate in these fantasies of masculine power; they are compelling. Yet I believe that a Shakespearean personification of language offers an alternative to the more limited impersonations of masculine or feminine discourse that pervade current critical theory. If any individual use of language can effectively question the structures and boundaries of genderized convention, it is Shakespeare's.

Beyond this dream of authorial androgyny, my idealization of Shakespeare enthrones him at the intersection of *author* in the personal sense and *language* in the impersonal sense. As the personification of language, he signifies an ideal wherein neither writer nor writing need be privileged or subordinated in relation to the other. In this sense Shakespeare's work both divides and bridges medieval and modern notions of textual production. It becomes a watershed of literary history, linking the culmination of anonymous or idealized texts, such as classical mythology and medieval scholasticism, to the incipience of secular self-consciousness and dramatic self-representation. It links textual faith with textual skepticism; it marks the goal of tradition and the origin of modernity.

By thus idealizing Shakespeare's poetic genius, I can share in his glory while repeatedly granting it to him, in a version of aggressive affection, a veneration that also appropriates the god's power. I can recharge my individual and collective faith in the (English) Word, and then replenish its verbal vigor by echoing it. Typically, Shakespeare's critics tend to identify with Shakespeare's language: we quote it, allude to it, paraphrase it. Whole books consist of one-half Shakespearean poetry and one-half critical prose. Like King Hamlet's Ghost, Shakespeare's language invites identification and appropriation. We listen to its story until it becomes our own, then we inscribe it in our tables to write down elsewhere. The ongoing discourse of Shakespeare criticism re-presents Shakespeare's art in another form; it is an echo as well as a voice. In addition, Shakespeare criticism is a translation into contemporary terms of issues central to current critical discourse— issues of representation, authority, sexuality, gender, history.

Commonplace observation shows that the history of characterizations of Shakespeare, like the history of Shakespearean productions, or editions, or critical essays, replicates the development of critical theory and taste—from Classicism to Romanticism to Modernism to our current post-Modernist reaction. For instance, nineteenth-century notions of Shakespeare's characters as unique individuals with histories, motives, and personalities have now shifted to conceptions of Shakespearean character as displaced, alienated, refracted into myriad hues and images. Today's Shakespeare is "subjectivized" by distancing and projective identification. He represents the author who projects himself imaginatively on a surface (a stage), where he sees the reintegration of his fragmentary self, or at least a dramatic reorganization of fragments into a temporary yet illusory unity.[36] Such a transformation of Shakespeare into a postmodern figure is inevitable. It reveals both Shakespeare and our current circumstance; the Bard is both our contemporary and for all time. As the mirror in which each age sees itself, Shakespeare provides the constancy of mirroring (form) and the variety of mirrored images (content).[37]

Narcissism provides a theoretical key here. Psychoanalytic theories of narcissism are multiple and complex. I will sketch versions by Winnicott, Lacan, and Lichtenstein. For Winnicott, "the precursor of the mirror is the mother's face." The infant sees itself reflected in the way in which its mother looks at and responds to it. This primary interrelationship inaugurates the development of a shared imaginative and social space, "the beginning of a significant exchange with the world, a two-way process in which self-enrichment alternates with the discovery of meaning in the world of seen things."[38] For Lacan, the space between infant and image is less beneficially mutual and enriching, since the mother is replaced by an actual mirror before which the child imagines an alienated integrity, a fiction of the "I." In the mirror-stage is constructed "the statue in which man projects himself, [and] the phantoms that dominate him." "The mirror-stage is *a drama*" (my italics). Identity for Lacan is always mistaken: the primary instance of *méconnaissance*.[39] Lichtenstein posits the symbiotic matrix of early mother-infant mirroring as the basis for "the existential structure of human reality" and stresses the precariousness of that structure. Since it depends on reflection, being is "always questionable" (like Hamlet's Ghost); it must be acquired, created, and maintained throughout life. Re-petitions (seeking again) of mirroring in the larger social world are essential to identity-maintenance. Identity then serves, in a shift of the image, as a window through which we perceive reality in our own terms. The mirror-window is the ego's original "frame of reference."[40]

Psychoanalysis provides theory; Shakespeare provides dramatic and linguistic enactments of theory. *Hamlet* remains the central text. "The purpose of playing," Hamlet asserts,

> both at the first and now, was and is, to hold as 'twere the mirror up to nature: to show virtue her feature, scorn her own image, and the very age and body of the time his form and pressure.   (3.2.20–24)

Although these lines are sometimes quoted to emphasize the social frame of Shakespearean drama, they are equally possessed by the personal. Hamlet's parents haunt his phrases: his "most seeming virtuous" mother, now scorned, and the aged body of his father who comes in questionable form to pressure his son. After looking in the dramatic mirror he constructs

("The play's the thing"), he assaults his mother with a metaphoric mirror in which she sees her maculate soul. Ultimately he stares into the mirror-face of his last image, Yorick, the jesting death's head that he orders to his lady's chamber.

Both we and Shakespeare are like Hamlet. The plays are the mirror in which we find reflected images of ourselves, and they are the ground on which Shakespeare saw his own multiple identity dramatically represented. Shakespeare inhabited a reality that could be made to order according to the blueprints of imagination. He could stage a scene, act in it, watch it, criticize it, change it. In him the "participating" and "observing" egos were co-creating partners. By projecting self-representations onto a re-flecting stage peopled by shadows, Shakespeare could see his own face.

Recall Cassius's question to Brutus, "Can you see your face?" Brutus answers that he cannot, "for the eye sees not itself / But by reflection, by some other things." Cassius then offers to mirror Brutus to himself: "I, your glass, / Will modestly discover to yourself / That of yourself which you yet know not of" (*Julius Caesar* 1.2.51–70). The moment is well-known and prefigures the more extended analysis of mirroring in *Troilus and Cressida*, Act Three, Scene Three, which I want now to revisit.[41]

> *Achilles.*   What are you reading?
> *Ulysses.*   A strange fellow here
> Writes me that man, how dearly ever parted,
> How much in having, or without or in,
> Cannot make boast to have that which he hath,
> Nor feels not what he owes, but by reflection;
> As when his virtues, aiming upon others,
> Heat them, and they retort that heat again
> To the first giver.
> *Achilles.*   This is not strange, Ulysses.
> The beauty that is borne here in the face
> The bearer knows not, but commends itself
> To others' eyes; nor doth the eye itself,
> That most pure spirit of sense, behold itself,
> Not going from itself; but eye to eye opposed,
> Salutes each other with each other's form;
> For speculation turns not to itself,
> Till it hath travell'd and is mirror'd there
> Where it may see itself. This is not strange at all.

Ulysses.   I do not strain at the position—
It is familiar—but at the author's drift,
Who in his circumstance expressly proves
That no man is the lord of any thing,
Though in and of him there be much consisting,
Till he communicate his parts to others;
Nor doth he of himself know them for aught,
Till he behold them formed in th' applause
Where th' are extended; who like an arch reverb'rate
The voice again, or like a gate of steel,
Fronting the sun, receives and renders back
His figure and his heat. I was much rapt in this.
                          (*Troilus and Cressida*   3.3.95–123)

Typically vivid and various, Shakespeare's language appeals to our senses of sight ("face," "eye"), sound ("applause"), and touch ("heat"). Its metaphors use imagery from Renaissance science: chemistry, optics, acoustics.[42] It puns, playfully and significantly ("eye," "part," "borne," "sun"). Gradually the speech makes manifest what was structurally latent from the start, the analogy to theater and self-exhibition. It makes us think not only about the philosophical and ethical issue of virtue showing itself in order to know itself through external validation but about Ulysses's motives in instructing Achilles in his duty by subtly appealing to his pride. The language makes us follow it, through a syntax that mirrors sense. Achilles's narcissistic reply consists of links of echoed terms, so that the speech proceeds by repetition and reverberation—a rhetorical self-reflection. Achilles, who clearly and simply understands both Renaissance ocular physics and the unnamed author's philosophical point, finds his understanding just slightly shifted by Ulysses—exactly as Achilles's repeated "It is not *strange*" is slightly shifted by Ulysses's reply, "I do not *strain*." Ulysses echoes Achilles with a devious difference, the art of mimicry in the service of politics. Whoever the author is, Ulysses reflects his argument, turning its "drift" into the channel of his own intention. He does not *identify* the author, but he does identify *with* him. Reading is an eye ("I") reflecting on a text. We are all rapt in it. Shakespeare here provides a visual and tangible image of what I have been discussing in abstract, idealized terms. He sets up a mirror for all to see, though it takes close reading and visualization of the passage to see it. The text reflects its meaning when energized by the mimetic power of what Henry James called "our interpretive heat, which adds the last beauty" to the "unwinking and inscrutable" face of serene authorial divinity.[43]

The moment demonstrates salient points of psychoanalytic theories of theatrical performance as narcissistic, exhibitionistic, and relational. An actor—or a modern person acting—is an eye gazing in a mirror, or a man extending his parts before an other, or someone seeking mutual correspondence. Shakespeare's language at several points suggests phallic and coital senses: "man, how dearly ever parted"; "man, . . . his parts"; "formed in th' applause / Where th' are extended"; "gate of steel"; "his figure and his heat." At the level of character, Ulysses cleverly appeals to Achilles's virility—as in, "Come on, man, show your stuff!" The speech rests on a subliminal equation: acting is a species of (phallic) exhibitionism.[44] The dramatic moment is intensely suggestive, verifying Henry James's assertion that Shakespeare possessed "the most potent aptitude for vivid reflection ever lodged in a human frame."[45]

No less suggestive is the teasing question of the identity of that "strange fellow" whose text Ulysses reads. It is very tempting to identify him as Shakespeare. Perhaps Ulysses is reading *Julius Caesar*—there was evidently no Quarto, but there must have been a script lying around at the Globe. He might be reading the Sonnets, another particularly apt text, or even *Troilus and Cressida*, the most apt (and textually problematic). Of course he could be reading his own speech.

In this speculative and imaginative identification, Shakespeare becomes the unnamed author of the text-within-the-text, the ghostly authority who expressly proves whatever case we construct from him. The effects of the author's pen—his poetic quill—are translated, through actor's voice or reader's representation, into a speculative understanding of original intent. Such mirroring is recursive. Shakespeare presents Ulysses reading a text by Shakespeare, in a scene where an actor recites a script written by Shakespeare while pretending to read a book by an unknown "strange fellow" who is simultaneously Shakespeare, the real author who designed the scene, and not Shakespeare. For the book is probably only a prop, mere blank pages, the perfect medium for projection—unless the actor playing Ulysses is having trouble with his lines, in which case the prop book is a real one, inscribing the actual text of Ulysses's speech.

Speculation lies at the core of both the dramatic and the interpretive scene. For one of the central lines of the quoted passage is textually corrupt. The line, "Till it hath *travell'd* and is *mirror'd*," is in both Quarto and Folio (the only authentic texts) actually thus: "Till it hath *trauail'd* and is *married*." Modern editorial conjecture has emended reasonably, but changing "travail'd" to "travell'd" dilutes the energy of the line by literally extracting the *work* from it (and the associations of *labor* as in pregnancy), and translating "married" into "mirror'd" loses in erotic intimacy what it gains in ocular accuracy.

Travailed or traveled? Married or mirrored? Which is the real Shakespeare? How can we ever know? What is a reader or editor to do? Such permutative possibilities in Shakespearean meanings are all too frequent. How can we establish an authoritative text when the words themselves won't stay still? Stability can be established temporarily, through "definitive" editions, but the unruly vitality of Shakespeare's text should (one can only hope) outlast all attempts to tame it.

Epilogue: Yorick's Skull, Miranda's Memory

Yorick's Skull

Gravedigger.   Here's a skull now hath lien you i' th' earth three and twenty years.
Hamlet.   Whose was it?
Gravedigger.   A whoreson mad fellow's it was. Whose do you think it was?
Hamlet.   Nay, I know not.
Gravedigger.   A pestilence on him for a mad rogue! 'a poured a flagon of Rhenish on my head once. This same skull, sir, was, sir, Yorick's skull, the King's jester.   [*Takes the skull*].
Hamlet.   This?
Gravedigger.   E'en that.
Hamlet.   Alas, poor Yorick! I knew him, Horatio, a fellow of infinite jest, of most excellent fancy. He hath bore me on his back a thousand times, and now how abhorr'd in my imagination it is! my gorge rises at it. Here hung those lips that I have kiss'd I know not how oft. Where be your gibes now, your gambols, your songs, your flashes of merriment, that were wont to set the table on a roar? Not one now to mock your own grinning— quite chop-fall'n. Now get you to my lady's chamber and tell her, let her paint an inch thick, to this favor she must come; make her laugh at that.   (5.1.173–95)

Perhaps the most famous image among all cultural representations of Shakespeare is the figure of Hamlet gazing at a skull and delivering these lines. The moment deserves a psychoanalytic question. Not *qui parle?* but to whom does he speak? Addressing this question will unfold multiple layers of past, present, and future, re-animating the gravid gestures of memory inherent in this profound and emblematic scene.

First, Hamlet is speaking to Horatio about one Yorick, or about his memory of the man. His reminiscence reveals a momentary glimpse of an entirely new character—the happy young prince at play, carried by a madcap courtly jester. Momentarily we visit a time and place before this dank, rotten, contaminated Denmark, when play was real and joy was genuine. It is, for an instant, a palpable nostalgia. If we project an imaginary childhood for Hamlet (as Shakespeare does here), we might see Yorick entertaining the boy during his father's absences (say, at war). The poison of loss is so potent, however, that this brief moment of innocent play is ruined by a super-sensitivity to what Lear called the "smell of mortality" (4.6.133) and an abhorrent imagination that transmutes the living playmate into a decayed corpse. The substitute figure (the living Yorick) suddenly collapses into the real one (the dead father). The symbol figuratively and literally decomposes.

Yorick was the king's jester as well as the prince's colleague in horseplay. As such, he presumably had a ready repertoire of jokes, games, taunts, and wordplay, protected by the custom of tolerating the fool even when he satirized the court. He was uniquely licensed to jest and censure. Hamlet assumes a similar role when he dons his antic disposition, and it seems plausible to imagine that many of his own clever devices as the new, unlicensed court jester derive from his experiences with Yorick.[1] Yorick may therefore be an original model for Hamlet's impersonation in the first half of the play. Furthermore, the terms in which Hamlet recalls him, as a fellow of infinite jest and excellent fancy, echo his speech to Rosencrantz and Guildenstern about the piece of work that is man, infinite in faculties and admirable in form, but who is ultimately, like Yorick, a "quintessence of dust" (2.2.303-8).

Both as idealized playmate and decayed corpse, Yorick takes his place in the sad parade of symbolic fathers that populate the play: the Ghost of King Hamlet, King Fortinbras, Old Norway, Claudius, Polonius, Priam, the Player King.[2] The skull provides yet another occasion for Hamlet to encounter a paternal representative, "seek[ing his] noble father in the dust," as Gertrude termed it (1.2.71). Yorick thus becomes a final recuperation of the Ghost, a last appearance of that figure returned from the grave who can now be re-interred, put to rest, silenced. Here then is the definitive re-incarnation of the Ghost—the spirit made flesh, or bone. Whereas the earlier Ghost was a displaced ventriloquism of Hamlet's unconscious wishes and fears ("O my prophetic soul! my uncle?" [1.5.40-41]), the skull is a mute emblem to whom and for whom Hamlet speaks.

Yorick is yet more. When Hamlet orders the recalled jester "to [his] lady's chamber" to mirror her final figuration, his language shifts from a description of the clown to a description of woman, whose cosmetic surface hides a contaminated source. ("I have heard of your paintings well enough," he tells Ophelia. "You jig and amble, and you lisp . . ." [3.1.141–44].) The figure of the painted woman also reflects Hamlet's own disguises and hypocrisies, when his exterior costume or expression concealed his interior thoughts, feelings, or designs. As the visage of the skull shifts toward an image of a woman's face, the sensual language of kissing and disgust may be pressed toward another register of ambivalent eroticism, recalling previous debased images of Ophelia and Gertrude.[3]

The echoes are made more mordant by the irony that Hamlet, as he speaks these lines, is standing next to Ophelia's newly made grave. As ambassador of mortality, Yorick does not have to travel far to attain the lady's chamber. Hamlet says more than he knows, means more than he says. Further, the sexual symbolism of the open grave of the woman, within which her rivals dispute their rights to love and mourn, merely dramatizes what the language portends. For the graveyard is the ultimate version of the female garden gone to seed; the final locus mirrors the earlier one.[4]

Yorick's skull is also another kind of mirror—a conventional *memento mori*, like many kept on the nightstands or writing desks of those philosophically inclined in Shakespeare's audience.[5] The skull is the ultimate mirror up to nature, which Hamlet now holds partly as jest (in his relation to the gravedigger and Horatio), partly as theater (in his exhibition to the audience), and partly in a dawning realization that this dusty object also mirrors himself. To this favor he too will come. The skull is the primordial mask that cannot be removed (nor indeed put on), the most profound natural make-up: an eschatological cosmetic that hides nothing and reveals all. *Res ipsa*, one is tempted to say, *das Ding*: "unaccommodated man" stripped to the bone, the king now truly a thing of nothing.[6] The skull is an emblem of ultimate *infancy* (speechlessness), the face beyond expression, verbal or gestural, "sans teeth, sans eyes, sans taste, sans every thing," as Jaques, Hamlet's comic cousin in melancholy, darkly predicts (*As You Like It*, 2.7.166).

Yorick is thus a multifaceted, multidimensional mirror of memory and projection, something like a time machine with a transferential trajectory, that transports Hamlet through several temporal layers, "looking before and after" (4.4.37), so that he revisits the past—his childhood, the original loss of his father, his own antic disposition, the Ghost and other iterations of the father, his distorted images of Ophelia and Gertrude—and then envisions the future, his lady dead, and his own death, initially imagined abstractly and conventionally through the *memento mori*, but gradually understood as specific, local, and impending: in the next scene he will declare his readiness for death (5.2.222). His retrospective look through specular, familiar masks becomes a preview of the end of the line, personal and political.[7] Finally, in addressing Yorick's skull Hamlet is talking to himself. This scene of morbid self-reflection is a partial soliloquy on which we eavesdrop. It is a moment of early-modern psychoanalytic meditation.

Yorick—or Yorick's skull—is a palpable pun, a highly overdetermined locus of intersecting figures and significances. As a tangible piece of that mortality toward which the tragedy of *Hamlet* inexorably proceeds, the skull embodies what seems an ultimate ground—the absolutism of the grave. Individual identities may be questionable, but in the end we are all the same, dust to stop a bung-hole (5.1.202–04). Yet precisely this egalitarian anonymity of the graveyard undoes the specific interpretations Hamlet and we have so carefully produced around the emblem of the skull.

Return to the beginning. The gravedigger disinters a skull, shows it to Hamlet, and asks him whose it was. He cannot say, of course. How could he? How could anyone, including the gravedigger? What he has uncovered is a skull like any skull, whose identity can only be conferred by the stories he tells about it. The privilege of the living is to fashion tales of the dead (see, for instance, Hamlet's last request of Horatio), and it is a likely perquisite of gravediggers to repopulate their morbid landscape with a society of acquaintances whose stories they recall and recount. As I read the scene, the gravedigger takes a skull at random from the general population and re-animates it with affection and respect. He takes dust and makes it Caesar before he returns it to dust. The "character" of "Yorick" is thus a temporary construction of apparently individual identity out of a random, arbitrary, featureless object.[8] The scene demonstrates the narrative production of character out of accidental material, not as soliloquy only but with social validation (the gravedigger specifically identifies Yorick, and Horatio listens to the tale). "Yorick" is thus what *remains*, as corporeal disintegration and as narrative surplus. It is a character, certainly, and it is also a text to be read, by Hamlet and by us, with all the revealing reconstructions of self and other that reading permits and requires.

"Here's fine revolution," as Hamlet remarks about the final progress of professions in the graveyard, "and we had the trick to see't. Did these bones cost no more the breeding, but to play at loggats with 'em? Mine ache to think on't" (5.1.90–92).[9] In this ultimate playground (the final stage) individual distinctions of profession or character collapse into the similitude and anonymity of dust—if we have the trick, or critical perspective, to see the mystery. As Hamlet tosses about bones and quips, he is simultaneously playing with others' pasts and his own future. He is bones at play (an animated skeleton) playing with bones.

Such a sudden and severe gesture toward the liminal boundary between life and death veers close to the morbid wit of Beckett, but without Beckett's grim, deadpan nihilism. Hamlet's final stage is not the desolate wasteland of the global graveyard in *Endgame*, where another Hamlet abbreviated in name and body (the paraplegic Hamm) marks time and occupies space by obsessive and futile moves, waiting for the end. There is vitality as well as melancholy in Shakespeare's keen distillation of the game of life—a *jouissance*, even. Hamlet's aching bones even evoke more than the quick metaphysical wit of Donne. The language gestures toward an empathic identification with every anonymous skeleton even as it emphasizes the individual, narcissistic insult that the particular character feels. Perhaps here we find the deepest core of Hamlet's inarticulate "that within": a merger of mind and body, affect and articulation, that instills itself in the marrow of his being. It does not show, it aches—but with pain or desire? [10]

Yorick's skull is an *embodied figure*—primarily of the father and his filial reflections. It is a tangible artifact of paternal absence, accessible to physical apprehension. For another style of imaginative apprehension, let us move from the figure of the father as external object to the image of the mother as internal object.

Miranda's Memory

Remember me.

(*Hamlet*, 1.5.91)

What seest thou else
In the dark backward and abysm of time?
(*The Tempest*, 1.2.49–50)

The two moments are similar: a father challenges the memory of his child. The Ghost's charge to his son is a command, while the magus interrogates his daughter. Both moments are efforts at patriarchal inculcation. King Hamlet's charge of paternal remembrance serves to displace another insistent memory from the Prince's mind, that of his mother, Gertrude, whose perfidies obsess her son. "Leave *her* to heaven," orders the Ghost (1.5.86); "remember *me*." Prospero's inquiry follows immediately upon Miranda's hazy recollections of maternal nurturance. In effect his question repeats with a difference the Ghost's command: "Remember *me*?"

Pros.   Canst thou remember
A time before we came unto this cell?
I do not think thou canst, for then thou wast not
Out three years old.
Mir. Certainly, sir, I can.
Pros.   By what? by any other house or person?
Of any thing the image tell me, that
Hath kept with thy remembrance.
Mir. 'Tis far off,
And rather like a dream than an assurance
That my remembrance warrants. Had I not
Four or five women once that tended on me?
Pros.   Thou hadst, and more, Miranda. But how is it
That this lives in thy mind? What seest thou else
In the dark backward and abysm of time?
If thou remembrest aught ere thou cam'st here,
How thou cam'st here thou mayst.
Mir. But that I do not.
Pros.   Twelve year since, Miranda, twelve year since,
Thy father was the Duke of Milan, and
A prince of power.
Mir. Sir, are not you my father?
Pros.   Thy mother was a piece of virtue, and
She said thou wast my daughter; and thy father
Was Duke of Milan; and his only heir
And princess; no worse issued.   (1.2.38–59)

The play of language in these lines is broad and deep. It can initially be approached through the functional fiction of character. As I imagine him, Prospero is strangely defensive in this exchange with his daughter. First he asks her a question, then suggests that she cannot answer it. When

Miranda says that she certainly can, he sharply interrogates her: "By what? by any other house or person?" Can someone else have been tampering with her memory before he has chosen to invoke and instruct it?

Miranda dimly recalls a matrix of four or five women, but no father. "But why," Prospero in effect asks, "do you remember *this*? What about *me*?" His project is evidently to inscribe a powerful paternal presence within the palace of memory, displacing any pre-existent maternal images.[11] This effort occurs *before* the oblique and questionable reference to Miranda's mother as "a piece of virtue"—an allusion that glances at those dark suspicions of infidelity that haunt such tragedies as *Hamlet, Lear*, and *Othello*. Paternal anxieties are suggested by the repetition of "twelve years," the displaced, third-person identification ("Thy father was the Duke, and a prince of power") and Miranda's curious question ("Are not you my father?").

This dual wish of paternal inscription and maternal displacement is the background against which to explore the deep relations of *Hamlet* and *The Tempest* as two styles of drama in the "revenge play" type: tragedy and romance. Although their genres differ, both plays are structurally revenge dramas; they recall a past in order to re-create an initial crime and thereby avenge it. They thus dramatize *styles of memory*, re-mindings of the past as aesthetically reconstructed narratives of original traumata.[12] Both plays aim to restore an illicitly seized position in the family and in the court. Both are tales of fraternal usurpation and maternal ambiguity or betrayal. In each, an extended narrative by a father provides the rationale and sets the stage for the enactment of revenge. The Ghost's story violently opens Hamlet's ears; Prospero's history is a tale that, Miranda notes, "would cure deafness" (1.2.106).

Both moments of paternal-filial narration dramatize memory as a tale told to a single auditor (Hamlet, Miranda) and later elaborated as a play shown to an audience (the Mousetrap, the Masque). There are important differences, of course. In *Hamlet*, the filial auditor is to be disturbed by horror, anger, and vengeful obsession ("Pity me *not*," says the Ghost). In *The Tempest*, the auditor is to be moved by pity for the paternal narrator as well as indignation against his wicked brother. When Prospero continues his story of usurpation and expulsion, a pitiful tale of a wronged father and a crying child thrown from their home in the dark of night, Miranda responds: "Alack, for pity! / I, not remembering how I cried out then, / Will cry it o'er again" (1.2.132–34).

In brief, the revenge scheme of *The Tempest* is both abreactive and therapeutic. It awakens past griefs in order to express and eventually exorcise them; it is repetition in the service of "working through."[13] *Hamlet* seeks to arouse the past in order to repeat it in raw retaliation, to make its agent "the slave to memory" (3.2.188); its revenge scheme is traumatic.[14] In the revenge romance of *The Tempest*, Prospero works through fantastic enactments of vengeance—such as the shipwreck, the apparent deaths of Alonso and Ferdinand, the raid of the Harpies, the attack of dogs in the antimasque—to the "rarer action" of virtuous forgiveness. Whereas the play begins with stormy division and fragmentation, as the nautical fraternity dissolves into snarling selfishness, the dramatic catastrophe presents a crystallized choreography of reparations and closure. The idealized goal of art in *The Tempest* is to work through anger and grief, subduing passion just as the music of the island soothes Ferdinand's traumatic sense of loss:

> Sitting on a bank,
> Weeping again the King my father's wrack,
> This music crept by me upon the waters,
> Allaying both their fury and my passion
> With its sweet air.   (1.2.390–94)

Ariel's ensuing song, "Full fadom five thy father lies," further translates grief into re-creation, effectively re-membering the lost father: "those are pearls that were his eyes" (1.2.399). Again, memorial representation is in the service of magical restorations of paternal images. But if father lies at fathom five, are there other images at deeper depths, in the "abysm of time?"

Vestiges of the occluded or submerged mother can be glimpsed in almost every reference to the past in the play. For instance, there is the larger context of that famous phrase, "What's past is prologue." This sentiment, frequently privileged as a citation of Shakespeare's wisdom about history, is voiced by the villain of the piece, Antonio, as he tries to persuade Sebastian to seize the occasion of Ferdinand's death to advance their own careers through regicide. His logical point is that the heir apparent to Naples, Claribel, is absent and cannot interfere, and his references to her are charged with exaggeration, but the lines resonate well beyond the character's immediate rhetorical purpose:

> *Ant.*   Will you grant with me
> That Ferdinand is drown'd?

Seb.   He's gone.
Ant.   Then tell me,
Who's the next heir of Naples?
Seb.   Claribel.
Ant.   She that is Queen of Tunis; she that dwells
Ten leagues beyond man's life; she that from Naples
Can have no note, unless the sun were post—
The man i' th' moon's too slow—till new-born chins
Be rough and razorable; she that from whom
We were all sea-swallow'd, though some cast again,
And that by destiny, to perform an act
Whereof what's past is prologue; what to come,
In yours and my discharge.   (2.1.243–54)

The passage collocates time and space, distance and duration—and especially the progress of a man ("till new-born chins be rough and razorable")—within an image of powerful feminine agency. A submerged maternal metaphor powers this passage; it encloses and "casts" masculine action, in terms that are simultaneously bodily and theatrical: "seaswallowed" to be "cast . . . by destiny to perform an act." A primitive image of incorporation and (re)birth underlies, as ground, those stages of intention on which such men as Antonio and Prospero will act; the word "discharge" points to both masculine performance and maternal issue, as well as to a final release. This collocation of time, fate, and femininity echoes Prospero's earlier language of "the dark backward and abysm of time," when he anxiously seeks to *recover* Miranda's memory of maternal care, both in the sense of disclosing it and glossing it over.

This evocative phrase, "the dark backward and abysm of time," is one of the richest examples of the deep play of language that permeates *The Tempest*. The senses, sounds, and shapes of the phrase press its words to their limits and beyond. Unlike Hamlet's appeal to human intellection and discursive history ("such large discourse, / Looking before and after" [4.4.36–37]), the phrase evinces dream as much as memory, as Miranda says. Imagined developmentally, the primitive space of darkness and absence precedes any awareness of time, subjective experience, or conscious articulation. Not only does the phrase's meaning gesture toward ideas of limitless origin and temporal and spatial vacancy, the sounds themselves echo uncannily. The vowels and consonants of "dark" are recursively repeated in "backward"; the alliterative "d"s and "b"s ride the current of the "a" sound, keeping the mouth open to mime those most primitive of proto-words (*"da," "ba," "ma"*), until the vowel shifts to "i" (first short, then long) and the mouth closes on the sounds of "m," while the voice, now silent, becomes a soft exhalation of breath.[15] The phrase figuratively, literally, and physically represents language in a process of regression, moving back through the symbolic register to the edge of the imaginary. In its effort to articulate the primary ground of memory, language itself offers to disintegrate into aboriginal components of articulation: mere phonemes, vowels, labials, dentals—the sentence as sounddance.[16]

Shakespeare's phrase gestures toward a preverbal dawn of consciousness at the deepest limits of human memory, when language as music was indeed the food of love.[17] It is one instance of a style Barthes evokes in his description of the full pleasure of the text, the *jouissance* of phonetic aspects of literature: "the pulsional incidents, the language lined with flesh, a text where we can hear the grain of the throat, the patina of consonants, the voluptuousness of vowels, a whole carnal stereophony: the articulation of the body, of the tongue, not that of meaning, of language."[18]

Kristeva's idea of the semiotic *chora* is pertinent here. She takes the term from Plato's creation myth, *The Timaeus*, where it alludes to place, space, or an amorphous container that pre-exists objects or language; in a note she calls it "a mother and wet nurse."[19] She relates the idea to prelinguistic psychological structures: "The *chora* is a modality of significance in which the linguistic sign is not yet articulated as the absence of an object and as the distinction between real and symbolic." "The mother's body is therefore what mediates the symbolic law organizing social relations and becomes the ordering principle of the semiotic *chora*." She then cites Mallarmé, "*Le mystère dans les lettres*," as a poet who gestures toward this primitive preverbal place: "Indifferent to language, enigmatic and feminine, this space underlying the written is rhythmic, unfettered, irreducible to its intelligible verbal translation; it is musical, anterior to judgement, but restrained by a single guarantee: syntax."[20] Reading Shakespeare's phrase ("dark backward and abysm of time"), our intellectual senses rely on syntax, symbolism, and thought, while our emotional and physical senses engage prelinguistic, semiotic registers of experience.

Skull and *memory*: container and contained, external form and internal matter. Both are sites: psychological, anatomical, architectural, and conceptual spaces that hold and produce recollected narratives. "This distracted globe"; "my lady's chamber"; "the undiscover'd country"—mind, womb, and death. Because they can be read, they are types of texts, whose explication is reflexive: both gate and mirror. They are also types of memorials, and metaphorically types of theater: abysses that show. Both objects push the limits of language. The skull presses toward termination, while memory reaches toward origin. Together they can frame the field of Shakespeare's play of language. A provisional table of Shakespearean elements may be useful; meet it is I set it down.

SKULL	*MEMORY*
father	mother
corpus delicti	*pia mater*
Narcissus	Echo
external object	internal object
command	wish
revenge	restoration
termination	continuity
grave	womb
dust	earth
mask	face
line	circle
mirror	gate
stage	ground
character	text
patron	muse
oedipal	pre-oedipal
subject	self
lack	absence
gap	space
alienation	relation
Lacan	Winnicott

As detailed in Chapter Seven and my conceptual effort to delineate various qualities of Shakespeare's "Nothing," the artifice of articulated distinctions in this table produces an implosive pressure: these elements want to recombine. The splittings in Shakespeare's art operate separately and divisively, but they also interrelate and eventually cohere. They fuse together (con-fuse); they *cleave*. "Two houses, both alike in dignity"; "two distincts, division none"; "a natural perspective, that is and is not."[21] Perhaps criticism is the art of making distinctions to produce a more coherent confusion.

Notes

Prologue. "Cordelia's Skirt"

1. Sigmund Freud, "Recommendations to Physicians Practicing Psycho-Analysis" (1911), *The Standard Edition of the Complete Psychological Works of Sigmund Freud*, ed. James Strachey, 24 vols. (London: Hogarth Press, 1966–74), 12, 109–20. Meredith Skura, in *The Literary Use of the Psychoanalytic Process* (New Haven, Conn.: Yale University Press, 1981) quotes Phyllis Greenacre on the analyst's "polymorphous perceptiveness." Describing psychoanalysis as "a new way of *reading*," Shoshana Felman writes that its practice is an interpretation of "the *excess*" in a subject's discourse, and that the unconscious is not only that which is read but also that which reads: see "Renewing the Practice of Reading, or Freud's Unprecedented Lesson" in *Jacques Lacan and the Adventure of Insight: Psychoanalysis in Contemporary Culture* (Cambridge, Mass.: Harvard University Press, 1987), pp. 19–25. The best way to perceive and practice psychoanalytic criticism is as a process of imaginatively interpreting linguistic experience and not as a procedure of formulaic application of a set of theories to a literary work. The former is like self-conscious play, while the latter can be like an autopsy.

2. See my essay, "Freud and the Interpenetration of Dreams," *Diacritics* 9 (1979), 98–110.

3. For a description of this unique educational experience, see Norman N. Holland and Murray M. Schwartz, "The Delphi Seminar," *College English* 36 (1975), 789–800.

4. *Mon ami français*, Robert Silhol, shared this Gallic wisdom. The most popular source of the idea is Roland Barthes, who described a text not as a site from which meaning is transmitted from author to reader, but as a site of possibilities, "a multi-dimensional space in which a variety of writings, none of them original, blend and clash": see "From Work to Text," and "The Death of the Author" in *Image-Music-Text*, trans. Stephen Heath (New York: Hill and Wang, 1977), pp. 155–64; pp. 142–47; p. 146. Following Barthes and other theorists like Fish and Iser, Harry Berger sensibly suggests, "Suppose we construe *text* not as a thing but as a function: *text* is the value we give to whatever we treat as an object of interpretation, and subject to the fate of reading": see "Bodies and Texts," *Representations* 17 (1987), 144–66; p. 150.

Berger's suggestion addresses the question from the perspective of *reception*. The question of the Shakespearean text is made more complex by the reciprocal question of *production*. E. A. J. Honigmann, in *The Stability of Shakespeare's*

Text (Lincoln: University of Nebraska Press, 1965), and Gerald Eades Bentley, in *The Profession of the Dramatist in Shakespeare's Time, 1590–1642* (Princeton, N.J.: Princeton University Press, 1971), provide substantial scholarship on this question. Honigmann consistently refers to Shakespeare as author of various drafts of the plays and explicitly warns against a current tendency to replace authorial with "printing-house practices," thereby substituting one kind of overconfidence for another (p. 6). He usually puts "textual instability" in quotation marks, and the final gesture in the book proper is toward the ultimate value of the texts as Shakespeare's own "reading" (p. 171). Bentley notes that Shakespeare wrote exclusively for the Lord Chamberlain's Men (later the King's Men) from the early 1590s to his retirement. While it was common for plays that survived into print to be revised, often under orders of the company, the agent of revisions would likely be that person most qualified to perform them: the author. Since Shakespeare was the exclusive author, as well as company shareholder, he was by clear inference the revisor: see pp. 261–63 for Bentley's sketch of customary practices of ownership and publication of plays. A powerful argument about the collaborative nature of artistic production is presented by Stephen Greenblatt in "The Circulation of Social Energy" in *Shakespearean Negotiations: The Circulation of Social Energy in Renaissance England* (Berkeley: University of California Press, 1988), pp. 1–20. I accept ninety percent of Greenblatt's ideas, subscribe to his Seven Abjurations of Principle, and prefer contingency over totalization anytime. His notion of "institutional improvisation" neither banishes the author nor marginalizes him, but places him within a community whose social energies inform the work he produces. My project is to "read" that "work," conceptualized as a "text," and always available to "performance," imagined or actual.

5. The event was in March 1979. I again thank Meredith Skura and Coppélia Kahn for inviting me to make the NEMLA presentation.

6. An amplified version of this paper was published in *Representing Shakespeare: New Psychoanalytic Essays*, ed. Murray M. Schwartz and Coppélia Kahn (Baltimore: Johns Hopkins University Press, 1980), pp. 244–63. Slightly modified, it now manifests itself as Chapter Seven of this book.

7. Some versions of resistance persist. In his *William Shakespeare* (Oxford: Blackwell, 1986), Terry Eagleton refers to my published essay. In a footnote (p. 107) he discusses the possibility that the meaning of "no thing" *might* be allowable, but that in no case are we to think that when asked for her response to her father's "What can you say?" Cordelia replies "Female genitals, my lord." Right: she doesn't say that. But the language does, or more precisely, the language puts the crucial term into play for resonance later with more specific bodily meanings (for those with ears to hear).

8. See A. C. Bradley, *Shakespearean Tragedy* (London: St. Martin's, 1904), pp. 321–24. Knight describes his "Principles of Shakespearean Interpretation" in *The Wheel of Fire: Interpretations of Shakespearean Tragedy* (London: Methuen, 1930), pp. 1–16. He argues for the pre-eminence of imaginative "interpretation" over judgmental "criticism," posits a poetic spatial dimension beyond temporal narrative so that each play can be read as "an expanded metaphor," rejects the notion

of character as too linked to intention and ethics, and asserts that the dramatic function of the plays is irrelevant to their secrets.

In an essay that reviews his own famous contribution to the question ("How Many Children Had Lady Macbeth?"), L. C. Knights begins with an illustrative juxtaposition of Bradley and Knight: see "The Question of Character in Shakespeare," *Further Explorations* (Stanford, Ca.: Stanford University Press, 1965), pp. 186–204. Knights provides a brisk history of the issue since Maurice Morgann and Samuel Johnson, notes the hazard of focusing on individual characters at the expense of "the structure of ideas" in the plays, and commends G. Wilson Knight's holistic approach to their imaginative logic.

9. See Henry George Liddell and Robert Scott, *A Greek-English Lexicon*, revised and augmented by Henry S. Jones (Oxford: Clarendon Press, 1968), s.v.

10. The only other Shakespearean occurrence of the term "poetical" is in *Twelfth Night*, 1.5.194–96, where it is immediately followed by the same judgment, that it is "feign'd." Shakespeare's evident attitude toward the term "poet" is at best ambiguous: see for example his famous yoking of "the lunatic, the lover, and the poet" in *A Midsummer Night's Dream* (5.1.7). When I use the term, I intend to return it to its roots and rescue it from such an ambiguous attitude, even if it is Shakespeare's.

11. The tangle of conscious and unconscious motivations represented in "the will" is well described in the philosophy of Arthur Schopenhauer and the psychology of Sigmund Freud. Schopenhauer's privilegings of irrational impulse and unconscious psychic structure prefigure Freud's more systematic subordinations of rationality. Freud's most direct reference to Schopenhauer is in a remark about the theory of repression, which he considered original until Otto Rank showed him a passage in *The World as Will and Idea* (1819). See "On the History of the Psycho-Analytic Movement" (1914), *Standard Edition* 14, 15–16; also *An Autobiographical Study* (1925), *Standard Edition*, 20, 59–60. At one point Freud writes that Schopenhauer's "unconscious 'Will' is equivalent to the mental instincts of psychoanalysis": see "A Difficulty in the Path of Psycho-Analytic Treatment" (1917), *Standard Edition*, 17, 143–44. Freud's most succinct discussions of the relation between will and wish, and conscious *vs.* unconscious intention, are in *Totem and Taboo* (1913), Standard Edition, 13, 84–85 (where he quotes *Hamlet*), and "A Difficulty in the Path of Psycho-Analysis," pp. 141–44 (where he cites Schopenhauer).

12. The OED extensively maps the lexical field. A more efficient gloss can be obtained in C. T. Onions, *A Shakespeare Glossary*, 2nd ed. (Oxford: Clarendon Press, 1953), and Eric Partridge, *Shakespeare's Bawdy: A Literary and Psychological Essay and a Comprehensive Glossary*, rev. ed. (London: Routledge and Kegan Paul, 1968). In his entry on "will," Partridge avers that "in Shakespeare, the nexus between the sexual act and literary creation is closer, more potent, more subtly psychosomatic than in any other writer" (p. 219).

13. Coleridge's analysis of this speech to show "the passionless character of Iago" is hence only part of the story. "It is all will in intellect," Coleridge noted, "and therefore he is here a bold partisan of a truth, but yet of a truth converted into a falsehood by the absence of all the necessary modifications caused by the frail

nature of man" (*Notes on Shakespeare*, quoted in *A New Variorum Edition*, ed. H. H. Furness [New York: Lippincott, 1886], p. 82).

14. The word "corrigible" first means "corrective," but the term has both active and passive senses, and Shakespeare's only other usage applies it passively (when Mark Antony tries to persuade Eros to kill him so he can escape the fate of submissive display in Rome, "bending down / His corrigible neck" to victorious Caesar [*Antony and Cleopatra*, 4.13.72–77]).

15. Further attention to the play of language in these lines might develop the ideas of the eradication of time ("tine" is a modern editorial emendation of Q_1 and F_1 "Time," which should mean "thyme" except that such an herb doesn't need weeding out) and the distraction of genders—themes crucial to *Othello*.

16. About writing, Freud noted that "unluckily, an author's creative power does not always obey his will: the work proceeds as it can, and often presents itself to the author as something independent or even alien." See "Moses and Monotheism" (1939), *Standard Edition*, 23, 104. See also his *Introductory Lectures on Psycho-Analysis* (1915–17), 16, 379. Ben Jonson's famous complaint about his fellow poet reveals his ideas about Shakespeare's unruly art: "His wit was in his own power; would the rule of it had been so too." See *Timber: or Discoveries* (c. 1630); quoted in F. E. Halliday, *Shakespeare and His Critics* (New York: Schocken, 1958), p. 50.

17. The modern juridical custom of swearing on a text (the Bible) is a displacement and sublimation of a more primitive gesture of assurance by testicular oath (grasping the testicles) as a sign of veracity and a symbolic indication of what was at risk in the case of false testimony. See Joseph Shipley, *The Origins of English Words: A Discursive Dictionary of Indo-European Roots* (Baltimore: Johns Hopkins University Press, 1984), *s.v.* "tre."

18. See "A Constant Will to Publish: Shakespeare's Dead Hand," in *Will Power: Essays on Shakespearean Authority* (Detroit: Wayne State University Press, 1993), pp. 184–237. Willson describes Jacobean society as one "where the will was becoming what etymology implies—a symbolic phallus for the impotent testator" (p. 196).

19. See E. K. Chambers, *William Shakespeare: A Study of Facts and Problems*, 2 vols. (Oxford: Clarendon Press, 1930), 1, 504–6.

20. See Derrida's description of the anxious interrelation of "center" and "freeplay" as aspects of "structure," in his critique of Lévi-Strauss: "Structure, Sign, and Play in the Discourse of the Human Sciences," in *The Structuralist Controversy: The Languages of Criticism and the Sciences of Man*, ed. Richard Macksey and Eugenio Donato (Baltimore: Johns Hopkins University Press, 1970), pp. 247–65. For an excellent introduction to the ideas and practices of play in society and language, especially as theorized by Nietzsche, Heidegger, Gadamer, and Derrida, see James Hans, *The Play of the World* (Amherst: University of Massachusetts Press, 1981). Hans wants to retain much of the deconstructionist theory of freeplay, but he also wants to recuperate agency and intention as fundamental human attributes that direct language even as they are directed by it. Like "free association," the freeplay of language is not absolutely free. It is bounded on one side by personal desire and on another by social communication. Although Hans

does not make the connection, his description of play as "an activity that points to the fundamental activity of man, the back-and-forth movement of encounter and exchange with the world . . . out of which understanding comes" (p. x) is closely related to Winnicott's psychoanalytic theory of play as described in "Playing: A Theoretical Statement," in *Playing and Reality* (London: Tavistock, 1971), pp. 38–52.

21. My uses of psychoanalytic theory as presented by Freud, Lacan, and Winnicott will recur throughout the book. For an excellent overview of contemporary theories of play and the early psychological development of the self, as modeled in the Renaissance, see Anna Nardo, *The Ludic Self in Seventeenth-Century English Literature* (Albany: SUNY Press, 1991). She also offers valuable speculations about the wider cultural contexts of the idea of "play" in the early modern period: see "Play and Historical Process," pp. 35–40. As well as psychological works, I have benefitted from several historical and theoretical works. An early source is Anne Righter's *Shakespeare and the Idea of the Play* (London: Chatto and Windus, 1964); see especially the sections on "Play or Illusion" (pp. 57–63) and "The Play Metaphor" (pp. 64–86) for her remarks on the gradual creation of a theatrical play-space as bounded illusion, separate from reality and to a degree self-contained. A more substantial source is Robert Weimann's masterful study of the cultural history of play as produced and transmitted by ritual, games, folk-plays, mysteries, and moralities, in *Shakespeare and the Popular Tradition in the Theater: Studies in the Social Dimension of Dramatic Form and Function*, ed. Robert Schwartz (Baltimore: Johns Hopkins University Press, 1978). For a careful exploration of those aspects of early modern pedagogy and poetics that presented different sides to questions and took pleasure in paradoxes and rhetorical elaborations of disputed principles, see Joel Altman, *The Tudor Play of Mind: Rhetorical Inquiry and the Development of Elizabethan Drama* (Berkeley: University of California Press, 1978). For a lively exploration of what it meant to be a player in Shakespeare's time, see Meredith Skura, *Shakespeare the Actor and the Purposes of Playing* (Chicago: University of Chicago Press, 1993).

22. "No object is in a constant relationship with pleasure (Lacan, apropos of Sade). For the writer, however, this object exists: it is not the language, it is the *mother tongue*. The writer is someone who plays with the mother's body . . . : in order to glorify it, to embellish it, or in order to dismember it, to take it to the limit of what can be known about the body: I would go so far as to take bliss (*jouissance*) in a *disfiguration* of the language." See *The Pleasure of the Text*, trans. Richard Miller (New York: Hill and Wang, 1975), p. 37.

23. The most recent and thorough demonstration of Shakespeare's anxious relation to the maternal body is by Janet Adelman, in *Suffocating Mothers: Fantasies of Maternal Origin in Shakespeare's Plays*, Hamlet *to* The Tempest (New York: Routledge, 1992). Katherine Eisaman Maus, not a psychoanalytic critic, examines the conventional tropes of the analogy between literary creation and procreation in "A Womb of His Own: Male Renaissance Poets and the Female Body," in *Inwardness and Theater in the English Renaissance* (Chicago: University of Chicago Press, 1995), pp. 182–209; see especially pp. 182–98.

Introduction. *"Hamlet's Inky Cloak"*

1. Except where otherwise noted, quotations from Shakespeare are from *The Riverside Shakespeare*, ed. G. Blakemore Evans et al. (Boston: Houghton Mifflin, 1974).

2. *Par exemple*, Jacques Lacan, who comments on the French translation of "id" into "ça" in "The Freudian Thing, or the Meaning of the Return to Freud in Psychoanalysis" (1956), in *Écrits: A Selection*, trans. Alan Sheridan (New York: Norton, 1977), pp. 114–45; especially pp. 128–29 and 121–23. Ellie Ragland Sullivan writes that "in opposition to the *Cogito*, Lacan offers *Ça parle*—"It speaks"—that is, the unconscious subject (*Séminaire* XI, p. 45)": see *Jacques Lacan and the Philosophy of Psychoanalysis* (Urbana: University of Illinois Press, 1986), p. 12.

3. Precisely because the power of dramatic enactment is so seductive, I stress the literariness of Shakespeare. Let me add that I also enjoy stage productions, even mediocre ones, as well as critical books that proceed from positions opposed to mine, especially very good ones, like Michael Goldman's *Acting and Action in Shakespearean Tragedy* (Princeton, N.J.: Princeton University Press, 1985), a palpable demonstration of the value of enacted readings in imagining Shakespearean character. My argument is that an actor begins with *reading*, then shapes and refines that reading, enlarging some possibilities of the text while limiting others. (According to Robert Weimann, the Greek term *hypokrites* means "interpreter" as well as "answerer" [the second actor]. A related term is *exegetes*: see *Shakespeare and the Popular Tradition in the Theater: Studies in the Social Dimension of Dramatic Form and Function*, ed. Robert Schwartz (Baltimore: Johns Hopkins University Press, 1978), p. 2.) One can also extend the boundaries of "language" to include gesture, with the reminder that genuine "Shakespearean" gesture (i.e., a movement not described yet evidently mandated) can be hard to tease out of the text. David Bevington's *Action Is Eloquence: The Language of Gesture in Shakespeare* (Cambridge, Mass.: Harvard University Press, 1984) extensively considers the dramaturgical components of costume, stage directions, properties, gestures, and spatial arrangements. As much as his book is about nonverbal elements, however, it is also about Shakespeare's vivid verbal descriptions of gesture (such as Ophelia's description of the distracted Hamlet).

4. The OED cites 1532 as its first instance of both terms, *denotation* and *connotation*.

5. For a specific interpretation of Hamlet as an effect of writing, see Daniel Sibony, "*Hamlet*: A Writing-Effect," *Yale French Studies* 55–56 (1977), 53–93. The most extensive scholarly and theoretical elaboration of this post-structuralist approach is by Jonathan Goldberg, "Hamlet's Hand," *Shakespeare Quarterly* 39 (1988), 307–27.

6. I borrow this particular example from Harold Fisch, "Character as Linguistic Sign," *New Literary History* 21 (1990), 593–94. For a specific essay on "reading" the female body in *Measure for Measure*, including Juliet's, Isabella's, and Mistress Elbow's, see Mario DiGangi, "Pleasure and Danger: Measuring Female Sexuality in *Measure for Measure*," *ELH* [English Literary History] 60 (1993), 589–609.

7. For a daring critique of this traditional "stage versus page" debate, see Harry Berger, *Imaginary Audition: Shakespeare on Stage and Page* (Berkeley: University of California Press, 1989), especially pp. 9–42, on "slit-eyed analysis" and "wide-eyed playgoing." In his critique of what he terms the "New Histrionicism," Berger challenges the claim that the authentic Shakespeare lies in dramatic enactments of the plays and develops a distinction between "stage-centered" and "text-centered" styles of reading.

8. Another layer of meaning here alludes to the maculate sheath of "too, too sullied flesh," the skin of fallen, sinful man. Hamlet alludes to it when he forces Gertrude to turn her eyes into her soul, where she sees "such black and grained spots / As will not leave their tinct" (3.4.89–91). See Ned Lukacher, *Primal Scenes: Literature, Philosophy, Psychoanalysis* (Ithaca, N.Y.: Cornell University Press, 1986), pp. 218–220; and Janet Adelman, "Man and Wife Is One Flesh: *Hamlet* and the Confrontation with the Maternal Body," in *Suffocating Mothers: Fantasies of Maternal Origin in Shakespeare's Plays*, Hamlet *to* The Tempest (New York: Routledge, 1992), pp. 11–37. One of the fascinating aspects of melancholia is its simultaneous status as an affected style (especially popular in the Renaissance) and an affective disease. It wholly blurs the line between seeming and being. For an excellent study of the cultural meanings of melancholy in the early modern and modern periods, see Juliana Schiesari, *The Gendering of Melancholy: Feminism, Psychoanalysis, and the Symbolics of Loss in Renaissance Literature* (Ithaca, N.Y.: Cornell University Press, 1992).

9. In his wonderful book on *The Properties of* Othello (Amherst: University of Massachusetts Press, 1989), James Calderwood studies similarities between Iago's unseen flag and Desdemona's all-too-visible handkerchief.

10. Several essays have explored the rich symbolic potentials of the handkerchief. Two of the best are by Lynda Boose, "Othello's Handkerchief: 'The Recognizance and Pledge of Love,'" *English Literary Renaissance* 5 (1975), 360–74, and Peter Rudnytsky, "The Purloined Handkerchief in *Othello*," in *The Psychoanalytic Study of Literature*, ed. Joseph Reppen and Maurice Charney (Hillsdale, N.J.: Analytic Press, 1985). For a thorough review of symbolic interpretations of this object, see Adelman, *Suffocating Mothers*, pp. 67–71.

11. In *Reading Shakespeare's Characters: Rhetoric, Ethics, and Identity* (Amherst: University of Massachusetts Press, 1992), Christy Desmet reviews Iago's pernicious effects on Othello's language and syntax. Describing the Moor as defined by the figure of hyperbole, she notes that "Iago's characteristic figure is *meiosis* [reduction]": see pp. 97–98. James Calderwood, in *The Properties of* Othello, describes Iago's negative "gravitational field" that ruins true knowledge, turning "know" into "no": see pp. 130–31. See also Madeleine Doran's chapter on "Iago's *If*—Conditional and Subjunctive in *Othello*," in *Shakespeare's Dramatic Language* (Madison: University of Wisconsin Press, 1976), pp. 63–91.

12. The same anecdote is reported by Meredith Skura in *The Literary Use of the Psychoanalytic Process* (New Haven, Conn.: Yale University Press, 1981), p. 260. While it is surely possible that identical wit occurred to different students in different locations, it's also possible that I told others of my experience.

13. See D. W. Winnicott, *Playing and Reality* (London: Tavistock, 1970).

This little book, actually a collection of brief essays on psychoanalytic theory and clinical practice, is a remarkable resource of thinking about the relation of imaginative to social experience. It presents a quintessential object-relations aesthetic.

14. I do not consider myself a theorist. Theoretical approaches to the question of the limits of criticism are best studied elsewhere: for instance in E. D. Hirsch's classic *Validity in Interpretation* (Charlottesville: University of Virginia Press, 1975), Paul Ricoeur's "Metaphor and the Main Problem of Hermeneutics," *New Literary History* 6 (1974), 95–110, or Umberto Eco's *The Limits of Interpretation* (Bloomington: Indiana University Press, 1991), which is less concerned with enforcement than with discovery. When I think of theory I think of Freud, who liked to quote Charcot's adage: "*La théorie, c'est bon, mais ça n'empêche pas d'exister*" ("Theory's good, but that doesn't prevent things from existing" [like critical readings]). Shoshana Felman writes that "the practice, the partially unconscious, analytic reading practice, always inescapably precedes the theory": see *Jacques Lacan and the Adventure of Insight: Psychoanalysis in Contemporary Culture* (Cambridge, Mass.: Harvard University Press, 1987), p. 24. Lacan is quoted as saying: "Interpretation is not open to all meanings. It is not just any interpretation. It is a *significant* interpretation, one that must not be missed." See "From Interpretation to the Transference," in *The Four Fundamental Concepts of Psycho-Analysis*, ed. Jacques-Alain Miller (New York: Norton, 1978), p. 250.

15. On the expanded linguistic resources available to early modern English, see Helge Kökeritz, *Shakespeare's Pronunciation* (New Haven, Conn.: Yale University Press, 1953), p. 54. For a basic introduction to the changing language of Elizabethan England—its expanding vocabulary, flexible structures, rhetorical devices and literary styles, with hundreds of examples from Shakespeare and his contemporaries—see S. S. Hussey, *The Literary Language of Shakespeare* (Essex: Longman, 1982). For a social view of the expanding energies in Elizabethan language and culture available to Shakespeare's genius, see Robert Weimann, "Metaphor and Historical Criticism: Shakespeare's Imagery Revisited," in *Structure and Society in Literary History: Studies in the History and Theory of Historical Criticism* (Charlottesville: University of Virginia Press, 1976), pp. 227–33. Weimann wisely notes the dependence of new styles of expression on existing traditional modes of understanding. On some plausible psychological effects of this interaction of plenitude and tradition, see William Kerrigan, "The Articulation of the Ego in the English Renaissance," in Joseph Smith, ed., *The Literary Freud: Mechanisms of Defense and the Poetic Will*, Psychiatry and the Humanities, vol. 4 (New Haven, Conn.: Yale University Press, 1980), pp. 261–308.

16. "Joyce's Agon with Shakespeare" in *The Western Canon: The Books and School of the Ages* (New York: Harcourt Brace, 1994), pp. 428, 429.

17. *The Western Canon*, p. 431.

18. Or as Lacan wrote it, "*Joyce le sinthome*"—using an archaic spelling to pun on Saint Thomas, the patron of doubt. See Ellie Ragland-Sullivan, "Lacan's Seminars on James Joyce: Writing as Symptom and 'Singular Solution,'" in *Compromise Formations: Current Directions in Psychoanalytic Criticism*, ed. Vera Camden (Kent, Ohio: Kent State University Press, 1989), pp. 61–85, p. 65.

19. For a brilliant analysis of the production of a new style of literary subjec-

tivity in Shakespeare, see Joel Fineman, *Shakespeare's Perjured Eye: The Invention of Poetic Subjectivity in the Sonnets* (Berkeley: University of California Press, 1986).

20. Stanley Cavell, "Macbeth Appalled," *Raritan* 12 (1992–93), 1, 1–15; 2, 1–15; 1, 15.

21. An intermediate position is suggested by Howard Felperin, who comments on the status and site of Shakespeare's language: "By foregrounding the fallen nature of human speech and backgrounding any divine or redemptive 'reality' to which it refers, Shakespeare dramatizes, in linguistic terms, the condition of secularity within which we all, wittingly or not, inescapably dwell; language being, in Heidegger's phrase, the house we live in." See " 'Tongue-Tied Our Queen?' Deconstruction of Presence in *The Winter's Tale*," *Shakespeare and the Question of Theory*, ed. Patricia Parker and Geoffrey Hartman (New York: Methuen, 1985), pp. 3–18; 16. Felperin's essay is reprinted as Chapter Three in his book, *The Uses of the Canon: Elizabethan Literature and Contemporary Theory* (Oxford: Clarendon Press, 1990), pp. 35–55.

22. "He is inconceivably wise. . . . He is strong, as nature is strong. . . ." "Shakespeare, or The Poet," *Representative Men: Seven Lectures* (1850), *Ralph Waldo Emerson: Essays and Lectures*, ed. Joel Porte (New York: Library of America, 1983), pp. 710–26; 722. This Emersonian apotheosis is continued most grandly by Harold Bloom in "Shakespeare, Center of the Canon" in *The Western Canon*, pp. 45–75.

23. For a critical review of some of these appropriations, see Michael Bristol, *Shakespeare's America, America's Shakespeare* (London: Routledge, 1990). For details on Barnum's plan, see Stephen Booth, "Shakespeare at Valley Forge: The International Shakespeare Association Congress, 1976," *Shakespeare Quarterly* 27 (1976), 231–42. For an informative and entertaining history of the fortunes of Shakespeare in America, see Lawrence Levine, *Highbrow/Lowbrow: The Emergence of Cultural Hierarchy in America* (Cambridge, Mass.: Harvard University Press, 1988), pp. 13–81. Levine's book describes multiple vigorous appropriations of Shakespeare throughout nineteenth- and twentieth-century America, from melodrama to Yiddish theater to advertising to cartoons. Reading this book, along with Michael Bristol's *Shakespeare's America, America's Shakespeare* (London: Routledge, 1990) and Gary Taylor's *Reinventing Shakespeare: A Cultural History from the Restoration to the Present* (New York: Oxford University Press, 1989), promotes conviction that Shakespeare will survive anything, from commercialism to criticism.

24. See Urkowitz, *Shakespeare's Revision of King Lear* (Berkeley: University of California Press, 1980). Foster's claim for Shakespeare as the "W.S." who authored "A Funeral Elegy for Master William Peter" (London, 1612) was originally published as *"Elegy by W.S.": A Study in Attribution* (Newark: University of Delaware Press, 1989). Foster repeats the claim, using computerized reading strategies, in *"A Funeral Elegy*: W[illiam] S[hakespeare]'s 'Best-Speaking Witnesses,' " *PMLA* III (1996), 1080–1105. Wanamaker's *New Globe* project, begun in 1987 after many years of fund raising, is almost complete. A preliminary season is scheduled for late 1996; the official Grand Opening is planned for 1999, the four-hundredth anniversary of the opening of the original. For the latest information on the project, visit its official World Wide Web site: *http://www.globe.jhe.net*, or

www.rdg.ac.uk.AcaDepts/In/Globe/home.html, the home page maintained at the University of Reading. Graham Holderness interviewed Sam Wanamaker in *The Shakespeare Myth* (Manchester: Manchester University Press, 1988), pp. 16–23. Wanamaker was not the least interested in Bardolatry, but in making the plays accessible to working-class audiences, as in Shakespeare's day. He comes across as a knowledgeable, sensitive, canny, passionate advocate of many aspects of "Shakespeare."

25. *The Letters of Ralph Waldo Emerson*, ed. Ralph Rusk (New York: Columbia University Press, 1939), vol. 4, p. 149. Quoted in Marjorie Garber, *Shakespeare's Ghost Writers* (New York: Methuen, 1987), p. 8.

26. "*Telmah*," in *That Shakespeherian Rag* (London: Methuen, 1986), pp. 92–119; also in Parker and Hartman, *Shakespeare and the Question of Theory*, pp. 310–32.

27. William Carlos Williams, *Spring and All* (1923), in *Imaginations*, ed. Webster Schott (New York: New Directions, 1970), pp. 149–50. It would be wonderful if Williams's American meditation on the liberation of language sprang from his reading of Gaunt's deathbed evocation of the past glories of England ("This royal throne of kings . . . "), but it is more likely that he was thinking of Gaunt's advice to the banished Bullingbrook to reconstruct his deprivation as imagined pleasure (*Richard II*, 1.3.277–309).

Chapter One. *"Limitations of Character, Limits of Language"*

1. "Of course you can't get away from the term ['character']," writes L.C. Knights. It is an inescapable figure for readers and audience alike: see "The Question of Character in Shakespeare," *Further Explorations* (Stanford, Ca.: Stanford University Press, 1965), pp. 186–204, p.193. Knights' essay is a sterling example of the difficulties of trying to take a critical position amid the quandary of treating characters as consistent persons or as mutable poetic figures. He concludes by appealing to each respondent's unconscious reaction to the plays (pp. 203–4).

2. An excellent history of the development of dramatic character and the apparently self-conscious hero in early modern drama remains David Bevington's *From* Mankind *to Marlowe: Growth of Structure in the Popular Drama of Tudor England* (Cambridge, Mass.: Harvard University Press, 1962); Robert Weimann also provides a valuable survey in *Shakespeare and the Popular Tradition in the Theater: Studies in the Social Dimension of Dramatic Form and Function*, ed. Robert Schwartz (Baltimore: Johns Hopkins University Press, 1978), pp. 196–207. For a useful sketch of shifts in critical emphases from Augustan interest in plot to Johnsonian emphasis on character, developed through the Romantics and A.C. Bradley, see Patrick Murray, "The Idea of Character in Shakespeare," in *That Shakespearian Scene: Some Twentieth-Century Perspectives* (London: Longmans, 1969) pp. 1–53.

3. *Artificial Persons: The Formation of Character in the Tragedies of Shakespeare* (Columbia: University of South Carolina Press, 1974).

4. See *Artificial Persons*, pp. 8–21, and especially the chapter on "The Motions of Men," pp. 22–66, which also provides a good review of Renaissance ideas on the "will" and "affections" (pp. 32–38). Although respectful of early modern concepts and conventions, Barroll's approach also assumes the applicability of Freudian theories. His comments about Bradley are on p. 249.

5. "The Character of 'Character,'" *New Literary History* 5 (1974), 384–402.

6. For an introduction to postmodern concepts of character, tracing the term to its origins in physical inscription, see Harold Fisch, "Character as Linguistic Sign," *New Literary History* 21 (1990), 593–94. Fisch notes that for all its psychological applications, the idea still belongs "essentially to *écriture*, to a linguistic ordering of reality" (p. 593). Following the traditions of Renaissance categories, such as Joseph Hall's *Characterisms of Virtues and Vices* (1608), he sensibly suggests that even psychological notions of character derive from rhetorical constructions of persons. Cynthia Marshall develops and deepens this argument (using Freud, Barthes, and Kristeva) in an essay on the "semiotics of character" that suggests the construction of character through an audience's empathic epistemology of response to physical signs and spoken words: see "Portia's Wound, Calphurnia's Dream: Reading Character in *Julius Caesar*," *English Literary Renaissance* 24 (1994), 471–88. For an account of character by an expert in theater that answers to many of Cixous's desires, see Herbert Blau, *Take Up the Bodies: Theater at the Vanishing Point* (Urbana: University of Illinois Press, 1982), pp. 276–82.

7. *A New Mimesis: Shakespeare and the Representation of Reality* (London: Methuen, 1983). For Auden's thesis, see *The Dyer's Hand and Other Essays* (New York: Random House, 1948).

8. *A New Mimesis*, p. 100. For Nuttall's consanguinity with Morgann, see pp. 163–77.

9. *The Subject of Tragedy: Identity and Difference in Renaissance Drama* (London: Methuen, 1985).

10. *Subject of Tragedy*, pp. 33–42, 52. This always alienated subject is the focus of a companion book, Francis Barker's *The Tremulous Private Body: Essays on Subjection* (London: Methuen, 1984), to which I will refer later.

11. Princeton, N.J.: Princeton University Press, 1989.

12. *Shakespeare—The Theater and the Book*, p. x.

13. *Shakespeare—The Theater and the Book*, pp. 128–30.

14. See Desmet, *Reading Shakespeare's Characters: Rhetoric, Ethics, and Identity* (Amherst: University of Massachusetts Press, 1992), especially Chapter Two, "Characterizing Shakespeare's Readers: Falstaff and the Motives of Character Criticism," pp. 35–58; States, *Hamlet and the Concept of Character* (Ithaca, N.Y.: Cornell University Press, 1992); and Kerrigan, "*Hamlet* in History: A Brief Polemical Guide from the Romantics to the Theorists" in *Hamlet's Perfection* (Baltimore: Johns Hopkins University Press, 1994), pp. 1–33, p. 31.

15. For Freud's first published remarks about Hamlet and the Oedipus complex, see *The Interpretation of Dreams* (1900), *Standard Edition*, 4, 264–66. Bloom's idealization of Hamlet can be found throughout *The Western Canon: The Books and School of the Ages* (New York: Harcourt Brace, 1994), for example on page 73.

16. *The "Inward" Language: Sonnets of Wyatt, Sidney, Shakespeare, and Donne* (Chicago: University of Chicago Press, 1983), p. 7.

17. See pp. 29–30, and Chapter One, "The 'Inward' Language," pp. 31–70.

18. See *The "Inward" Language*, pp. 61–62. Ferry quotes Hamlet's "Seems, madam?" speech, but only to note its conventional vocabulary, metaphor, and conceits. If Hamlet is a new kind of character, evidently his novelty is not revealed at this point.

19. See *The Tremulous Private Body*, pp. 34–40.

20. See *Inwardness and Theater in the English Renaissance* (Chicago: University of Chicago Press, 1995).

21. See *Inwardness and Theater*, pp. 3–9, 19–21, 26–34. From another, post-Lacanian perspective, Juliana Schiesari criticizes Barker and Terry Eagleton for idealizing Hamlet as a (masculine) "postmodern hero," ignoring the debased feminine significance of the "lack" they posit: see *The Gendering of Melancholia: Feminism, Psychoanalysis, and the Symbolics of Loss in Renaissance Literature* (Ithaca, N.Y.: Cornell University Press, 1992), pp. 236–43.

22. *Shakespeare's Perjured Eye: The Invention of Poetic Subjectivity in the Sonnets* (Berkeley: University of California Press, 1986).

23. It is in the Sonnets that Shakespeare's self-reflexive and recursive linguistic play is most distilled and sustained, and seems most obvious. Among the multitude of studies on those poems, the following—besides Fineman's brilliant book—are pertinent to my assumptions about the play of language: Kirby Farrell, *Shakespeare's Creation: The Language of Magic and Play* (Amherst: University of Massachusetts Press, 1975), esp. Part One, pp. 3–66; Stephen Booth, *An Essay on Shakespeare's Sonnets* (New Haven, Conn.: Yale University Press, 1970); and the fascinating endnotes to Booth's edition of *The Sonnets* (New Haven, Conn.: Yale University Press, 1977), which provide perhaps the best single source to the intricacies and multiplicities of Shakespeare's language.

24. *Shakespeare's Perjured Eye*, p 25, p. 29.

25. *Shakespeare's Perjured Eye*, p. 81.

26. See "Mimesis in *Hamlet*," in *Shakespeare and the Question of Theory*, ed. Patricia Parker and Geoffrey Hartman (New York: Methuen, 1985), pp. 275–91. In *Shakespeare and the Popular Tradition*, Weimann reads Hamlet's "Seems" speech as a paradoxical announcement of the mimetic and antimimetic aspects of his character: see pp. 232–33.

27. By calling attention, in the "Seems" speech, to his costume and pose as stylized and inadequate artificial representations of an authentic inner state, Hamlet insists on being seen both as surface and depth. His aggressive reflection and deflection of questions (Gertrude's, our own) snap him into focus at the place of "theatricality" and the Lacanian "gaze" as described by Barbara Freedman in *Staging the Gaze: Postmodernism, Psychoanalysis, and Shakespearean Comedy* (Ithaca, N.Y.: Cornell University Press, 1991); see especially pp. 1–6. See also Stanley Cavell, "Hamlet's Burden of Proof," in *Disowning Knowledge in Six Plays of Shakespeare* (Cambridge: Cambridge University Press, 1987), especially pp. 187–88 on self-conscious display as "debarment" from humanity; and André Green, "Les miroirs

du théâtre," *Hamlet et* Hamlet: *Une interprétation psychanalytique de la représentation* (Paris: Balland, 1982), pp. 201–6.

28. *The Subject of Tragedy*, pp. 41–2. Quoting the "Seems" speech, Belsey cites Barker on merely "gestural" interiority: "Hamlet cannot be fully present to himself or to the audience in his own speeches and *this* is the heart of his mystery, his interiority, his essence" (p. 50). In short, his essence is his absence.

29. This is the most obvious and powerful psychological mode of understanding Hamlet's gesture toward an inarticulate interior. Among the many recent critics who characterize the function of mourning in the character and in the play, see Jacques Lacan, "Desire and the Interpretation of Desire in *Hamlet*," *Yale French Studies*, 55–56 (1977), 11–51; Richard Wheeler, *Shakespeare's Development and the Problem Comedies* (Berkeley: University of California Press, 1981), pp. 193–200; Green, *Hamlet et* Hamlet, pp. 58–61; Stanley Cavell, "Hamlet's Burden of Proof," pp. 185–86; Marjorie Garber, *Shakespeare's Ghost Writers: Literature as Uncanny Causality* (New York: Methuen, 1987), p. 149; and Julia Lupton and Kenneth Reinhard, *After Oedipus: Shakespeare and Psychoanalysis* (Ithaca, N.Y.: Cornell University Press, 1993), pp. 11–33.

30. See *Shakespeare and the Popular Voice* (Cambridge: Blackwell, 1989), pp. 93–119.

31. *Shakespeare's Perjured Eye*, p. 185.

32. A good review of traditional conceptions is provided by Margreta de Grazia, in "Shakespeare's View of Language: An Historical Perspective," *Shakespeare Quarterly* 29 (1978), 374–88. She argues that Shakespeare accepted the common sixteenth-century view of "Babel-Pentecost history," "that language is competent if the speaker's will is correct." By the seventeenth century, however, "linguistic pessimism" abounds; she cites Bacon, Browne, Descartes, Locke, and Hobbes. Similarly, Marion Trousdale states that "poetic language to the Elizabethan was always a conscious language and its origin and intent a rational one": see *Shakespeare and the Rhetoricians* (Chapel Hill: University of North Carolina Press, 1982), p. 81. Theory and training regularly reinforced the artifices of rhetorical elaboration, as Joel Altman demonstrates in *The Tudor Play of Mind: Rhetorical Inquiry and the Development of Elizabethan Drama* (Berkeley: University of California Press, 1978). Yet while this rational emphasis is true to a degree, the issue is not so simple. Even that most rational of Elizabethan rhetoricians, Francis Bacon, recognized the propensity of language to evade and elide stable referential meaning. For example, in his criticism of the "Idols of the Marketplace"—or the contaminated cultural commerce of language—he instanced the term "humid" and its tendency to dissipate, leak, or otherwise osmose into multiple tangential areas of related significance: see *The New Organon, Part II, Francis Bacon: A Selection of His Works*, ed. Sidney Warhaft (London: Macmillan, 1965), pp. 342–43. Trousdale explores the interplay of two rhetorical "structures" in language and criticism of language: the structure we find "in" the (historical) language, and the (critical) structure we bring "to" it that enables and configures what we find: see pp. 3–7. He calls the first structure "style" and the latter "meaning" (p. 155). From the perspective of either structure, "modes of composition entail modes of perception" (p. 13).

A less historical approach is offered by Keir Elam in *Shakespeare's Universe of Discourse: Language-Games in the Comedies* (Cambridge: Cambridge University Press, 1984). He distinguishes among three categories: *discourse* (language in use), *language* (the general tongue), and *speech* (oral delivery). These are useful and timely distinctions, except that Shakespeare did not exactly make them. For instance, see Hamlet's reference to the uniquely human "large discourse / Looking before and after" (4.4.36–37)—where "discourse" means a god-given capability of historical awareness and articulation (also the "discourse of reason" [1.2.150])—or the "excellent dumb discourse" of dancing spirits in *The Tempest* (3.3.39), or the "madness of discourse" that bifurcates Troilus's vision of his love (5.2.142). Such usages at least threaten the neatness of Elam's distinctions, or suggest that some twentieth-century linguistic categories may be awkward artifices to capture the vitality of Shakespeare's language. One difference between our approaches is instructive. When Elam quotes a passage, his typical move is to translate toward discursive sense (in other words), noting language-games and speech-acts. By contrast, my typical interpretive gesture turns back into the language, focusing on specific words and metaphors. Elam's project is to achieve ever-more-precise taxonomies of verbal utterances, at the expense of the specific values of words. His is a performative approach to language, not (like mine) a hermeneutic one. M.M. Mahood makes a remark about Sister Miriam Joseph's exhaustive study of Shakespeare's use of rhetorical figures that is pertinent here: "Naming the parts does not show us what makes the gun go off." See *Shakespeare's Wordplay* (London: Methuen, 1957), p. 51; Joseph's book is *Rhetoric in Shakespeare's Time: Literary Theory of Renaissance Europe* (1947; New York: Harbinger, 1962).

33. London: Cambridge University Press, 1935.

34. Another key early work in the field is Wolfgang Clemen's *Shakespeares Bilder* (1936), revised and published in English as *The Development of Shakespeare's Imagery* (Cambridge, Mass.: Harvard University Press, 1951).

35. *Shakespeare's Imagination: A Study in the Psychology of Association and Inspiration* (London: Lindsay Drummond, 1946).

36. For instance, he praises "the ability of a genius to stir our feelings to vibrate in harmony with his by making available for our appreciation relationships hitherto only dimly apprehended which satisfy profound and universal emotional demands": see *Shakespeare's Imagination*, pp. 130–41, p. 141.

37. *Shakespeare's Dramatic Language* (Madison: University of Wisconsin Press, 1976).

38. See *Shakespeare's Dramatic Language*, p. 28, p. 32.

39. *The Shakespearean Metaphor: Studies in Language and Form* (Totowa, N.J.: Rowman and Littlefield, 1978).

40. See "Metaphor and Historical Criticism: Shakespeare's Imagery Revisited" in *Structure and Society in Literary History: Studies in the History and Theory of Historical Criticism* (Charlottesville: University of Virginia Press, 1976), pp. 188–233.

41. "Metaphor and Historical Criticism," pp. 196–203. Weimann mentions G. Wilson Knight in this connection.

42. "Metaphor and Historical Criticism," p. 194.

43. "Metaphor and Historical Criticism," pp. 215–17. Tuve's book is *Elizabethan and Metaphysical Imagery: Renaissance Poetic and Twentieth-Century Critics* (Chicago: University of Chicago Press, 1947).

44. *The Interpretation of Language*, 2 vols. (New York: Jason Aronson, 1973). The concept of "language" in psychoanalytic theory is vast and difficult. Readers interested in pursuing the question might profitably begin with Marshall Edelson, *Language and Interpretation in Psychoanalysis* (Chicago: University of Chicago, 1975); John Forrester, *Language and the Origins of Psychoanalysis* (New York: Columbia University Press, 1980); Hans Loewald, "Primary Process, Secondary Process, and Language" in *Papers on Psychoanalysis* (New Haven, Conn.: Yale University Press, 1980), pp. 178–206; and Robert Rogers, *Metaphor: A Psychoanalytic View* (Berkeley: University of California Press, 1978.) For Lacan's modifications, see Anthony Wilden's translation and commentary on "The Rome Discourse" in *The Language of the Self: The Function of Language in Psychoanalysis* (Baltimore: Johns Hopkins University Press, 1968); and Jacques-Alain Miller, "Language: Much Ado About What?" in *Lacan and the Subject of Language*, ed. Ellie Ragland-Sullivan and Mark Bracher (New York: Routledge, 1991), pp. 21–35.

45. *The Interpretation of Language*, 1, 85–86.

46. *Shakespeare's Wordplay*, p. 30. In a footnote she cites Freud's *Jokes and Their Relation to the Unconscious*. Stephen Greenblatt makes a similar observation: "Dallying with words is the principal Shakespearean representation of erotic heat": see "Fiction and Friction" in *Shakespearean Negotiations: The Circulation of Social Energy in Renaissance England* (Berkeley: University of California Press, 1988), p. 90.

47. *Shakespeare's Wordplay*, pp. 174–75.

48. *Shakespeare's Wordplay*, p. 28. Mahood's caution is shared as well by another meticulous reader of Shakespeare's puns, Stephen Booth. See his extended notes to his edition of *The Sonnets* (1974), in which he consistently evokes then resists latent puns in Shakespeare's language. A much less resistant reader of sexual elements is William Carroll: see "The Virgin Not: Sexuality and Language in Shakespeare," *Shakespeare Survey* 46 (1994), 107–19.

49. Fineman writes: "There are always fewer words than meanings because, through the medium of 'translation' (etymologies, false homophones, cross-language cognates, etc.), any given word possesses, at least potentially, a plurality of significations. The 'world' 'slides,' therefore, because the equivocality of the 'word' undoes the univocality of the 'world'": *Shakespeare's Perjured Eye*, p. 348 n. 39. As Fineman knew, the terms "word" and "world" were homophones in Shakespeare's day.

50. Julia Lupton and Kenneth Reinhard begin their rigorously Lacanian critique of the interrelation of Shakespeare and psychoanalysis by quoting and then analyzing the "kin/kind" pun. See *After Oedipus*, pp. 1–3.

51. *Shakespearean Meanings* (Princeton, N.J.: Princeton University Press, 1968), pp. 24–25; quoted by Lawrence Danson in *Tragic Alphabet: Shakespeare's Drama of Language* (New Haven, Conn.: Yale University Press, 1974), p. 27 n. 2. Danson himself sees punning as a malady of language, a "sign of linguistic ill-health." For him, conflicted meanings in a character's speech indicate a conflict or

crisis as a stage on the way toward the "disintegration of language": see pp. 174–76. In an essay on "Shakespeare as 'Corrupter of Words,'" Michel Grivelet agrees: "Shakespeare's dramatic work has a dimension in which no comforting limits can be set to the deceptiveness of language. . . . Once let loose from reality, [words] run wild and proliferate in an unhealthy manner"—leading to a "potential delusion" and destructiveness inherent in Shakespeare's poetic power: see *Shakespeare Survey* 16 (1963), 70–76, 72. In the days before signifying chains were unlinked from "reality," precisely the opposite claim could be made: Kenneth Muir wrote in 1950 that puns in Shakespeare "seem to shoot out roots in all directions, so that the poetry is firmly based on reality" (quoted in Walter Redfern, *Puns* [Oxford: Blackwell, 1984], p. 47). Today such an observation about the efflorescence of multidirectional etymology would more likely base itself in the unstable semantic surplus of interlinked signifiers, and not in "firm reality." On the subversive nature of puns, see Jonathan Culler, "The Call of the Phoneme: Introduction" in *On Puns: The Foundation of Letters*, ed. Culler (Oxford: Blackwell, 1988), pp. 1–16. For a demonstration of puns as radically destabilizing language and referentiality in *Hamlet*, see Margaret Ferguson, "*Hamlet*: Letters and Spirits," in Parker and Hartman, eds., *Shakespeare and the Question of Theory*, pp. 275–91.

52. See *Shakespeare and the Popular Tradition*, pp. 135–37. Weimann reviews concepts of early modern wordplay and its re-situation in the context of theater: see pp. 133–51. In a note, he reluctantly remarks that "Freud's interpretation of wordplay is, no doubt, illuminating, and sometimes profoundly so: but how relevant is the psychological approach to a collective tradition antedating the rise of individualism?" (p. 283, n. 68). Although his own praise of Freud's profound illumination implicitly answers his question, a further response might be to note that *language* (not just customs of wordplay) is a collective tradition that precedes any individual speaker's entry into it (whether or not such a speaker is yet considered an "individual"), and that any psychoanalytic study of language (such as Freud's, Lacan's, or Thass-Thienemann's) is simultaneously a social anthropology and personal psychology of linguistic usage.

53. *Explorations in Shakespeare's Language: Some Problems of Word Meaning in the Dramatic Text* (London: Longman Group, 1962).

54. *Explorations in Shakespeare's Language*, pp. 21–29.

55. *The Dramatic Use of Bawdy in Shakespeare* (London: Longman Group, 1974), p. 9.

56. *Dramatic Use of Bawdy*, p. 164.

57. Booth, ed., *The Sonnets*, pp. 441–43.

58. Although more interested in linguistic structure than literary content, Roman Jakobson and Lawrence Jones briefly note the sexual punning in Sonnet 129: see *Shakespeare's Verbal Art in "Th' Expense of Spirit"* (Paris: Mouton, 1970), pp. 14–15.

For a conservative, moralistic reaction to "oversophisticated," merely "literary" readings, see N. F. Blake, *Shakespeare's Language: An Introduction* (London: Macmillan, 1983). A more philosophically and dramatically oriented effort to restrict Shakespearean meanings is developed by Harriet Hawkins in *The Devil's Party: Critical Counter-Interpretations of Shakespearean Drama* (Oxford: Clarendon Press, 1985). She follows "Sir Karl Popper's insistence" that interpretive claims should be falsifiable, otherwise they're not open to scrutiny and hence unworthy of belief. As reliable sources of falsifiability she offers three components: "the texts themselves," "audience responses over centuries," and "the facts of theatrical life" (pp. 128–29). Once examined, the clarity of these components blurs. First, to be blunt, there is no such thing as a text itself. Until animated by a reader (this includes actors) the words-on-the-page are mere marks. (This notion of the autonomous self-evident text will be addressed in Chapter Two.) Second, the measurement of "audience responses over centuries" would be a daunting task. I suppose what Hawkins means is the "typical" or "normal" response of any (normal) audience to a play when presented conventionally. People don't generally laugh when Lear banishes Cordelia. People don't generally hear the full range of meanings in Cordelia's fateful "Nothing," either. One function of Shakespeare criticism is precisely to articulate those meanings of the language that audiences or readers do not generally hear. Audience responses to individual characters, once charted, would be all over the map. As to "the facts of life" in the theater, I suppose she means that any linguistic sense that cannot be staged is illegitimate. She is especially harsh on sexualized readings of the text because they are "critical interpretations-by-free-association" and cannot be refuted, and because such insights cannot be staged (see pp. 139–40, n. 15). "Who cares," she asks, "what Shakespeare's lines actually say, if it's what you think (or what Freud may have thought) they might mean that counts?" She then remarkably suggests that censorship ("Bowdlerization") is preferable to the free licensing of sexual meanings, but then reconsiders her own impulse and opines that "the best way to discover the outer limits to legitimate interpretation is by examining specific instances" (pp. 121–23). With this latter statement I fully agree: see Chapter Three.

59. Harry Berger, *Imaginary Audition: Shakespeare on Stage and Page* (Berkeley: University of California Press, 1989), pp. 146–48. Although I fully agree with the conclusion, this example may not be the best. As a pun the syntax is awkward. For a similar instance, consider the regular recurrence of the word "broke" in Richard the Second's final soliloquy (5.5.42–66). For example: "How sour sweet music is / When time is broke, and no proportion kept!" Within a few lines, the exact word resounds three times, reinforced by its echo in Bullingbrook's name (also spelled "Bolingbroke") which Richard voices twice. There can be little question that the pun is intentional: a minor sonic instance of the larger political interruption. The question is whether intent is to be ascribed to the character, Richard, or to the poet, Shakespeare. Either choice is defensible, and making it can determine how the character of Richard is imagined and enacted. I will consider less evident puns in Chapter Three.

60. See Terence Hawkes, *Shakespeare's Talking Animals: Language and Drama in Society* (London: Edward Arnold, 1973), p. 3. Hawkes cites Muriel Bradbrook for an estimated literacy rate of thirty to fifty percent among men in Shakespeare's London. Citing the work of Walter Ong, he asserts that Shakespeare's audience had "an oral set of mind": see p. 49.

61. See *Shakespeare's Talking Animals*, pp. 24–26, 86. Writing in the early 1970s, Hawkes cites Marshall McLuhan on this point: see pp. 223 ff.

62. There are of course social and economic answers to this question, but it remains as well an issue of intellectual and emotional comprehension, at least as I experience it in my own teaching.

63. Milton is cited by Walter Raleigh (the twentieth-century figure); quoted in Terence Hawkes, *That Shakespeherian Rag: Essays on a Critical Process* (London: Methuen, 1986), p. 59. For Nietzsche's superior view, see "Human, All-Too-Human" (1878), *Complete Works*, ed. Oscar Levy, 18 vols. (New York: Russell and Russell, 1909–11), 6, 177. Lamb's remark is recorded in "The Tragedies of Shakespeare," *The Reflector* (1811); reprinted in D. Nicholl Smith, *Shakespeare Criticism: A Selection* (Oxford: Oxford University Press, 1944), pp. 230–40. The irony in Lamb's case is that his readings as reflected in his shallow retellings of major plays (with his wife, Mary) became a way for generations of children to learn about Shakespeare *without* having to read him.

64. *That Shakespeherian Rag*, pp. 76–77, 87.

65. See *Explorations in Shakespeare's Language*, pp. 124–25. M. R. Ridley, editor of the 1958 Arden edition of *Othello*, sees no reason to comment on the term at all. Partridge cites *2 Henry IV* and *Romeo and Juliet* (2.3.97–103) for "occupy" and *Measure for Measure* for "occupation." He adds that "perhaps, too, there is a prophetic relevancy" in Othello's usage: see Eric Partridge, *Shakespeare's Bawdy* (London: Routledge and Kegan Paul, 1968), p. 155.

66. Gurr's paper was not published, as far as I can tell. Recently several other Americans have elaborated Hulme's tiny point into fulcrums for major arguments about the interrelations of sexuality, militarism, and narration in the play: see Mark Rose, "Othello's Occupation: Shakespeare and the Romance of Chivalry," *English Literary Renaissance* 15 (1985), 293–311; Tom McBride, "Othello's Orotund Occupation," *Texas Studies in Literature and Language* 30 (1988), 412–30; and James Calderwood, *The Properties of Othello* (Amherst: University of Massachusetts Press, 1989), pp. 71–91.

Chapter Two. "Paranoia, Criticism, and Malvolio"

1. Released in 1971, the film was directed by Nicholas Meyer from his screenplay based on his novel.

2. Arthur Conan Doyle, *The Hound of the Baskervilles. The Complete Sherlock Holmes: The Long Stories* (London: John Murray, 1929), p. 401.

3. For an immensely broad-ranging essay on the interpretation of signs, marks, traces, and other evidence to produce the "semiotic" or "conjectural paradigm" that informs the work of art historians, detectives, and psychoanalysts in their uses of discrete pieces of evidence (clues) to construct generalizations and conclusions, see Carlo Ginzburg, "Morelli, Freud, and Sherlock Holmes: Clues and Scientific Method," trans. Anne Davin and Susanna Graham-Jones, *History Workshop* 9 (1980), 5–36.

4. Sigmund Freud, *Introductory Lectures on Psycho-Analysis* (1915–16). *Standard Edition* 15, 66–67.

5. See, for example, Paul Ricoeur, *Freud and Philosophy: An Essay on Interpretation*, trans. Denis Savage (New Haven, Conn.: Yale University Press, 1970), p. 32.

6. Freud, *Standard Edition*, 12, 3–84.

7. *Standard Edition*, 12, 83–84.

8. For Freud's remark about the similarity between paranoid delusions and philosophical systems, see his "Preface to Reik's *Ritual: Psycho-Analytic Studies*" (1919), *Standard Edition*, 17, 261. In one of his last papers, "Constructions in Analysis" (1937), Freud briefly pursued "the seduction of an analogy: The delusions of patients appear to me to be the equivalents of the constructions which we build up in the course of an analytic treatment": *Standard Edition*, 23, 257–69, 268. While some might cite this sentence to prove that psychoanalysis itself is delusory, I prefer to understand it in terms of the "constructive" nature of all interpretive efforts, including symptoms and interpretations. For a demonstration of the "interpretation-work" that mirrors the Freudian "dream-work," see my essay on "Freud and the Interpenetration of Dreams," *Diacritics* 43 (1979), 98–110.

9. David Shapiro, "Paranoid Style," in *Neurotic Styles* (New York: Basic Books, 1965), p. 66.

10. *Neurotic Styles*, pp. 70–71.

11. Edward Wasiolek, "Texts are Made and Not Given: A Reply to a Critique," *Critical Inquiry* 2 (Winter 1975), 386–91. See his essay, "Wanted: A New Contextualism," *Critical Inquiry* 1 (March 1975), 623–39. See also Barbara Herrnstein Smith, "In the Margins of Discourse," *Critical Inquiry* 1 (June 1975), 769–98. James Kincaid's notion of "coherent readers and incoherent texts" is especially relevant here, both as a mediating position between the monolith and the abyss (as the editors of *Critical Inquiry* describe the contemporary critical argument), and as a useful way to approach Malvolio's situation in *Twelfth Night*, which I discuss below. See Kincaid's contribution to the discussion of "The Limits of Pluralism," *Critical Inquiry* 3 (Summer 1977), 781–800.

12. Geoffrey Hartman, "Literary Criticism and Its Discontents," *Critical Inquiry* 3 (1976), 203–20.

13. Cary Nelson, "Reading Criticism," *PMLA* 91 (1976), 803. See also Murray M. Schwartz, "Where Is Literature?" *College English* 36 (1975), 756–65; reprinted in *Transitional Objects and Potential Spaces: Literary Uses of D.W. Winnicott*, ed. Peter Rudnytsky (New York: Columbia University Press, 1993), pp. 50–62.

14. The critical style of Stanley Fish, in one of his earlier theoretical poses, participates in such an assumption: see *Surprised by Sin: The Reader in* Paradise Lost (Berkeley: University of California Press, 1971), or his defense of "affective stylistics" in "Literature in the Reader," *New Literary History* 2 (1970), 123–62. Of course the fantasy of omnipotent author is well located in Milton; a similar excusable hazard affects Shakespeareans.

15. See Shapiro, *Neurotic Styles*, pp. 73 ff.

16. John Hollander notes this analogy in his excellent essay, "*Twelfth Night* and the Morality of Indulgence," *Sewanee Review* 67 (1959), 220–38.

17. See Norman Holland's chapter on *Twelfth Night* in *The Shakespearean Imagination* (Bloomington: Indiana University Press, 1964), pp. 180–96.

18. The term "graphomania" comes from Keir Elam, who describes it as "a sanguine faith in the calligraphic or . . . typographic sign and its time-defeating fixity"—a component of "semiotic credulity . . . in esoteric circles." Elam also refers to myths about Hebrew and sacred letters, associated with cabbalistic magic and the presumed powers of anagrams and acrostics. Malvolio deciphers a "debased tetragrammaton" not as a name of God but as his own name, due to his "monstrous narcissism": see *Shakespeare's Universe of Discourse: Language-Games in the Comedies* (Cambridge: Cambridge University Press, 1984), pp. 159–64. J. Leeds Barroll reads the scene as a parody of Puritan literal exegesis of scripture: see *Artificial Persons: The Formation of Character in the Tragedies of Shakespeare* (Columbia: University of South Carolina Press, 1974), p. 158. For a wonderful variety of hermeneutic solutions to the riddle, see J. O. Halliwell, in H. H. Furness's Variorum *Twelfth Night* (Philadelphia: J. B. Lippincott, 1901), p. 168, n. 102; Theodore C. Hoepfer, "M. O. A. I.—*Twelfth Night*," *Notes & Queries* 5 (1958), 193; F. G. Fleay, in Furness's Variorum *Twelfth Night*, p. 168, n. 102; Leslie Hotson, *The First Night of "Twelfth Night"* (New York: Macmillan, 1954), pp. 165–66; Lee Sheridan Cox, "The Riddle in *Twelfth Night*," *Shakespeare Quarterly* 13 (1962), 360; Leonard Manheim, "The Mythical Joys of Shakespeare; or, What You *Will*," in *Shakespeare Encomium*, ed. Anne Paolucci, CUNY City College Papers I (New York, 1964); Inge Leimberg, "'M.O.A.I.': Trying to Share the Joke in *Twelfth Night* 2.5 (A Critical Hypothesis)," in *Connotations* (Munster) I (1991), 191–96; and Robert Fleissner, "Malvolio's Manipulated Name," *Names* 39 (1991), 95–102. For a Lacanian reading, see Laurie Osborne, "Letters, Lovers, Lacan: Malvolio's Not-so-Purloined Letter," *Assays* 5 (1989), 63–89.

In "Naming Loss: Mourning and Representation in *Twelfth Night*," Barbara Freedman manages an adroit juggling of Freud, Lacan, Derrida, and object-relations psychoanalysis as she reviews "the scene of the play and of criticism, analysis terminable and interminable." Her essay is an excellent introduction to the different ideas and practices of Freudian and post-Freudian theories, especially about issues of loss, repetition, and representation. See *Staging the Gaze: Postmodernism, Psychoanalysis, and Shakespearean Comedy* (Ithaca, N.Y.: Cornell University Press, 1991), pp. 192–235. Stevie Davies has written a rich essay on Malvolio's regressive relation to language and his audience: see "Textual Strategy: Malvolio, the Puritans, and the Audience," in *Twelfth Night: Penguin Critical Studies* (London: Penguin, 1993), pp. 88–112.

19. Stephen Booth remarks that "Sherlock Holmes himself would accept Maria's letter as a love letter from Olivia to Malvolio": see *"Twelfth Night* 1.1: The Audience as Malvolio," in Peter Erickson and Coppélia Kahn, eds., *Shakespeare's "Rough Magic": Renaissance Essays in Honor of C. L. Barber*, ed. Peter Erickson and Coppélia Kahn (Newark: University of Delaware Press, 1985), p. 166.

20. "*Twelfth Night* and the Tyranny of Interpretation," *ELH [English Literary History]* 53 (1986), 481–82. Freund's excellent essay draws a distinction between styles of reading that is immediately pertinent to my project here. She differentiates between the "mimetic critic," for whom language belongs to the character that speaks it, and the "semiotic critic," for whom character belongs to language ("a

cipher enmeshed in textuality"). The goal of semiotic criticism is to discover "not meaning but the conditions of meaning." But, she continues, even "subjectless semiotic criticism" can be tempted into analyses of dramatic speeches emanating from characters, thereby revealing "its residue of hermeneutic hunger": see pp. 486–88.

21. The bawdy spelling lesson in *Twelfth Night* was evidently not noted publicly until 1933, by David Garnett in *The New Statesman*. See Eric Partridge, *Shakespeare's Bawdy*, rev. ed. (London: Routledge and Kegan Paul, 1968), pp. 160–61. It was partially explicated by Helge Kökeritz in *Shakespeare's Pronunciation* (New Haven, Conn.: Yale University Press, 1953), p. 133. See also E. A. M. Colman, *The Dramatic Use of Bawdy in Shakespeare* (London: Longman Group, 1974), p. 85. Notions of female genitalia as a "cut" pertain to those childish hypotheses described by Freud, maintained in common vulgarisms of language, and implicitly theorized by Lacan in his use, for example, of *coupure* (see below). Malvolio's literalized object is thus ambi-referential: it points crudely to the sexualized body as well as to post-structuralist and psychoanalytic theory. Although tempting, I will not pursue this particular reconstruction of *Twelfth Night, or What You Will*, into this arena. Suture self. (Lacan's notion of *coupure* is detailed with bodily referents in "The Subversion of the Subject and the Dialectic of Desire in the Freudian Unconscious," in *Écrits: A Selection*, trans. Alan Sheridan [New York: Norton, 1977], pp. 292–325; pp. 314–15. The largest frame of reference is Lacan's divisive linguistics in "The Agency of the Letter in the Unconscious," where he coyly shifts the sight/ site of remarked genital difference from the body to lavatory signs: the scheme "*S/s*" produces a radical *coupure* in language that bars any subject's unmediated access to it [see *Écrits*, pp. 146–78; 149 ff.] For the relation of this idea to "suture," see Kaja Silverman, *The Subject of Semiotics* [New York: Oxford University Press, 1983], pp. 194–236.)

22. In some of his last work, Joel Fineman also addressed this figure of the violated letter: see "Shakespeare's *Will*: The Temporality of Rape," *Representations* 10 (1987), 70–71.

23. Kenneth Burke, "Trial Translation (from *Twelfth Night*)," in *The Philosophy of Literary Form* (New York: Vintage, 1957), pp. 291–95.

24. For a remarkably energetic effort to demonstrate the essential "nonsense" of these opening lines, in which grammatical subjects and verb referents tend to shift, see Booth, "*Twelfth Night* 1.1," 150–55. Although he is more than usually clever, the argument is not convincing. For instance, one moment that he cites as a problem—the movement in lines 2–3 from Orsino ("me") to "appetite"—is a precise syntactic demonstration of the split and projection described in the following lines: Orsino's appetite is getting away from him and taking on a life of its own.

25. *Twelfth Night*, ed. Lothian and Craik (London: Methuen, 1975), p. 5 (note).

26. *Henry V*, 5.2.289 (where the bawdiness is most clear); *Romeo and Juliet*, 2.1.24. See also Partridge, *Shakespeare's Bawdy*, where some, but by no means all, of these meanings are spelled out.

27. *Troilus and Cressida*, 4.5.54; *Measure for Measure*, 3.2.59; *Henry V*, 3.3.14.

The term "fresh" had the same romantic-sexual connotations in the Elizabethan vocabulary that it has today.

28. A justification of the Folio punctuation of this passage, by Barry Adams, mentions by the way that the "spirit of love" may refer to Cupid, and then implies in a footnote that this sense may be frankly sexual (citing the bawdy lines from *Henry V*). See "Orsino and the Spirit of Love: Text, Syntax, and Sense in *Twelfth Night*, I.i.1–15," *Shakespeare Quarterly* 29 (1978), 57. Booth sustains an elaborate and exhaustive demolition of the logic of these lines: see "*Twelfth Night*, 1.1," pp. 155–59. He also cites "the traditional courtly love situation in which the frustrated lover pleads with his beloved who, although made for love, will admit no male into her vagina (her 'nought')." W. Thomas MacCary, who is especially attentive to the erotic resonances of Orsino's language, sees Orsino's bottomless love as an emblem of his abysmal narcissism: see *Friends and Lovers: The Phenomenology of Desire in Shakespearean Comedy* (New York: Columbia University Press, 1985), pp. 186–91.

29. A similar dynamic of projection and retaliation underlies and animates many of Shakespeare's plays (and poems), both comedies and tragedies. It represents a primitive, oral narcissism and anxiety, whereby characters become the victims of their own denied and projected appetites. "Is it not," asks Lear, "as this mouth should tear this hand / For lifting food to 't?" (*King Lear*, 3.4.15–16). Compare Orsino, the little bear, to the actual bear who savagely pursues and devours Antigonus in *The Winter's Tale* (3.3)—another embodiment of irrational, dangerous appetite. For an excellent interpretation of this and other bears in Shakespeare, see Murray Schwartz, "*The Winter's Tale*: Loss and Transformation," *American Imago* 32 (1975), 158–62. For an insightful reading of the Actaeon myth in the plays, see Meredith Skura, *Shakespeare the Actor and the Purposes of Playing* (Chicago: University of Chicago Press, 1993), pp. 134–37.

30. Of course the full process involves introjection as well as projection (Lacan calls this an "inmixing of Otherness")—plus an array of personal interpretive strategies that create the relationship between reader and text that characterizes any particular experience of that text: see Schwartz, "Where Is Literature?"

31. For a similar response to these lines from *Hamlet*, see Geoffrey Hartman, *The Fate of Reading* (Chicago: University of Chicago Press, 1975), p. 19.

32. See J. Dennis Huston's comments on Malvolio's "masturbatory" self-conceit, in "'When I Came to Man's Estate': *Twelfth Night* and Problems of Identity," *Modern Language Quarterly* 33 (1972), 274–88. MacCary sees in Malvolio "the negative paradigm of all that goes on erotically in the play": "His perversion is that he does not love at all. . . . He cannot see beyond himself to others, even to see himself in others." See *Friends and Lovers*, p. 186, p.p. 186, 189. Commenting on Derrida's collapsing of all interpretation into the groundless freeplay of writing, James Hans states: "All interpretation is active, but all interpretation also plays back into the freeplay of the world, where that activity is subject to confirmation or denial." A theory that admits no social referentiality is literally unquestionable, left to play with itself as "a masturbatory system incapable of impregnating any other field of play": see *The Play of the World* (Amherst: University of Massachusetts Press, 1981), pp. 100–102.

Chapter Three. "Supersonic Criticism: Pushing the Envelope"

1. *William Shakespeare: A Reader's Guide*, quoted in O. J. Campbell, ed., *The Reader's Encyclopedia of Shakespeare* (New York: Thomas Crowell, 1966), p. 831b.

2. Elizabeth Freund considers the moment from a different perspective that also highlights the issue of interpretation. After quoting much of the conversation, she writes: "Ulysses' citation extends a double summons: it enables reading by providing us with a theory of reading, according to which the object is reconstituted by careful reflection, but it also disables reading because, according to the theory, the object of reading is infinitely inaccessible, perhaps nonexistent." " 'Ariachne's Broken Woof': The Rhetoric of Citation in *Troilus and Cressida*," in *Shakespeare and the Question of Theory*, ed. Patricia Parker and Geoffrey Hartman (New York: Methuen, 1985), p. 28.

3. The issue of readerly interpolation is especially acute in this passage from *Troilus and Cressida*, since one of the central lines is textually questionable. The line, "Till it hath travell'd and is mirror'd . . ." is in both Quarto and Folio actually thus: "Till it hath *trauail'd* and is *married*. . . ." I will reconsider these lines at the end of Chapter Eight.

4. For helpful psychoanalytic and philosophical commentary on the question of individual frames of reference, see Heinz Lichtenstein, "Narcissism and Primary Identity," in *The Dilemma of Human Identity* (New York: Jason Aronson, 1978), pp. 207–21.

5. W. Thomas MacCary notes the implicit cannibalism in the phrase: see *Friends and Lovers: The Phenomenology of Desire in Shakespearean Comedy* (New York: Columbia University Press, 1985), pp. 163–64.

6. See Leslie Fiedler, *The Stranger in Shakespeare* (New York: Stein and Day, 1972), pp. 124–25; and Marc Shell, "The Wether and the Ewe," in *Money, Language and Thought: Literary and Philosophical Economies from the Medieval to the Modern Era* (New Haven, Conn.: Yale University Press, 1982).

7. Caroline Walker Bynum, "The Female Body and Religious Practice in the Later Middle Ages," in *Fragments for a History of the Human Body*, ed. Michel Feher et al. (New York: Zone, 1989), I, p. 164. Marc Shell's latest book, *Art and Money* (Chicago: University of Chicago Press, 1995), has a section on "The Holy Foreskin" that prominently features *The Merchant of Venice*: see pp. 30–37.

8. In *The Dramatic Use of Bawdy in Shakespeare* (London: Longman Group, 1974), E. A. M. Colman comments on the sexual senses of Shylock's lost stones. He considers the moment "bawdy-bizarre" and farcical: see pp. 75–76. To further pursue the bizarre, we might consider the echo of the word "ship" in Shylock's initial greeting, and note the economic anxiety about Antonio's anthropomorphic merchant ships that "sail / Like signiors and rich burghers on the flood" (1.1.9–10) where they are imperilled by rocks and narrows "where the carcasses of many a tall ship lie buried" (3.1.5–6). Thus heard, Shylock's appetite pursues Antonio across all the currents of the play.

9. For a review of these arguments, see Janet Adelman, *Suffocating Mothers:*

Fantasies of Maternal Origin in Shakespeare's Plays (New York: Routledge, 1992), pp. 354–55 (n. 54).

10. Similar observations are made by M. M. Mahood, *Shakespeare's Wordplay* (London: Methuen, 1957), pp. 146–47; Howard Felperin, "Tongue-Tied Our Queen?: Deconstruction of Presence in *The Winter's Tale*," in Parker and Hartman, eds., *Shakespeare and the Question of Theory*, pp. 7–10; Ruth Nevo, *Shakespeare's Other Language* (New York: Methuen, 1987), pp. 103–4; Stanley Cavell, "Recounting Gains, Showing Losses (A Reading of *The Winter's Tale*)," in *Disowning Knowledge in Six Plays by Shakespeare* (Cambridge: Cambridge University Press, 1987), pp. 209–10; Adelman, *Suffocating Mothers*, pp. 220–21; and Gillian West, "Fueling the Flames: Inadvertent Double Entendre in *The Winter's Tale*, Act I, Scene ii," *English Studies* (Netherlands) 74 (1993), 520–23. Meredith Skura is excellent on the various lubricities of language, ethics, and person in the play: see *The Literary Use of the Psychoanalytic Process* (New Haven, Conn.: Yale University Press, 1981), pp. 243–70. In Chapter Seven I will return to this scene.

11. See, for example, Carolyn Brown, "Isabella's Beating Fantasies," *American Imago* 43 (1986), 67–80; and "Erotic Religious Flagellation and Shakespeare's *Measure for Measure*," *English Literary Renaissance* 16 (1986), 139–65. Writing of this and similar diagnostic readings of Isabella, Katherine Maus proposes an intriguing twist. She suggests that Isabella's resistance to Angelo and her repressive self-restraint are "a way of protecting her mental virginity," refusing to be "known," and that critical inquiries into her character repeat Angelo's assault on her integrity: see *Inwardness and Theater in the English Renaissance* (Chicago: University of Chicago Press, 1995), p. 167.

12. See Richard Wheeler, *Shakespeare's Development and the Problem Comedies: Turn and Counter-Turn* (Berkeley: University of California Press, 1981), p. 111, and Janet Adelman, "Bed Tricks," in *Shakespeare's Personality*, ed. Norman Holland et al. (Berkeley: University of California Press, 1990), pp. 169–70.

13. By contrast, Keir Elam breaks down Isabella's statement in terms of speech-act sequentiae and thereby obliterates the specific language by translating it into presumed intents and effects: see *Shakespeare's Universe of Discourse: Language-Games in the Comedies* (Cambridge: Cambridge University Press, 1984), pp. 7–8. He analyzes the language but neglects the words; poetic *play* is sacrificed to linguistic *work*. Thus is poetry lost in translation.

14. As Robert Watson puts it, though with less emphasis on the possibility of Isabella's agency: "Throughout the play, Isabella is . . . steadily drawn into the marketplace of the physical": see "False Immortality in *Measure for Measure*: Comic Means, Tragic Ends," *Shakespeare Quarterly* 41 (1990), 411–32, p. 427. This essay is revised and reprinted as Chapter Three in Watson's book, *The Rest Is Silence: Death as Annihilation in the English Renaissance* (Berkeley: University of California Press, 1994), pp. 103–32.

15. For a description of Isabella as a construction of masculine fantasy, see Kathleen McLuskie, "The Patriarchal Bard: Feminist Criticism and Shakespeare: *King Lear* and *Measure for Measure*," in *Shakespeare: New Essays in Cultural Materialism*, ed. Jonathan Dollimore and Alan Sinfield (Ithaca, N.Y.: Cornell University Press, 1985), pp. 88–108, especially pp. 96–97.

16. For corresponding lascivious apprehensions of the various ambiguities of language, ethic, and person in this extraordinary play, see Wheeler, *Shakespeare's Development*, pp. 92–153, and Skura, *The Literary Use of the Psychoanalytic Process*, pp. 243–70.

17. J. Leeds Barroll links Malvolio and Angelo as characters whose lusts emerge as they read the objects of their desire. Angelo acts out what Malvolio fantasizes: power over a woman. See *Artificial Persons: The Formation of Character in the Tragedies of Shakespeare* (Columbia: University of South Carolina Press, 1974), pp. 159–65.

18. See William Empson, " 'Sense' in *Measure for Measure*," in *The Structure of Complex Words* (London: Chatto and Windus, 1951), pp. 270–88, for full treatment of the various senses of the term "sense" in the play.

19. For an analysis of Shakespeare's refusal to admit any form of successful mediation into the rhetorical debates and moral problems of the play, see Richard Fly, "Ragozine's Head: Comic Solutions Through Fraudulent Mediation in *Measure for Measure*," in *Shakespeare's Mediated World* (Amherst: University of Massachusetts Press, 1976), pp. 55–83. Cristy Desmet describes Isabella as an expert rhetorician who uses the "master trope" of analogy in her argument with Angelo, but who is caught in a bind. As she pursues her own argument she is being read in terms of another; as she asks Angelo to extend his imaginative identification, he begins to explore his "affection" toward her. See *Reading Shakespeare's Characters: Rhetoric, Ethics, and Identity* (Amherst: University of Massachusetts Press, 1992), pp. 144–53.

20. See Ella Freeman Sharpe, "Psycho-Physical Problems Revealed in Language: An Examination of Metaphor" (1940), *Collected Papers on Psycho-Analysis*, ed. Marjorie Brierley (London: Hogarth Press, 1950), pp. 155–69. The most extensive analysis of the carnal components of language is Theodore Thass-Thienemann's *The Interpretation of Language*, 2 vols. (New York: Jason Aronson, 1973); see especially "The Symbolism of the Body," I, 203–400. "The body-self has set the primary pattern for all subsequent understanding of the world" (I. 211). As Empson wrote, "Language is full of sleeping metaphors, and the words for mental processes are all derived from words for physical processes": see *The Structure of Complex Words* (London: Chatto and Windus, 1951), p. 331. Freud's classic statement is, "The ego is first and foremost a body-ego"—later restated by Erik Erikson as, "The ego is founded on the ground-plan of the body."

21. Rose, "Sexuality in *Hamlet* and *Measure for Measure*," in *Alternative Shakespeares*, ed. John Drakakis (London: Methuen, 1987), pp. 95–118.

22. *A Preface to Shakespeare* (London, 1765). In his *Dictionary* (1755), Johnson defines "quibble" as "a low conceit depending on the sound of words; a pun." At the entry on "punster," he notes: "a low wit who endeavours at reputation by double meaning." Johnson's censure is elaborated by William Empson in terms that clearly admit what is at stake—the manly mastery of language. "It shows lack of decision and will-power," Empson writes, "a feminine pleasure in yielding to the mesmerism of language, in getting one's way, if at all, by deceit and flattery, for a poet to be so fearfully susceptible to puns. Many of us could wish the Bard had been more manly in his literary habits." Empson's comment is from *Seven Types of Am-*

biguity (1930); it is quoted by Walter Redfern in *Puns* (Oxford: Blackwell, 1984), p. 46. For an elaborate critique of masculist assumptions about Cleopatra and language, see Ania Loomba, "The 'Infinite Variety' of Patriarchal Discourse," *Gender, Race, Renaissance Drama* (New York: St. Martin's Press, 1989), pp. 65–79.

23. *Explorations in Shakespeare's Language: Some Problems of Word Meaning in the Dramatic Text* (London: Longman Group, 1962), pp. 92–93.

24. The "country pun" is also available and provisionally significant in Hamlet's famous lines about "death, / The undiscover'd country from whose bourn / No traveller returns" (3.2.77–79)—a thought that "puzzles the will": see Avi Erlich, *Hamlet's Absent Father* (Princeton, N.J.: Princeton University Press, 1977), p. 188; and Adelman, *Suffocating Mothers*, p. 27.

25. Linda Charnes quickly alludes to the phallic and homoerotic nature of this encounter: see *Notorious Identity: Materializing the Subject in Shakespeare* (Cambridge, Mass.: Harvard University Press, 1993), pp. 97–98.

26. Barroll sees the Ulysses-Achilles scene (like the similar Cassius-Brutus scene in *Julius Caesar*) as producing a mutual mirroring of merely human faces that distorts the theological "transcendentalist" idea of the self: see *Artificial Persons*, pp. 176–77. James Calderwood, in *The Properties of* Othello (Amherst: University of Massachusetts Press, 1989), quickly reads the scene as a prefiguration of Hegel, Freud, and Lacan on the formation of self by reflection from an other: see pp. 41–42.

27. For a psychoanalytic reading of Achilles's identity, see W. Thomas MacCary, *Childlike Achilles* (New York: Columbia University Press, 1982).

28. Meredith Skura sees the gate of steel image as "one of Shakespeare's more formidable images for an audience": see *Shakespeare the Actor and the Purposes of Playing* (Chicago: University of Chicago Press, 1993), p. 290, n. 26. See also pp. 154–55 on the audience as a means of maintaining identity for an actor or author.

29. Pushing the limits of sexuality and society to the extreme produces large-scale personal and cultural anxiety as described by Marc Shell in *The End of Kinship: Measure for Measure, Incest, and the Ideal of Universal Siblinghood* (Stanford, Ca.: Stanford University Press, 1988).

30. Booth's talk was published as "Close Reading Without Readings," in *Shakespeare Reread: The Texts in New Contexts*, ed. Russ McDonald, (Ithaca, N.Y.: Cornell University Press, 1994), pp. 42–55. A previous version of this chapter resides in that volume as well.

31. Berger, "Psychoanalyzing the Shakespeare Text: The First Three Scenes of the *Henriad*," in Parker and Hartman, eds., *Shakespeare and the Question of Theory*, p. 226.

32. The particular details of Booth's pitfalls are not, of course, for me to analyze. In general it seems clear that his temporary ecstasies of intellectual order when reading Shakespeare ("the happiest moment the human mind ever knows," he writes in *An Essay on Shakespeare's Sonnets* [New Haven, Conn.: Yale University Press, 1969], p. 14) are darkly mirrored by a concern about disorder or "craziness"—cracks in the perfect psychic whole: see his worry about seeming "to be a crazy advocate of crazy interpretations" in his edition of *The Sonnets*, p. 371. The

great value of literature—or the value of great literature—is to provide a holding environment for potential mental disorder, to "cradle" the mind in the "superior strength" of the "fabric" of a play like *Hamlet*: see "On the Value of *Hamlet*," in *Reinterpretations of Elizabethan Drama*, ed. Norman Rabkin (New York: Columbia University Press, 1969), pp. 175–76. Although Booth is histrionically non-psychoanalytic, his presumed theory of literary response merges nicely with psycho-analytic hypotheses about the value of art, such as Anton Ehrenzweig's classic statement that art provides "an enriching experience of envelopment and unconscious integration . . . [;] the work of art acts as a containing 'womb' which receives frag-mented projections of the artist's self": see *The Hidden Order of Art* (New York: International Universities Press, 1970), p. 185.

Chapter Four. *"The Famous Analyses of* Henry the Fourth*"*

1. Maurice Morgann, *Shakespearian Criticism*, ed. Daniel Fineman (Oxford: Clarendon Press, 1972). Fineman's Introduction reviews critical controversies over the status of character in Shakespeare studies up to the mid-twentieth century: see pp. 11–36.

2. See A. C. Bradley, "The Rejection of Falstaff," *Oxford Lectures on Poetry* (1909) (London: Macmillan, 1950); L. L. Schucking, *Character Problems in Shake-speare's Plays: A Guide to the Better Understanding of the Dramatist* (London: Har-rap and Co., 1922); J. I. M. Stewart, "The Birth and Death of Falstaff," *Character and Motive in Shakespeare* (New York: Longmans, 1949); Ernst Kris, "Prince Hal's Conflict," *Psychoanalytic Explorations in Art* (New York: International Universities Press, 1952), pp. 273–88. Kris's seminal essay on the psychoanalysis of a literary character has been reprinted, along with several critiques, in George Moraitis and Sidney Pollock, eds., *Psychoanalytic Studies of Biography* (New York: International Universities Press, 1987). Most recently, Harold Bloom discovers in Falstaff, along-side Hamlet, the verbal self-consciousness that constitutes modern literary character itself. See *The Western Canon: The Books and School of the Ages* (New York: Harcourt Brace, 1994), pp. 47–50.

3. For a summary of psychoanalytic approaches to *1 Henry IV* up to 1964, see Norman Holland, *Psychoanalysis and Shakespeare* (New York: McGraw Hill, 1966), pp. 206–10. I will refer to salient items since 1964 in what follows.

4. A lucid tripartite psychic mapping of *1 Henry IV* is by Norman Holland, *The Shakespearean Imagination* (Bloomington: Indiana University Press, 1964), pp. 109–29. The embodiment of uncontrolled wishes and mortal mischief in Falstaff relates to the emblem of "Riot" incarnate, and to the psycho-anthropological read-ing of C. L. Barber in *Shakespeare's Festive Comedy* (Princeton, N.J.: Princeton University Press, 1959), pp. 192–213. The most thorough mapping of Freudian structural categories onto the dramatized *psychomachia* in the *Henry IV* plays is by Robert Watson, *Shakespeare and the Hazards of Ambition* (Cambridge, Mass.: Harvard University Press, 1984), pp. 47–75. Even nonpsychoanalytic critics find

Freudian terms tempting in this case. M. M. Mahood remarks that Falstaff "represents freedom from all the normal inhibitions, [and] even succeeds in breaking down those of the Lord Chief Justice, that walking embodiment of Freud's censor, to the point where he, too, begins to pun": see *Shakespeare's Wordplay*, p. 29.

5. The standard oedipal view is by Kris. For a sophisticated reading of the process of identity-formation through rivalry with the father, see Coppélia Kahn, *Man's Estate: Masculine Identity in Shakespeare* (Berkeley: University of California Press, 1981), pp. 69–79. Kahn develops her analysis into a consideration of masculine imitations of the mother-son relation, thus merging into the "object-relations" view I sketch below. Harry Berger's work on the displacements of oedipal feelings and representations in *Richard II* uses a kind of family systems theory approach to teasing out latent meanings and relations between characters: see "Psychoanalyzing the Shakespeare Text: The First Three Scenes of the *Henriad*," in *Shakespeare and the Question of Theory*, ed. Patricia Parker and Geoffrey Hartman (New York: Methuen, 1985), pp. 210–29. Watson amplifies the standard oedipal view to include Hal's identification with paternal power through his defeat of Hotspur: see *Shakespeare and the Hazards of Ambition*, p. 63.

6. Colin McCabe, in "Toward a Modern Trivium—English Studies Today," *Critical Quarterly* 26 (1984), notes that Mortimer's Welsh wife represents the seductive nonverbal power of female sexuality (pp. 71–72). Phyllis Rackin draws strong analogies between Wales, women, and female sexuality: "the country of the Others, a world of witchcraft and magic, of mysterious music, and also of unspeakable atrocity." See "Genealogical Anxiety and Female Authority: The Return of the Repressed in Shakespeare's Histories," in *Contending Kingdoms: Historical, Psychological, and Feminist Approaches to the Literature of Sixteenth-Century England and France*, ed. Marie-Rose Logan and Peter Rudnytsky (Detroit: Wayne State University Press, 1991), pp. 323–45, p. 332.

7. The earliest psychoanalytic characterization of Falstaff, as "the pleasure-seeking principle," is by Franz Alexander: "Some Notes on Falstaff," *Psychoanalytic Quarterly* 22 (1933), 592–606.

8. "A fat man," writes Auden, "is a cross between a very young child and a pregnant mother." See "The Prince's Dog," in *The Dyer's Hand and Other Essays* (New York: Random House, 1948), p. 195. For further discussion of this idea, see Kahn, *Man's Estate*, pp. 72–73, and Richard Wheeler, *Shakespeare's Development and the Problem Comedies: Turn and Counter-Turn* (Berkeley: University of California Press, 1981), pp. 165–67. The most extensive analysis is by Valerie Traub, in *Desire and Anxiety: Circulations of Sexuality in Shakespearean Drama* (London: Routledge, 1992), which is discussed below. In his essay on Falstaff, Morgann (1777) noted "the unaffected freedom and wonderful pregnancy of his wit and humour" (Fineman, ed., *Shakespearian Criticism*, p. 194).

9. *Shakespeare's Development and the Problem Comedies*, p. 166.

10. Traub, "Prince Hal's Falstaff: Positioning Psychoanalysis and the Female Reproductive Body," *Shakespeare Quarterly* 40 (1989), 456–74; reprinted as Chapter Two in her book, *Desire and Anxiety*. She also quotes McCabe ("Toward a Modern Trivium"): "Falstaff's body constitutes a polymorphously perverse threat to the possibility of representation." For an account of the social and psychological

functions of Elizabethan genealogy and history to support patriarchal structures and marginalize women, see Rackin, "Genealogical Anxiety and Female Authority." Two sentences from this excellent essay are especially pertinent here:

Patriarchal history was designed to construct a verbal substitute for the visible physical connection between a mother and her children, to authenticate the relationships between fathers and sons, and to suppress and supplant the role of the mother. (p. 324)

Never present in patriarchal history, women could only be represented, and what they represented was the material physical life that patriarchal discourse could never completely capture or control. (p. 336)

11. *Man's Estate*, pp. 72–73.

12. See Jonathan Goldberg, "Hamlet's Hand," *Shakespeare Quarterly* 39 (1988), 307–27, for an extensive examination of Elizabethan handwriting practices and a theoretical extension to the idea of Hamlet as written character.

13. See Watson, *Shakespeare and the Hazards of Ambition*, pp. 62–64.

14. Terry Eagleton notes another difference. "Hotspur is an old-fashioned idealist," he writes, "who desires a language adequate to action and vice-versa; Falstaff has not the slightest wish to integrate the two, but flourishes in the gulf between them." See *William Shakespeare* (Oxford: Blackwell, 1986), p. 17.

15. For a thorough survey of the different languages in the play, see W.F. Bolton, "Linguistic Variety in *1–2 Henry IV*," in *Shakespeare's English: Language in the History Plays* (Oxford: Blackwell, 1992), pp. 151–85. Bolton provides many examples of different styles, with some gestures toward characterization, especially of Hal's mimetic appropriations of Falstaff and Hotspur. For cogent remarks on the blending of political, sexual, and linguistic power in the play, and their relation to the project of a national language, see McCabe, "Toward a Modern Trivium."

16. *Man's Estate*, p. 69.

17. *Patriarchal Structures in Shakespeare's Drama* (Berkeley: University of California Press, 1985), p. 42.

18. Watson, *Shakespeare and the Hazards of Ambition*, pp. 57–58; Traub, *Desire and Anxiety*, p. 60.

19. Watson (*Shakespeare and the Hazards of Ambition*, pp. 48–50) cites Hotspur's reference to "the maidenhead of our affairs" (4.1.59) and quotes his arrogant reply to Glendower's claim that an earthquake announced his birth:

> Oft the teeming earth
> Is with a kind of colic pinch'd and vex'd
> By the imprisoning of unruly wind
> Within her womb . . . .
>
> . . . .
> . . . At your birth
> Our grandam earth, having this distemp'rature,
> In passion shook.   (3.1.26–34)

(Notice the iteration of the term "distemp'rature" in 5.1.3.) In the deep fantasy structure of the language of this play, or the play of this language, the unruly uterine wind of this passage replicates the whistling wind in the regal poem that begins Act Five.

20. "Man and Wife Is One Flesh: *Hamlet* and the Confrontation with the Maternal Body," in *Suffocating Mothers: Fantasies of Maternal Origin in Shakespeare's Plays* (New York: Routledge, 1992), p. 36.

21. *Standard Edition*, 19, 3–66; 56.

22. These ideas are implicit in Winnicott, for instance in "Mirror-Role of Mother and Family in Child Development" in *Playing and Reality* (London: Tavistock, 1970), pp. 111–18. For the explicit restatements by Bollas, see *The Shadow of the Object: Psychoanalysis of the Unthought Known* (New York: Columbia University Press, 1987), pp. 9–10.

23. Lacan speaks for himself in "The mirror stage as formative of the function of the I as revealed in psychoanalytic experience," in *Écrits: A Selection*, trans. Alan Sheridan (New York: Norton, 1977), pp. 1–7; and "The subversion of the subject and the dialectic of desire in the Freudian unconscious," in *Écrits*, pp. 292–325. I make no claim to full representation of his concept of the subject nor would I undertake to explicate his various schemata. For selective secondary explication, see Kaja Silverman, *The Subject of Semiotics* (New York: Oxford University Press, 1983), pp. 126–93; Ellie Ragland Sullivan, *Jacques Lacan and the Philosophy of Psychoanalysis* (Urbana: University of Illinois Press, 1986), pp. 1–16; and Malcolm Bowie, *Lacan* (Cambridge, Mass.: Harvard University Press, 1991), pp. 186–90.

24. *The Seminar of Jacques Lacan: Book II: The Ego in Freud's Theory and in the Technique of Psychoanalysis*, ed. Jacques-Alain Miller (New York: Norton, 1988), p. 155.

25. As Adam Phillips has noted, at crucial moments Winnicott's language harbors religious residues: see his critical biography, *Winnicott* (Cambridge, Mass.: Harvard University Press, 1988), pp. 3, 155 (n. 5), 97, 130.

26. See Lichtenstein's collected essays, *The Dilemma of Human Identity* (New York: Jason Aronson, 1977), especially "Identity and Sexuality," pp. 49–122, and "Narcissism and Primary Identity," pp. 207–21.

27. Lichtenstein, "Narcissism and Primary Identity," in *Dilemma of Human Identity*, p. 215, p. 218. The concept of the "identity theme" is elaborated by Norman Holland, *The I* (New Haven, Conn.: Yale University Press, 1986).

28. Published in *Transport to Summer* (1947) and in *The Collected Poems of Wallace Stevens* (New York: Alfred Knopf, 1965), pp. 339–46.

29. *Hamlet et* Hamlet (Paris: Ballard, 1982), p. 60.

30. Freud's version of this ideal developmental and therapeutic moment is: "*Wo es war, soll ich werden*" ("Where it was, I will be"): see *New Introductory Lectures on Psycho-Analysis* (1933), *Standard Edition* 22, p. 80. Lacan notes a telling historical and psychological shift in French idiom: "The '*ce suis-je*' of the time of Villon has become reversed in the '*c'est moi*' of modern man." See "The Function and Field of Speech and Language in Psychoanalysis," in *Écrits*, p. 70. That exemplary adventurer of early modernity, Hamlet, asserts himself at a most propitious

historical moment. For a Lacanian reading of Hamlet's spontaneity as an expression of his desire and its relation to chance and change, see William Beatty Warner, "The Case of Hamlet, Prince of Denmark," in *Chance and the Text of Experience: Freud, Nietzsche, and Shakespeare's* Hamlet (Ithaca, N.Y.: Cornell University Press, 1986), pp. 215–98, especially pp. 246–63.

31. See "Ego Distortion in Terms of True and False Self" in *Maturational Processes and the Facilitating Environment: Studies in the Theory of Emotional Development* (London: Hogarth Press, 1965), pp. 140–52.

32. See "Communicating and Not Communicating Leading to a Study of Certain Opposites" in *Maturational Processes and the Facilitating Environment*, pp. 179–92.

33. See *Winnicott*, pp. 138–52.

34. Recent readings of *Hamlet* paint a much darker picture of this internalized relation to the mother. Adelman's brilliant essay argues that Hamlet's appeal to "an inviolable core of selfhood" that cannot be shown or known is a defense against his fear of contamination by the sullied world that engulfs him. Since the source of this contamination is his fantasy of a debased and threatening maternal body, however, his "that within" also paradoxically marks the unavoidable link to the matter of the mother. See "Man and Wife Is One Flesh," especially pp. 29–30. See also Juliana Schiesari, *The Gendering of Melancholia: Feminism, Psychoanalysis, and the Symbolics of Loss in Renaissance Drama* (Ithaca, N.Y.: Cornell University Press, 1992), for a Lacanian and Kristevan account of Hamlet's melancholy that differs from Adelman's Kleinian and Winnicottian perspective. In a recent dissertation, Marsha Ginsberg links psychoanalytic ideas about melancholy and the maternal to classical, medieval, and early modern sciences of physiology, sexuality, and psychology. See *Reconceiving Melancholy: Gynecological Moles of Difference in Shakespeare's* Hamlet *and* Richard II (Ph.D. Dissertation, SUNY Buffalo, 1996). Patricia Parker develops an intense and provocative reading of the links between maternal sexuality and "show" in "*Othello* and *Hamlet*: Dilation, Spying, and the 'Secret Place' of Woman," in *Shakespeare Reread: The Texts in New Contexts*, ed. Russ McDonald (Ithaca, N.Y.: Cornell University Press, 1994), pp. 105–46.

35. "Invisible Bullets: Renaissance Authority and Its Subversion, *Henry IV* and *Henry V*," in *Shakespeare: New Essays in Cultural Materialism*, ed. Jonathan Dollimore and Alan Sinfield (Ithaca, N.Y.: Cornell University Press, 1985), pp. 18–47.

36. "Invisible Bullets," p. 33, p. 35.

37. In *Literary Theory/Renaissance Texts*, ed. Patricia Parker and David Quint (Baltimore: Johns Hopkins University Press, 1986), pp. 210–24; reprinted in Greenblatt, *Learning to Curse: Essays in Early Modern Culture* (New York: Routledge, 1990), pp. 131–45. The thesis is also noted by Joel Fineman in *Shakespeare's Perjured Eye: The Invention of Poetic Subjectivity in the Sonnets* (Berkeley: University of California Press, 1986), p. 47.

38. "Psychoanalysis and Renaissance Culture," p. 133. Although Greenblatt offers no proof of this assertion, similar claims are made by J. Leeds Barroll in *Artificial Persons: The Formation of Character in the Tragedies of Shakespeare* (Colum-

bia: University of South Carolina Press, 1974), p. 73, pp. 85–88, and Anne Ferry in *The "Inward" Language: Sonnets of Wyatt, Sidney, Shakespeare, and Donne* (Chicago: University of Chicago Press, 1983), pp. 31–70.

39. "Psychoanalysis and Renaissance Culture," pp. 134–35, p. 138.

40. "Psychoanalysis and Renaissance Culture," p. 137, p. 141, p. 145 (n. 7).

41. Freud's most succinct account of the development of the ego is in *The Ego and the Id* (1923), *Standard Edition*, 19, 3–68. He discusses the pleasure and reality principles in "Formulations on the Two Principles of Mental Functioning" (1911), *Standard Edition*, 12, 213–26. For a theoretical essay that refashions Greenblatt's strictly oedipal model into a process of identification, see Freud, "The Dissolution of the Oedipus Complex" (1924), *Standard Edition*, 19, 173–82.

42. "Psychoanalysis and Renaissance Culture," p. 138.

43. *William Shakespeare*, p. 13.

44. *Renaissance Self-Fashioning: From More to Shakespeare* (Chicago: University of Chicago Press, 1981), p. 256.

45. Eloquent and subtle restatements of Winnicott can be found in Bollas, *The Shadow of the Object*: see Introduction, pp. 9–10, and "The Self as Object," pp. 41–63. For a review of psychoanalytic literature on the self that does not rely on Lacan or Winnicott, see Otto Kernberg, "The Dynamic Unconscious and the Self," in Raphael Stern, ed., *Theories of the Unconscious*, ed. Raphael Stern (Hillsdale, N.J.: Analytic Press, 1987), pp. 3–25. See also the response by Marcia Cavell in the same volume, pp. 58–63.

46. Lichtenstein, "Narcissism and Primary Identity," p. 218. For further postmodern elaborations of the question of personal identity as a struggle between inscribed or prescribed "character" and an individual will to originality, enacted through play or a staging of self in Shakespeare, see Linda Charnes, *Notorious Identity: Materializing the Subject in Shakespeare* (Cambridge, Mass.: Harvard University Press, 1993), pp. 1–19. Later she writes that "by deconstructing the legend of Troilus and Cressida, Shakespeare reconstructs theater and drama as a new site not for representing 'identity' but for staging 'kinds of selves'" (p. 102).

47. A brilliant and thorough analysis of the dispute is offered by Meredith Skura in "Discourse and the Individual: The Case of Colonialism in *The Tempest*," *Shakespeare Quarterly* 40 (1989), 42–69.

Chapter Five. "Hyperbolic Desire: Shakespeare's Lucrece*"*

1. *The Poems*, ed. F. T. Prince (London: Methuen, 1960). All subsequent quotations from *Lucrece* are from this Arden edition.

2. For an essay that dovetails with many of my observations, see Jonathan Crewe, "Shakespeare's Figure of Lucrece: Writing Rape," in *Trials of Authorship: Anterior Forms and Poetic Reconstruction from Wyatt to Shakespeare* (Berkeley: University of California Press, 1990), pp. 141–63.

3. The best Renaissance representative of this style of narrative psychodramatic allegory is Spenser. For an excellent description of the Spenserian back-

ground against which *Lucrece* is most profitably read, see Leonard Barkan, *Nature's Work of Art: The Human Body as Image of the World* (New Haven, Conn.: Yale University Press, 1975), especially Chapter Five, "*The Faerie Queene*: Allegory, Iconography, and the Human Body."

4. *Macbeth* is the richest dramatic parallel here, to the point of exact echoes. As Macbeth moves "with Tarquin's ravishing strides" toward the bloody business of regicide, he occupies the identical arena of dream and allegory, enacting Lust and "Murther" (*Macbeth*, 2.1.49–56). M.C. Bradbrook calls Tarquin's soliloquies "a first cartoon for the study of *Macbeth*": see *Shakespeare and Elizabethan Poetry* (London: Chatto and Windus, 1951), p. 112. For an extensive mapping of the dreamscape of *Macbeth*, see Chapter Six in this book.

5. Shakespeare's language is manifestly bawdy here. "Pride" has frequent connotations of male arousal, and the physiology of tumescence is clear (see Angelo's erection in *Measure for Measure*, 2.4.5–6; and Sonnet 151, where the signification is exact). E. A. M. Colman notes in Tarquin's "pride"-full advance toward Lucrece's chamber that "one can detect here a suggestion of Tarquin's being led along by his own erect penis" (*The Dramatic Use of Bawdy in Shakespeare* [London: Longman Group, 1974], p. 160). This insight is repeated almost verbatim by Saad El-Gabalawy in "The Ethical Question of Lucrece: A Case of Rape," *Mosaic* 12 (1979), 80. Katharine Maus also hears the echoes: see "Taking Tropes Seriously: Language and Violence in Shakespeare's *Rape of Lucrece*," *Shakespeare Quarterly* 37 (1986), 74.

6. Joel Fineman notes how Shakespeare's description of Lucrece's rape is displaced onto the details of Tarquin's progress toward her room, which he terms "a kind of pornographic *effictio*": see "Shakespeare's *Will*: The Temporality of Rape," *Representations* 20 (1987), 25–76, 39. Reprinted in Fineman, *The Subjectivity Effect in Western Literary Tradition: Essays Toward the Release of Shakespeare's Will* (Cambridge, Mass.: MIT Press, 1991), pp. 165–221.

7. The term "peculiar" carries its etymology of *pecus*, livestock—that portion of a herd given to the herdsman; it is thus related to *pecunia* (cattle, money). See Eric Partridge, *Origins: A Short Etymological Dictionary of Modern English* (New York: Macmillan, 1961), *s.v.* The term is infrequent in Shakespeare, and its contexts are suggestive. For instance, Iago to Othello on the fraternity of cuckolds: "There's millions now alive / That nightly lies in those unproper beds / Which they dare swear peculiar" (*Othello*, 4.1.67–69). Or Pompey the Bawd to Mistress Overdone on Claudio's crime of unlicensed fornication: "But what's his offence?" she asks. "Groping for trouts in a peculiar river," he replies (*Measure for Measure*, 1.2.83–84). Shakespeare uses the Latin *pecus* in *Love's Labour's Lost* (4.2.92).

8. Stimpson, "Shakespeare and the Soil of Rape," in *The Woman's Part: Feminist Criticism of Shakespeare*, ed. Ruth Lenz, Gayle Greene, and Carol Neely (Urbana: University of Illinois Press, 1980), p. 58; Vickers, "'The Blazon of Sweet Beauty's Best': Shakespeare's *Lucrece*," in *Shakespeare and the Question of Theory*, ed. Patricia Parker and Geoffrey Hartman (New York: Methuen, 1985), p. 102. Both of these readers also review the parallel structure in *Cymbeline* as a parody of the dynamic of rape and male rivalry. Some female critics have extended this observation of masculine complicity to include male readers of Shakespeare's poem. Harriet

Hawkins objects to contemporary critics of *Lucrece* who dare to discover moral ambiguities or locate any violation in Tarquin. In her view such efforts merely add insult to injury and are "critical rapes of Lucrece": see *The Devil's Party: Critical Counter-Interpretations of Shakespearean Drama* (Oxford: Clarendon Press, 1985), p. 157. She cites Susan Brownmiller's sociological study of rape, *Against Our Will: Men, Women and Rape* (New York: Simon and Schuster, 1975), and asserts that Shakespeare's poem presents "identical conclusions" about rapists' motivations. In an intriguing poststructuralist mirror-move, Jonathan Crewe emphasizes his point about characters as figures or representations by contrast with Brownmiller's book: see "Shakespeare's Figure of Lucrece: Writing Rape," pp. 153–63. Annabel Patterson writes that "disturbingly, the first half of the poem identifies closely with Tarquin, who is always seen from the inside and who, after the rape, is hideously disappointed." She then rebukes Joel Fineman for taking such pleasure in his close reading as to "produce an effect equivalent to rape in what it does to Lucrece." To her, Fineman's analysis of lines 676–79 "is the postmodern equivalent of the reprehensible tradition whereby it was assumed that Lucrece partially assented to or at least involuntarily enjoyed her rape." Yet after thus blaming Fineman, Patterson admits that Shakespeare's poem, whose core scene she labels a "painting on black velvet," can itself be held responsible for "such insinuations": see *Reading Between the Lines* (Madison: University of Wisconsin Press, 1993), pp. 302–4. Such speculations may be furthered by William Empson's rather brazen assertion that Lucrece "took an involuntary pleasure in the rape" and therefore felt guilty; he continues to confess that "the reader perhaps is also guilty, having taken a sexual pleasure in these descriptions of sexual wrong": see "The Narrative Poems," in *Essays on Shakespeare* (Cambridge: Cambridge University Press, 1986), p. 11.

  9. Fineman, in a tour de force elaboration of reciprocal and recursive "postings" in the poem, traces the themes of self-conscious writing from the level of microscopic literariness (the "porno-graphic" "erotic theater" of textuality) to the level of macroscopic poststructuralist theory of the construction of the literary subject. See "Shakespeare's *Will*," pp. 25–76.

  10. But Hamlet's terms repeat the problem of a masculine perspective (Hyperion, the satyr). Feminist critics have explored the flaws in the unstable construction of masculine subjectivity and the radical ambivalence about woman as idealized and debased object. See, for example, Madelon Gohlke [Sprengnether], " 'I wooed thee with my sword': Shakespeare's Tragic Paradigms," in *Representing Shakespeare: New Psychoanalytic Essays*, ed. Murray M. Schwartz and Coppélia Kahn (Baltimore: Johns Hopkins University Press, 1980), pp. 170–87; or Valerie Traub on the impossibility of representing a feminine subject in strictly patriarchal, phallogocentric discourse: see *Desire and Anxiety: Circulations of Sexuality in Shakespearean Drama* (New York: Routledge, 1992), pp. 25–49, especially pp. 46–47. The source of this radical ambivalence is theorized by Janet Adelman in *Suffocating Mothers: Fantasies of Maternal Origin in Shakespeare's Plays* (New York: Routledge, 1992).

  11. See Sam Hynes, "The Rape of Tarquin," *Shakespeare Quarterly* (1959), 451–53. Hynes also notes the parallels of Tarquin's internal insurrection with Macbeth's. A. C. Hamilton notes that "Tarquin's desire for Lucrece turns into

a desire to destroy himself through sin": see *The Early Shakespeare* (San Marino, Ca.: Huntington Library, 1967), p. 174.

12. See Coppélia Kahn, "The Rape in Shakespeare's *Lucrece*," *Shakespeare Studies* 9 (1976), pp. 58–60.

13. Jerome Kramer and Judith Kaminsky, "'These Contraries Such Unity Do Hold': Structure in *The Rape of Lucrece*," *Mosaic* 10 (1977), 143–55.

14. The symbolism, frequently noted in current criticism, is hardly Freudian. Shakespeare takes pains to establish it in *Romeo and Juliet*, and it echoes through *Macbeth* and *Antony and Cleopatra*. For erotic depictions of Lucrece's suicide, see Ian Donaldson, *The Rapes of Lucrece: A Myth and Its Transformations* (Oxford: Clarendon, 1982). Discussing Lucas Cranach's early-sixteenth-century drawing of a naked, placid Lucrece pressing a long dagger into her abdomen, Donaldson quotes Michel Leiris's *L'Age d'homme* (Paris, Gallimard, 1946): "Elle s'apprêtant à annuler l'effet du viol qu'elle a subi, par un geste pareil" (p. 17, n. 36)—"She prepares herself to annul the effect of the violation she has suffered, by a similar gesture" (my translation). An intemperate reading comes from Roy Battenhouse, who terms Lucrece's suicide "martyrdom in an obscene mode, a religious 'dying' which Shakespeare hints, figuratively, is a kind of masturbatory self-rape": see *Shakespearean Tragedy: Its Art and Its Christian Premises* (Bloomington: Indiana University Press, 1969), p. 28.

15. Renaissance physiologies of sex, which derived from classic and medieval theories of conception and "humours," held that procreation resulted from an actual commingling of "spirits" or bloods during coitus. For Shakespearean echoes, see Leontes's obsessions in *The Winter's Tale*: "Too hot, too hot! / To mingle friendship far is mingling bloods" (1.2.108–9).

16. "Iconography and Rhetoric in Shakespeare's *Lucrece*," *Shakespeare Studies* 14 (1981), 16–18. From a different perspective, Laura Bromley remarks that "Lucrece comes to embody the evil within Tarquin, fulfilling the prophecy about the consequences of his act which he chose to ignore." See "Lucrece's Recreation," *Shakespeare Quarterly* 34 (1983), 200–211, 205.

17. Kahn cites the Roman tradition of Vesta and the concept of "the virginal wife": see "The Rape in Shakespeare's *Lucrece*," p. 50.

18. Ovid, *Amores*, I.xiii.40. The topos is a familiar one in Renaissance poetry. Shakespeare locates the wish in its conventional romantic context in *Romeo and Juliet*.

19. William Butler Yeats, "Leda and the Swan" (1923), *The Collected Poems*, 2nd ed. (London: Macmillan, 1950), p. 241.

20. The representational status of this artifact, be it painting or weaving, remains indeterminate. See Harold Walley, "*The Rape of Lucrece* and Shakespearean Tragedy," *PMLA* 76 (1961), 480–87; and S. Clark Hulse, "'A Piece of Skilful Painting' in Shakespeare's *Lucrece*," *Shakespeare Survey* 31 (1978), 13–22.

21. David Bevington describes how Lucrece, with the Narrator's complicity, searches the Troy-piece for a representational model to manage her traumatic circumstance, only to be faced with the disillusioning fact that appearances—real or aesthetic—can deceive: see *Action Is Eloquence: The Language of Gesture in Shakespeare* (Cambridge, Mass.: Harvard University Press, 1984), pp. 23–26.

22. For an excellent reading of the relations between Shakespeare's and Ovid's versions of the story, which finds an Ovidian subtext of feminine reaction and revenge that is "repressed in both Shakespeare's text and scholarship about the text" in order to emphasize a phallocentric social order, see Jane Newman, "'And Let Mild Women to Him Lose Their Mildness': Philomela, Female Violence, and Shakespeare's *The Rape of Lucrece*," *Shakespeare Quarterly* 45 (1994), 304–26, 317–18.

23. "The Ethical Question of Lucrece: A Case of Rape," *Mosaic* 12 (1979), 82–86.

24. Fineman has an elegant and powerful paragraph on this stanza: see "Shakespeare's *Will*," p. 59.

25. Quoted in F. T. Prince, ed., *The Poems*, p. 199. For a gruesome biblical parallel to this political display of the woman's body, see the story of "Beth" in the Book of Judges (19), as analyzed by Mieke Bal in "The Rape of Narrative and the Narrative of Rape," in Elaine Scarry, ed., *Literature and the Body: Essays on Populations and Persons*, ed. Elaine Scarry (Baltimore: Johns Hopkins University Press, 1988), pp. 1–32;, especially p. 18.

26. *Mythology and the Renaissance Tradition* (New York: Norton, 1963), p. 152. Patterson makes a related remark when she notes that "what delays the reader for 1,855 lines is primarily psychological and rhetorical filler": see *Reading Between the Lines*, p. 301.

27. Recent criticism addresses the central issue of rhetorical figures as a direct topic of the poem. Excellent articles are by Heather Dubrow, "The Rape of Clio: Attitudes to History in Shakespeare's *Lucrece*," *English Literary Renaissance* 16 (1986), 425–41; Maus, "Taking Tropes Seriously," and Fineman, "Shakespeare's *Will*." Although Maus begins by asserting that *Lucrece* is about "two people making important decisions" (p. 67), her essay demonstrates how the two characters of Lucrece and Tarquin use and abuse metaphors to rationalize intentions and conclusions already formed. As I read her essay, she considers Lucrece and Tarquin not finally as characters but as enactments of stylized tropes, or *literalized figures*.

28. See Crewe, "Shakespeare's Figure of Lucrece," for consideration of Lucrece as a site of *difference* (gender, political, property) and the object of male gazes and readings.

29. "Shakespeare's *Will*," p. 41.

30. Stephanie Jed, in the Appendix to her provocative book on the historical and emblematic instance of Lucretia, translates the key Renaissance document that is the basis of her study. It advances in judicial terms the thesis that Lucretia's suicide is an admission of guilt: "A woman will not be thought to be innocent who afflicts herself with punishment as a criminal." See *Chaste Thinking: The Rape of Lucretia and the Birth of Humanism* (Bloomington: Indiana University Press, 1989), p. 150.

31. The published title during Shakespeare's lifetime was simply *Lucrece*. An editor augmented the title in the Quarto of 1616; tradition retains the emendation. As Fineman points out, however, the running title on the original page headings is "The Rape of Lucrece"—thereby admitting an ambiguity of subjective and objective genitive: see "Shakespeare's *Will*," p. 72, n. 21.

32. Crewe notes that rape is not the "constitutive" subject of the poem,

nor is it an "extratextual" "social fact": see "Shakespeare's Figure of Lucrece,' pp. 142–43.

33. Mallarmé, "Mimique," quoted in Jacques Derrida, *Dissemination*, trans. Barbara Johnson (Chicago: University of Chicago Press, 1981), pp. xx, xxii. For Derrida's commentary on the passage, see pp. 209–22.

34. Several critics address, though in different ways, this genderized division. Kramer and Kaminsky cite the opposition between Tarquin's aggressive action and Lucrece's exhaustive tirades, noting that Tarquin strides in linear motive while Lucrece wanders through her rooms: see " 'These Contraries Such Unity Do Hold,' " p. 153. Dubrow examines sex-roles as delineated in the poem in terms of history: Lucrece responds passively and is thereby "victimized into history"; Tarquin is the active agent of historical (epic) inscription: see "The Rape of Clio." Jed argues that classical and Renaissance narratives of Lucretia contruct a trope of personal privacy as an aspect of the distinction between (violable) body and (inviolable) mind, producing a style of writing that is "literary" or "humanist"—a kind of "chaste thinking," separable from the contaminated discourse of commerce or even standard history: see *Chaste Thinking*. For an alternative view of Lucrece as an active heroine, see Bromley, "Lucrece's Recreation."

35. "Taking Tropes Seriously," p. 75.

36. Hulse speculates that the marble/wax image is "a model for the rape itself: that is, Tarquin . . . stamps his evil in the wax that is Lucrece": see " 'A Piece of Skilful Painting,' " p. 20. More than simply a model of evil marking innocence, however, the image pertains to writing itself. The association of writing and rape is a theme of Fineman's essay, addressed most directly in a long note in which he considers the interchangeablity of "the violence of desire and the desire of violence": see "Shakespeare's *Will*," pp. 70–71. See also Bal, "Rape of Narrative."

Chapter Six. *"Phantasmagoric* Macbeth*"*

1. *"Macbeth* and the Metaphysic of Evil," in *The Wheel of Fire*, rev. ed. (London: Methuen, 1949), p. 58.

2. Quotations are from the Arden Edition of *Macbeth*, ed. Kenneth Muir (London: Methuen, 1962).

3. " 'A New Gorgon': Visual Effects in *Macbeth*," in *Focus on* Macbeth, ed. J. R. Brown (London: Routledge and Kegan Paul, 1982).

4. "Some Character Types Met with in Psycho-Analytic Work" (1916), *Standard Edition*, 4, 316–31.

5. For a detailed review of psychoanalytic interpretations of the regicide as parricide, see Norman Holland, *Psychoanalysis and Shakespeare* (New York: McGraw Hill, 1966), pp. 219–30. After 1964, see L. Vesny-Wagner, "*Macbeth*: 'Fair is Foul and Foul is Fair,' " *American Imago* 25 (1968), 242–57; Victor Calef, "Lady Macbeth and Infanticide," *Journal of the American Psychoanalytic Association* 17 (1969), 528–48; Susan Bachmann, "Daggers in Men's Smiles," *International Review of Psycho-Analysis* 5 (1978), 97–104; and Robert N. Watson, " 'Thriftless

Ambition,' Foolish Wishes, and the Tragedy of *Macbeth*," in *Shakespeare and the Hazards of Ambition* (Cambridge, Mass.: Harvard University Press, 1984), pp. 83–141. For a useful account of the oedipal, patricidal interpretation, which also includes a Kleinian perspective of the jealous infant, see Patrick Roberts, *The Psychology of Tragic Drama* (London: Routledge and Kegan Paul, 1975), pp. 206–11. Noting that Macbeth decides to kill Duncan after the King chooses Malcolm as his heir, Norman Rabkin writes: "It is as if Macbeth decides to kill Duncan out of the rage of a disappointed sibling": see *Shakespeare and the Problem of Meaning* (Chicago: University of Chicago Press, 1981), pp. 105–8. A Freudian reading of Fuseli's watercolor illustration (1766) of the Macbeths just after the deed (based on Garrick's production) also finds the oedipal design, with Lady Macbeth in the role of mother: see S.L. Carr and P. Knapp, "Seeing Through *Macbeth*," *PMLA* 96 (1981), 837–47. Two related essays that elaborate oedipal and pre-oedipal readings of the play are Pierre Janton, "Sonship and Fatherhood in *Macbeth*," *Cahiers élisabethains* 35 (1989), and Anny Crunelle-Vanrigh, "*Macbeth*: Oedipus Transposed," *Cahiers élisabethains* 43–44 (1993), 21–33. The most exhaustive recent psychoanalytic study of the play is by Janet Adelman, "Escaping the Matrix: The Construction of Masculinity in *Macbeth* and *Coriolanus*," in *Suffocating Mothers: Fantasies of Maternal Origin in Shakespeare's Plays* (New York: Routledge, 1992), pp. 130–46. Another provocative essay is by Marjorie Garber, "Macbeth: The Male Medusa," in *Shakespeare's Ghost Writers: Literature as Uncanny Causality* (New York: Methuen, 1987), pp. 87–123.

6. See *Hamlet*, 3.2.360ff ("Soft, now to my mother . . . "). For a provocative paragraph on these fantasies in *Macbeth*, see Richard Wheeler, *Shakespeare's Development and the Problem Comedies: Turn and Counter-Turn* (Berkeley: University of California Press, 1981), pp. 145–46. Another valuable essay is by Dennis Biggins, "Sexuality, Witchcraft, and Violence in *Macbeth*," *Shakespeare Studies* 8 (1975), 255–77; see also Watson, *Shakespeare and the Hazards of Ambition*, pp. 99–100. A critic of Roman Polanski's film has noted the director's erotization of the regicide: see Virginia Wexman, "*Macbeth* and Polanski's Theme of Regression," *University of Dayton Review* 14 (1979), 80–90. In an informative essay on "Obstetrics and Gynecology in *Macbeth*," Alice Fox explicates the connotations of breech birth in the description of Duncan's murder: see *Shakespeare Studies* 12 (1979), 127–41; also E. Silling, "Another Meaning of "Breech'd," *MSE* [Modern Studies in English] 14 (1974). James Calderwood reads the sexual allusions in the regicide as the sign of "a metaphorically displaced act of copulation between Lord and Lady Macbeth" whose consequences bear tragic fruit: see *"If It Were Done": Macbeth and Tragic Action* (Berkeley: University of California Press, 1986), pp. 43–47.

7. Harry Berger, in his essay on "The Early Scenes of *Macbeth*: Preface to a New Interpretation," *ELH* [English Literary History] 47 (1980), 1–31, finds Duncan "vaguely androgynous" as the source of paternal blood and maternal milk. In a paper delivered to the 1981 MLA Special Session on "Marriage and the Family in Shakespeare," David Sundelson stressed the "horrifying fusion of sexes" that ideas of androgyny evoke in the tragedies (as opposed to the comedies) and remarked of the "new Gorgon" that is Duncan's corpse: "The father's ravaged body becomes

the annihilating mother." See also D. W. Harding, "Woman's Fantasy of Manhood," *Shakespeare Quarterly* 20 (1969), 245–53; Dianne Hunter, "Shakespearian Myth-making in *Macbeth*: Cultural Crisis and Return to Origins," in *Myth and Shakespeare*, ed. I. Reid (Victoria, Australia, 1980), pp. 176–85; and Adelman, *Suffocating Mothers*, p. 132.

8. For further anatomical reconstruction of the castle, see Elizabeth Sacks, *Shakespeare's Images of Pregnancy* (New York: St. Martin's Press, 1980), pp. 78ff, and Ruth Nevo, *Tragic Form in Shakespeare* (Princeton, N.J.: Princeton University Press, 1972), pp. 226–27. The 1983 BBC television production filmed a blood-red sunset through half-open, teeth-like gates, just as Duncan and Banquo were describing the castle's pleasantries. The traditional image of the Hellmouth is of course related.

9. As critics have noted, the figure of Macduff is profoundly ambivalent. He ultimately appears as the heroic response to Macbeth's evil, but his own tragedy and his uncanny status as "not of woman born" link him to that dread of the feminine that empowers the play. See Adelman, *Suffocating Mothers*, p. 144, pp. 320–21.

10. "The Naked Babe and the Cloak of Manliness," in *The Well Wrought Urn* (New York: Harcourt, Brace, and World, 1947).

11. "The Theatre of the Mind: An Essay on *Macbeth*," *ELH* 42 (1975), 328–49; 348–49.

12. "The Babe That Milks: An Organic Study of *Macbeth*," in *The Design Within: Psychoanalytic Approaches to Shakespeare*, ed. M. D. Faber (New York: Science House, 1970), pp. 251–79, p. 265.

13. Joan Klein finds this religious image in Macbeth's evocation of infant Pity: see her essay, "Lady Macbeth 'Infirm of Purpose,'" in *The Woman's Part: Feminist Criticism of Shakespeare*, ed. Ruth Lenz, Gayle Greene, and Carol Neely (Urbana: University of Illinois Press, 1980), p. 242.

14. For a variety of insightful analyses of this event, see L. C. Knights, "How Many Children Had Lady Macbeth?" (1933) in *Explorations: Essays in Criticism* (London: Chatto and Windus, 1946), pp. 13–50; Victor Calef, "Lady Macbeth and Infanticide," *Journal of the American Psychoanalytic Association* 17 (1969), 528–48; Maynard Mack, *Killing the King: Three Studies in Shakespeare's Tragic Structure* (New Haven, Conn.: Yale University Press, 1973); Murray Schwartz, "Shakespeare Through Contemporary Psychoanalysis," in *Representing Shakespeare: New Psychoanalytic Essays*, ed. Murray M. Schwartz and Coppélia Kahn (Baltimore: Johns Hopkins University Press, 1980), pp. 28–29; and Berger, "Early Scenes of *Macbeth*," pp. 27–28. In *Action Is Eloquence: The Language of Gesture in Shakespeare* (Cambridge, Mass.: Harvard University Press, 1984), David Bevington traces the pattern of "aborted hospitality" of broken feasts in the play: see pp. 157–58.

15. *The Anatomy of Melancholy* (1628), 3 vols. (London: Everyman's Library, 1932), I, 330ff.; I, 215.

16. Fox discovers a language of nursing in Macbeth's final soliloquy about the player who "struts and frets his hour." She notes OED evidence that "strut" can mean to bulge, or swell (as with milk), and "fret" can mean to gnaw: see "Obstetrics and Gynecology in *Macbeth*," p. 132, p. 140, n. 18.

17. See D. W. Winnicott, *The Maturational Processes and the Facilitating Environment* (London: Hogarth Press, 1965); and Margaret Mahler, *The Psychological Birth of the Human Infant* (New York: Basic Books, 1975).

18. Booth, *King Lear, Macbeth, Indefinition, and Tragedy* (New Haven, Conn.: Yale University Press, 1983), p. 99; Berger, "The Early Scenes of *Macbeth*: Preface to a New Interpretation," *ELH* 47 (1980), 1–31, 13.

19. "The Babe That Milks," pp. 268–69, 271. See also Hunter, "Shakespearian Myth-Making in *Macbeth*"; Watson, *Shakespeare and the Hazards of Ambition*, pp. 100–105; and Adelman, *Suffocating Mothers*, pp. 142–43.

20. Jacques Guillemeau, *Child-birth or, The happie deliverie of women* (London, 1612); quoted in Fox, "Obstetrics and Gynecology in *Macbeth*," p. 130.

21. "Obstetrics and Gynecology in *Macbeth*," p. 136. Barron suggests a similar point: see "The Babe That Milks," p. 277, n. 16.

22. See R. V. Schnucker, "The English Puritans and Pregnancy, Delivery, and Breast-Feeding," *History of Childhood Quarterly* 1 (1974), 637–58.

23. Commentators have noted the mirroring syntax in a variety of ways. Most useful are Laurence Michel, *The Thing Contained: A Theory of the Tragic* (Bloomington: Indiana University Press, 1976), pp. 52–53; Berger, "The Early Scenes of *Macbeth*"; and Booth, *King Lear, Macbeth, Indefinition, and Tragedy*, pp. 88–89. On doubling and rivalry, see Joel Fineman, "Fratricide and Cuckoldry: Shakespeare's Doubles," in Schwartz and Kahn, eds., *Representing Shakespeare*, pp. 70–109; René Girard, *Violence and the Sacred* (Baltimore: Johns Hopkins University Press, 1978); Coppélia Kahn, *Man's Estate: Masculine Identity in Shakespeare* (Berkeley: University of California Press, 1981); Watson, *Shakespeare and the Hazards of Ambition*; and Adelman, *Suffocating Mothers*.

24. "Mirror-Role of Mother and Family in Child Development," in *Playing and Reality* (London: Tavistock Publications, 1971), p. 111.

25. Winnicott, *The Maturational Processes*, pp. 151–52.

26. "The Use of an Object and Relating through Identifications," in *Playing and Reality*, pp. 86–94.

27. *Suffocating Mothers*, p. 135.

28. *Suffocating Mothers*, p. 138.

29. See Schwartz, "Shakespeare Through Contemporary Psychoanalysis," pp. 28–29.

30. See "Transitional Objects and Transitional Phenomena," in *Playing and Reality*, pp. 1–25.

31. See Marjorie Garber, *Dream in Shakespeare* (New Haven, Conn.: Yale University Press, 1974), pp. 113–14, and John Bayley, *Shakespearean Tragedy* (London: Routledge and Kegan Paul, 1981), p. 188). Berger, however, presents a good case for Banquo's implicit blame in the regicide: see "Early Scenes of *Macbeth*," pp. 29–30. In Holinshed's account, Banquo is Macbeth's accomplice.

32. "*Macbeth* and the Metaphysic of Evil," p. 153.

33. J. I. M. Stewart was one of the first critics to describe Macbeth's "almost hypnoidal state": "he is like a man moving in a blood-drenched trance, subject to visual and auditory hallucinations, uncertain of the boundaries of actuality and dream" (*Character and Motive in Shakespeare* [New York: Longmans, 1949], p. 93).

For more on the perspective of *Macbeth* as dream, see Simon Lesser, "*Macbeth*: Drama and Dream," in *The Whispered Meanings*, ed. Richard Noland and Robert Sprich (Amherst: University of Massachusetts Press, 1977); and Kay Stockholder, *Dream Works: Lovers and Families in Shakespeare's Plays* (Toronto: University of Toronto Press, 1987), pp. 100–17.

34. *The Dyer's Hand*. Stephen Booth elaborates this claim, although he considers the Malcolm-Macduff scene a dramaturgical "irritation": see *King Lear, Macbeth, Indefinition, and Tragedy*, pp. 105–11. Perhaps the most fervent assertion of our complicity with Macbeth came from Arthur Quiller-Couch, in *Shakespeare's Workmanship* (London, 1918). His lengthy remarks are quoted in Laurence Lerner, ed., *Shakespeare's Tragedies* (Baltimore: Penguin, 1963), pp. 175–78.

35. See Robert Egan, "His Hour Upon the Stage: Role-Playing in *Macbeth*," *Centennial Review* 22 (1968), 327–45; and Ide, "Theatre of the Mind."

36. "The Theater of Cruelty," in *Writing and Difference*, trans. Alan Bass (Chicago: University of Chicago Press, 1978), p. 242.

37. Fergusson, "*Macbeth* and the Imitation of an Action," in *The Human Image in Dramatic Literature* (Garden City, N.Y.: Doubleday, 1957); Rabkin, *Shakespeare and the Problem of Meaning*, p. 103; Ramsey, "The Perversion of Manliness in *Macbeth*," *Studies in English Literature: 1500–1900* 13 (1973), 290; Bloom, *The Western Canon: The Books and School of the Ages* (New York: Harcourt Brace, 1994), p. 393.

38. Stage productions confront a problem here. As Peter Hall said in an interview, "This is very difficult to do: it has to be absolutely real to Macbeth because he does see a dagger. The audience only see a dagger if he sees a dagger. That is a wonderful image." See "Directing *Macbeth*" in Brown, ed., *Focus on* Macbeth, p. 241). Modern film technology allowed Polanski to solve this problem. When Macbeth (played by Jon Finch) looks at the dagger, it appears; when he looks away, it disappears. Its evident existence to the senses (Macbeth's sight and our own) is thus precisely contingent on Macbeth's "seeing" it.

39. *The Masks of Macbeth* (Berkeley: University of California Press, 1970), Appendix.

40. "Obstetrics and Gynecology in *Macbeth*," p. 132. I imagine at least one theatrical production has presented a pregnant Queen.

41. Winnicott, "Transitional Objects," p. 96. Critics like Rosenberg (and A.C. Bradley) are not the only readers who seek certainty. A British Professor of Mental Health has diagnosed Macbeth's pathology: "On the International Classification of Diseases, Macbeth's illness would be classified as a psychogenic paranoid psychosis": see D.R. Davis, "Hurt Minds," in Brown, ed., *Focus on* Macbeth, pp. 210–28. The same expert suggests that timely therapeutic intervention might have saved Macbeth's marriage (not to mention Duncan's life).

42. For a thoughtful and imaginative analysis of projected audience response to this anxiety of unanswerability, see Booth, *King Lear, Macbeth, Indefinition, and Tragedy*.

43. Lawrence Danson makes a remark about the Jesuit doctrine of equivocation that is relevant here. "I think Shakespeare may have felt," he writes, that the doctrine "constituted an attack upon all the bases of rational discourse. For the

doctrine, with its all-purpose escape clause about 'mental reservation,' perverts the nature of language, which must be public and exoteric, into something private and esoteric. . . . The doctrine gives a sort of metaphysical warrant to solipsism, and elevates individual fantasy to a status equal with public reality": see *Tragic Alphabet: Shakespeare's Drama of Language* (New Haven, Conn.: Yale University Press, 1974), p. 133. I speculate that Shakespeare intended to attack the bases of rational discourse in *Macbeth*. Indeed, the notion of equality between individual fantasy and public reality states the dilemma and mystery of the play and our responses to it. See also the brief remarks on *Macbeth* by Steven Mullaney, "Lying Like Truth: Riddle, Representation, and Treason in Renaissance England," *ELH* 47 (1980), 32, 38.

44. "Language Most Shows a Man? Language and Speaker in *Macbeth*," in *Shakespeare's Styles: Essays in Honour of Kenneth Muir*, ed. Phillip Edwards et al. (Cambridge: Cambridge University Press, 1980), pp. 67–77; 75. See also Peter Stallybrass, "*Macbeth* and Witchcraft," and R. Grove, "Multiplying Villainies of Nature," in Brown ed., *Focus on Macbeth*.

45. King Lear, Macbeth, *Indefinition, and Tragedy*.

46. *Shakespeare and the Common Understanding* (New York: Free Press, 1967), p. 11.

47. See Thomas Cartelli, "Banquo's Ghost: The Shared Vision," *Theatre Journal* 38 (1983), 389–405. Calderwood's excellent treatment of the question describes an epistemological paradox for the audience that fits well with my suggestion about the status of Lady Macbeth's child: see *"If It Were Done"*, pp. 127–31.

48. After noting the symbolic aptness of the Macbeths' childlessness, and the evident pertinence of Lady Macbeth's child, Empson concludes that the question must finally be left in doubt. "It is the only crux of the play," he wrote, "which need be regarded as a radical dramatic ambiguity": see *Essays on Shakespeare* (Cambridge: Cambridge University Press, 1986), pp. 142–43. Writing of another moment in *Macbeth*, Stewart states, "If the audience can be made to grope among motives which are insubstantial, phantasmagoric and contradictory they will be approximating to the condition of the protagonist": see *Character and Motive*, p. 96.

49. "Epistemology and Tragedy: A Reading of *Othello*," *Daedalus* 108 (1979); reprinted as "Othello and the Stake of the Other" in *Disowning Knowledge in Six Plays by Shakespeare* (Cambridge: Cambridge University Press, 1987), pp. 125–42.

50. *Shakespearean Tragedy* (London: Cambridge University Press, 1904), p. 40. For the famous reply by L. C. Knights, see "How Many Children Had Lady Macbeth?"

51. In her study of the function of witchcraft belief as representing a deep contest between matriarchal and patriarchal social powers, Dympna Callaghan states: "In *Macbeth* the kingdom of darkness is unequivocally female, unequivocally matriarchal, and the fantasy of incipient rebellion of demonic forces is crucial to the maintenance of the godly rule it is supposed to overthrow": see "Wicked Women in *Macbeth*," in *Reconsidering the Renaissance*, ed. Mario DiCesare (Binghamton, N.Y.: Medieval and Renaissance Text Society, 1992), pp. 358–59. My only quarrel with this assertion is her emphasis on "unequivocal."

52. Cavell considers the issue of Macbeth's displaced relation to his intention

and the position of Lady Macbeth as "other": see "Macbeth Appalled," *Raritan* 12 (1992–93), 1, 1–15; 2, 1–15; 2, 10–11. He suggests that Lady Macbeth enters like a conjured apparition (just as, I would add, Macbeth comes to her call at the moment of regicide).

53. See *Comic Women, Tragic Men* (Stanford, Ca.: Stanford University Press, 1982), pp. 19, 93, 105. Bamber's book sympathetically yet critically revises Leslie Fiedler's concept of woman as Other in *The Stranger in Shakespeare* (New York: Stein and Day, 1972), pp. 43–84.

54. The auger hole is a specific link to the witches, both in terms of their fantastic abilities to "worm" into places and events and in the exact terms of Scot's *Discoverie of Witchcraft* (1584), a text Shakespeare evidently read. See Stephen Greenblatt, "Shakespeare Bewitched," in Jeffrey Cox and Larry Reynolds, eds., *New Historical Literary Study: Essays on Reproducing Texts, Representing History*, ed. Jeffrey Cox and Larry Reynolds (Princeton, N.J.: Princeton University Press, 1993), p. 125.

55. The Arden editor, Kenneth Muir, gives *entrails* as the meaning of "chaudron," citing a Dekker play (the *OED* also gives this definition under "chaldron," an obsolete form of "chawdron"). However, the rhyming terms were synonyms as well (under "chaudron," the *OED* gives *cauldron*, from the French). Their cognation derives from the image of a container, either a container of viscera (a kettle of entrails) or a visceral container (entrails themselves). See also Barron, "The Babe That Milks," p. 269.

56. Michael Goldman is especially good at evoking potential physical styles of the weird sisters: see *Acting and Action in Shakespearean Tragedy* (Princeton, N.J.: Princeton University Press, 1985).

57. See Hunter, "Shakespearian myth-making in *Macbeth*," for a development of these parallels. The larger theoretical issue I am treating here is openly discovered by Coppélia Kahn's review of feminist psychoanalytic theory in "Excavating 'Those Dim Minoan Regions': Maternal Subtexts in Patriarchal Literature," *Diacritics* 12 (1982), 32–41.

58. In her own imaginative recreation of *Macbeth*, Marjorie Garber suggests that the ghost author of the play is Lady Macbeth, as "a tale told by a sleepwalker." See "*Macbeth*: The Male Medusa," p. 87.

59. A standard "phallic" interpretation is by Ruth Nevo, *Tragic Form in Shakespeare* (Princeton, N.J.: Princeton University Press, 1972), pp. 233–34.

60. For a consideration of castration anxiety and the defense of doubling in the play, see Garber, "*Macbeth*: The Male Medusa," pp. 103–10.

61. See, for example, "The Splitting of the Ego in the Process of Defense" (1938), *Standard Edition*, 23, 271–78.

62. See Barbara Freedman, "Egeon's Debt: Self-Division and Self-Redemption in *The Comedy of Errors*," *English Literary Renaissance* 10 (1981), 360–83. A later, Lacanian revision of this essay was published in her book, *Staging the Gaze: Postmodernism, Psychoanalysis, and Shakespearean Comedy* (Ithaca, N.Y.: Cornell University Press, 1991): see "Reading Errantly: Misrecognition and the Uncanny," pp. 78–113.

63. I am using the definition of isomorphism provided by Douglas Hof-

stadter, who relates the mathematical idea to language and interpretation and who considers the issue of isomorphism the key to the question of consciousness itself. See his book, *Gödel, Escher, Bach: An Eternal Golden Braid* (New York: Basic Books, 1979), p. 9, pp. 49–50, p. 82.

64. A strong assertion of the isomorphic relation between Shakespeare and Freud is by Harold Bloom, who privileges Shakespeare and sees Freud as an anxious and defensive follower: see "Freud: A Shakespearean Reading," *The Western Canon*, pp. 371–94.

65. *The History of Sexuality*, trans. Robert Hurley (New York: Vintage, 1978), pp. 145–50.

66. For another instance of Shakespeare's cultural premonition—or more likely Foucault's intellectual prejudice for the eighteenth century—see Robert Watson's commentary on the effects of Foucauldian "bio-power" in the social policing and "domestication" of personal sexuality in *Measure for Measure*: see "False Immortality in *Measure for Measure*: Comic Means, Tragic Ends," *Shakespeare Quarterly* 41 (1990), 415–16; reprinted in Watson, *The Rest Is Silence: Death as Annihilation in the English Renaissance* (Berkeley: University of California Press, 1994), pp. 103–32.

67. See Foucault, *History of Sexuality*, p. 104, and Davis, "Hurt Minds," p. 20. In his "Theoretical" concluding section to *Studies on Hysteria*, co-authored with Freud (1893–95), Josef Breuer writes: "The split-off mind is the devil with which the unsophisticated observation of early superstitious times believed that these patients were possessed": see *Standard Edition*, 2, 249–50.

68. I am not citing cognation, just hearing a pun. Shakespeare uses the anatomical term ("pia mater") in *Love's Labour's Lost* (4.2.68) and *Troilus and Cressida* (2.1.77). Twice in *The Comedy of Errors* he uses "mated" in connection to madness (3.2.54, 5.1.282). The *OED* quotes the Doctor's line to illustrate one sense, derived from the Old French *mater*: "To put out of countenance; to render helpless by terror, shame, or discouragement; to daunt, abash; to stupefy." Under "mated," the *OED* gives "confounded, amazed"; most of these meanings relate to the position of "checkmate" in chess.

69. The most thorough study of this relation, not only imagined, is Adelman's *Suffocating Mothers*.

70. In a valuable extension and sharpening of the idea of *Macbeth* as dream or wish, Robert Watson sees the events as a catastrophic fulfillment of the "foolish wish" of folktales: see *Shakespeare and the Hazards of Ambition*, pp. 86–88.

71. A good account of the "great witch-hunt" that obsessed western Europe from the late sixteenth through most of the seventeenth century is by Norman Cohn, *Europe's Inner Demons* (New York: Basic Books, 1975). Although England was more legalistic and less severe than other countries (and preferred hanging to burning), Scotland seems to have been especially fierce in its persecution: see Cohn, pp. 253–55.

72. "Macbeth Appalled," 1, 1.

73. "*Macbeth*: The Male Medusa," p. 91.

74. See *A Thematic Introduction to Shakespeare* (New York: Empire State College, 1974), p. 26. See also Michel, *The Thing Contained*, p. 56.

75. In his chapter on *"Macbeth*: Counter-*Hamlet*," James Calderwood elaborates the thesis of tragic complementarity, in terms of issues of time, action, and thought: see *"If It Were Done"*, pp. 3–31.

76. See J.H. Summers, "The Anger of Prospero," *Michigan Quarterly Review* 12 (1973), 116–35; Peter Lindenbaum, "Prospero's Anger," *Massachusetts Review* 25 (1984), 161–71; and Richard Abrams, *"The Tempest* and the Concept of the Machiavellian Playwright," *English Literary Renaissance* 8 (1978), 43–66.

77. "A Commentary on *The Tempest*" (c. 1785–90), *Shakespearian Criticism*, ed. Daniel Fineman (Oxford: Clarendon Press, 1972), p. 338.

78. "Shakespeare Bewitched," p. 120.

79. "Shakespeare Bewitched," p. 123. See also Cavell, "Macbeth Appalled," 2, 5. On Prospero as magician and the cultural hazards of practicing magic, see Alvin Kernan, *The Playwright as Magician: Shakespeare's Image of the Poet in the English Public Theater* (New Haven, Conn.: Yale University Press, 1979), pp. 156–59.

80. Marjorie Garber would likely locate the scene in a reflected surface, as a defensive transformation of such dangerous (female) power—specifically Perseus's mirror-shield against Medusa: see *"Macbeth*: The Male Medusa," p. 117.

81. *"Macbeth* and the Imitation of an Action."

82. "Things I Owe to the Ancients" (1888), *Twilight of the Idols*, trans. A.M. Lodovici (New York, 1909–11; rep. 1964), 16: 112–20; 120. I am aware of the longstanding controversies over the psychological location and function of *catharsis* and do not wish to restrict its meaning to audience response. Indeed, the free-floating consanguinity between character's reaction and audience response is central to my theme. *Mimesis* can concern psychological "action" as well.

83. Greenblatt argues that whereas Scot's skepticism (in *The Discoverie of Witchcraft*) removes witches from reality and relocates them in theater, Shakespeare's art uses theater to restore the state of psychic credulity essential to witchcraft belief. Shakespeare is thus "in the position of the witch" who conjures and makes us believe: see "Shakespeare Bewitched," pp. 126–27.

84. "Things I Owe to the Ancients" (1888) in *Twilight of the Idols*, trans. A.M. Lodovici. *Complete Works*, 16, 120. In "Macbeth Appalled," Cavell finds a parallel between Macbeth and Nietzsche's figure of "the Pale Criminal" in *Thus Spoke Zarathustra*, whose whole self is "taken over by an image of the performance of the deed" that defines him, identifies him, as a criminal, so that he suffers "subjective extinction as it were in the doing of what he does" (2, 13).

Chapter Seven. "Shakespeare's Nothing"

1. Shakespeare's bawdy usage of "nothing" in *Hamlet* has been noted by most commentators. See Thomas Pyles, "Ophelia's 'Nothing,'" *Modern Language Notes* 64 (1949), 322–23; and Eric Partridge, *Shakespeare's Bawdy*, rev. ed. (London: Routledge and Kegan Paul, 1968). Its use in *King Lear* is noted by Samuel Abrams and Leonard Shengold, "The Meaning of 'Nothing': (I) A Note on 'Nothing' (II) More about the Meaning of 'Nothing,'" *Psychoanalytic Quarterly* 43 (1974),

115–19. Pyles, who assumed that this sort of naughtiness would have produced "guffaws" and "leers" from Shakespeare's audience, considered it "safe to assume that Shakespeare was perfectly well aware of the 'loose' meaning of *nothing* and *naught(y)* in the venereal vocabulary of his day."

2. The word "thing" is unique. Practically meaningless in itself, it can fill in any blank, replacing any other noun. It has a kind of semantic omnipotence by displacement. For the possible etymological origins of the phallic sense of "thing," see Theodore Thass-Thienemann, *The Interpretation of Language*, 2 vols. (New York: Jason Aronson, 1973) 2, 61–63. On "nothing," see 2, 69–70.

3. Ella Freeman Sharpe reads "folds of favor" as a reference to the maternal breast, which "child Lear" has been denied. See her essay, "From *King Lear* to *The Tempest*" (1946), *Collected Papers on Psycho-Analysis* (London: Hogarth Press, 1968), pp. 229–30.

4. The first and second Quarto editions have "small"; the first Folio has "great." Either reading is defensible. (Lear, I imagine, would prefer the Folio text.)

5. "Nuncle" is an Elizabethan dialect form, with the "n" transferred from "mine uncle."

6. See Norman O. Brown, "Nothing," in *Love's Body* (New York: Random House, 1966), pp. 256–66. On silences in *King Lear*, see Jill Levenson, "What the Silence Said: Still Points in *King Lear*," in *Shakespeare 1971: Proceedings of the World Shakespeare Congress, Vancouver, August 1971* , ed. Clifford Leech and J. M. R. Margeson (Toronto: University of Toronto Press, 1972), pp. 215–29; Emily Leider, "Plainness of Style in *King Lear*," *Shakespeare Quarterly* 21 (1970), 45–53; and Richard Fly, "Revelations of Darkness: The Language of Silence in *King Lear*," *Bucknell Review* 20 (1972), 73–92.

7. See Murray Schwartz, "Leontes' Jealousy in *The Winter's Tale*," *American Imago* 30 (1973), 250–73. Schwartz describes the "Affection!" passage as "an abstract version of the primal scene, the intercourse of something and nothing" (pp. 264–65). In a reading of the speech that places it in early modern psychological and medical contexts, David Ward understands it as Leontes's attempt at self-diagnosis. Ward holds the terminology close to an historical lexicon; his goal is to produce logical connections within the passionate speech. Attention to unconscious associations is not part of his project, which is hence limited: see "Affection, Intention, and Dreams in *The Winter's Tale*," *Modern Language Review* 82 (1987), 545–54.

8. Stanley Cavell finds in Leontes's "nothing" speech a pathological skepticism searching for some epistemological basis on its way to desperate nihilism: see "Recounting Gains, Showing Losses (A Reading of *The Winter's Tale*)," in *Disowning Knowledge in Six Plays by Shakespeare* (Cambridge: Cambridge University Press, 1987), pp. 85–90.

9. See my remarks on this scene in Chapter Three. Valerie Traub interprets Leontes's paranoia as an expression of masculine anxiety when confronted with the "enormous powers of signification" contained in the female body: see *Desire and Anxiety: Circulations of Sexuality in Shakespearean Drama* (New York: Routledge, 1992), p. 44. In other words, Leontes's psychological excess is in response to (his fantasy of) female procreative excess.

10. Robert Watson notes the highly suggestive language of the scene and judges that "Leontes has become illiterate in the courtly *langue* that explains and justifies the sexual *paroles*": see *Shakespeare and the Hazards of Ambition* (Cambridge, Mass.: Harvard University Press, 1984), p. 234, p. 240. I would modify this perspective. In his super-subtle audition, Leontes brings a paranoid frame of reference that obliterates rhetorical distinctions between courtly convention and sexual metaphor. His suspicious ears undo the customary sublimation that permits sensual flirtation in the guise of flowery civility. In this sense he is not illiterate but hyperliterate. His interpretation restores the literal meanings of the words; he brings language back to its senses (even as he loses his own).

11. For commentary on traditional theological and philosophical notions of creation ex nihilo in the Renaissance, see William R. Elton, *King Lear and the Gods* (San Marino, Ca.: The Huntington Library, 1968), especially pp. 179–90; and Paul A. Jorgensen, "Much Ado About 'Nothing,'" *Shakespeare Quarterly* 5 (1954), 287–95.

12. See Helge Kökeritz, *Shakespeare's Pronunciation* (New Haven, Conn.: Yale University Press, 1953). The Latin *nota*, meaning mark of designation, is related to *nosco* ("I begin to know") and thus to our word "know." Several of Shakespeare's senses and uses of the word "nothing," as well as the auditory pun on "noting," are cited in Jorgensen, "Much Ado About 'Nothing'." In a suggestive essay, Patricia Parker explores the full sexual significances of the sign and sound of "o": see "*Othello* and *Hamlet*: Dilation, Spying, and the 'Secret Place' of Woman," in *Shakespeare Reread: The Texts in New Contexts*, ed. Russ McDonald (Ithaca, N.Y.: Cornell University Press, 1994), pp. 104–46.

13. See Bruno Munari, *The Discovery of the Circle*, trans. Marcello and Edna Maestro (New York: George Wittenborn, 1966), p. 65.

14. This is a central and continuing theme in Freudian theory. Freud's essay, "Negation" (1925), offers a brief statement: see *Standard Edition*, 19, 235–41. See also David Bleich, "New Considerations of the Infantile Acquisition of Language and Symbolic Thought," *Psychoanalytic Review* 63 (1976), 49–72; Joseph Smith, "Language and the Genealogy of the Absent Object," in *Psychiatry and the Humanities*, ed. Joseph Smith (New Haven, Conn.: Yale University Press, 1976), pp. 145–70; and my Epilogue.

15. See Jacques Lacan, *The Language of the Self: The Function of Language in Psychoanalysis*, trans. with notes and commentary by Anthony Wilden (Baltimore: Johns Hopkins University Press, 1968), p. 217. For a semiotic essay on the dialectic of writing and nothingness that cites Derrida, see Jean-Louis Schefer, "*La mort, le corps, rien*," *Sub-stance* 14 (1976), 117–25. Besides Lacan, these Gallic myths of primordial absence and "zero degree" writing are most eloquently related by Derrida and Barthes.

Among narrative myths of origin, there seem to be two primary versions. In Judaeo-Christian mythology, the Beginning is characterized by a *void* (Old Testament), and by a *word* (New Testament). The two myths together create the primary dialectic of void and word, nothing and noting, which Joyce captures in his most significant pun: "In the buginning is the woid, in the muddle is the sounddance" (*Finnegans Wake*, 378.29).

Ex nihilo myths, of nothing at the nodal point, recur throughout human thought. All of our counting numbers literally start from, and derive from, zero. Proof of their mathematical generation (by Gottlob Frege, Bertrand Russell, and other theorists) is elaborate: see Martin Gardner's "Mathematical Games" section of *Scientific American* 232 (February 1975), 98–101. Modern astrophysical speculation about "black holes" posits an all-engulfing emptiness that is often imaged as a mouth, or "the navel of the universe," and which has at its core something termed a "naked singularity"—an entity which one excitable science writer considers a "gorgon-like horror": see Dietrick E. Thomson, "The Blob that Ate Physics," *Science News* 108 (July 12, 1975), 28–29. Gardner has reviewed the literature on this mysterious phenomenon in "The Holes in Black Holes," *New York Review of Books* (September 29, 1977), 22–24. Twenty years later the trope of dangerous sexual engulfment persists in narrations of this science: the latest Scientific American Library volume, by Mitchell Begelman and Martin Rees, is titled *Gravity's Fatal Attraction: Black Holes in the Universe* (New York: Scientific American Library, 1996). Gary Taylor has appropriated the image in the final chapter of *Reinventing Shakespeare: A Cultural History from the Restoration to the Present* (New York: Oxford University Press, 1989), titled "Singularity" (pp. 373–411), where he addresses the question—or rather interrogates the assumption—of Shakespeare's unique, supreme genius. Taylor's conclusions are vigorous, biased, resistant (even antagonistic) to current academic criticism. His final trope is clever and compelling: Where Shakespeare was once a star, he has now collapsed under the weight of excessive attention and praise, so that he is now a black hole that "warps cultural space-time" and traps all possible readings (see pp. 410–11).

16. See Freud, *Beyond the Pleasure Principle* (1920), *Standard Edition*, 18, 3–65. The incident is central to Lacanian theory: see *The Language of the Self* (also known as "The Rome Discourse").

17. The quartos have "yawne," the folios, "ayme." In an impossibly perfect play of language both words coexist. Audiences search for meaning, their mouths agape.

18. See Georges Poulet, *The Metamorphoses of the Circle*, trans. Carley Dawson and Elliott Coleman (Baltimore: Johns Hopkins University Press, 1966), especially pp. xxii–xxiv.

19. See my essay, "Rape and Revenge in *Titus Andronicus*," *English Literary Renaissance* 8 (1978), 159–82.

20. See Alvin Kernan, *The Playwright as Magician: Shakespeare's Image of the Poet in the English Public Theater* (New Haven, Conn.: Yale University Press, 1979), pp. 133–34. In a Christian version of the scheme of magical transformation, Cynthia Marshall describes analogies between church and theater as sacred spaces: see *Last Things and Last Plays: Shakespearean Eschatology* (Carbondale: Southern Illinois University Press, 1991), pp. 107–15. Meredith Skura also reviews multiple personal and cultural meanings of Shakespeare's circles: see *Shakespeare the Actor and the Purposes of Playing* (Chicago: University of Chicago Press, 1993), pp. 225–34.

21. *Finnegans Wake*, 353–22. Anthony Burgess glosses this phrase as, "optimistically, the re-creation of meaning out of nothing." See his *Re Joyce* (New York:

Norton, 1965), p. 239. "An infinite deal of nothing" is Bassanio's opinion of Gratiano's loquacity in *The Merchant of Venice* (1.1.114).

22. "Search" derives from Middle English *serchen* or *cerchen*, out of Old and Middle French *cercher* or *chercher*, from the Latin *circum* and *circare* ("to go around or about"). See Eric Partridge, *Origins: A Short Etymological Dictionary of Modern English*, third ed. (New York: Macmillan, 1961); s.v. "circulate," "search."

23. E. A. M. Colman provides a hesitant, circumspect handling of the puns in "nothing" and "O" in these lines: see *The Dramatic Use of Bawdy in Shakespeare* (London: Longman Group, 1974), pp. 16–18, p. 71. Today's auditors and editors likely have readier ears and eyes.

24. See Partridge, *Shakespeare's Bawdy*, p. 152.

25. The term "*fécondation*" is J.B. Petit's: see "'This wooden O': Théâtre et signe dans les choeurs de *Henry V*," *Études Anglaises* 21 (1968), 286–92. For an excellent brief evocation of the imaginative range of Shakespeare's stage, see A.B. Kernan, "This Goodly Frame, the Stage: The Interior Theater of Imagination in English Renaissance Drama," *Shakespeare Quarterly* 25 (1974), 1–5; revised and included in *The Playwright as Magician*. On the pregnancy of words and the potency of images, see Inga-Stina Ewbank, "'More pregnantly than words': Some Uses and Limitations of Visual Symbols," *Shakespeare Survey* 24 (1971), 13–18.

26. See René Spitz, "The Primal Cavity: A Contribution to the Genesis of Perception and Its Role for Psychoanalytic Theory," in *No and Yes: On the Genesis of Human Communication* (New York: International Universities Press, 1957); and Spitz, *The First Year of Life* (New York: International Universities Press, 1965). Excellent use of Spitz's theories has been made by Donald Kaplan, in "Theatre Architecture: A Derivation of the Primal Cavity," *The Drama Review* 12 (1968), 105–16. Using Spitz's notion of "primal dialogues"—nonverbal communications between infant and mother—Kaplan argues that "a theatre . . . structures an opportunity for a primal dialogue between the audience and the actors" (p. 109). No dramatist was more aware of this opportunity, and its primitive origins, than Shakespeare. See also Skura, "Circles and Centers," in *Shakespeare the Actor*, pp. 225–34. In an essay on *Henry V*, Krystian Cznerniecki notes the aural and visual puns on "O." He uses the brand of psychoanalysis promoted by Nicholas Abraham and Maria Torok to press his interpretation toward metaphoric recuperations of mourning and introjection: the wooden O that is impossibly crammed with represented objects becomes "the O of the bereaved mouth." See "The Jest Digested: Perspectives on History in *Henry V*," in *On Puns: The Foundation of Letters*, ed. Jonathan Culler (Oxford: Blackwell, 1988), pp. 62–82; especially pp. 62–66.

27. "'This wooden O,'" p. 291.

28. After quoting the famous lines from Theseus's speech about the imagination, and citing the gentleman's remark about the effect of Ophelia's mad discourse on her audience, Jorgensen writes: "One must not, of course, try to build Shakespeare's concept of imaginative creation upon the fanciful, and at best figurative, references to Nothing in these passages. At the same time, analogy with the doctrine of divine creation, which was neither fanciful nor figurative, helps explain the remarkable persistence with which the concept of nothingness, and usually the

word itself, appears in his statements on poetry and dreams": see "Much Ado About 'Nothing.'" I am arguing that the primary analogy is not with "divine creation" (a doctrine both fanciful and figurative, even though believed), but with natural human procreation. Moreover, I *am* willing to build an idea of Shakespearean imaginative productivity on these various fancies and figures of Nothing.

29. See K. T. S. Campbell, "'The Phoenix and the Turtle' as a Signpost of Shakespeare's Development," *British Journal of Aesthetics* 10 (1970), 169–79.

30. See Poulet, *Metamorphoses of the Circle*, pp. 15–31.

31. "*King Lear*: The Quality of Nothing," in Howard Babb, ed., *Essays in Stylistic Analysis* (New York, 1972), p. 242.

32. See Ralph Berry, "'To Say "One"': An Essay on *Hamlet*," *Shakespeare Survey* 28 (1975), 107–15; reprinted in *The Shakespearean Metaphor: Studies in Language and Form* (Totowa, N.J.: Rowman and Littlefield, 1978), pp. 61–73.

33. The pun comes from Brown, *Love's Body*, p. 262: "I'm no one. I'm a noun."

34. Murray Schwartz concludes his study of *The Winter's Tale* by writing, "Finally Shakespeare . . . looks toward reality and fantasy simultaneously, toward loss, the beginning of death, and toward re-creation, its negation. He gives us nothing and all": see "*The Winter's Tale*: Loss and Transformation," *American Imago* 32 (1975), 158–98, 198.

Chapter Eight. "What Is Shakespeare?"

1. *The Sketchbook of Geoffrey Crayon, Gent. Washington Irving: History, Tales & Sketches*, ed. J. W. Tuttleton (New York: Library of America, 1983), pp. 983–1001.

2. Hawthorne, *The English Notebooks*, ed. R. Stewart (New York: Russell and Russell, 1962), pp. 129–34. Two other famous American writers also resisted the call of Bardolatry. Melville predicted that an American talent would surpass Shakespeare, and Poe observed that most overvaluation of Shakespeare proceeded from ignorance and hearsay. See Lawrence Levine, "Shakespeare in America," in *Highbrow/Lowbrow: The Emergence of Cultural Hierarchy in America* (Cambridge, Mass.: Harvard University Press, 1988), pp. 129–34.

3. Clemens, *Is Shakespeare Dead?* (New York: Harper, 1906). For James's remarks, see Leon Edel, *Henry James: The Master: 1901–1916* (Philadelphia: Lippincott, 1972), pp. 145–46.

4. James, "The Birthplace," in *The Better Sort* (Freeport, New York: Books for Libraries Press, 1903), pp. 245–311. For a similar application of James's story, see Marjorie Garber, *Shakespeare's Ghost Writers: Literature as Uncanny Causality* (New York: Methuen, 1987), pp. 9–10. Garber provides a set of proposals for understanding the tenacity of the authorship controversy as a social phenomenon and suggests a blend of Freudian and Derridean ideas (the uncanny, the supplement) to situate the problem within the plays themselves.

5. "The Birthplace," p. 263.

6. "The Birthplace," pp. 283–84.

7. "Introduction" to *The Tempest* (1907). *Selected Literary Criticism*, ed. Morris Shapira (New York: McGraw-Hill, 1964), pp. 297–310.

8. "Introduction" to *The Tempest*, pp. 297–98.

9. Yeats, "At Stratford-on-Avon" in *Essays and Introductions* (New York: Macmillan, 1961), pp. 106–7; Joyce, *Ulysses* (New York: Modern Library, 1961), p. 197; Hazlitt, *Lectures on the English Poets* (London, 1818) (quoted in F. E. Halliday, *Shakespeare and His Critics* [New York: Schocken, 1958], p.88); Borges, "Everything and Nothing," in *Labyrinths*, ed. Donald Yates and James Irby (New York: New Directions, 1964), pp. 248–49.

10. Leah Marcus cites Edmund Malone's whitewashing of the Stratford bust of Shakespeare as an emblem of the "denial of Shakespeare's topicality," replacing local color with marble-like idealization: see *Puzzling Shakespeare: Local Reading and Its Discontents* (Berkeley: University of California Press, 1988), pp. 213–14. The bust was painted in 1793 and remained so until 1861.

11. See Barthes, "The Death of the Author," and Foucault, "What Is an Author?" in *Language, Counter-Memory, Practice: Selected Essays and Interviews*, ed. Donald F. Bouchard (Ithaca, N.Y.: Cornell University Press, 1977), pp. 113–38.

12. See Harold Bloom, *The Anxiety of Influence* (New York: Oxford University Press, 1973), p. 11. Bloom's contention is grandly elaborated in *The Western Canon: The Books and School of the Ages* (New York: Harcourt Brace, 1994). In the later book the idealized figure of Shakespeare appears throughout: see especially "Shakespeare, Center of the Canon," pp. 45–75. At times it is a mere equation: "Shakespeare is the canon" (p. 50), creator of self-conscious language itself. Joel Fineman's idealizations are more sophisticated and at least as grand. In *Shakespeare's Perjured Eye: The Invention of Poetic Subjectivity in the Sonnets* (Berkeley: University of California Press, 1986) he posits Shakespeare as the inventor of modern subjectivity and ultimately asserts that after Shakespeare all literature is "Shakespearean"—any other kind must be outside of language and history: see p. 29, pp. 79–82, p. 296.

13. See Peter Erickson, "Shakespeare and the Author Function," in *Shakespeare's "Rough Magic": Renaissance Essays in Honor of C. L. Barber*, ed. Peter Erickson and Coppélia Kahn (Newark: University Delaware Press, 1985), pp. 245–55. For a suggestion that the Renaissance invention of the author already carried Foucauldian features of restriction and censorship, see Marcus, *Puzzling Shakespeare*, p. 29.

14. "The Death of the Author," p. 145.

15. See my theoretical interlude in Chapter Four.

16. *The World, the Text, and the Critic* (Cambridge, Mass.: Harvard University Press, 1983), pp. 196–99. The *Great Expectations* scene is in Chapter 31.

17. *That Shakespeherian Rag: Essays on a Critical Process* (London: Methuen, 1986), pp. 74–75.

18. Thus begins Ben Jonson's famous prefatory poem to the First Folio (1623). My italics indicate the rival poet's gratuitous denial of envy and the inference that praise is extracted through confession. Notice also how the parenthesis brackets

Shakespeare's name, in a momentary syntactic subordination; the halting progress of the line imitates the hesitation of its author.

19. In her Epilogue to *Notorious Identity: Materializing the Subject in Shakespeare* (Cambridge, Mass.: Harvard University Press, 1993), Linda Charnes notes the late-twentieth-century transformation of Shakespeare into a "commodity identity" for commercial and political purposes—"a form of symbolic capital that circulates in the culture like unalloyed gold coin": see pp. 155–59; 155. Shakespeare is thus given only token recognition that yet carries value.

20. *Shakespeare's Lives* (Oxford: Oxford University Press, 1970), p. ix.

21. Robert Greene, *A Groats-Worth of Wit* (London, 1592), quoted in Halliday, *Shakespeare and His Critics*, p. 45.

22. Thomas Freeman, *Runne and a Great Cast* (London, 1614), quoted in Halliday, *Shakespeare and His Critics*, p. 47.

23. *Essay on the Dramatic Poetry of the Last Age* (London, 1672), quoted in Halliday, *Shakespeare and His Critics*, p. 57.

24. *Human, All-Too-Human, Complete Works*, vol. 6, p. 176.

25. "At Stratford-on-Avon," p. 107.

26. See Schoenbaum, *Shakespeare's Lives*, p. 298.

27. Howard Felperin states that "Shakespeare never succumbs to the rhetorical pressure of the traditional forms he employs, to their built-in claims to have made sense of the world, but keeps them always in brackets and puts them ultimately into question": see *Shakespearean Representation: Mimesis and Modernity in Elizabethan Tragedy* (Princeton, N.J.: Princeton University Press, 1977), p. 106. Joel Fineman notes Shakespeare's tendency to deploy and exhaust tropes, genres, and literary structures. Shakespeare uses the interplay of traditional categories of opposition, complementary, and paradox (here Fineman cites Norman Rabkin and Robert Grudin) to produce "a profound Shakespearean meditation" by deploying such structures while simultaneously putting them into question. Shakespeare, in other words, is his own deconstructor. See *Shakespeare's Perjured Eye*, p. 333, n. 35.

28. *Palladis Tamia: Wit's Treasury* (London, 1598), quoted in Halliday, *Shakespeare and His Critics*, p. 45.

29. *Shakespearean Criticism*, ed. Thomas Raysor, 2 vols. (London: Everyman's Library, 1960), vol. 2, pp. 146–47.

30. Edward Pechter, *What Was Shakespeare? Renaissance Plays and Changing Critical Practice* (Ithaca, N.Y.: Cornell University Press, 1995), p. 3. Besides Pechter's superb review, there are several other recent histories of Bardolatry. For example, see Graham Holderness, "Bardolatry: Or the Cultural Materialist's Guide to Stratford-Upon-Avon," in *The Shakespeare Myth*, ed. Graham Holderness (Manchester: Manchester University Press, 1988), pp. 2–15; Howard Felperin's survey of eighteenth- and nineteenth-century constructions that shows how the notion of "ahistorical" idealism has a history, in "Historicizing Bardolatry: Or, Where Could Coleridge have been Coming from?" in *The Uses of the Canon: Elizabethan Literature and Contemporary Theory* (Oxford: Clarendon Press, 1990), pp. 1–15; and Leah Marcus's brief synopsis of "the demise of the transcendent Bard" during the iconoclastic 1960s and 1970s, in *Puzzling Shakespeare*, pp. 23–32. William Beatty Warner offers an astute view of some motives and uses of cultural constructions of an

idealized and idolized Shakespeare: see *Chance and the Text of Experience: Freud, Nietzsche, and Shakespeare's* Hamlet (Ithaca, N.Y.: Cornell University Press, 1986), pp. 217–22.

31. *Lectures on the English Poets* (London, 1818), quoted in Halliday, *Shakespeare and His Critics*, p. 91.

32. See "The Articulation of the Ego in the English Renaissance," *The Literary Freud: Mechanisms of Defense and the Poetic Will*, ed. Joseph Smith, Psychiatry and the Humanities, vol. 4 (New Haven, Conn.: Yale University Press, 1980), pp. 273–74.

33. See Foucault, "What Is an Author?", p. 123.

34. "Introduction" to *The Tempest*, p. 302.

35. See Caroline Spurgeon, *Shakespeare's Imagery and What It Tells Us* (London: Cambridge University Press, 1935), pp. 6–8.

36. For a representative essay from this perspective, see Michael McCanles, "Shakespeare, Intertextuality, and the Decentered Self," in Douglas Atkins, ed., *Shakespeare and Deconstruction*, ed. Douglas Atkins (New York: Peter Lang, 1988), pp. 193–212.

37. This sort of claim is not limited to literary critics. Peter Brook, in a BBC television program, *A Muse of Fire* (BBC/Time-Life, 1983), opined that Shakespeare's own perspective is invisible in the plays: "He served the expression of an omnidirectional reality."

38. Winnicott, "Mirror-Role of Mother and Family in Child Development," in *Playing and Reality* (London: Tavistock Publications, 1971).

39. Lacan, "The mirror stage as formative of the function of the I as revealed in psychoanalytic experience," in *Écrits: A Selection*, trans. Alan Sheridan (New York: Norton, 1977), pp. 1–7.

40. Lichtenstein, "Narcissism and Primary Identity," in *The Dilemma of Human Identity* (New York: Jason Aronson, 1977), pp. 207–21.

41. A previous interpretation of this passage can be found in Chapter Three.

42. For a review of philosophical and scientific theories of speculation from Plato and Aristotle through Neoplatonism to the Renaissance, see Kent Kraft, "Mind's Mirrors: Some Early Versions of Contemporary Specular Discourse," in *The Play of the Self*, ed. Ronald Bogue and Mihai Spariosu (Albany: SUNY Press, 1994), pp. 39–66.

43. "Introduction" to *The Tempest*," p. 298.

44. See Otto Fenichel, "On Acting," *Psychoanalytic Quarterly* 15 (1946), 144–60, and Jonas Barish, *The Antitheatrical Prejudice* (Berkeley: University of California Press, 1981).

45. "Introduction" to *The Tempest*, p. 305.

Epilogue. "Yorick's Skull, Miranda's Memory"

1. On Hamlet as the courtly clown whose uses of language subvert conventional signifiers, see Lacan, "Desire and the Interpretation of Desire in *Hamlet*," *Yale French Studies* 55–56 (1977), pp. 11–52, 33–34.

2. Ella Freeman Sharpe confidently identifies Yorick with "the real father of the poet's youth, . . . rich, prosperous, and merry," here brought back as both tribute and guilty memory: see *Collected Papers on Psycho-Analysis* (London: Hogarth Press, 1968), p. 260. Most psychoanalytic critics have followed Freud's assumption that Shakespeare wrote *Hamlet* in response to his father's death. Biographical facts are unclear on this point, but it is likely that John Shakespeare was alive, if not well, when his son composed the play. John Shakespeare died in September 1601, at age 70, a very advanced age for the times. *Hamlet* is typically dated between 1599 and 1602. For a succinct review of the issue, see Harold Jenkins's Introduction to the Arden Edition (London: Methuen, 1982), pp. 1–13. Jenkins concludes that the play was being acted in 1600, albeit without some topical passages possibly added later. If Shakespeare-as-Hamlet is looking at his father's death, he is likely looking into the future. It's a near future, however, and perspectives can be powered by wishes, as Henry the Fourth famously pointed out to his son (*2 Henry IV*, 4.5.92). For psychoanalytic interpretation of Yorick as the "good father," see K.R. Eissler, *Discourse on Hamlet and* Hamlet: *A Psychoanalytic Inquiry* (New York: International Universities Press, 1971), pp. 84–85; and William Kerrigan, *Hamlet's Perfection* (Baltimore: Johns Hopkins University Press, 1994), pp. 133–34.

3. In a bold reading, Avi Erlich literalizes hints in the passage to construct a homosexual fantasy of Hamlet riding Yorick as a passive, feminized object. He further interprets Hamlet's transformation of the skull from a representation of active manhood to empty skull to figure of woman as a type of castration: see *Hamlet's Absent Father* (Princeton, N..J. .J.: Princeton University Press, 1977), pp. 140–41.

4. For a thorough reading of the woman-as-garden image in the play, see Janet Adelman, "Man and Wife is One Flesh: *Hamlet* and the Confrontation with the Maternal Body," in *Suffocating Mothers: Fantasies of Maternal Origin in Shakespeare's Plays* (New York: Routledge, 1992), pp. 11–37. Although at points her characterization of (the fantasized) Gertrude suggests the further equation of maternal garden and maternal grave (for example, "Gertrude is death's mouth," p. 27), Adelman does not fully explore the analogy. A classic "Freudian" analysis of the scene produces symbolic readings of objects (skulls = paternal testicles; grave = mother's body): see Norman Symons, "The Graveyard Scene in *Hamlet*," *International Journal of Psycho-Analysis* 9 (1928), 96–119. A more recent similar reading is by M.D. Faber, "*Hamlet* and the Inner World of Objects," in *The Undiscover'd Country: New Essays on Psychoanalysis and Shakespeare*, ed. J. B. Sokol (London: Free Association Press, 1993), pp. 57–90. Faber traces links of association from Yorick to the figure of "mother as betrayer" and reads the image of "my lady's chamber" as a prefiguration of the "bunghole" and "beer barrel" of ensuing lines—all images of the debased maternal body (see pp. 81–83). On the psychic and mythic relation between unrepresentable death and the figure of the maternal body, see Kristeva, *Black Sun: Depression and Melancholia*, trans. Leon Roudiez (New York: Columbia University Press, 1989), pp. 26–27.

5. The cover art for this book is a typical representation of the genre, popular in northern Europe in the early seventeenth century. Such *vanitas* paintings were

inspired by the lines in Ecclesiastes 12:8 ("Vanity of vanities, saith the preacher. All is vanity"). This specific type of small allegorical still-life was devised in Holland. Pieter Claesz's version was painted in 1623, the year of Shakespeare's First Folio. Beyond this coincidence, the tableau is appropriately Shakespearean. A poet's quill rests on a manuscript, guarded by a chop-fallen skull that apparently grips some loose pages in its partial mouth. The subject speaks now only through post-mortem testimony; its tongue is text. The wine has been drawn, drunk, or spilled; the brief candle is out. The time-piece is open but its hands are not visible; probably it has run down. Unlike other examples of the genre, which typically include iconography of other ultimately empty human efforts like music, drawing, or science, Claesz's painting focusses on writing. For information about the *vanitas* type, see *Microsoft Art Gallery: The Collection of the National Gallery, London* (Microsoft, 1994). This particular work is not in the collection (it's at the Metropolitan Museum in New York), but information about the genre and other examples are available on the CD-ROM.

6. See *King Lear*, 3.4.106–7 ("Thou art the thing itself: unaccommodated man is no more . . ."), and *Hamlet*, 4.2.27–30 ("The body is with the King, but the King is not with the body. The King is a thing . . . of nothing"). Stanley Cavell suggests that Hamlet is finally looking at what he always anyway sees in others, their "everyday skeletal manner": see "Hamlet's Burden of Proof," in *Disowning Knowledge in Six Plays by Shakespeare* (Cambridge: Cambridge University Press, 1987), p. 186. In Lacanian terms, it may be that Hamlet is here trying to gaze at "the real," or at "the hole in the real": see Lacan, "Desire and the Interpretation of Desire in *Hamlet*," pp. 37–38. Graham Hammill suggests (personal communication) that the skull is an instance of the Lacanian *objet a*, whose materiality or link with the real "threatens the symbolic universe of the play."

7. Kerrigan evokes a full sense of the vastness of the graveyard scene, inside the play and outside of it: see "The Last Mystery," in *Hamlet's Perfection*, pp. 122–51. An especially apt observation is that the gravedigger began his trade on the "very day that young Hamlet was born" (5.1.147). He is digging Ophelia's grave today, and will likely be digging Hamlet's grave tomorrow. "Symbolically," Kerrigan notes, "he has been digging it from the day Hamlet was born" (p. 128). Hamlet's readiness merely catches up to that of his grave. Robert Watson makes a similar observation: see *The Rest is Silence: Death as Annihilation in the English Renaissance* (Berkeley: University of California Press, 1994), p. 92.

8. Richard Fly assumes the accuracy of the gravedigger's memory, yet also stresses the universal loss of difference in the graveyard—including persons, professions, and meanings of words. See "Accommodating Death: The Ending of *Hamlet*," *Studies in English Literature 1500–1900* 24 (1984), 257–274, especially pp. 266–67 and Note.

9. The game of loggats was a kind of bowling, with bones substituted for wooden pins: see Forbes Sieveking's account of early modern games in *Shakespeare's England: An Account of the Life and Manners of His Age*, 2 vols. (Oxford: Clarendon Press, 1916), 2, 466; and Harold Jenkins's skeptical citation in the Arden edition of *Hamlet* (London: Methuen, 1982), p. 381, n. 91.

10. Readers will note that I am reluctant to specify the nature of Hamlet's "that within." By this point I hope that its significance as a mark of the aboriginal link between infantile self and maternal source is apparent, or at least implicit. That link connects the individual unconscious and the primal social world: a bond that sustains the deepest desires and dreads. See the theoretical interlude in Chapter Four (especially Note 34).

11. In an essay on "Prospero's Wife," Stephen Orgel makes good use of previous psychoanalytic commentary on the absent and demonized mother in *The Tempest*, especially as located in other marginal and mysterious female characters, such as Sycorax, Ceres, and Medea: see *Representations* 8 (1984), 1–13. In "Shakespeare's Tempest," *American Imago* 39 (1982), 219–37, Jerry McGuire notes how Prospero replaces (maternal) memory with (paternal) history—or "maternal poetics" with "paternal rhetoric"—so that "the silent image of the mother is submitted to a naming by the male, . . . brought under the post-Oedipal canopy of his language and law" (p. 229).

12. Several essays iterate this fundamental idea, which is best expressed in one of the best essays on *The Tempest*, Harry Berger's "Miraculous Harp: A Reading of *The Tempest*," in *Second World and Green World: Studies in Renaissance Fiction-Making* (Berkeley: University of California Press, 1988), pp. 147–85. See also Orgel, "Prospero's Wife"; and Stephen Greenblatt, "Martial Law in the Land of Cockaigne," in *Shakespearean Negotiations: The Circulation of Social Energy in Renaissance England* (Berkeley: University of California Press, 1988), pp. 129–63. On the fusion of corporeal and intellectual space in *The Tempest*, see Cary Nelson, "Prospero's Island: The Visionary Body of *The Tempest*," in *The Incarnate Word: Literature as Verbal Space* (Urbana: University of Illinois Press, 1973), pp. 53–79. Both Nelson and Adelman are very insightful about the deep metaphoric relation between island and mother.

13. See Freud, "Remembering, Repeating, and Working Through: Further Recommendations on the Technique of Psycho-Analysis II" (1914), *Standard Edition*, 12, 146–56.

14. As Nigel Alexander puts it, "*The Tempest* is designed to allay anxieties about the past and give the audience a glimpse of a hopeful future. *Hamlet* raises anxieties about the past and buries all hope for the future": see *Poison, Play, and Duel* (Lincoln: University of Nebraska Press, 1970), p. 38. For a treatment of *Hamlet* in terms of Freudian repetition compulsion and symptomatic acting-out, see Marjorie Garber, "*Hamlet*: Giving Up the Ghost," in *Shakespeare's Ghost Writers*.

15. This is the realm of "baby talk": see Marcia Cavell, "Baby Talk," in *The Psychoanalytic Mind: From Freud to Philosophy* (Cambridge, Mass.: Harvard University Press, 1993); and Steven Pinker, "Baby Born Talking—Describes Heaven," in *The Language Instinct: How the Mind Creates Language* (New York: William Morrow, 1994), pp. 262–96. On primitive phonemic sounds, see Thass-Thienemann, *The Interpretation of Language*, 2, 34–36; and Pinker, *The Language Instinct*, p. 171. For a nontechnical linguistic essay on the origins of primitive phonemes out of the nursery—the "optimal" consonants and vowels for early mutterance—see Roman Jakobson, "Why 'Mama' and 'Papa'?" in *On Language*, ed.

Linda Waugh and Monique Monville-Burston (Cambridge, Mass.: Harvard University Press, 1990), pp. 305–14. A related essay is Jakobson's "The Spell of the Speech Sound," a review of several linguistic and psychological theories of sound meanings and symbolisms (*On Language*, pp. 422–47). On the evolution of primordial language and aboriginal phonemes, see Mary Foster, "Body Process in the Evolution of Language," in *Giving the Body Its Due*, ed. Maxine Sheets-Johnstone (Albany: SUNY Press, 1992), pp. 208–30. An anthropological linguist, Foster understands language "as an analogic system with its deepest roots in bodily mimicry" (p. 228).

16. See Joyce, *Finnegans Wake*, 378.29: "In the buginning is the woid, in the muddle is the sounddance."

17. Marcia Cavell discusses the developmental possibility of preverbal subjective experience in her chapter, "Behind the Veil of Language," in *The Psychoanalytic Mind*, pp. 107–20 (see pp. 113–17 for an explicit critique of Lacan). She cites an unpublished paper by J. McDowell on the emergence of articulated experience from such an aboriginal matrix (pp. 116–17). For a lucid account of psychological theories of the development of language, see Daniel Stern, "The Sense of a Verbal Self," in *The Interpersonal World of the Infant: A View from Psychoanalysis and Developmental Psychology* (New York: Basic Books, 1985), pp. 162–82; and "Unformulated Experience," *Contemporary Psychoanalysis* 19 (1987), 71–99. Stern cites research and theory on the origins of meaning as "negotiated" experience, and the double-edged effect of language to enable shared conversation while privileging the articulatable self, thus cutting off core areas of affective experience. "Language forces a space," he writes, "between interpersonal experience as lived and as represented": see *Interpersonal World*, p. 182. See also D.W. Winnicott on "the non-communicating central self, forever immune from the reality principle, and forever silent." in "Communicating and Not Communicating Leading to a Study of Certain Opposites," *The Maturational Processes and the Facilitating Environment* (London: Hogarth Press, 1965), p. 187. For Winnicott, this secret, silent core is a space of authenticity, a presence that connects unconsciously to a nurturing (maternal) absence. For Lacan, the center is a void, a loss forever mourned, alack, alack. A few contemporary psychoanalysts have attempted to find language to point to this preverbal space: see Christopher Bollas on "The Unthought Known," in *The Shadow of the Object: Psychoanalysis of the Unthought Known* (New York: Columbia University Press, 1987), pp. 277–83.

18. Roland Barthes, *The Pleasure of the Text*, trans. Richard Miller (New York: Hill and Wang, 1975), pp. 66–67.

19. See "Revolution in Poetic Language," *The Kristeva Reader*, ed. Toril Moi (New York: Columbia University Press, 1986), pp. 89–136; the note is on p. 127 (n. 14).

20. Quotations are from "Revolution in Poetic Language," pp. 93–97.

21. *Romeo and Juliet*, Prologue, 1; "The Phoenix and the Turtle," 27; *Twelfth Night*, 5.1.216. The word "cleave" is an English instance of a primitive semantic phenomenon Freud considered in his brief essay on "The Antithetical Meaning of Primal Words" (1910), *Standard Edition*, 11, 153–61.

Epigraphs to this volume

Julia Kristeva, *Black Sun: Depression and Melancholia*, trans. Leon Roudiez (New York; Columbia University Press, 1989), p. 22.
D.W. Winnicott, "Primitive Emotional Development" (1945), *Collected Papers: Through Pediatrics to Psycho-Analysis* (New York: Basic Books, 1975), p. 150.

Index

Abraham, Nicholas, 221
Abrams, Richard, 217
Achilles (*Troilus and Cressida*), 40–41, 49–50, 156–57, 198
Adams, Barry, 194
Adelman, Janet, 63, 107, 177, 179, 195, 196, 198, 203, 206, 210, 211, 212, 216, 226, 228
Alexander, Nigel, 228
Altman, Joel, 177, 185
Angelo (*Measure for Measure*), 46–47, 50, 82, 197, 205
Antony and Cleopatra, 120–21, 176
Aretino, Pietro, 88
Aristotle, 123–24
Armstrong, Edward, 17, 186
As You Like It, xiv, xviii, 141, 162
Auden, W. H., 12, 57, 109, 183, 200
authorship, xii, xvii–xviii, 10, 14, 24, 30, 38, 40, 90, 95, 106, 144–49, 150, 152–54, 157–58, 173, 174, 176, 191, 198, 223, 225

Bachmann, Susan, 209
Bacon, Francis, 185
Bakhtin, Mikhail, 58
Bal, Mieke, 208, 209
Bamber, Linda, 115, 215
Banquo (*Macbeth*), 100, 102, 105, 109, 113, 120
Barber, C. L., 57, 199
Barish, Jonas, 225
Barkan, Leonard, 205
Barker, Francis, 15, 17, 183, 184, 185
Barnum, Phineas T., 9, 181
Barroll, J. Leeds, 11, 183, 192, 197, 198, 203
Barron, David, 102, 105, 212, 215
Barthes, Roland, xviii, 145, 147, 169, 173, 177, 183, 220, 223, 229
Battenhouse, Roy, 207
Bayley, John, 212
Beckett, Samuel, 7, 8, 164

Begelman, Mitchell, 220
Belsey, Catherine, 12–13, 17, 185
Bentley, Gerald Eades, 174
Berger, Harry, 22–23, 52–54, 103, 173, 179, 189, 200, 210, 211, 212, 228
Berry, Ralph, 18, 222
Bevington, David, 178, 182, 207, 211
Biggins, Dennis, 210
black holes, 220
Blake, N. F., 188
Blau, Herbert, 183
Bleich, David, 219
Bloom, Harold, 8, 14, 110, 146, 181, 183, 199, 213, 216, 223
Bollas, Christopher, 65, 202, 204, 229
Bolton, W. F., 201
Boose, Lynda, 179
Booth, Stephen, 22, 51–54, 103, 113, 181, 184, 187, 192, 193, 194, 198, 212, 213
Borges, Jorge, 145, 223
Bowers, A. Robin, 85, 207
Bowie, Malcolm, 202
Bradbrook, Muriel, 189, 205
Bradley, A. C., xiii, 11, 55, 114, 174–75, 183, 199, 213
Breuer, Josef, 216
Bristol, Michael, 181
Bromley, Laura, 207, 209
Brook, Peter, 33, 132, 225
Brooke, Nicholas, 112–13, 214
Brooks, Cleanth, 102, 113, 211
Brown, Carolyn, 196
Brown, Norman, 218, 222
Brownmiller, Susan, 206
Brutus (*Julius Caesar*), 108
Burckhardt, Sigurd, 21, 141
Burgess, Anthony, 221
Burke, Kenneth, 35, 193
Burton, Robert, 103, 211
Bush, Douglas, 90, 208
Bynum, Caroline Walker, 195

Caesarean section, 104–105
Calderwood, James, 179, 190, 198, 210, 214,
    217
Calef, Victor, 209, 211
Callaghan, Dympna, 214
Campbell, O. J., 195, 222
Carew, Richard, 88
Carr, S. L., 210
Carroll, William, 187
Cartelli, Thomas, 214
catharsis, 123–24, 217
Catherine of Siena, 43
Cavell, Marcia, 204, 228, 229
Cavell, Stanley, 8–9, 114, 121, 123, 181, 184,
    185, 196, 214, 217, 219, 227
Chambers, E.K., 176
character, xii–xiv, 1–3, 11–17, 55, 64, 76, 154,
    163, 178, 182, 183, 192, 199, 204, 208
Charcot, Jean Martin, 180
Charnes, Linda, 198, 204, 224
chora (Kristeva), 169, 229
Cixous, Hélène, 12, 183
Claesz, Pieter, 227
Claribel (*Tempest*), 167–68
Clemen, Wolfgang, 18, 186
Clemens, Samuel, 9, 144, 223
Cleopatra (*Anthony and Cleopatra*), 48, 50,
    120, 153, 198
Cohn, Norman, 216
Coleridge, Samuel, 151, 175
Collatine (*Rape of Lucrece*), 76–79, 81–82,
    84, 86, 88–90
Colman, E.A.M., 22, 193, 195, 205, 221
Comedy of Errors, 118, 215, 216
Cordelia (*King Lear*), xii–xiii, 83, 125–128,
    135, 174, 189
Coriolanus, 105–06, 115, 130, 142
Cox, Lee Sheridan, 192
Cranach, Lucas, 207
Cressida (*Troilus and Cressida*), 50
Crewe, Jonathan, 204, 206, 208
Crunelle-Vanrigh, Anny, 210
Culler, Jonathan, 188
Cymbeline, 94, 205
Cznerniecki, Krystian, 221

Danson, Lawrence, 187, 213
Dante, 135–36
Davies, Stevie, 192
Davis, D. R., 213, 216
de Beauvoir, Simone, 115

de Grazia, Margreta, 185
Delphi Seminar, xi, 173
Derrida, Jacques, 93–94, 109, 132, 148, 176,
    192, 194, 209, 220, 223
Descartes, René, 13, 14, 147
Desdemona (*Othello*), 4–5, 25, 83, 93, 114,
    179
Desmet, Christy, 13, 179, 183, 197
Dickens, Charles, 148, 223
DiGangi, Mario, 178
Donaldson, Ian, 207
Donne, John, 164
Doran, Madeleine, 18, 179
Doyle, Arthur Conan, 26, 190
Dryden, John, 150
Dubrow, Heather, 208, 209
Duncan (*Macbeth*), 97–102, 117, 210

Eagleton, Terry, 73, 174, 184, 201
Ecclesiastes, 54, 226
Eco, Umberto, 180
Edel, Leon, 223
Edelson, Marshall, 187
Edmund (*King Lear*), 51
Egan, Robert, 213
ego, 6, 55–56, 59, 63, 64–65, 72, 107, 147, 155,
    156, 180, 197, 202–3, 204, 215, 225
Ehrenzweig, Anton, 199
Eissler, K. R., 226
El-Gabalawy, Saad, 88, 205
Elam, Keir, 186, 192, 196
Eliot, T. S., 47
Elton, William, 219
Emerson, Ralph Waldo, 9, 181, 182
Empson, William, 197, 206, 214
equivocation, 110–13, 213–14
Erickson, Peter, 57, 61, 223
Erikson, Erik, 197
Erlich, Avi, 198, 226
Ewbank, Inga-Stina, 221

Faber, M. D., 226
Falstaff (*1 Henry IV*), 14, 55–60, 62, 63, 71,
    120, 199–200, 201
Farrell, Kirby, 184
Felman, Shoshana, 173, 180
Felperin, Howard, 181, 196, 224
Fenichel, Otto, 225
Ferguson, Margaret, 188
Fergusson, Francis, 110, 123, 213
Ferry, Anne, 14–15, 204

Fiedler, Leslie, 195, 215
Fineman, Joel, 16, 17, 20, 91, 181, 184, 187, 193, 199, 203, 205, 206, 208, 209, 212, 223, 224
First Folio, 24
Fisch, Harold, 178
Fish, Stanley, 173, 191
Fleay, F.G., 192
Fleissner, Robert, 192
Fly, Richard, 197, 218, 227
Folger, Henry Clay, 9
Forrester, John, 187
Fort! Da! (game), 132–33
Foster, Dennis, 9, 181
Foster, Mary, 229
Foucault, Michel, xii, 17, 119, 145–46, 216, 223, 225
Fox, Alice, 105, 111, 210, 211
frame of reference, 4, 41, 155, 195, 219
free association, xi–xii, 22, 54, 176
Freedman, Barbara, 184, 192, 215
Freeman, Thomas, 224
Frege, Gottlob, 220
Freud, Sigmund, xi, xvi, 14, 20, 22, 26–29, 52, 64, 72, 98, 100, 117–19, 132, 133, 173, 175, 176, 180, 183, 187, 188, 189, 190–91, 192, 193, 197, 202, 204, 216, 219–20, 228, 229
Freund, Elizabeth, 34, 192, 195
Frost, Robert, 54
Furness, Horace Howard, 9

Garber, Marjorie, 121, 182, 185, 210, 212, 215, 217, 223, 228
Gardner, Martin, 220
Garnett, David, 193
gate, 40–41, 49–50, 54, 157–58, 170, 198
Gertrude (*Hamlet*), xiv, 2, 47, 114, 125, 161, 162–63, 165, 179, 185, 226
Ginsberg, Marsha, 203
Ginzburg, Carlo, 190
Girard, René, 212
Gloucester (*King Lear*), 125–26, 135, 139
Goldberg, Jonathan, 178, 201
Goldman, Michael, 178, 215
Green, André, 68, 184, 185
Greenacre, Phyllis, 173
Greenblatt, Stephen, 70–74, 123, 174, 187, 204, 215, 217, 228
Greene, Robert, 150, 224
Grivelet, Michel, 188

Grove, R., 214
Grudin, Robert, 224
Guerre, Martin, 71–72
Guillemeau, Jacques, 212
Gurr, Andrew, 25, 190

Hal (*1 Henry IV*), 55–63, 71
Hall, Joseph, 183, 213
Halliwell, J.O., 192
Hamilton, A.C., 206
Hamlet, xii, xiii, xiv, xviii, 1–4, 14–17, 20–21, 48, 63–64, 66, 68–70, 83, 125, 126, 128, 141, 146, 147, 149, 150, 155, 156, 160–64, 166, 168, 178, 179, 183, 184, 185, 186, 199, 201, 202–3, 206, 225, 226
Hamlet, xvi, 2, 4, 13, 14, 15–17, 37–38, 47, 48, 58, 68, 70, 73, 112, 114, 118, 119, 122, 133, 139, 141, 142, 147, 148, 155, 163, 164, 166–67, 175, 185, 188, 194, 198, 199, 201, 210, 222, 226, 227, 228
Hammill, Graham, 227
Hans, James, 176, 194
Harbage, Alfred, 39, 145
Harding, D. W., 211
Hartman, Geoffrey, 31, 191, 194
Hawkes, Terence, 9, 23–24, 148, 182, 189
Hawkins, Harriet, 188, 206
Hawthorne, Nathaniel, 143, 145, 222
Hazlitt, William, 145, 152, 223
Hecuba (*Rape of Lucrece*), 14, 87
Helen (*Rape of Lucrece*), 49, 86–88
Henry (*1 Henry IV*), 55–56, 59, 61–63
Henry IV Part One, 55–63, 70, 199
Henry IV Part Two, 22, 56, 70, 120, 226
Henry V, 57, 120, 137, 193, 221
Hirsch, E. D., 180
Hoepfer, Theodore, 192
Hofstadter, Douglas, 215–16
Holderness, Graham, 182, 224
Holland, Norman, 191, 199, 202, 209
Hollander, John, 191
Holmes, Sherlock, 26–27, 190, 192
Honigmann, E.A.J., 173
Hotson, Leslie, 192
Hotspur (*1 Henry IV*), 55–56, 57, 59–60, 62, 63, 201
Hulme, Hilda, 21–22, 25, 49
Hulse, S. Clark, 207, 209
Hunter, Dianne, 211, 212, 215
Hussey, S.S., 180
Huston, Dennis, 194

hymen, 93–96
Hynes, Sam, 206
hysteria, 114, 120, 216

Iago (*Othello*), xv–xvi, 3, 4–5, 120, 175, 179
Ide, Richard, 102
idealization, 8, 9, 78–79, 81–83, 85, 86, 89,
    91, 93, 100, 145, 146, 148–49, 152–54, 161,
    181, 183, 184, 206, 223, 225
identification, 12, 16, 50, 57, 59, 60, 63–65,
    66, 70, 72, 84, 87–88, 106, 117, 146, 149,
    152, 154, 158, 164, 197, 200, 204, 212
identity, 13, 16, 49–50, 60, 63–66, 69–70,
    71–73, 105, 106–7, 142, 147, 151–52, 155,
    198, 204
imaginary (Lacan), 64, 65, 73, 86, 169
Imogen (*Cymbeline*), 83
infanticide, 100–103, 107–8, 209
interim, 108–10, 122
Irving, Washington, 143, 145, 222
Isabella (*Measure for Measure*), 44–47, 50,
    82
isomorphism, 118–19, 215

Jakobson, Roman, 188, 228
James, Henry, 144–45, 153, 157–58, 223
Janton, Pierre, 210
Jed, Stephanie, 208, 209
Jenkins, Harold, 226, 227
Johnson, Samuel, 12, 48, 153, 175, 197
Jonson, Ben, 146, 148, 151, 176, 224
Jorgensen, Paul, 219, 222
Joseph, Miriam, 186
jouissance, 8, 164, 169, 177
Joyce, James, 7–8, 136, 140, 145, 180, 220,
    229
Julius Caesar, xvi–xvii, 108, 156, 158, 183

Kahn, Coppélia 57, 58, 61, 174, 200, 207, 212,
    215
Kaminsky, Judith, 207, 209
Kaplan, Donald, 221
Keats, John, 113
Kernan, Alvin, 217, 221
Kernberg, Otto, 204
Kerrigan, William, 13, 152, 180, 183, 226, 227
Kincaid, James, 191
King Lear, 51, 118, 120, 125–28, 129, 131, 132–
    33, 134, 135, 139, 140, 141, 142, 151, 161, 166,
    227
Klein, Joan, 211

Knapp, P., 210
Knapp, Robert, 13
Knight, G. Wilson, xiii, 18, 97, 109, 174, 175,
    186
Knights, L. C., 12, 175, 182, 211, 214
Kökeritz, Helge, 180, 193, 219
Kott, Jan, 7
Kraft, Kent, 225
Kramer, Jerome, 207, 209
Kris, Ernst, 55, 199, 200
Kristeva, Julia, 58, 169, 183, 203, 226, 229

Lacan, Jacques, 7, 8–9, 17, 64–67, 70, 86,
    115, 131–32, 134, 155, 170, 177, 178, 180, 184,
    185, 187, 188, 192, 193, 194, 202, 220, 225,
    227, 229
Lady Macbeth, 97–101, 102–3, 107, 115–17,
    119–20, 121, 210, 215
Lady Macbeth's child, 102–4, 107, 111–14,
    214
Lady Macduff (*Macbeth*), 99
Lamb, Charles, 24, 190
language, xiii, 2, 4, 7–10, 13, 16, 17–25, 50,
    60, 66, 68, 70, 131, 132, 152–54, 169, 178,
    180, 181, 185–188, 192, 197, 198, 219, 228,
    229
play of language, xii–xiii, xviii, 2–6, 10, 21,
    25, 36, 42–47, 51–53, 61, 77, 134, 165, 168–
    70, 176, 184, 194, 202, 220
puns, wordplay, xii, xiv, xvi, xvii, xviii, 2, 17,
    20–23, 36, 39, 47–49, 60, 62, 65, 82, 107,
    132–34, 137–38, 140, 153, 157, 161, 163, 180,
    187–89, 195, 197, 198, 200, 216, 219, 220,
    221, 222
Lavinia (*Titus Andronicus*), 93, 139
Lee, Sidney, 144
Leech, Clifford, 218
Leider, Emily, 218
Leimberg, Inge, 192
Leiris, Michel, 207
Leontes (*Winter's Tale*), 43, 81, 129–30, 207,
    218, 219
Lesser, Simon, 213
Levenson, Jill, 218
Levine, Lawrence, 181, 222
Lichtenstein, Heinz, 66, 74, 155, 195, 225
Lindenbaum, Peter, 217
Locke, John, 14
Loewald, Hans, 187
Loomba, Ania, 198
Love's Labour's Lost, 120, 205, 216

Lucrece (*Rape of Lucrece*), 34, 76–96, 208
Lukacher, Ned, 179
Lupton, Julia, 185, 187

Macbeth (and *Macbeth*), 21, 24, 25, 52, 81, 83,
    93, 97–124, 139, 140, 205
MacCary, W. Thomas, 194, 195, 198
Macdonwald (*Macbeth*), 104, 105
Macduff (*Macbeth*), 102, 105, 109, 211
Mack, Maynard, 211
Mahler, Margaret, 212
Mahood, M. M., 20, 186, 187, 196, 200
Malcolm (*Macbeth*), 102, 109, 213
Mallarmé, Stéphane, 93, 94, 169, 209
Malone, Edmund, 223
Malvolio (*Twelfth Night*), 32–38, 39, 46, 48,
    50, 191, 192, 194, 197
Manheim, Leonard, 192
Marcus, Leah, 223
Margeson, J.M.R., 218
Mark Antony (*Antony and Cleopatra*), 176
Mark Antony (*Julius Caesar*), xvi–xvii
Marlowe, Christopher, 90, 147, 151
Marshall, Cynthia, 183, 221
Maus, Katherine Eisaman, 15, 95, 177, 196,
    205, 208
McBride, Tom, 190
McCabe, Colin, 200
McCanles, Michael, 225
McDowell, J., 229
McGuire, Jerry, 228
McLuhan, Marshall, 189
McLuskie, Kathleen, 196
Measure for Measure, 4, 44–47, 82, 178, 193,
    196, 205, 216
méconnaissance, 146, 155
melancholia, 1, 4, 103, 162, 164, 179, 184, 203,
    211, 226
Melville, Herman, 9, 222
memento mori, 162. See also *vanitas*
memory, 64, 95–96, 119–20, 141, 160–170,
    226, 227, 228
Merchant of Venice, xvii, 42–43, 80, 195, 221
Mercutio (*Romeo and Juliet*), 6, 129, 137
Meres, Francis, 151
Meyer, Nicholas, 190
Michel, Laurence, 212, 216
Midsummer Night's Dream, 95, 131, 175
Miller, Jacques-Alain, 187
Milton, John, 24, 190, 191
Miranda (*Tempest*), 164–166, 168

mirror, xi, 10, 41, 49–50, 54, 57, 64, 66–68,
    74–75, 84, 87, 89, 93, 94, 99, 103, 105–6,
    108, 139, 141, 149, 151–52, 154–59, 162, 170,
    191, 195, 198, 202, 212, 217, 225
Morgann, Maurice, 12, 55, 122, 175, 183, 200
mother (maternal body) xviii–xix, 7, 49–50,
    57–58, 61–66, 68, 74, 83, 86–87, 98–99,
    100–103, 105–7, 110, 114, 116, 120, 132, 135,
    139, 141, 155, 165–69, 177, 200, 201, 203,
    210–11, 215, 218, 226, 228, 229
Muir, Kenneth, 188, 209, 215
Mullaney, Steven, 214
Munari, Bruno, 219
Murray, Peter, 182

narcissism, 32, 38, 49–50, 57, 66, 74, 106,
    151–52, 155, 157–58, 164, 192, 194, 202
Nardo, Anna, 177
Nelson, Cary, 31, 191, 228
Nevo, Ruth, 196, 211, 215
New Criticism, xi, 18
Newman, Jane, 208
Nietzsche, Friedrich, 8, 24, 67, 124, 145, 150,
    176, 190, 217
Nuttall, A.D., 12, 13, 183

object relations, 6–7, 49–50, 55, 57–58, 64–
    68, 74, 106–8, 158, 180
Oedipus complex, 14, 86, 97–98, 183, 204
Ong, Walter, 189
Onions, C.T., 175
Ophelia (*Hamlet*), xii, 126, 133, 162, 163, 222
Orgel, Stephen, 228
Orsino (*Twelfth Night*), 35–37, 193, 194
Osborne, Laurie, 192
Othello (and *Othello*), xvi, 4, 5, 25, 81, 83, 92,
    112, 114, 130, 166, 176, 205, 219
Ovid, 85, 87, 89, 106, 151, 207, 208

Palmer, D. J., 97
paranoia, 26–32, 34, 37–38, 219
Parker, Patricia, 203, 219
Partridge, Eric, 175, 190, 193, 205, 218, 221
Patterson, Annabel, 17, 206, 208
Pechter, Edward, 224
Penelope, 87, 89
Persephone, 87
Petit, J.-P., 139, 221
Phillips, Adam, 70, 202
Philomela, 87
Phoenix and the Turtle, 229

Pierce, Franklin, 143
Pinker, Steven, 228
Plato, 93, 169
Poe, Edgar Allan, 222
Polanski, Roman, 210, 213
Popper, Karl, 189
potential space, 108, 110–13, 123, 142, 191
Poulet, Georges, 220, 222
primal dialogue, 139, 168–69, 221–22, 228–29
primal scene, 79, 86, 94, 179, 218
Prince, F.T., 204
Prospero (*Tempest*), 122, 136, 141–42, 165–66, 168, 217
psychoanalytic criticism, xiii, xix, 6–7, 23, 45, 49, 53–54, 55–59, 97, 100, 199, 226
psychoanalytic theory, xi, 20, 63–70, 71–74, 103, 106–7, 119, 131, 151, 155, 158, 187, 193, 215, 229
psychomachia, 14, 55, 77, 78, 199
pun. *See* language
Pyles, Thomas, 218

Quiller-Couch, Arthur, 213

Rabkin, Norman, 110, 113, 210, 213, 224
Rackin, Phyllis, 200, 201
Ragland-Sullivan, 8, 178, 180, 202
Ramsey, Jerald, 110, 213
Rank, Otto, 175
rape, 34, 49, 50, 76, 77, 79, 81–86, 89–96, 99, 117, 205–6, 207, 208, 209, 220
Rape of Lucrece, 76–96
reading, xi, xvii, 30–31, 33–35, 37–38, 41, 46, 47, 50–54, 56, 85, 87, 133–34, 157, 158, 163, 178, 180, 186, 189, 191, 192–93, 195
real (Lacan), 227
Redfern, Walter, 198
Rees, Martin, 220
Reinhard, Kenneth, 185, 187
revenge play, 166–67
Richard II, 1–2, 10, 19, 53, 58, 120, 147, 150, 151, 182, 189, 200
Ricoeur, Paul, 180, 191
Ridley, M.R., 190
Righter, Anne, 177
Roberts, Patrick, 210
Rogers, Robert, 187
Romeo and Juliet, xiv, 6, 103, 129, 135, 136, 137, 193, 207, 229

Rose, Jacqueline, 47–48, 190
Rosenberg, Marvin, 111, 213
Rudnytsky, Peter, 179
Russell, Bertrand, 220

Sacks, Elizabeth, 211
Said, Edward, 148
Schefer, Jean-Louis, 220
Schiesari, Julia, 179, 184, 203
Schnucker, R.V., 212
Schoenbaum, Samuel, 150, 224
Schopenhauer, Arthur, 175
Schreber (Freud's case history), 27–28
Schucking, L.L., 55, 199
Schwartz, Murray, 122, 173, 174, 191, 194, 211, 212, 218, 222
Scot, Reginald, 215, 217
self, 3, 5, 14, 15–16, 23, 37, 49, 63–65, 68, 69–70, 71–74, 79, 106–08, 115, 121, 137, 147, 154, 163, 177, 198, 199, 203, 204
Shakespeare, John, 226
Shakespeare, William:
    author-effect, xii, 6, 45;
    criticism, 74–75;
    cultural figure, 143–59;
    imagination, 114–24, 134–42;
    language, 2–4, 7–8, 143–59;
    last will and testament, xvi–xvii;
    literary ideal, xvii–xviii, 143–59;
    writing, 93–96. *See also* individual plays, poems, characters
Shapiro, David, 29–31, 191
Sharpe, Ella Freeman, 197, 218, 226
Shell, Marc, 195, 198
Shengold, Leonard, 218
Shipley, Joseph, 176
Shylock (*Merchant of Venice*), 42–43, 195
Sibony, Daniel, 178
Sieveking, Forbes, 227
Silhol, Robert, 173
Silling, E., 210
Silverman, Kaja, 193, 202
Sinon (*Rape of Lucrece*), 88–89
Skura, Meredith, 173, 174, 177, 179, 194, 196, 198, 204, 221
Smith, Barbara Herrnstein, 191
Smith, Joseph, 219
Sonnet 116, 90
Sonnet 129, 22, 36, 80, 188
Sonnet 130, 135

Sonnet 135, xiv
Sonnets, 16, 140, 184, 187
Spenser, Edmund, 95, 146, 151, 204
Spitz, René, 221
splitting, 13, 14, 99–100, 117–18, 119, 171, 193, 215, 216
Sprengnether, Madelon, 206
Spurgeon, Caroline, 17, 18, 225
Stallybrass, Peter, 214
States, Bert, 13, 183
Stern, Daniel, 229
Stevens, Wallace, 66–68
Stewart, J.I.M., 55, 199, 212, 214
Stimpson, Catherine, 82, 205
Stockholder, Kay, 213
Stoll, E.E., 12
subject, 8, 12–16, 63–65, 70, 73–75, 173, 178, 183, 193, 202, 206, 227
Summers, Joseph, 217
Sundelson, David, 210
symbolic (Lacan), 8, 73, 86, 132, 169, 227
Symons, Norman, 226

Tarquin (*Rape of Lucrece*), 76–96, 99, 117, 205, 206
Taylor, Gary, 181, 220
Tempest, 118, 122, 140, 166, 168, 186, 204, 228
text (see also gate, mirror), 4, 17, 18, 21–22, 23, 30–32, 35–38, 41, 46, 53–54, 68, 77, 147–48, 157, 158–59, 163, 169–70, 173, 176, 178, 189, 194
Thass-Thienemann, Theodore, 20, 188, 197, 218
Theseus (*Midsummer Night's Dream*), 131, 133, 140, 222
Thomson, Dietrick, 220
Timon of Athens, 46
Titus Andronicus, 93, 135, 139, 220
Torok, Maria, 221
transitional object, 110–13, 191, 212
Traub, Valerie, 57–58, 62, 200, 206, 219
Troilus and Cressida, 39, 50, 147, 156, 158, 193, 195, 204, 216
Trousdale, Marion, 185
true self (Winnicott), 63–65, 70, 203
Tuve, Rosamund, 19, 187
Twain, Mark. *See* Samuel Clemens

Twelfth Night, xiv, xviii, 32, 34–35, 37, 39, 118, 175, 193, 194, 229

Ulysses (*Troilus and Cressida*), 40–41, 49–50, 156–158
unconscious, xiii, xvi, xviii, 1, 3, 20, 27, 31, 42, 45, 51–54, 64–66, 69–70, 113–20, 122, 218, 228
Urkowitz, Steven, 9, 181

vanitas, 226–27
Venus and Adonis, 95
Vesny-Wagner, L., 209
Vickers, Nancy, 82, 205

Walley, Harold, 207
Wanamaker, Sam, 9, 181–82
Ward, David, 218
Warner, William Beatty, 203, 225
Wasiolek, Edward, 31, 191
Watson, Robert N., 62, 196, 199, 200, 201, 209, 210, 212, 216, 219, 227
Weimann, Robert, 16, 18, 19, 21, 177, 178, 180, 182, 184, 188
West, Gillian, 196
Wexman, Virginia, 210
Wheeler, Richard, 57, 185, 196, 197, 200, 210
Wilden, Anthony, 132, 187, 220
will, xiv–xviii, 3, 70, 76, 78–79, 91, 92, 175, 176, 183, 198
Willbern, David, 173, 191, 220
Williams, William Carlos, 10, 182
Willson, Richard, xvii, 176
Winnicott, D.W., 65–66, 70, 106–7, 108, 110, 112, 155, 170, 177, 179–80, 202, 204, 212, 213, 225, 229
Winter's Tale, 43, 129–30, 222
witches, 99–101, 106, 109, 111, 114–22, 200, 214, 215, 216, 217
wordplay. *See* language
writing, xii, xvii, 1, 3–4, 5–7, 8, 13, 23, 37–38, 59, 69–70, 76, 82, 92–96, 131, 139, 147, 153–54, 169, 173, 176, 178, 183, 189, 194, 201, 206, 209, 220, 227

Yeats, William Butler, 86, 145, 150, 207, 223
Yorick (*Hamlet*), 156, 160–64, 226

Permissions

Earlier versions of the following chapters have appeared previously and are reprinted by permission of the editors and presses.

Chapter Two was published in *University of Hartford Studies in Literature* 11 (1979), 1–23. Chapter Three was published in Russ McDonald, ed., *Shakespeare Reread: The Texts in New Contexts* (Ithaca, N.Y.: Cornell University Press, 1994), pp. 170–90.

Chapter Five initially appeared as "Rape, Writing, Hyperbole: Shakespeare's *Lucrece*," in Vera Camden, ed., *Compromise Formations: Current Directions in Psychoanalytic Criticism* (Kent: Kent State University Press, 1989), pp. 182–98. It is reprinted with permission of Kent State University Press. A revised version was published as "Hyperbolic Desire: Shakespeare's *Lucrece*," in Peter Rudnytsky and Marie-Rose Logan, eds., *Contending Kingdoms: Historical, Psychological, and Feminist Approaches to the Literature of Sixteenth-Century England and France* (Detroit: Wayne State University Press, 1991), pp. 202–24.

Chapter Six was published in *English Literary Renaissance* 16.3 (1986), 520–49.

Chapter Seven appeared in Murray M. Schwartz and Coppélia Kahn, eds., *Representing Shakespeare: New Psychoanalytic Essays* (Baltimore: Johns Hopkins University Press, 1980), pp. 244–63. It is reprinted by permission of the Johns Hopkins University Press.

Chapter Eight, was published in Norman Holland, Sidney Homan, and Bernard Paris, eds., *Shakespeare's Personality* (Berkeley: University of California Press, 1989), pp. 226–43. It is reprinted by permission of the University of California Press.

Most of the chapters had earlier oral iterations. I am grateful to the Renaissance Society of America and the Northeast Modern Language Association for opportunities to discuss "Shakespeare's Nothing" in the late 1970s. A seminar at the 1981 World Shakespeare Congress let me present my ideas on "Phantasmagoric *Macbeth*." A conference on "Shakespeare's Personality" at the University of Florida in 1985 was an occasion for "What Is Shakespeare?" My ideas about *Lucrece* first took shape for the Fourth International Conference in Literature and Psychoanalysis, at Kent State University in 1987. The 1989 meeting of the Shakespeare Association of America gave me a forum for "The Famous Analyses of *Henry the Fourth*." "Pushing the Envelope" had a previous iteration as "How Not to Read Shakespeare," at the 1991 College English Association of Ohio meeting, and the 1992 Shakespeare Association of America meeting. An early version of the Epilogue was presented at Cornell University in 1992; later versions were part of the Victor Johnson lecture series in the Buffalo English department in 1995, a seminar at the World Shakespeare Congress in Los Angeles in 1996, and the Thirteenth International Conference in Literature and Psychoanalysis in Boston in 1996.